BEHIND
THE LINES

ALSO BY JEFFREY B. MILLER

Stapleton International Airport: The First Fifty Years
Pruett Publishing, Boulder, CO, 1983.
The first history book about a major U.S. airport.

Facing Your Fifties: Every Man's Reference to Mid-life Health,
co-author, Dr. Gordon Ehlers, M. Evans & Co., New York, 2002.
Included as one of only three health books in *Publishers Weekly's*
"Best Books of 2002."

Honor Bound, unpublished.
An 850-page historical novel about the Commission for
Relief in Belgium, Belgium, and World War I.

ABOUT THIS BOOK

Behind the Lines follows a handful of Belgians in German-occupied Belgium and a group of Americans in the Commission for Relief in Belgium (CRB) from August 1914 through December 1914. The book is the first in a series that will span the time from August 1914 until April 1917, when America enters the war and the CRB delegates have to leave Belgium. The second book will cover January 1915 through spring 1916 and is planned for publication in 2015. The third book will cover summer 1916 through April 1917 and is planned for publication in 2016. More information can be found at www.WWIBehindTheLines.com.

ABOUT THE AUTHOR

Jeffrey B. Miller has been a writer, editor, and author for nearly forty years. His career includes starting six magazines (city, regional, and national), being editor in chief of five in-flight magazines, and serving as director of communications for AAA Colorado, where he supervised its magazine, public relations, public affairs, traffic safety programs, and website. He lives in Denver with his wife, Susan Burdick, and is working on the next book in the *Behind the Lines* series.

BEHIND
THE LINES

*WWI's little-known story of German occupation,
Belgian resistance, and the band of Yanks
who saved millions from starvation.*

Beginnings, 1914

Jeffrey B. Miller

MILBROWN PRESS, DENVER
www.WWIBehindTheLines.com

Special discounts are available for quantity purchases.

Published in the United States of America.

Milbrown Press is an imprint of JBM Publishing Company.

 Milbrown Press

Jeff Miller
Milbrown Press
1265 South Columbine St.
Denver, CO 80210
(303) 503-1739

www.WWIBehindTheLines.com
jbmwriter@aol.com

ISBN: 978-0-9906893-0-0 (paperback)
ISBN: 978-0-9906893-1-7 (ebook)

Library of Congress Control Number: 2014914989

Cover photographs. Front: public domain; *War Bread*, E. E. Hunt (Henry Holt & Co., 1916); Back, left to right (all public domain): multiple sources; Herbert Hoover Presidential Library Archives; author's archives.

PBC

Text design by Pratt Brothers Composition

Front cover design by Laurie Shields Design

To my grandparents, Milton M. Brown and
Erica Bunge Brown, who started it all.

To Susan Burdick—my north star, my
inspiration, my friend, my one true love.

Contents

OCTOBER 1914
STUMBLING TOWARD ORGANIZATION

NOVEMBER 1914
COMING TOGETHER

DECEMBER 1914
UNCERTAINTY PREVAILS

Foreword

Precisely 100 years ago, in 1914, the world descended into chaos. The cataclysm known initially as the World War or the Great War, and subsequently as the First World War or World War I, powerfully resonates today. We can trace the ascent of the United States to a position of global preeminence, the unraveling of European imperial control over many parts of the world, and the political demarcation of a fractious modern Middle East to this war and its immediate aftermath.

Although the war is best known for the industrialized slaughter of millions of soldiers along the western front and the innovative and horrific use of chemical weapons, machine guns, tanks, and submarines, as well as the strategic bombing of civilian population centers, it is a conflict that is nevertheless poorly understood. Compared with the Second World War, few Americans study the prior war in depth. European audiences are generally more familiar with World War I's contours, but it remains an enigma. Fierce scholarly debates still rage over its origins, conduct, and consequences.

Collectively, the war's centennial is providing historians, writers, and journalists many new opportunities to reexamine this titanic conflict and to establish its connections to a globalized world today, to link the two eras spanning a century.

A wave of new scholarly writing and documentary films connected to the war's anniversary promises to bombard us with images of the past. Surely many of these reflections on World War I will mostly reinforce what we already know. We are generally familiar with the diplomatic and ethnonational disputes that triggered the war and prevented its swift conclusion and with the slaughter of millions on an ever-expanding and ever-more-destructive battlefield. Reflections on this century-old conflict will certainly further canonize the enduring sense of the war's futility, the failures of imagination and implementation by statesmen and generals, and a glowing appreciation for the valorous troops swept into a tragic vortex.

It remains to be seen what effect, if any, a new wave of research and writing on the war will have on shaping these powerfully held popular memories.

The growing field of histories on humanitarianism and humanitarian interventions ranks prominently among new areas of scholarly interest in World War I. Once the almost-exclusive province of nurses' and ambulance drivers' memoirs, the emergent front of humanitarian studies has cast a wider net to encompass the activities of international relief organizations, transnational disease-abatement campaigns, nation-building initiatives, and the dynamics of state-sponsored social welfare programs for soldiers' dependents and permanently disabled troops.

We are presently developing a deeper understanding of the power struggles between and interactions among the swirling constellation of humanitarian actors, state and private donors, and recipients of aid. Just as states and societies waging World War I focused considerable attention on industrial mobilization for the purposes of waging war, they also developed humanitarian countermeasures to mitigate war's destructive effects on soldiers, their families, and millions of others engulfed by its violence.

Those involved in humanitarian efforts exercised profound influence over the war's conduct and outcome. They helped to shape policy and strategy among belligerent and neutral powers alike. As they gave hope to many beleaguered peoples who lacked the means to provide for themselves, humanitarians demonstrated outstanding life-sustaining alternatives to unbridled destruction.

Behind the Lines reveals one of the most remarkable humanitarian enterprises undertaken during World War I. In this historically accurate and gripping account, Jeff Miller traces the activities of the Commission for Relief in Belgium, the CRB, an ingenious organization established in October 1914 to import food and to ensure its distribution within German-occupied Belgium (and subsequently northern France).

Belgium, the most highly industrialized and densely populated country in Europe, urgently needed international assistance from willing neutral powers that would intercede on its behalf. It was threatened by starvation because of its acute dependency on foreign food imports, Germany's acts of destruction and/or forcible acquisition of native agricultural stockpiles and livestock as it conquered Belgium, and Britain's erection of a strict naval blockade along the Belgian coast to deny its German adversary imported war materials, including food.

Emerging as the CRB's indomitable and dynamic leader was a figure that few Americans today associate with gallantry, effective leadership, or managerial success: Herbert Hoover.

This man, whose reputation in the United States would forever be linked to the Great Depression of the 1930s, was nevertheless the guiding force that orchestrated the nation-saving food relief of Belgium and northern France.

Hoover and his deputies, whom he called a "band of crusaders," were comprised mostly of American university students and developed the CRB into a highly efficient, neutral international relief organization. They negotiated and maintained the consent of the belligerent governments of Britain, Germany, and France, and the neutral powers, including the United States and Holland, to permit the distribution of foodstuffs across occupied Belgium and France. The CRB secured nearly $1 billion in funding (nearly $20 billion in 2014 dollars) to purchase millions of tons of food, and it developed a global logistics system reliant on a fleet of ocean-going ships and canal boats to transport the food to Belgian and French communities.

CRB officials—known to many as "delegates"—worked closely with tens of thousands of Belgian and French counterparts to distribute the food and feed more than 9 million Belgian and French civilians. And they voluntarily (and without salary) rendered this humanitarian service during a war that constantly threatened to kill or maim them personally.

Remarkably, the CRBers (as they called themselves) pulled it off—the rescue of a nation from starvation—despite the improbability of success, the lack of precedents upon which to rely, the extraordinary and constantly changing difficulties associated with shifting war policies and strategies, and formidable constraints on finances and food supplies.

Never before had private individuals rallied to prevent the wholesale starvation of a nation and actually designed and implemented a successful program that accomplished this purpose. They halted what would have surely been a national calamity.

Although it is little known today outside scholarly circles and among Belgians—who, since 2006, have been exposed to a multi-year historical commemoration program titled "Remembering Herbert Hoover and the Commission for Relief in Belgium"—the CRB made several profound impacts on the world.

First, it demonstrated that humanitarian countermeasures could be devised to resist the tidal wave of carnage unleashed by industrial empires waging total war. Never again could someone claim that relief in wartime was an absolute impossibility—the CRB had shown otherwise.

Second, the CRB awakened expectations among suffering peoples across war-ravaged Europe that they should receive prompt and efficient assistance, just as the Belgians had received. Many Europeans identified the United States and American society as a font of genuine benevolence and unlimited humanitarian aid. When the channels of American aid were slowed or distinctly shaped by geostrategic motivations, once-grateful foreign populations expressed frustration and distrusted American intentions.

Third, Americans, who had always harbored beliefs about their special status in the world, found in the CRB's accomplishments even more evidence to substantiate their exceptionalism. Many Americans were inspired by "saving Belgium" to embark upon even greater adventures in saving lives and remaking other societies during the war and its aftermath, although it would take a second global war to fully convince American society to embrace this perpetual mission.

Throughout the twentieth century and beyond, Americans have espoused a Wilsonian foreign policy of fighting "for the rights and liberties of small nations," such as Belgium, and of making the world "safe for democracy" (Woodrow Wilson, *The War Message of President Woodrow Wilson*, Washington, D.C., 1917, page 19). These transformative visions have urged continual American involvement in the affairs of peoples across the globe.

Fourth, the CRB was the conceptual seed from which many other international humanitarian agencies have sprung. Advocacy for human rights and the routine delivery of humanitarian assistance and disaster relief is a hallmark of modern society. Expectations of efficiency and transparency among aid organizations are routine today, but they were a novelty when the CRB first publicized its ledgers as a way to demonstrate its comparative advantages to rival aid organizations. It is easy to overlook the ways in which the CRB and its humanitarian counterparts in World War I established essential precedents for the delivery of relief during crises and the underlying arguments about the ethical burdens to do so lest millions unnecessarily perish.

Fifth, despite the previous points, the CRB was a novel response to a particular problem. The improvised solutions conceived by Hoover and his companions are not universally applicable to the innumerable, complex humanitarian crises today. Still, we can glean from them many principles for effective relief administration and for inspiration in undertaking seemingly impossible tasks.

As important as the CRB was to averting the starvation of millions and to establishing precedents for ever-wider interventionist practices, the personal story of the Americans engaged in this relief work has not been widely circulated. Certainly some memoirs were published and read with interest a century ago, but their stories have mostly been forgotten, subsumed in a broader war narrative of empires waging industrial war.

Over the past decade, historians, including myself, have been unearthing parts of the CRB story using the organizational records and personal papers of CRB officials to establish its role in American society during the war and within the broader tapestry of relief organizations. But what we have been missing until now is a thorough and intimate portrait of the Americans who saved Belgium from starvation.

In *Behind the Lines*, Jeff Miller has written a vividly detailed account of the Americans who rescued Belgium. Miller, who is an independent scholar and writer, is directly connected to Belgian relief by his grandfather, Milton M. Brown, who labored alongside Hoover to safeguard the Belgians a century ago, and by his grandmother, Erica Bunge Brown, who experienced the German invasion of her country firsthand.

Inspired by his grandparents' tales and entrusted with their diaries and related materials documenting their wartime adventures, Miller has for decades relentlessly pursued the CRB. His steadfast purpose has been to share its story with a wide audience. He has ransacked the archival papers of the CRBers and conducted extensive research into their lives. This volume represents the first installment in a series Miller is writing to showcase the dramatic history of the CRB within the context of German-occupied Belgium. Among its revelations are that Americans were deeply involved in World War I from the outset. *Behind the Lines* depicts Americans who were living and traveling in Belgium and Britain responding to the outbreak of war. Miller shows how American diplomats and businessmen working in foreign capitals perceived the cataclysm, how American journalists-turned-war-correspondents reported their firsthand experiences traveling through war zones, and how Americans studying in European universities reconsidered their studies in light of the opportunities war presented. He also shows us from diaries and related sources the responses of Belgians to the German invasion.

As Miller takes his readers *Behind the Lines*, he firmly establishes that Americans were deeply engaged in European affairs as part of a broader transatlantic relationship that enlarged during a period between the 1870s and 1914 called the *Belle Époque*, the "beautiful age," when steam travel and undersea telegraphic networks strengthened the connections across the North Atlantic world.

By addressing the humanitarian reaction of Americans to Belgian distress, Miller recasts the familiar saga of Americans first becoming "involved" in World War I when the United States declared war on Germany and Austria-Hungary in 1917. Instead, he shows that Americans energetically participated in the war from its opening salvos in 1914.

Oriented around German-occupied Belgium and the life-sustaining food relief campaign of the CRB, *Behind the Lines* also illuminates the constructive problem-solving innovations to address war-induced suffering.

Hoover's humanitarian statecraft conducted while chairman of the CRB pitted warring nations against each other and secured a tenuous lifeline for the Belgian population. Among contemporaries of his time, Hoover was commonly ranked as great a statesman, as were President Woodrow Wilson and his European counterparts. Hoover did not bear

his cross alone in the crusade to save Belgium. He was joined by a remarkable and unlikely group of diplomats, businessmen, engineers, students, and hundreds of thousands of others across the world.

In *Behind the Lines*, Miller has re-created a world that brings to life
a whole ensemble uncommonly associated with America's participation
in the "Great" War. Rather than focusing on the familiar celebrities such
as President Wilson or General John J. Pershing, Miller highlights un-
sung heroes, including a war correspondent who became a life-giver, E. E.
Hunt; a Rhodes scholar from North Dakota, David T. Nelson; an independent scion of a Belgian banker who joined a clandestine resistance
movement, Erica Bunge; and a Belgian businessman, Eugene van Doren,
and Catholic priest, Abbé Vincent de Moor, who teamed up to inspire a
nation and infuriate the German occupiers. These individuals and many
more compose a rich tapestry Miller weaves together to depict the tri-
umphs and tragedies of World War I.

Just as if it were taken from today's headlines, *Behind the Lines* features
invading armies, ransacked villages, desperate refugees, warlord generals,
and stalwart aid workers clinging to the hope that their actions will make
the difference between life and death for victimized peoples.

Miller's spellbinding story should help its readers, especially its American audience who views the war through lenses occluded by the even
more catastrophic Second World War, to understand the reasons why
Americans of an earlier age rallied to the defense of humanity against
aggression. Partly by design and partly by chance, Americans embraced
the cause of Belgian relief and came to view it as a symbol with profound
importance. Americans eventually recognized their relief as but a prelude
to a greater role in the liberation and restoration of an independent, free
Belgium. This familiar "liberators, not conquerors" refrain in American
history has a powerful example in this catalytic war.

Behind the Lines is a book that not only enriches our understanding of
World War I but also provides insights into an arena of enduring global
concern: human rights and humanitarian intervention.

For at least twenty-five years, politicians, pundits, and scholars have
regularly debated the political propriety, ethics, and logistics of humanitarian relief. Many critics allege aid workers do more harm than good and
stress the defensibility of inaction amid complex emergencies while many
advocates seek to mobilize global responses to avert even larger disasters.
Both critics and proponents of what is frequently called "the responsibility

to protect" doctrine of humanitarian intervention have overlooked the foundational humanitarian precedents of World War I.

This pivotal era that Jeff Miller lavishly describes established the institutional and popular foundations for international humanitarian aid. Virtually all the problems and promises of foreign aid today were revealed a century ago. The very ideas of rescuing foreign populations endangered by famine, war, and other forms of distress are not new, even though so many current-day policymakers and commentators overlook their antecedents. They would be wiser for reading this book.

Dr. Branden Little, History Professor
Weber State University
July 2014

www.weber.edu/History/faculty/brandenlittle.html

Preface

The concept of this book lies in the early 1980s when I received an inheritance of the CRB-related letters, journals, and photos of my grandfather, Milton M. Brown, and the edited diary and photos of my grandmother, Erica Bunge Brown. (Bunge is pronounced "Boong-ah.") As a young man I had been interested in the stories my grandfather had told about his time in German-occupied Belgium as one of Herbert Hoover's CRB delegates. His stories seemed always to be about Hoover or the other American delegates; rarely did he speak of the Belgians of that time or how he had met my grandmother. My grandmother rarely spoke of that time, although I'm not sure of that because I was a teenager then and had the attention span of a gnat. In the end, most of the stories I remember came not from my grandparents but from my mother, Erica Sophie Lucy Brown Miller, who had heard many of them from her parents.

Before receiving my grandparents' material, I had graduated from the University of Denver with a BA degree in history. I wanted to be a writer, magazine editor, and book author. My passion was historical novels, so, of course, I decided to write a historical novel about my grandparents and the CRB. But I didn't want the book to be just about my family's participation. Besides learning about Herbert Hoover and the CRB, I researched in depth three other delegates (Joe Green, Maurice Pate, and Fred Eckstein) and two U.S. diplomats (Brand Whitlock and Hugh Gibson). I also read a wealth of books written by other delegates about their service in the CRB.

After two full-time years of researching and writing, I produced an 850-page historical novel, *Honor Bound*. During the writing process, my mother had been my Belgian historical consultant, my brother Eric had been my concept editor, and my cousin Evie Newell had been my copy editor. When it came time to sell the book, I had a few nibbles from a handful of agents and publishers who wanted to read the entire book, but no contract was offered.

As the years passed I did become a writer, a magazine editor, and a book author and in the process had to face the fact that my writing strength was in nonfiction, not fiction. I put away *Honor Bound* and thought I would someday convert it to creative nonfiction.

In February 2009 I was diagnosed with stage 4 throat cancer and began a year I'd prefer to forget. Once I was declared cancer free (thank you, doctors and nurses), it took me a few years to totally reengage with life. I felt like a mountain goat on the shifting sands of a beach, with no solid rock to regain my footing.

Then in December 2012, while exercising in my basement on a NordicTrack machine, I suddenly "saw" myself working on, and completing, a history of the CRB. I ran upstairs and told my wife in the melodramatic way I have, "I'm back!"

And thus I began the journey that has led to this book.

Because I had previously written two books that were published by traditional book publishers, I knew that if I wanted to find a traditional publisher interested in taking on my book and printing it in 2014 (the 100-year anniversary of the start of World War I and the CRB), I would have had to have completed the manuscript in 2012. So, the same day I committed to the project, I committed to self-publishing the book in 2014.

I quickly discovered that it was a brave new world out there since my last book was published in 2002. And the research world had changed dramatically since the advent of the Internet. Nevertheless, I still spent a week of research at each of three institutions: the Herbert Hoover Presidential Library and Museum Archives in West Branch, Iowa; the Hoover Institution Library and Archives at Stanford University, California; and Princeton University's Seeley G. Mudd Manuscript Library in Princeton, New Jersey. I ended up collecting copies of letters, documents, and journals from approximately 30 of the more than 185 CRB delegates who had served. I also reacquainted myself with the two years of research I had done in the 1980s, and I read numerous books about Belgium and World War I, collecting more than 120 volumes on the topic.

My initial 2012 concept was to write one book solely on the CRB delegates. A handful of excellent books have been published about the major international players and the tremendous diplomatic negotiations that were necessary to establish and operate the largest food and relief drive the world had ever seen. To me, though, those books tell the story at the 30,000-foot level. Granted, it's an important story to tell, but I wanted to tell the story of the boots-on-the-ground CRB delegates who had done the work inside German-occupied Belgium.

As I dug deeper into the material, however, I realized I did not want to write a book simply on the CRB delegates. To fully understand and appreciate the young Americans' stories, readers had to also have a working knowledge of the war and of Belgium behind "the ring of steel," as Hoover termed it.

Suddenly the project morphed into a gigantic book, and I was faced with a critical decision: Write one large book that would miss the 100-year anniversary of the CRB's founding (October 1914) and not include many of the small details that I feel make a book come alive, or write three books that include much of what has never been published before, with the first book in the series being published in 2014. Obviously, I chose the latter.

I hope it was a wise choice, although only time will tell.

What I do know is that this is a great story of one of America's finest humanitarian achievements, and it deserves to be told. For a long time these men and women have been lying quietly—silent through the years because no one has asked them to speak. In this book I hope you feel that they are now standing proudly and telling their stories.

—JEFFREY B. MILLER

Acknowledgments

No book is a one-person project. I've been fortunate to have a team of professionals who have agreed to help me make this book the best possible. The process of team building started for me in the research stage. I am grateful for the warm, welcoming, and helpful assistance of Matthew T. Schaefer, archivist at the Herbert Hoover Presidential Library and Museum Archives, West Branch, Iowa; to Carol A. Leadenham, assistant archivist for reference, and David Jacobs, archival specialist, at the Hoover Institution Library and Archives at Stanford University, California; and to Emma Harrold at Oxford University Archives, United Kingdom. I was also assisted in research in Iowa by professional researcher Wesley Beck.

During this stage I was fortunate to have had a chance meeting at the Herbert Hoover Presidential Library and Museum Archives with Dr. Branden Little, a history professor who teaches at Weber State University in Ogden, Utah. He has been studying the CRB and many other humanitarian relief efforts for more than a decade. In the highly competitive world of academic research and writing, Little is unusual in his friendly openness and his willingness to share his knowledge of historical sources and give of his time. I'm proud to say that he has become a friend who has aided me in countless ways, big and small. He read the manuscript for any major historical inaccuracies, and he wrote the foreword.

I must also thank the ever-gracious George Nash, a scholar and biographer of Herbert Hoover. An extremely accessible and friendly man, he has been constantly supportive since I first began working on this project. He was kind enough to read the first section of the book and gave me wise counsel regarding it and numerous proposed front covers.

During the research stage, I was also fortunate enough to come in contact with a handful of descendants of CRB delegates. They were tremendously helpful and willing to share any information they had about their relatives. They included Dr. Erskine Carmichael, nephew of Oliver C. Carmichael; John P. Nelson, son of delegate David T. Nelson; Sherman and Prentiss Gray, son and grandson, respectively, of delegate Prentiss Gray; and Margaret Hunt, granddaughter of delegate E. E. Hunt.

Outside of the CRB "family," I was also helped in numerous ways by Marc Brans, a Belgian amateur historian who lives outside of Antwerp, and by a New Jersey high school student, Hanl Park, who created a masterful video on the CRB for National History Day. (The video earned him a trip to the national round and can be seen at www.WWIBehindTheLines. com.)

In the writing, editing, and proofing stages, I am thankful to some general readers—my siblings Carolyn, Buck, and Leslie, my cousin Evie Newell, and Larry Yoder—who gave good advice and suggestions. I gained valuable insights from an editorial evaluation that was completed by professional book editor Mark Chimsky. I am indebted to professional editor Tom Locke, who ably handled the heavy lifting of editing and standardizing the text and having it conform to *The Chicago Manual of Style*. I'm thankful for the sharp eye of proofreader Laura Furney and for the highly specialized talents of freelance book indexer Linda Gregonis. The book cover concept and design were beautifully developed by professional graphic designer—and friend—Laurie Shields of Laurie Shields Design. The back cover and interior pages were created by the talented team of Dan and Jim Pratt of Pratt Brothers Composition. And the book's website, www.WWIBehindTheLines.com, was created by the business-savvy team led by Mike Bren and Seth Daire of Crown Point Solutions.

Finally, while the book's dedication says it all, I must end where it all began, with thanks to my grandparents and to my wife, Susan Burdick. The story came to me because of my grandparents; my being a writer came in large part because of Susan's unreserved love and support. I owe her all that I am—and more.

Author's Note

One of my professional goals has always been to write a history book that would be read by people who say they "never read history books." Through the years I've been inspired by the best history storytellers—writers such as Barbara W. Tuchman, David McCullough, Doris Kearns Goodwin, and Laura Hillenbrand. It remains to be seen whether or not I have come close to my goal.

So what is my job as a writer of history?

To me it is to capture a moment in time so that it comes alive and can be seen, felt, and otherwise experienced by those who read it. If, at the end of my book, readers feel they have met and become familiar with the main characters as living, breathing people, then I've done my job.

I can't speak for the reader, but for me, after years of research, these main characters are very much alive. I want to help young Erica Bunge survive the bombardment of Antwerp and fight the Germans. I want to be beside first-year Rhodes scholar David Nelson as he walks alone toward the Belgian border not knowing what to expect. I want to hear Hugh Gibson's sad, dry wit as he struggles to comprehend the scene before him of Germans who are still burning and looting Louvain. I want to politely scold Émile Francqui for putting unnecessary roadblocks in the way of the CRB. I want to ask Herbert Hoover if the manipulation of others is always acceptable if it's for the greater good. And I want to have a beer and intense conversation with war-correspondent-turned-compassionate-relief-worker E. E. Hunt about what he learned while fleeing with refugees from Belgium into Holland.

But does my vision of these people, places, and events match up with what other history scholars have written? Is my book "accurate"?

I think of history in fluid terms. I feel that capturing one moment in time is like capturing one moment in the bend of a river. What does the bend really look like? It all depends on your perspective. The pebble on the submerged riverbed sees it differently than the reeds on the right bank, the trees on the left, the bird gliding overhead, the fish battling upstream, and the bit of flotsam floating by.

I have collected, cataloged, read, and assimilated the documents, letters, journals, and photos of close to fifty different people. I've studied and read about War World I and Belgium.

This book contains my vision of who those people were and what they did. It is my vision. It is my perspective of the bend in the river.

More than thirty years ago I read a blurb in the front of a book. Today, the author's name and book title are long gone from my mind, but the words he wrote in that blurb have stuck with me: "I write; let the reader beware."

I might not have written what some academics would consider a scholarly history book. My formal training is in journalism and magazine writing, not scholarship and academic writing. I have possibly bent—or even broken—a few academic rules of history writing. If I have done so, my only defense is that I did so in an attempt to make the reading experience smooth and enjoyable for general readers.

An example is attribution within the text. If an item is historically common knowledge and/or in multiple sources, I did not attribute it in the text because it would have slowed down reading and been needlessly disruptive. However, the item is sometimes quoted to show I did not phrase it in that particular way or that I did not make it up. And it will be properly attributed in the notes at the end of the book—the source is confirmed, just not in the text.

Some readers might take exception to the way certain words are spelled in the book. In most cases, the words are spelled as they appeared in primary source materials. It is true that spelling has changed in a hundred years, and it's true that some names of towns, cities, and even buildings have changed. I felt, however, it was best to stay true to the time period and its original documents. An example is the famous Belgian city named Louvain/Leuven. I know that today it is known by the Flemish name of Leuven, but in the vast majority of 1914 materials I reviewed the city was referred to by the French name of Louvain. I, therefore, chose to retain Louvain throughout the book (with first reference indicating the Flemish spelling of Leuven).

I also know that when it comes to the book's scope and coverage, I have barely touched upon the varied Belgian, English, French, and German activities during the war. Simply put, I did not have the time, the space, or the expertise to do so. It helps to know that for the past 100 years there have been numerous great books that have covered each nationality's activities far better than I could ever do.

With those caveats in mind, I hope the reader enjoys reading *Behind the Lines,* my loving tribute to the men and women of Belgium and the CRB during World War I.

Black indicates countries that would form the Central Powers while those in white would become the Allies and associated countries. Gray shows neutral countries. It's interesting to note that on this map, used in a major history book of the war, Belgium (BEL.) is marked as being part of the Allies, even though it was neutral in "prewar Europe." (Brigadier General S. L. A. Marshall, *The American Heritage History of World War I*, American Heritage Publishing Co./Bonanza Books, 1982.)

Reader Aids
Primary People in the Book

Oliver C. Carmichael—Twenty-three-year-old Rhodes scholar Carmichael was from Alabama and had scheduled a trip to Scotland during Oxford's six-week Christmas break before he heard of Hoover's need for neutral observers to go into German-occupied Belgium. If his account is correct, he and a fellow CRB delegate helped to smuggle from Belgium into Holland Cardinal Mercier's famous pastoral letter, which inflamed world opinion against the Germans and inspired the Belgians to resist their occupiers.

Perrin C. Galpin—He was a second-year man at Oxford when Hoover contacted him directly to see if he could round up volunteers to become CRB delegates. Galpin organized meetings, corresponded with Hoover and his executive committee, and chose the first twenty-five men from Oxford who went into Belgium. He personally went into Belgium with the second wave of recruits.

Hugh Gibson—The secretary to the U.S. Legation in Belgium, Gibson was thirty-one and nearing the middle of his career as a diplomat when the war broke out. He earned admiration and respect for his hard work, dedication to helping the Belgians, and fearless traveling through the country as the war was still in its pre-trenches stage. He would be loved for his unfailing sense of humor and dry, sarcastic wit.

Herbert Clark Hoover—A highly successful forty-year-old U.S. mining engineer, Hoover was living in London before the war and searching for a way to get into public service or politics. When war erupted he jumped right in to organize assistance for stranded American tourists trying to get back home. When Belgian representatives from various cities and provinces came to England looking for a way to avert seemingly inevitable starvation within their country, he took over and started the Commission for Relief in Belgium, which became the largest food and relief drive the world had ever known.

Edward Eyre Hunt (E. E. Hunt)—A sensitive and artistic magazine journalist in America, Hunt became a war correspondent so he could see the war up close and personal. When he did get a clear vision of what was happening—especially in Belgium—he became an important chief delegate in Hoover's CRB, helping to create and develop the processes of relief within the city and province of Antwerp, which encompassed 1 million people in 1914.

David T. Nelson—In late November 1914 Nelson was a first-year Rhodes scholar ready to embark on six weeks' vacation from Oxford. When the twenty-three-year-old from North Dakota heard that Hoover was looking for volunteers to go into German-occupied Belgium as neutral observers to ensure the food would not be taken by the Germans, he signed up. Of all the CRB delegates, he was the only one who had to walk solo into Belgium with only the clothes on his back and what was in his pockets.

Brand Whitlock—When Whitlock was appointed minister of the U.S. Legation in Belgium in early 1914, he was looking forward to working on his novels at the traditionally noneventful post. He would be thoroughly tested by the war and the potential starvation of 9 million people in Belgium and northern France. In the end, he would become a figure who was both respected and ridiculed, beloved and belittled.

THE BELGIANS

Edouard Bunge—A wealthy Antwerp merchant, Bunge was vice president of the provincial relief committee for Antwerp Province, owner of Chateau Oude Gracht on the Hoogboom estate, and widowed father of five daughters—three of whom, Erica, Eva, and Hilda, were living with him when the war broke out.

Erica Bunge—A twenty-two-year-old woman from a wealthy Belgian family, Erica Bunge was unusual because she had graduated from agricultural college in England and helped run the farm on the family's Hoogboom estate. During the German occupation of Belgium, she would help in a soldiers' hospital, volunteer at a soup kitchen, and work late at night in the underground against the Germans.

Abbé Vincent de Moor—A man of the Catholic cloth, de Moor was not only a priest but a clandestine operative for British intelligence. He became partners with Eugene van Doren on an underground newspaper that would inspire a nation but lead to the imprisonment of many and the execution of a few, including a young Belgian woman named Gabrielle Petit.

Émile Francqui—One of the most powerful and ruthless financial men in Belgium before the war, Francqui would lead the Comité National, the Belgian counterpart to the CRB that handled the actual distribution of the CRB food throughout the country. He and Hoover had met before and disliked each other immensely. With his passion for his country and his dominating personality, Francqui would create numerous problems for Hoover and the CRB.

Eugene van Doren—A Belgian cardboard manufacturer, van Doren so hated the Germans that he took up clandestine work for de Moor before helping to develop the idea for an underground newspaper, *La Libre Belgique*. His work and the newspaper would inspire the nation and would lead to a German reward of 50,000 francs for the capture of the newspaper's publisher, whose identity was unknown to the Germans.

BEHIND
THE LINES

"All that is necessary for evil to triumph is for good men to do nothing."

ATTRIBUTED TO EDMUND BURKE,
BUT SPECIFIC PHRASEOLOGY IS DISPUTED

ONE

A Story Few Have Heard

"There Once Was a Nice Little Town in That Place"

On a cold evening in late November 1914, a German officer was drinking with a boisterous group of fellow officers in the luxurious Hotel Astoria. Situated in Brussels, Belgium, on Rue Royale near the city's major park, the hotel was in the fashionable upper part of town and had been commandeered by the German occupation forces for their officers, staffs, and privileged guests.

Nearly four months before, on Tuesday, August 4, the German Army had started World War I by invading neutral Belgium on its way to its real objective, France. The German officer had been a part of that invading force. A "fine-looking man" with "agreeable manners," he was in his mid-thirties and had lived in England for years before returning to Germany to become a cavalry officer in the kaiser's army.

Even though it was late—past midnight—and all the other Germans had stumbled off to bed, this cavalry officer stayed at the table and spoke in perfect English to two Americans, war correspondent E. E. Hunt and neutral observer Lieutenant Victor Daniel Herbster of the U.S. Navy, both of whom were visiting the German-occupied city.

Referring to the August days of the invasion, the German calmly stated that the Belgians "do not understand war, and they do not understand the rules of war. I remember once riding into a little town down here in the South of Belgium and finding my four scouts lying dead in the streets. Civilians had butchered horses and men—shot them from behind.

"I ordered my men to go into the houses and kill every one they found. Then I ordered them to burn the town."

The man sat back a moment, raised his glass, then took a drink.

"There once was a nice little town in that place. There is no such town now."

Hunt would never forget the German's calm, brutal words, and they would follow him when less than a month later, in December, he joined a small group of Americans who would try to save more than 9 million Belgian and French civilians from starving to death.

The interlacing stories of German brutality, Belgian resistance, the struggles against starvation, and the American men Hunt joined in the burgeoning Commission for Relief in Belgium (CRB), all began back in those chaotic days of August 1914, when the Germans attacked the little country. Few could have guessed it then, but the invasion acted like a toppling domino that would cause a tumbling together of extraordinary people into a chain reaction of life-and-death situations far from the trenches and killing fields of World War I.

And hanging in the balance were millions of civilian lives.

It is a story that few have heard.

AUGUST 1914

INVASION

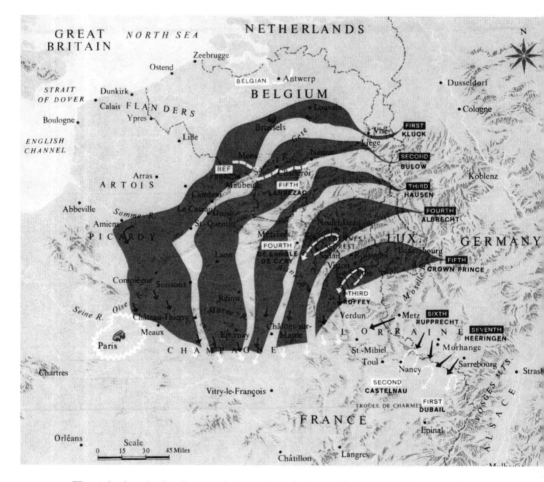

The paths that the five German field armies took through Belgium and France in August and where the British Expeditionary Force and the French unsuccessfully tried to stop them (broken white lines and arrows). (The American Heritage History of World War I, Brigadier General S. L. A. Marshall, American Heritage Publishing Co./Bonanza Books, 1982.)

Setting the Stage

Practically Inevitable

"To understand Germany, you must think in centuries."

While the German who said that believed he was speaking philosophically about his country alone, he was aptly describing the soul of every European power at the turn of the twentieth century. Major conflicts from the past—such as the Thirty Years' War (1618–1648), the Napoleonic Wars (1803–1815), and the Franco-Prussian War (1870–1871)—were still very much alive in the hearts, minds, and attitudes of many Europeans. As a result, each country's collective memory was as much comforting as it was confining and controlling.

So what happened next was practically inevitable.

By the summer of 1914, decades of European political posturing, diplomatic wrangling, treaty negotiations, and international skirmishes—inflamed by the June 28 assassination of Austria's Archduke Ferdinand and his wife, Sophie—led inescapably to Tuesday morning, August 4, when five German armies, numbering 1 million men, amassed along Germany's western border.

This was the largest invasion force ever assembled, and it was to follow Germany's revised Schlieffen Plan of attack, which called for the five armies to sweep in a wide westward arc through Belgium into France, overwhelming the French Army and capturing Paris to achieve a quick victory. Ensuring France's rapid defeat was essential, the German General Staff believed, so it could then shift troops to its eastern front and help its Austro-Hungarian allies defeat Russia before the tsar's armies could fully mobilize. It was critical to Germany's war plans that the sweep through Belgium be lightning fast, or the Germans would be caught in a prolonged and probably unwinnable two-front war.

Belgium was no stranger to invading armies. In fact, it was known as the cockpit of Europe, referring to the cockfighting ring where two fierce roosters would battle to exhaustion or death. On a map the three countries of Belgium, Holland, and Luxembourg (known as the Low Countries because much of their land is below sea level or slightly above) appeared as a rough-hewn wedge driven between France and Germany. In the past, Belgium had always been a region without its own country—pieces of which had belonged at times to France, Germany, Holland, Spain, and Austria. Its people were eyewitnesses to many other nations' battles across their land—most notably the Battle of Waterloo, on the outskirts of Brussels, where Napoleon had his final defeat in 1815.

In 1830, however, this region that would later become Belgium successfully revolted and seceded from Holland; enthroned King Leopold I on July 21, 1831; and was recognized by the international community as a country for the first time. While only slightly smaller than Maryland, Belgium makes up for its lack of girth with its critical spot on the European map: Germany and Luxembourg lie on its eastern border, the North Sea and the United Kingdom are to the west, Holland is to the north, and France is to the south.

No one could deny the strategic importance of Belgium's location, and in an obvious move to prevent the past from repeating itself, the 1839 Treaty of London declared the little country permanently neutral. The treaty proved critical to Belgium's survival and was signed by Great Britain, Austria, Prussia (the precursor of Germany), Russia, France, Holland, and Belgium. Each signatory pledged to respect Belgium's neutrality and to defend it from any invader. Even so, the pragmatic

Belgians knew their own history well enough that they maintained a small defensive army of fewer than 150,000 men. No one was going to take away their hard-fought freedom without a fight.

It was no surprise, then, how the Belgian government responded to an August 2, 1914, German ultimatum, which basically stated: If you stand aside as the kaiser's armies pass through to invade France, you will remain a sovereign nation, and no Belgian will be hurt; if you resist, we will destroy you. Germany had already declared war on Russia the day before (August 1), and it declared war on France on August 3, the same day Belgium courageously refused the German ulti

King Albert of Belgium was thirty-nine years old and little-known to the world before the start of World War I. (Public domain; multiple sources.)

matum and said it would not allow Germany to march through unopposed. That same day, in a rousing speech to the Belgian Parliament, King Albert declared: "I have faith in our destiny. A country which defends itself enforces the respect of all; such a country shall not perish. God will be with us in this just cause. Long live free Belgium!" The country then prepared as best it could for the coming onslaught, hoping its two major neutrality supporters, France and England, would honor their 1839 treaty commitment and come to its aid.

While the Belgians saw the Germans as aggressive invaders, the Germans described themselves, and their actions, quite differently. The Germans said they felt they had no choice but to fight, as explained by their chancellor, Theobald von Bethmann-Hollweg. On August 4, only a few hours after the invasion started, Bethmann-Hollweg gave a patriotic speech to the German Reichstag (parliament) that admitted Germany had violated Belgian neutrality but insisted it had the right to do so because its preemptive assault against France was in self-defense. Germany was fighting for its national survival, Bethmann-Hollweg maintained, because France was bent on avenging the German victories of the Franco-

Prussian War and had already developed a plan to attack Germany. The only way to thwart the French quest for revenge, the German authorities declared, was to attack first.

But violating Belgium's sacred neutrality was a huge gamble for Germany, which did not want to fight Britain as well as France and Russia. Germany hoped that Britain would not stand behind its 1839 treaty pledge to protect Belgium's neutrality. Bethmann-Hollweg even told the British ambassador to Germany, Sir Edward Goschen, that he found it hard to believe Britain would go to war over "a scrap of paper."

It was a statement that was quickly repeated—and condemned—around the world.

Within hours, Britain declared war on Germany, not only to honor the 1839 treaty but also to stop Germany's aggression. Britain's entrance into the war brought the last major power in Europe into the fight: Britain, Russia, and France as the Entente Powers or Allies against Germany, Austria-Hungary, and the Ottoman Empire (centered in modern Turkey) as the Central Powers. Across the Atlantic, the U.S. government, along with the majority of Americans, wanted to stay clear of the fight and declared neutrality on August 4, with President Woodrow Wilson detailing that neutrality to congress on August 19.

Back in Europe, it would take France and Britain precious days, if not weeks, to mount significant defensive maneuvers.

In the meantime, Belgium stood staunchly alone to defend its neutrality against one of the best-equipped and most mobile armies the world had ever seen.

Belgium Prepares for Invasion

With great precision and organization the Germans implemented their grand invasion plans. In fact, their general sense of preparedness was so well-known and accepted that they were given credit for some rather unorthodox (albeit untrue) war planning—most notably the absurdly unrealistic item reported as fact by the *New York Times* in a quote from a source: "In June the Germans ordered 80,000 road maps from the Brussels Motor Touring Club."

On the receiving end of the invasion, the Belgians had not thought to include a motorcar club in their war plans, so they were far less prepared—not to mention they thought they were protected by treaty-sanctioned neutrality. As such, in late July and the first few days of August, they reacted with barely controlled bedlam to the coming invasion.

Thirty-nine-year-old King Albert and the military, which had mobilized July 31, took charge of the country's defense and immediately began strategic destruction of land and property to slow Germany's advance. Nonessential bridges were blown up, critical river crossings were fortified, and the country's extensive canal system was sabotaged by some of the blown bridges and even sunken barges. Around and near Belgium's renowned fortress system (rings of massive forts protecting critical cities such as Liège and Antwerp), whole forests were cut down, and buildings were blown up to gain better firing line-of-sight against the invader. Tree stumps within the then-dead forests were cut to jagged edges, while sharpened wooden lances protruded from defensive mounds and trenches— all in an effort to slow down the enemy. In cities such as Antwerp and Brussels, major thoroughfares were torn up, tram tracks wrecked, barricades of motorcars and trolleys erected, trenches dug into streets, and barbed-wire fences were strung up by the untrained but highly enthusiastic *garde civique* (civilian guard).

For civilians, life had a feel of near-blind confusion. Martial law was declared in Brussels because of anti-German rioting. Countrywide, banks closed or suspended critical financial services. Black markets prospered as food prices soared. Travel became difficult. Military checkpoints were established on major roads. Trains and trams were rescheduled at a moment's notice or commandeered by the military. Motorcars were requisitioned or banned from nonessential travel, and most horses were seized by the military. (Even with the then-recent advent of mechanized travel, armies still relied heavily on horses for transportation of everything from soldiers and materials to artillery and field kitchens.) The only way for most Belgians to get around was to walk, and rarely was that out of their neighborhood or village.

Communication within Belgium was severely restricted. It was nearly impossible to make a phone call, send a telegram, or receive a letter. Newspapers were still being printed, but they were hard to find and, in many cases, filled with more rumors than reliable news. In an age without radio or television, and at a time when telephones were more novelty than necessity, Belgium had, in essence, returned to medieval times—life became centered around a person's tiny slice of the world, whether it was a small village in the country or a neighborhood within a city.

With such uncertainty and lack of credible information, Belgians became justifiably concerned, fearful, and suspicious. Every day brought countless new rumors that could never be substantiated. Anyone not personally known was thought to be a spy in the employ of the coming invaders.

Belgian Woman Erica Bunge—"We Are Desperate"

In Antwerp, according to British reporter and photographer R. Scotland Liddell, crowds turned on residents who were Germans, wrecking "all the little German cafes and saloon-bars in the dirty, narrow slum streets around the docks, many of them cesspools of iniquity that ought to have been wrecked long ago in any case. They threw stones through every window and plate-glass sign. They set some places on fire. They entered upstairs rooms and threw out the chairs on which many of them had sat the week before, and tables and ornaments, and even the cheap German pianos whose tinkling notes had been the source of mingled pleasure and disturbance in the neighbourhood."

Young Erica Bunge wrote in her diary on Sunday, August 2: "There is talk of throwing out foreigners from [Antwerp] and the country. Tomorrow the army will purchase 400 horses. It is very probable that ours will be requisitioned. Our cars are still here. Every foreigner has left."

A twenty-two-year-old Belgian from a wealthy merchant family, Erica, along with two of her four sisters, Eva and Hilda, lived a privileged life with their widowed father, Edouard Bunge. Before the war they had moved effortlessly between their large townhouse at 21 Rue Marie-Therese in Antwerp and their chateau named Oude Gracht, which was on Hoogboom estate twenty miles northeast of the city.

Of average height and build, Erica had long brown hair that she kept pinned up and an oval, open face and pale blue eyes, which darkened when angry. Her broad smile was slow to come, but also slow to fade once it appeared. Her laugh was hearty and deep.

As a child she had always been a bit different from other young girls. She enjoyed time with her father in his study at Oude Gracht, watching him handle the business papers that he pulled from his worn dispatch case, and even staying when he and his business associates managed their varied corporate affairs. Years later her father had turned to her as a trusted business associate, asking her advice about problems with his worldwide shipping company, his agricultural concerns in South America, and his

From left: Hilda, Eva, and Erica Bunge. (Author's family archives.)

rubber plantations in Malaysia. Her family was not surprised when she announced she wanted to go to agricultural college in England—a rarity for women in the early 1900s—and when she returned with her degree, she began to participate in the management of Hoogboom's farm.

Nearly every day before the war Erica had had a ritual that she loved. She would rise early before many of her family members were up, quietly go downstairs, and gather her coat and hat from the *vestiaire* (cloakroom) in the right front tower of the chateau. Most times Isidore, Oude Gracht's *maitré de hôtel* (head butler), was there to assist her with her coat. She would then pass through the great hall, listening to her shoes echo off the part of the parquet floor that wasn't covered by the large Turkoman rug. Taking the French doors onto the back stone terrace, she would stand for a moment and start her day by looking out over the estate's small lake. Many times she would see two black swans gliding gracefully across the still water. Sheep were nearly always grazing on the other side while birds chattered and sang to the rising sun. A tiny island, no more than 100 feet across, lay in the middle of the lake. A ring of thick pines edged the island with five taller pines in the center representing the five Bunge girls. She never knew which tree represented her, but she hoped it was the strongest. It didn't need to be the tallest—just the strongest.

Taking a deep breath, she would then walk down the stone steps to the rim of the white gravel that circled the house like a moat. She would walk to the side of the chateau where a cobblestoned lane led to the farm. The path crossed a wooden bridge spanning one of the property's numerous canals that fed the lake.

In a few minutes she would reach the farm, which was the size of a small village. Buildings lined three or four converging cobbled alleys, and there were long barns for cattle, horses, and sheep. Surrounding these were the houses of the farm superintendent, the gardener, and the game-keeper, as well as numerous smaller cottages for the farm tenants. All were red brick with thick thatched roofs, and they sported shutters and doors painted bright red and white.

Even at the early hour in which she would arrive at the farm, there would be workers already moving about. Dressed in traditional corduroy pants, coarse shirts, peasant caps, and *sabots* (wooden shoes), they would many times be working with the large draft horses, high-wheeled delivery wagons, or dog carts or simply be standing about talking and smoking as they waited for the day's instructions. They would respectfully raise their hats as Erica would go by; she would nod and say in Flemish, "*Goeiemorgen*," adding names when she knew them.

Walking to one of the smaller buildings, she would go in and meet with Verheyen, the farm's superintendent. He was hardened and big like many of the rest of the workers, but her father had said he had chosen him years before because his eyes had shown a shrewd intelligence and kindly nature.

When she had returned from British agricultural college, she was sure of herself and what she had learned. But in short order she had discovered from kindly Verheyen that academic knowledge sometimes had little to do with the realities of a working farm. He would always be waiting for her there in the mornings. When she was done conferring with Verheyen about the day's activities and the general operations of the farm, she would walk back to the chateau to join her family for breakfast.

By 1914, Erica was a serious-minded young woman who spoke thought-fully and always with conviction. She confided to her diary, however, that she longed for a partner who would be her equal, but she despaired of ever finding such a man. In early August 1914, as the German invasion began, her diary entries were filled only with war rumors and apprehensions of what would happen to her family and her country. Excerpts from her diary give insight into many Belgians' confusion, concern, and anxiety over the future.

Monday, August 3: "A day of terror in [Antwerp]. . . . The situation is very grave, the Germans have moved into Belgium and are coming from the North. We started to pack up everything and then we waited for news from Pereken [nickname for her father] who had to go to Brussels. At last a telegram by phone: news of the German invasion is denied, not a German soldier in Belgium. Do not worry, send a car for me as usual. . . . Three sacks of flour cost 70 francs."

Tuesday, August 4: "There is no more telephone for private people. The street [outside the Antwerp townhouse] is torn up in places and we can't get through. In the city there have been demonstrations against the Germans, the Consul and the Vice-Consul have left. . . . The Consulate's windows have been broken, also those of the German school. Stones and ladders were used."

Wednesday, August 5: "All the Germans were thrown out of Antwerp during the night . . . We are living from day to day. My God, don't let this war last long. . . . I went to Hoogboom, everything is quiet and calm. There is a lot of damage everywhere [from the digging of] trenches, many trees are down."

Friday, August 7: "I couldn't write yesterday, I was too sad and shattered. It was thought that Pereken was German! What an affront! An official came last night to ask Pereken if he would put something in the papers about what he does. . . . I hate those Germans, they are vile! . . . At Hoogboom there are a lot of [Belgian] soldiers [to set up defensive positions], and the cannons are on our land, pulled there by our oxen. At our place there were only small pine trees lost. Poor Guillot [the property's arborist] was howling when they touched his trees, and this morning he was taken to the hospital, totally out of his mind. . . . Spies are picked up everywhere, it's terrible, they are disguised as gendarmes, soldiers, anything. If only they could all be killed. . . . What news tomorrow?"

Saturday, August 8: "News is rare and everything is contradictory. We don't know anything officially. . . . Today we hear pessimistic news for the first time: there are many wounded, things are going badly, we really don't hear anything definite."

During the war, the Chateau Oude Gracht was home to Antwerp merchant Edouard Bunge and three of his five daughters, Erica, Eva, and Hilda. (Author's family archives.)

Sunday, August 9: "We wanted to go to Hoogboom but it was impossible. No permission."

Monday, August 10: "I went to Hoogboom, we were stopped nine times to show our permits. I arrived just in time. A detachment of [Belgian] Artillery is on our place, Commandant Nyssens, eight officers and junior officers, two orderlies, a stableman, and one cook are living in the chateau. We made ready 14 rooms, they all seemed very happy with the good beds and the baths. The soldiers have permission to bathe, to catch rabbits and other things; a good post! There are 400 infantry soldiers, a Commander and some officers, and the whole estate belongs to them! I hope they will respect it. . . . We came back [from Antwerp] by train and car. . . . The train was stopped before it reached the city and the permits were checked."

Tuesday/Wednesday, August 11/12: "No official news . . . Where are the Allies? . . . The waiting is awful, we cannot do anything. . . . We have 600 [Belgian] soldiers on the estate, 400 infantry and 200 artillery. Fifteen are in the chateau. 450 grams of meat a day, one loaf of bread, and the rest, 150 kilos of potatoes are taken per day. Soon there won't be anything left."

Thursday, August 13: "Where the devil are the French? . . . We don't hear anything, it's horrible to have to wait. . . . I went with Eva to collect donations for the Children's Soldiers' Fund."

Friday, August 14: "Still no news, we are desperate. The poor soldiers. We don't know anything new. The great battle must not have been fought yet. The [Belgian] Commandant [at Hoogboom] believes that the Germans will march on Antwerp and will try to take the forts. It would be awful. And we have to wait. . . . There has been a lot of work done digging trenches [on Hoogboom] by the infantry. Pereken is very tired, beaten down. . . . What will become of us? Personally I'm not afraid, it's so heartbreaking to think of those who are fighting."

Franc-tireurs—"Wholly Against the Laws of War"

Erica Bunge's concern for the Belgian troops was well-founded, and she would have undoubtedly included civilians in her thoughts if she had known how well prepared the German Army was to wage a horrific war. One of Germany's early statesmen, Otto von Bismarck (1815–1898), had written back in 1870 that to be truly successful an army had to have a strategy of destruction and intimidation, which was known as *schrecklichkeit*. "True strategy consists in striking your enemy and striking him hard," stated Bismarck. "Above all things you must inflict on the inhabitants of invaded territories the maximum of suffering, in order to discourage them from the struggle. . . . You must leave to the people . . . nothing but their eyes with which to weep."

And who was to inflict such devastation? They would be men who had been born and bred for war. As one World War I German officer explained, war "was not taught us at school, nor in the universities, nor even the barracks—we learned it in our mother's womb."

And it was their "father"—Kaiser Wilhelm—who issued an order the first week of August that stated, "After forty-three years of peace I call upon all Germans capable of bearing arms. We have to defend our most sacred possessions in fatherland and home against the reckless assault of enemies on all sides of us.

"That means hard fighting," the kaiser continued. "I am confident that the ancient warlike spirit still lives in the German people—that powerful, warlike spirit which attacks the enemy wherever it finds him, regardless of costs, and which in the past has been the dread and terror of our enemies."

As for Belgium, the Germans had little but disdain for such a small and insignificant country. Famous Belgian journalist Victor Jourdain wrote, "Belgium was represented [to the Germans] as a backward, barbarous, and cruel country, inhabited by a race of *franc-tireurs* [civilian guerrilla fighters]; a country where the civilians mutilated the prisoners, where the women poured boiling oil upon soldiers, where the young girls tore out the eyes of the wounded; a country, in short, whose inhabitants deserved no consideration and must be treated with the utmost rigour of martial law."

Jourdain continued, "The soldiers, as they set out [to invade Belgium], were taught that the war had been forced upon Germany and had been prepared by the Allies of the Triple Entente for two years, that they themselves were the army of civilization fighting the barbarians of Europe, that France was the home of immorality, England a self-seeking nation, and Belgium a country of franc-tireurs."

Franc-tireur was a word repeatedly used by the Germans when speaking of the invasion. While the French army defined the word as "sharpshooter" or "sniper," a more widely understood definition was "civilian or guerrilla fighter." Traditionally warfare was left to professional soldiers; noncombatants usually stayed just that. For a civilian to take up arms against a professional soldier was quite a shocking development. The Franco-Prussian War had acquainted German forces with civilian insurgents, and they were determined to prevent a recurrence when moving against Belgium and France. The German troops of 1914 considered "civilian resistance . . . to be wholly against the laws of war and proper military conduct."

Many Belgian burgomasters (mayors) believed the same, and in the early days of the invasion they posted placards and placed notices in local papers telling their residents to turn in all weapons, to do nothing aggressive against the Germans, and even, in some cases, to offer soldiers food and drink.

Nevertheless, from the start of the invasion the Germans insisted that Belgian *franc-tireurs* were killing their men, which left them no choice but to retaliate with the harshest of measures. Many Germans, from the kaiser and his generals down to the lowliest of foot soldiers, blamed *franc-tireurs* for inciting German reprisals, even though their belief was based on exaggerated fears of Belgian violence rather than actual sustained civilian resistance. The kaiser commented privately that "the population of Belgium behaved in a diabolical, not to say bestial, manner, not one iota better than the Cossacks. They tormented the wounded, beat them to death, killed doctors and medical orderlies, fired secretly . . . on men harmlessly standing in the street."

The German government officially stated: "Men of all professions, workers, manufacturers, doctors, professors, even clergymen—yes, even women and children, were taken with weapons in their hands, in the regions from which the regular troops had retired. They were shooting from houses or from gardens, from roofs and from cellars, from fields and from forests, on the Germans. They used means that would never be employed by regular troops, shot guns and lead shot, old revolvers and old pistols, and numerous were the men found mutilated or scalded with boiling tar or boiling water. In short, it is not to be doubted that the German wounded were struck and killed by the Belgian population, and also greatly mutilated; nor is it to be doubted that women and even girls participated in these shameful exploits. German wounded had their eyes punctured, their noses and ears and fingers and their sexual organs mutilated, their bodies ripped open; in other cases German soldiers were poisoned, sprayed with boiling liquid, or roasted, so that they suffered an atrocious death."

On the other side, Belgians accused German soldiers of countless atrocities against innocent civilians, everything from chopping off children's hands to raping and bayoneting pregnant women. Many Belgians and foreign observers swore these stories were true. Others, like Horace Green—a correspondent for the *New York Evening Post* who was in Belgium during the invasion—countered general public opinion when he stated: "The reports of unprovoked personal atrocities . . . have been hideously exaggerated. . . . In every war of invasion there is bound to occur a certain amount of plunder and rapine. The German system of reprisal is relentless; but the German private as an individual is no more barbaric than his brother in the French, the British, or the Belgian trenches."

While it's true that some of the Belgian stories were exaggerated or fabricated, many of them were horrifyingly accurate. And the stories—real or imagined—changed the way the rest of the world saw the war and its participants. "The controversy over whether the Belgians had ambushed the Germans or the Germans had massacred the Belgians profoundly shaped feeling about the war," stated historian Larry Zuckerman. "For many, Belgium defined a struggle between justice and lawlessness, civilization and barbarity. To a world that could not even have imagined death camps, bombed-out cities, or ethnic cleansing—or, in August 1914, the trench warfare that would soon bleed Europe—Belgium was a

A column of German foot soldiers during the August invasion. (Public domain: *Fighting in Flanders*, E. Alexander Powell, Charles Scribner's Sons, 1914.)

terrible shock. What had happened there challenged the axiom that cultured Europeans did not behave like savages."

Of all the stories of German atrocities committed during the invasion and immediately after, three became well known to all Belgians and achieved worldwide notoriety. Two were the stories of what happened to the picturesque frontier villages of Visé and Dinant while the third told of the horrors that descended upon the world-renowned university town of Louvain.

Visé—"Vanished From the Map"

The town of Visé did not have long to wait for its story to begin.

On that first day of the invasion, Tuesday, August 4, it was a hot and surprisingly clear summer day in the normally cool, cloudy, and wet country. At 8 a.m. German *uhlans* (lance-carrying cavalry) thundered across the border, signaling the start of what became the deadliest war the world had ever seen, and what Pope Benedict XV called "the suicide of civilized Europe." By evening six columns of German troops were two to three miles past the border.

Around noon the Germans entered the frontier village of Visé. Nestled on the right bank of the Meuse River, it boasted 3,800 people and 900 houses. When the Germans arrived, the Belgian soldiers withdrew from the town, crossed the Meuse, blew up the bridge behind them and settled onto the left bank, where they shot at any German who came close to the river.

According to historian Jeff Lipkes, within ten minutes of entering Visé, the Germans shot their first civilian. He was "Monsieur Istas, a cashier at the railway station, [who was] gunned down as he returned to work after an early lunch. . . . By evening, more than a dozen corpses littered the streets. Most of the murders seemed wholly arbitrary. . . . The Brouhas, father and son, brewers, were dragged out of their basement and executed in front of their house."

One of the town's barbers, Louis Kinable, was shot in front of his shop because he had a pair of clippers in his hand—hence he was seen as a *franc-tireur*. One boy was battered so badly by rifle butts "that his body could only be identified thanks to a card from his middle school proclaiming him an honors student." Meanwhile, a Berlin newspaper reported that a sixteen-year-old Belgian girl in Visé had been executed for mutilating German corpses.

On August 10 the Germans burned down Visé's church in the center of town, claiming its Gothic spire was being used by Belgian artillery to sight their cannons. Then, on the evening of August 15, eleven days after the town had been taken—and after the residents and their homes had been thoroughly searched for arms—the German troops began firing their weapons in response to what they said they thought were attacks by *franc-tireurs*. As terrified residents reacted to the guns, events escalated until the Germans were burning, looting, and killing. The destruction went on door-to-door for two days and nights. By August 18, the town was leveled, 631 citizens had been deported to Germany, twenty-three additional residents were dead, and more than 600 homes had been destroyed.

It was the "first systematic destruction of a Belgian town," according to one history of German atrocities. Systematic or not, as one observer later described it, all that remained were "heaps of brick and mortar like a ruined Pompeii, the only difference being that the bricks of the walls which still stand look newer." One German captain bluntly summed it up when he declared that Visé had simply "vanished from the map."

Dinant—"The Town Is *Gone*"

A few days later, it was Dinant's turn.

A town of more than 7,500, Dinant was the second largest in Namur Province and sat on the right bank of the Meuse River at a major crossing. Known for its stalactite caverns and chased copper and brass wares, and for being the birthplace of Adolphe Sax (the inventor of the saxophone), the town had survived for more than 700 years, squeezing itself in between the river and the base of barren limestone cliffs, which were crowned by a ruined fortress. The most distinctive element of the town's skyline was the 200-foot-high "curiously Oriental spire" of the Church of Notre Dame, a restored thirteenth-century Gothic structure located in the town's *grand place* (main square).

Because of its strategic position at a major river crossing and its close proximity to the French border, Dinant was quickly fortified by French troops when war was declared. After heavy fighting, though, the town was finally occupied by the Germans on Sunday, August 23. They promptly accused the residents of fighting alongside the regular troops and in retaliation began to destroy the town and kill its civilians.

That Sunday morning, according to later testimony in a committee of inquiry, "soldiers of the 108th Regiment of Infantry invaded the Church of the Premonastrensian [*sic*] Fathers, drove out the congregation, separated the women from the men, and shot 50 of the latter. Between 7 and 9 the same morning the soldiers gave themselves up to pillage and arson, going from house to house and driving the inhabitants into the street. Those who tried to escape were shot."

In some cases the Germans lined up people against a wall and executed them with machine guns. Monsieur Wasseige, the forty-three-year-old director of a Dinant bank, refused to open the bank's safe, so he and his two sons, Jacques, nineteen, and Pierre, twenty, along with about 100 others, were machine-gunned down in the town's square, *place d'armes*. The Germans forced Wasseige's three youngest children to witness the murder of their father and two brothers. Later, an American observer said, "We saw the wall with the machine-gun bullet marks, breast high, along its entire length."

Another person said, with cutting sarcasm: "Those killed [in Dinant] ranged in age from Felix Fivet, aged three weeks, to an old woman named Jadot, who was eighty. But then Felix probably fired on the German troops."

When the Germans were finally finished, they had "killed 674 people, deporting an unknown number and destroying 1,100 buildings." The town's distinctive church spire was gone, as was nearly everything else. "Dinant is far worse than anything I have seen, or even dreamed the war could bring about," said one American observer walking through the devastation later.

"The town is *gone*," said another American. "Part of the church is standing, and the walls of a number of buildings, but for the most part, there is nothing but a mess of scattered bricks to show where the houses had stood."

Louvain—"We Shall Make This Place a Desert"

The story of Louvain was different in some respects from the stories of Visé and Dinant, primarily because of its size and because it was already famous before the war began. Louvain (Leuven in Flemish) was a world-renowned university town only twenty miles west of Belgium's capital, Brussels. Home to more than 42,000 residents, it was famous for its Catholic university (founded in 1426) and incomparable library, which boasted 300,000 volumes and contained one of the world's greatest collections of rare medieval books and manuscripts. The Dyle River flowed through the town, and broad boulevards encircled it, having replaced the fourteenth-century ramparts that had protected Louvain for hundreds of years.

One journalist described the people as "brewers, lacemakers, and manufacturers of ornaments for churches. . . . The city [was] clean, sleepy, and pretty, with narrow twisting streets and smart shops and cafes set in flower gardens of the houses, with red roofs, green shutters, and white walls." Giving another perspective, the famous German travel author Karl Baedeker had declared Louvain "a dull place."

Regardless of its entertainment value, Louvain and its university library were world treasures that no one wanted to see damaged by war. Before the Germans appeared, the city had taken major steps to keep the peace. Belgian troops purposefully did not defend the town as a way of protecting it from German wrath; the local *garde civique* was disbanded, and all weapons in private hands were brought to the *hôtel de ville* (city hall). "All necessary measures had been taken to warn the inhabitants against protesting or shooting at the German soldiers. As elsewhere, weapons had been confiscated and posters warned the people not to take up arms;

reminders being issued daily in the newspapers and by the clergy," according to one historian.

The German entry into the city seemed to bode well. On August 19 the army paraded in with marching bands playing and soldiers singing loudly "Die Wacht am Rhein" ("The Watch on the Rhine," a patriotic anthem). Inhabitants remained calm but "were indeed terrified." The Germans—nervous themselves and constantly on guard for *franc-tireur* attacks—established a curfew of 8 p.m. and declared "house doors had to be kept open at night and windows lit. Every day, hostages were taken to guarantee the conduct of the citizens. New troop arrivals increased the concentration of soldiers in Louvain to at least 15,000." German commanders barracked soldiers in homes, and many of them looked the other way, or joined in, as their men looted whatever they wanted—everything from food and liquor to furniture and artwork.

On the evening of August 25, the real trouble began. Just before sunset sporadic shots were heard around town, which the Germans attributed to a significant attack by Belgian *franc-tireurs*. Residents believed the Germans were accidentally firing at each other. Regardless of how it started, the situation quickly escalated, and by nightfall, in almost complete darkness, it turned into a massive German rampage. Soldiers—many of them fearful and drinking—broke into houses, dragged out and shot residents, looted homes, and set buildings on fire. Horses "stampeded . . . and galloped riderless in all directions" as "panic spread like wildfire through the city."

The aged were not spared. "Hubert David-Fischbach . . . a man of eighty-three who had had German officers quartered in his house, was tied up and made to watch his house burn, beaten with bayonets, and finally shot. Others were killed during the night as they fled from their burning houses."

In the darkened and terrified city, the soldiers also broke into the university library and set it ablaze, using gas and other accelerants to do so; they then stopped any who tried to put the fire out. By some accounts it took nine to ten hours for all 300,000 books to burn.

But that wasn't the end of it. The German soldiers continued to rampage through the town for days. From August 25 through August 30 more than 248 Belgians were killed, hundreds were deported to Germany, and more than 2,000 structures—about a sixth of the city's buildings—were destroyed.

The ancient university town of Louvain in ruins after the Germans ransacked it August 25–30. (Public domain; multiple sources.)

On August 28, even though looting and burning were still going on, Hugh Gibson, the secretary of the U.S. Legation in Brussels, took a car and with three others drove east from Brussels to Louvain to see if the rumors of mass destruction coming from fleeing refugees were true. (There was no American embassy in Belgium, only the lesser diplomatic post of the U.S. Legation, located in Brussels, and the lesser-still consular offices, located in Antwerp, Brussels, Ghent, and Liège. The distinction between legation and embassy was slowly dropped after World War II.)

Gibson was able to travel around Belgium (albeit with difficulty) because he was a diplomat from a neutral country and had secured numerous passes and permits from the German military command to do so. Because the U.S. Legation was not well-equipped with vehicles, the motorcar Gibson used to go to Louvain had been donated by D. L. Blount, a young businessman living in Brussels, who also donated his services as driver. The Swedish and Mexican chargés d'affaires (heads of diplomatic missions, lower ranking than ambassador) went with them.

As the group approached Louvain, Gibson noticed: "The road was black with frightened civilians carrying away small bundles from the ruins of their homes. Ahead was a great column of dull gray smoke which completely hid the city. We could hear the muffled sound of firing ahead. Down the little street which led to the town, we could see dozens of white flags which had been hung out of the windows in a childish hope of averting trouble."

Gibson continued: "A lot of the houses were still burning, but most of them were nothing but blackened walls with smouldering timbers inside. Many of the front doors had been battered open in order to start the fires or to rout out the people who were in hiding. . . . Then we began to see more ghastly sights—poor civilians lying where they had been shot down as they ran—men and women—one old patriarch lying on his back in the sun, his great white beard nearly hiding his swollen face. All sorts of wreckage scattered over the street, hats and wooden shoes, German helmets, swords and saddles, bottles and all sorts of bundles which had been dropped and abandoned when the trouble began. . . . The boulevard looked as though it had been swept by a cyclone."

The group came across a German officer who spoke English and told them that because of the *franc-tireur* attacks an order had been given to destroy the city. "We shall make this place a desert," the officer declared to Gibson. "We shall wipe it out so that it will be hard to find where Louvain used to stand. For generations people will come here to see what we have done, and it will teach them to respect Germany and to think twice before they resist her. Not one stone on another, I tell you."

As the group surveyed the incredible destruction, one of the party wanted to take a photo with his Kodak. Very aware that he was in a city that was still under fire and filled with highly volatile German troops, the man, as Gibson later wrote, turned to the German officer and asked as politely as possible, "May I take a picture?"

The tired and distracted officer said magnanimously, "Certainly; go ahead. You will find some beautiful things over there on the corner in the house they are getting ready to burn."

Louvain burned and crumbled August 25 to August 30 when, reportedly, orders were finally received from Berlin to stop the destruction. Because of the city's renown, its story became much more than just another tale of German brutality. As newspaper journalist Arthur L. Humphreys explained, Louvain characterized "Belgium's ordeal to the outside world."

THREE

Marching Into Brussels

While Belgium's "ordeal" was a burden few countries had ever shouldered, its army did achieve the critical goal of slowing down the German invasion—although nothing at that stage had totally stopped the German juggernaut.

Liège, a large city in the east of Belgium near the German border, had been the first major objective of the invasion. While the city's ring of heavily fortified forts had held out longer than many expected, the Germans made short work of what the Belgians had thought were the forts' impregnable walls. The Germans accomplished this with their new 75-ton "Big Bertha" howitzer, which was designed to destroy concrete fortifications with its 2,052-pound projectiles. By August 17, Liège and its system of forts had fallen. The five German armies continued their arcing swing through Belgium and France.

On Thursday, August 20—a week before Louvain began to burn—Brussels, the capital of Belgium, was declared an open city, which meant both sides had acknowledged there would be no defensive resistance by the Belgians as the Germans marched in and no unprovoked destruction by the Germans. This saved the city from damage but meant the Belgians had to endure the pain of having the Germans march in as a conqueror that had paid nothing in battle to do so.

A Chance Meeting of a Businessman and an Abbé

During the morning of Thursday, August 20, on a hill within a newly built suburb east of Brussels, a small crowd of neighbors and passersby gathered. Such a coming together normally would have been filled with greetings, handshakes, embraces, and conversations, but that day nearly everyone stood silent and still. Those who did talk did so in frightened and anxious whispers. Parents held tightly to their children.

They had come to watch the beast enter their city. Off in the distance they saw the long, waving line of soldiers marching resolutely along "like some monstrous grey reptile." The head had long since passed from view, moving with relentless resolve toward the heart of the Belgian capital, while the end was miles away.

Standing in the small crowd on the hillside, watching this spectacle of massive force, were two men who were nearly a head taller than those around them. Neither man would ever have thought that a few inches of height would make the difference between life and death for people they had not yet met, nor give hope to an entire nation. History would say otherwise.

Eugene van Doren was "for a Belgian . . . uncommonly tall," slim, and with sloping shoulders. He had a scholarly look that was accented by close-cropped hair and pince-nez (glasses with a nose clip rather than ear pieces). At thirty-eight years old, with a wife and five young children, van Doren was a successful cardboard manufacturer with strongly held political beliefs. His blue eyes "were mild and thoughtful, but . . . they quickly reflect his feelings and occasionally flash with unexpected fire. His mouth, extremely mobile, smiles easily, and he has a ready laugh, when his eyes gleam boyishly." Altogether, he was a passionate, enthusiastic man who was never afraid to show both.

Standing not far away, the Abbé Vincent de Moor, vicar of the nearby Church of Saint Albert, was "no ordinary priest." He was "broad-minded, iron-willed, fearless and as strong as a horse," with black hair and the "jaw

Eugene van Doren, a thirty-eight-year-old Belgian cardboard manufacturer, became a driving force in the underground against the German occupation. (Underground News, The Complete Story of the Secret Newspaper That Made War History, Oscar E. Millard, Robert M. McBride and Company, 1938.)

of a fighter. There was devil in his dark eyes and his mouth was like a steel trap. But the hard mouth frequently softened into a broad smile which, with the twinkling eyes, gave the aggressive features an unexpected and wholly attractive gaiety." That day, no doubt, de Moor's jaw was set, and his mouth was tightly resolute.

If not for their height, the two men might have missed sharing a look of disgust and anger. Though they had never met, van Doren was compelled by the moment of eye contact to move through the crowd and introduce himself to the priest. "In that chance meeting van Doren found the man who was to become one of his staunchest allies and a life-long friend." And, together, they would accomplish the nearly impossible, all the while bedeviling the German civilian government, generating a 50,000-franc reward for their capture, and creating an obsession to stop them in the mind of the German governor general of Belgium, Baron Moritz Ferdinand von Bissing, a seventy-year-old Prussian officer.

But their actions would also lead ultimately to the imprisonment of many and the execution of some, including a heroic twenty-three-year-old Belgian girl, Gabrielle Petit, who gave up a chance for freedom and said good-bye to her fiancé so she could work for their cause. She was to be one of eleven women the Germans tried, convicted, and executed by firing squad in Belgium during World War I.

Brand Whitlock, U.S. Legation Minister

As van Doren and the abbé began to talk, closer to the city's center Brand Whitlock, the newly appointed minister to the U.S. Legation in

The Abbé Vincent de Moor (pictured in a later army uniform) was vicar of Saint Albert Church in Brussels and underground partner with van Doren. He also worked with British intelligence against the Germans. (Public domain; multiple sources.)

Belgium, was racing around in a motorcar, trying to find the advancing army.

Whitlock was forty-five years old and had taken office only seven months before. Born in Urbana, Ohio, he had had a successful career as a journalist, working as a reporter in Chicago before entering politics and becoming mayor of Toledo, Ohio, in 1905. He had been reelected in 1907, 1909, and 1911.

Whitlock was tall and slender, with a long, thin nose and eyes that had the "tense look of constantly straining to see something too close to him." With his rimless pince-nez, he had the appearance of a scholar or professor, and just like one, he longed for the solitude of a writer's garret. When President Wilson had appointed him to lead the U.S. Legation in Brussels, it was just what Whitlock had hoped for. The post was known as a quiet one, with more diplomatic show than substance. That suited Whitlock perfectly, for all he wanted to do was have time to write literary novels.

If he had known what the next four years would be like—and what history would call on him to do—he probably would not have taken the position. And while Whitlock was as yet little known in Belgium, he would, during the next few years, become a figure who was both respected and ridiculed, beloved and belittled. But in the spring and early summer of 1914, Whitlock saw Brussels and all of Belgium as blessed islands of solitude and peace for his work as a novelist.

All that changed on Saturday, August 1, as the war clouds had gathered. At six that morning, Whitlock was awakened by Omer, one of his servants, who told him that even though he had finished his Belgian national military service years ago, he had been called up and had come to say good-bye. Later, as Whitlock walked through Brussels, he noted "the dim, familiar streets seemed strangely deserted, and yet, almost palpably, panic, fear, stalked through them."

At the legation, crowds of American tourists showed up in a panic as their vacations were suddenly cut short. As Whitlock later wrote about the first days of August, "all our patience was absorbed by the crowds of Americans that filled the corridors of the Legation day and night. . . . Many of them were without money; their traveler's checks suddenly worthless, they were at their wits' end. I find a note in my journal to the effect that the women were often calmer, braver, more reasonable than the men."

Forty-five-year-old Brand Whitlock had taken the appointment of minister of the U.S. Legation in Belgium in February 1914 because he thought it would be a quiet, uneventful post. Less than two months later, the Germans invaded Belgium. (Public domain: Robert Arrowsmith papers, Hoover Institution Archives, Stanford University, Stanford, California.)

Whitlock told the story of a young, newly married couple from the Midwest who came to the legation and patiently waited their turn in the crowd. They were both school-teachers and were on their "bridal trip." For the first time in their lives they were in Europe and "doubtless for the first time in their lives away from home."

Whitlock explained, "All the bridegroom had was a ticket which, as he unrolled it, revealed yard on yard, in almost interminable convolutions, a series of coupons—coupons for everything, steamships, railways, trams, omnibuses, hotels, in short, one of those tourist tickets that provide for every need of a determined voyage, themselves the itinerary and the means of following it."

But now, with the advent of war and all its chaos and uncertainties, "the young couple found their coupons suddenly worthless: no one would accept them, not a steamship, railway, bus or hotel—and the bridegroom had no money; all that he and his wife had was invested in that preternaturally elongated ticket, which was to have supplied every possible human want, and to have spared them every care and annoyance, so long as they did not depart from the narrow, defined groove of travel it marked out for them. . . . The whole scene was vividly present—the little town, the high school, the Chautauqua, the faint apprehension of the thing called culture—my heart went out to them."

Whitlock wanted to do everything possible to help all stranded tourists and enlisted the offered aid of prominent Americans living in Brussels, including Dannie Heineman, Millard K. Shaler, William Hulse, and J. H. Fleming. As Whitlock explained, "Funds were raised, a house was rented where Americans might find shelter, and thus by the admirable and efficient efforts of these gentlemen, all the Americans who wished to go home were enabled to go to England and eventually to find their way to their own land." Through the next two weeks, these Americans, along with Whitlock, Gibson, and the rest of the U.S. Legation staff, would work to help the stranded tourists get out of Belgium and on their way home.

But on the day the Germans entered Brussels, Whitlock had just made his first big mark toward diplomatic fame. He was no doubt justifiably proud that the Germans were merely marching into Brussels, not fighting their way in. Whitlock, along with the Spanish minister in Brussels, Marquis de Villalobar y O'Neill, had helped to convince city leaders— most notably the larger-than-life Burgomaster Adolphe Max—to declare Brussels an open city and save it from the destruction that had befallen so many other places by then. It had been days and nights of tense negotiations, but in the end, the ancient monuments, medieval churches, and broad, tree-lined boulevards of Brussels (compared favorably by many to Paris) were spared from bombardment and devastation.

After that, all Whitlock wanted to do was see the great German army march into Brussels. It was history in the making, and he was well aware of the fact that Brussels had not seen foreign occupation since Napoleon in 1815; nor had any European capital been occupied by an enemy in forty-four years. Whitlock would not miss observing such a historic event.

He found what he thought was the main body of men near the city's majestic Cathedral of Saint Michael and Saint Gudula. He stood on the upstairs terrace and saw "riding in column of twos, in . . . field-gray uniforms, their black-and-white pennants fluttering from their lances, a squadron of German *hussars* [cavalry]. . . . It was very still, the crowds sullen and silent, there in the glitter of the sunlight—the horses' hoofs clattering on the stones of the uneven pavement, the lances swaying, the pennants fluttering and that deep-throated chant ["Heil dir im

Siegerkranz" or "Hail to Thee in Victor's Crown"] to the tune that the English know as 'God Save the King' and we as 'America,' and over us the gray facades of the stately old church. The scene had the aspect of medievalism; something terrible too, that almost savage chant and those gray horsemen pouring down out of the Middle Ages into modern civilization."

When no other soldiers followed after the cavalry, Whitlock and his group thought they had seen it all and drove away in their motorcar. Suddenly, as they rounded a corner, they came face-to-face with the main column. "All we had seen was but an advance-guard . . . for there, up and down the boulevard, under the spreading branches of the trees, as far as we could see, were undulating, glinting fields of bayonets, and a mighty gray, grim horde, a thing of steel, that came thundering on with shrill fifes and throbbing drums and clanging cymbals, nervous horses and lumbering guns and wild songs.

"And this was Germany!" he continued in a literary vein. "Not the stolid, good-natured, smiling German of the glass of beer and tasseled pipe, whiling away a Sunday afternoon in his peaceful beer-garden, while a band plays Strauss waltzes. . . . [It was] this dread thing, this Frankenstein, this monstrous anachronism, modern science yoked to the chariot of the autocratic and cruel will of the pagan world."

Hugh Gibson, U.S. Legation Secretary

Whitlock's able assistant, U.S. Legation Secretary Hugh Gibson—who would venture to Louvain eight days later—was also out and about in Brussels on the day the Germans marched in. He, too, wanted to be part of the historic event. Gibson, like Whitlock, was new to the legation in Brussels, although, unlike his boss, he wasn't new to diplomatic service. At thirty-one Gibson was energetic and passionate and filled with a lively, cutting sense of humor that was never far from the surface. Photos showed him to be a well-groomed, impeccably dressed and stylish man with an impish look.

Gibson had been born in Los Angeles and started in the foreign service in his twenties. Like many others in that field, he had pinballed from job to job: secretary of the U.S. Legation in Honduras (1908); second secretary of the American Embassy in London (1909–1910); private secretary to the assistant secretary of state in Washington, D.C. (1910–1911); and secretary of the U.S. Legation in Havana, Cuba (1911–1913).

Thirty-one-year-old Hugh Gibson was the secretary of the U.S. Legation in Belgium. He was energetic and passionate and filled with a lively, cutting sense of humor. (Public domain: Prentiss Gray papers, CRB portrait book, Herbert Hoover Presidential Library Archives, West Branch, Iowa.)

In a very short time at his new post in Brussels, Gibson had made a good name for himself, as "his wit and fearlessness were the talk of Brussels." He was nothing if not hardworking, and as one observer commented, Gibson always seemed to be the busiest person in the legation.

On this day, Gibson had heard that the bulk of the German soldiers were to march down the broad Chaussée de Louvain in the northeastern part of the city and then move right through the city to the other side, leaving behind an occupying force within the older, lower downtown. As he watched the first contingent of troops heading down the hill into the lower town, he and his companion/driver D. L. Blount decided to find a better vantage point from which to watch. They motored across and through some side streets and found a better viewing spot.

"There was a sullen and depressed crowd lining the streets," Gibson observed, "and not a sound was heard." The Germans, he supposed, were tramping through the city "to impress the populace with their force and discipline." For Gibson, it certainly worked: "I never expect to see [it] equaled as long as I live. They poured down the hill in a steady stream without a pause or a break; not an order was shouted nor a word exchanged among the officers or men. All the orders and signals were given by whistles and signs. The silence was a large element of the impressiveness."

First came hundreds of lancers—soldiers on horseback in the full regalia of *pickelhaubens* (spiked helmets) and long lances, and officers with electric searchlights on their chests that were attached to batteries that were in their saddlebags. The Germans were so precise and prepared that when the occasional horse, which was shod for campaigning in the country, slipped on the smooth cobble pavements, "a man was there with a coarse cloth to put under his head and another to go under his forefeet, so that he would not hurt himself slipping and pawing at the cobbles."

Later, as Gibson and Blount moved on, they came across Whitlock. The minister was accompanied by "the ladies of the family who had been brought out to watch the passing show. We [Gibson and Blount] had hesitated to bring them out at the beginning for fear that there might be riots. . . . Fortunately, there was nothing of the sort." A short time later, the newly expanded group all motored out to the country to watch "the steady stream nearer its source; still pouring in, company after company, regiment after regiment, with apparently no end in sight."

In conclusion of a long day, Gibson wrote with his characteristically dry sense of humor, "We watched until after seven [p.m.], and decided that the rest would have to get in without our assistance."

Gibson also noted that for the Belgians watching the Germans marching into Brussels, "the humiliation has been terrible. The Belgians have always had a tremendous city patriotism . . . and it must hurt them more than it could possibly hurt any other people."

Some reports say it took three days for the army to pass through the city.

FOUR

London

American Tourists in Harm's Way

In late July and early August, as war tensions grew before the actual invasion, anywhere from 100,000 to 200,000 American tourists (an accurate count was impossible) found their European vacations brought to an abrupt end. Suddenly, letters of credit, traveler's checks, and sometimes even paper money were no longer accepted at banks, hotels, restaurants, and shops. Telephone and telegraph services were restricted, limited, or simply overwhelmed. Most modes of travel, including horse-drawn, automotive, rail, and ship, were canceled, unavailable, or overbooked.

A trickle of travelers who had been alert to the first signs of trouble had quickly made their way from the continent to England in hopes of finding early passage home. That trickle soon turned into a raging flood— Belgian and French ports were overwhelmed by those trying to get to England, while English ports and train stations were inundated with harried travelers who were lucky enough to have secured passage across the English Channel.

None was luckier—or, more likely, better served by being wealthy—than Mrs. Otto H. Kahn, wife of a famous American investment banker, collector, and philanthropist. According to a *New York Times* story, she was traveling with an entourage that included her four children, a dozen servants, two automobiles, and sixty-five trunks. The group somehow caught the last channel boat from Dieppe, France, to Newhaven, England, on invasion day, August 4. As for her sixty-five trunks, "she was lucky enough to get this record-breaking quantity of baggage through owing to the exertions of a special agent of an American express company." She was forced, however, to leave the autos behind.

Hers, though, was a one-in-a-million story. More representative was the tale told by W. E. Walters of Boston. He caught the last train from Paris to Dieppe at 9:30 a.m. Sunday, August 2. He recounted to the *New York Times* how the crowds had started gathering at the Paris station at 6 a.m., and 15 percent were Americans. "Eventually, tired of waiting for the gates to open, the crowd poured forward, smashed the gates, overflowed the platforms and the tracks, and fought desperately for places on the train. Even after the train was pulling out men tried to jump on, or held to the window sills in the hope that friends inside would pull them in. Once on, all were wedged so tightly in their seats or standing places that they were unable to move during the long hours of the run to Dieppe."

Under these kinds of chaotic conditions, nearly all American travelers were happy to simply get themselves off the continent and to England, with or without bags. When they got there, though, they were confused and bewildered as to what they should do next. They were still far from home and in desperate need of help, especially because all British sailings to America had been indefinitely suspended.

Organized Assistance Stumbles Into Existence

Walter Hines Page, the U.S. ambassador to Britain, cabled the State Department: "Thousands of perfectly solvent Americans possess letters of credit but can not cash them. No banking transactions have taken place since the closing of banking hours on August 1." And because the only way to get across the Atlantic was by steamship, it wasn't surprising when the *New York Times* reported on August 5, "It is estimated that it may take four months to bring home the many thousands of Americans who are marooned in Europe."

But those trapped American tourists also needed immediate assistance with housing, food, and clothes. Most turned to the London offices of the U.S. Embassy and U.S. Consulate for help. Both offices and their staffs were instantly overwhelmed and knew that any substantial help from the U.S. government—such as gold to handle the financial crisis, extra personnel for processing multiple tasks, and ships for transport back—would likely take weeks to organize and get across the Atlantic.

Into this void stepped American businessmen, as well as men and women of substantial means, who were then living in London or had been stranded there because of the war. They all wanted to help their countrymen. By Tuesday, August 4, the American Citizens' Committee had been formed, and its headquarters was in the main ballroom of the luxurious Savoy Hotel in London. That day the American Express office also reopened after being closed since Saturday, August 1. The manager estimated that his office had handed out $200,000 to more than 6,000 people on reopening day, with no one receiving more than $30. Tens of thousands more still needed help.

Beleaguered and exhausted Americans also sought assistance from Robert Skinner, U.S. consul general, at the consulate, which had a separate office from the U.S. Embassy. As fate would have it, the consulate was only a block away from the office of young American mining engineer Herbert Clark Hoover.

Hoover had been born and raised until eleven in West Branch, Iowa, a small "Quaker settlement of poke bonnets and abolitionist politics." He remembered life there to be one of "breakfasts of milk and mush, an aunt who held winter sledding to be a godless activity and parents who were dead by his tenth birthday."

That hardscrabble start was followed by attendance at newly opened Stanford University in Northern California, where he earned a degree in geology. Years of hard work and international travel to mining operations in such out-of-the-way places as Australia and China had transformed him into an extraordinarily successful businessman. He served as director on "eighteen financial and mining companies with total capital in the range of $55 million. He controlled investments in major Australian, Burmese, South African, and Russian mines. In terms of sheer size alone, his Russian mining and forestry holdings had a combined area larger than Belgium."

At the start of the war, Herbert C. Hoover was a forty-year-old mining engineer who was a no-nonsense, ambitious, roll-up-your-sleeves-and-get-it-done kind of American. He would go on to organize and build the Commission for Relief in Belgium (CRB), which would become the largest food and relief drive the world had ever seen. During four years of war, more than 9 million Belgians and northern French would be saved from starvation by the efforts of the CRB and its Belgian counterpart, the Comité National. (Public domain: Herbert Hoover Presidential Library Archives, West Branch, Iowa.)

Hoover was a no-nonsense, ambitious, roll-up-your-sleeves-and-get-it-done kind of American who was highly skilled at tackling complex problems and organizing massive operations. He also had little patience for trivial things, such as clothes, as evidenced by one colleague's dry remark that "his dress never varies—he merely writes to his tailor, 'Send me another suit,' and seldom gives himself the bother of a try-on."

In August 1914, Hoover and his wife, Lou Henry Hoover, were living in London and trying to secure European nations' participation in the upcoming Panama-Pacific International Exposition to be held in San Francisco in 1915. They both realized their mission was stillborn the moment the war started.

Additionally, though, Hoover, who would turn forty on August 10, was contemplating what he should do in his next stage of life. He was restless and not content to sit back and manage his worldwide mining operations. Options included the presidency of Stanford University and the purchase of a California newspaper as two different pathways into public service and politics—two areas that deeply interested the mining engineer. He was a wealthy man, but as one associate later wrote, "He didn't want to become just richer. He wanted sincerely . . . to do public service and help people, but in a wholesale way. I don't think he was terribly sympathetic to the fellow selling lead pencils on the corner, but I think he was very desirous to create a society where that fellow wouldn't be selling lead pencils on the corner."

On the chaotic German invasion day, Hoover showed up at the U.S. Consulate and offered his assistance. While there is a question as to whether he came unsolicited or if Skinner called and asked for his help, there is no doubt Hoover jumped in that day with both feet. According to historian George Nash, Hoover gathered "all the cash he could find in his office and from business associates, and telephoning his wife for £100 more at their home, [Hoover] opened an office at the consulate that very afternoon. Here, with some assistants, he proceeded to loan small sums (at no interest and often without security) to more than three hundred Americans who had no other cash to live on."

As the days went by, Hoover became better acquainted with the needs of the people and more aware of the other assistance groups that had been formed in London. And, in doing so, he also learned much about the intricacies involved in charity work, which demanded not only an understandable amount of diplomacy but also a surprising amount of subtle intrigues and backdoor maneuverings.

Lou Hoover immediately became involved in the American Citizens' Committee and began serving the needs of American women at the Savoy Hotel. "The all-male [American] Citizens' Committee promptly added her to its membership—the only woman to be so selected."

Hoover Makes His Move for Dominance

Hoover, seeing a chance to serve the public as he had hoped, decided to move forward independently from the American Citizens' Committee and on Wednesday, August 5, brought together a group of respected Americans living in London, many of whom were business associates and mining engineers he had known for years. They formed the Committee of American Residents (also known as the Relief Committee, or Residents' Committee), with Hoover as its chairman, and immediately went to work building a viable operation to try and meet the tremendous need.

Reflecting Hoover's ability to see quickly to the heart of any problem, his Residents' Committee chose to focus on the primary concern of many stranded American travelers: money. His group quickly established two funds—one that would loan money to those who could afford to pay it back and one that was for charitable giving. The group then began soliciting money from private citizens to bankroll both funds. Hoover personally gave £1,000 to the loan fund and £500 to the benevolent fund.

As the *New York Times* reported on August 6, "Another who did admirable relief work was Herbert Clark Hoover, a California mining man, who opened an office of his own in the American Consulate and advanced sums of $25 or more in coin to over 300 Americans who had nothing but paper money. He declares that he will continue to do so till his stock is exhausted."

But Hoover didn't want to be just "another" relief worker. Neglecting not even the smallest item, Hoover and his committee "moved rapidly.... Within twenty-four hours of its founding it had its own stationery and masthead. Within forty-eight hours it established a branch adjacent to the Citizens' Committee's headquarters in the Savoy as well as three other locations." And to man those locations and do the basic relief work, Hoover began recruiting volunteers such as Edward Curtis, an American student studying at Cambridge who had heard of the need and came to help.

Hoover also showed that he understood the power of the press and how to use it. On August 8 American papers ran a press release his group had sent out earlier. Hoover was not letting fate take its course; he would tell fate where it should go and hope it got there soon after. Part of the press release, as published in the *New York Times*, read, "With the object of co-ordinating the system of giving assistance to traveling Americans and restoring order among the somewhat chaotic conditions arising from the multiplicity of committees[,] an authoritative committee of American residents in London was formed today under official auspices. Walter Hines Page, the American Ambassador, has been appointed honorary chairman, and Consul General Robert Skinner vice chairman."

There were two problems with this statement: One, the American Citizens' Committee was still very much alive and active and would beg to differ with Hoover's group about its being the "authoritative committee." And two, Page had not yet agreed to serve as honorary chairman (but he would do so later).

Unimportant details, some might have believed, when there were tens of thousands of travelers in need of help. Even so, Hoover's Residents' Committee and the American Citizens' Committee did work together over the course of the next two weeks—the demand was simply too big for any one grassroots group to handle at that stage. So, the Citizens' Committee "worked mainly with banks in New York and London to open channels of cash and credit. Hoover's group took charge of immediate relief."

But Hoover's actions during this time seem to indicate he would have preferred to have been the sole organizer of relief. He probably felt he could be more efficient and effective making quick decisions without having to consult or coordinate with other groups—much as any good mining manager had to do when in distant lands and far from owners or boardroom politics. Undoubtedly, Hoover simply wanted to do what came naturally after all those years of mining work.

In the meantime, the American government had been flooded with official and unofficial pleas for help. Even though President Wilson was focused on his gravely ill wife (she died August 7 of the chronic kidney ailment Bright's disease), he was aware of, and sympathetic to, the travelers' plights and moved the government to action. On August 5 congress unanimously appropriated $2.5 million to assist American travelers; the secretaries of state, treasury, and war met and developed a plan for aiding the travelers; and by the evening of August 6 the armored cruiser USS *Tennessee* set sail from New York. Aboard was the American Relief Expedition— comprised of the assistant secretary of war, Henry Breckinridge, more than twenty army officers, numerous clerks and treasury officials, and millions of dollars in gold. The ship and its precious cargo arrived in England on August 16. The cavalry had arrived.

That didn't mean the crisis was over. There was still a lot of work to do. But now the stakes were much higher—the U.S. government's substantial financial resources were available to be distributed to needy American travelers, but any work using government funds would be much more scrutinized than work by private individuals using private funds.

The big question was: Which group would be chosen to distribute the funds?

During the previous few weeks, Hoover had built his Residents' Committee, sparred with the Citizens' Committee, and vied for the attention and support of Page—not to mention helped thousands of American travelers. Throughout, it became apparent that the young, energetic mining engineer was not afraid to do what was needed to protect and expand his traveler-assistance group. In a series of maneuvers, which many times utilized the power, resources, and support of Page's position as U.S. ambassador, Hoover and his group emerged as the preeminent organization responsible for aiding American travelers. It was a testament to his innate organizational skills and his ability to convince diplomats, businessmen, and the press that his way was the best way.

On August 17, Breckinridge and Page formally invited Hoover and his group to, in Hoover's words, "take over the entire distribution of funds in London." That was followed two days later by the disbanding of the American Citizens' Committee and the transfer of all its duties to Hoover's group.

While part of the reason the transfer took place was that many of the American Citizens' Committee officers were themselves heading home, it was still a victory for Hoover. And coupled with the fact that Hoover and his group were now responsible for distributing the U.S. government funds, it meant he was the number one relief game in town.

Through the rest of August, Hoover would turn his considerable skills and business acumen to aiding all American travelers trying to get home from England. During the week of August 16–22, eighteen ships sailed for America carrying 20,000 U.S. citizens. On August 29 Hoover and his American Residents' Committee issued a detailed report on what had been done so far. While the report no doubt pleased the American government, it reflected Hoover's admirable desire to always be transparent about the financial operations of any group he led. The report showed that an estimated 14,000 U. S. Citizens were departing that last week of August for America, while 45,000 had been helped with passage home from August 5 through August 29. Additionally, in the month of August, 4,135 people had been given some form of financial assistance.

Even though it had been nearly a month since the war began, problems were still arising. More than 3,000 Americans arrived from the continent during the last week of August, and on August 28 the majority of 800 stranded Americans had no housing for the night. "Many were absolutely without financial means, being principally the wives and children of naturalized Germans who have been visiting relatives in Germany, but are now anxious to get back to America." Hoover and his committee found them all places to stay.

Still the travelers kept coming, and Hoover kept working to solve their problems.

In those last days of August with little end in sight, Hoover undoubtedly had no idea that within two short months he would be called upon to do so much more. But the next time the consequences of failure would not be simple traveler inconveniences; it would be potential starvation for millions.

FIVE

Back in America

Starting in late July and throughout August, war-related news made the front page of nearly every newspaper in America. First came the coverage of European diplomats working to avoid war, the posturing of political figures, and the proclamations of national unity by each European country. Then came the actual war news—overall strategies, statements by generals, battle plans, confusing reports from the field, conflicting stories of atrocities and casualties, and human interest pieces about the average foot soldier or the frightened civilian. And, whenever possible, photos of the devastation and destruction were used by publishers and editors to bring home the realities of war to the American public.

While most Americans supported neutrality, there were definitely divided loyalties, as indicated by demographic breakdowns alone: The 1910 census showed that 13.5 million, or 15 percent, of Americans were foreign born. And of those, the two largest groups were from the United Kingdom (2,573,000) and Germany (2,501,000). These population numbers did not take into consideration the millions who were only one or two generations away from leaving their home countries. Sympathies—if not outright support—were definitely divided between the Allies and the Central Powers.

Generally, though, the nation's mood and feeling were that this was Europe's fight and the United States should have nothing to do with it. Even though the United States had declared neutrality on August 4, President Wilson addressed congress on August 19 to clarify America's policy of neutrality.

"The effect of the war upon the United States," Wilson proclaimed, "will depend upon what American citizens say and do. Every man who really loves America will act and speak in the true spirit of neutrality, which is the spirit of impartiality and fairness and friendliness to all concerned."

Wilson specifically acknowledged and addressed the large partisan groups in America. "The people of the United States are drawn from many nations, and chiefly from the nations now at war. It is natural and inevitable that there should be the utmost variety of sympathy and desire among them with regards to the issues and circumstances of the conflict. Some will wish one nation, others another, to succeed in the momentous struggle. It will be easy to excite passion and difficult to allay it."

The president went on to caution those who would incite others, and he warned his "fellow countrymen . . . against that deepest, most subtle, most essential breach of neutrality which may spring out of partisanship, out of passionately taking sides."

Wilson felt America's "duty" in the conflict was as "the one great nation of peace, the one people holding itself ready to play a part of impartial mediation and speak the counsels of peace and accommodation, not as a partisan, but as a friend."

In no uncertain terms, the president was telling the country that he would not tolerate any form of civil war at home over Europe's struggle. America would be a bastion of peace, a sanctuary, in a world rapidly deteriorating into total war.

Wilson was speaking to a nation that had been changing drastically during the last few decades. In August 1914, America was in the midst of a major demographic shift it had never seen before. For the first time in its history, more people were living in cities than on the more than 6 million farms that dotted the countryside. At that time, slightly more than 50 percent of the approximately 99 million citizens were urban dwellers.

That didn't mean, however, that people were living on top of each other. Because of the country's massive size, America's density was a very low 31 people per square mile, compared with France's 189, Germany's 310, the United Kingdom's 374, and Belgium's impressive 652, which made the little Low Country the most densely populated country in the world. And only three U.S. cities had more than 1 million residents: New York was the largest, with 4.7 million; followed by Chicago, with 2.1 million; and Philadelphia, with 1.5 million.

In August 1914 unemployment was approximately 7.9 percent, and many people made less than two dollars a day. The average cost of a year's food supply for an average worker's family was between $439 and $493, depending on the area of the country. That meant that if there was only one breadwinner in the family, more than half the yearly wages would have gone for food.

Most Americans didn't go to college or university—less than 0.5 percent of the total population attended a school of higher learning. And more than 5.5 million U.S. citizens could not read. Those who did learn learned by reading the Bible and other classical pieces of literature and by attending tent Chautauquas that would visit a town like a traveling circus, setting up big tents that contained lectures, musical performances, dramatic readings, and other cultural events.

Probably the biggest event—besides the start of World War I—that took place in the world in August was the opening of the Panama Canal on August 15. It had taken ten years and $375 million to build and was the single most expensive construction project in U.S. history. While it was a distinctly American project, it was something the entire world should have celebrated. Great things had been planned for the official opening, but it became a very modest affair when World War I broke out. Not one international dignitary showed up.

As America quietly celebrated the building of something incredible and useful for all people, a large part of the rest of the world was engaged in tearing itself apart. As British Foreign Minister Sir Edward Grey famously put it, "The lamps are going out all over Europe; we shall not see them lit again in our lifetime."

American newspapers ran as many details as possible of that tearing apart. And right from the start, Belgium was a significant part of that news coverage. Its treaty-guaranteed neutrality was a pivotal point in shaping the war, and its location on Germany's path to France dictated that Americans would soon be learning the names of Belgian villages, towns, and cities, not to mention the feats of its courageous little army and tall, stately looking King Albert. Most of all, Belgium received U.S. news coverage about German atrocities such as the burning of Louvain.

Rarely in August, though, was there mention of the critical Belgian harvest, which had basically been lost through destruction by troops, requisitions by both armies, and because no one was there to gather it in. Nor did Americans learn of Belgium's heavy reliance on the importation of food and clothes that had always been paid for by exports from its numerous industries, which now lay shuttered or in ruins.

Beyond the battlefields, a perfect storm of potential starvation for millions was converging on Belgium, and few had any idea it was coming.

By September, more and more Belgians throughout the country had no choice but to join the soup-kitchen lines as the country quickly consumed its dwindling supplies. (Public domain: *In Occupied Belgium*, Robert Withington, The Cornhill Co., 1921.)

SEPTEMBER 1914

BEGINNINGS OF HUNGER
AND RETALIATION

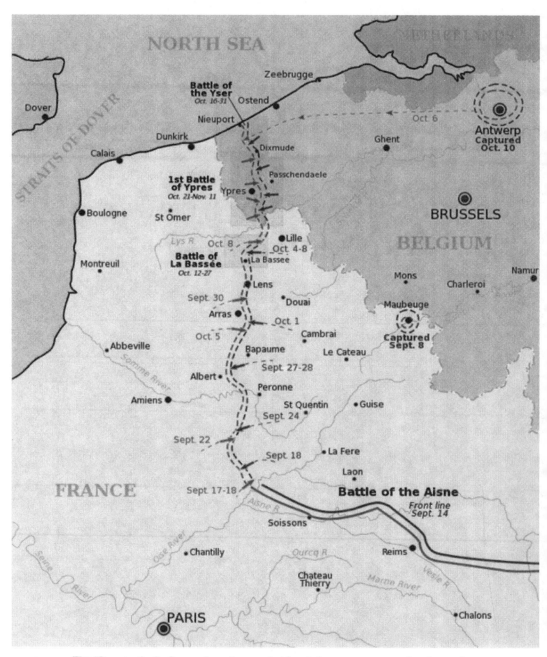

NORTH SEA

NETHERLANDS

Dover

Zeebrugge

**Battle of
the Yser**
Oct. 16-31   Ostend

Nieuport

Oct. 6

Antwerp
Captured
Oct. 10

STRAITS OF DOVER

Dunkirk

Calais

Dixmude

Ghent

Boulogne

St Omer

**1st Battle
of Ypres**
Oct. 21-Nov. 11   Ypres

Passchendaele

BRUSSELS

BELGIUM

Montreuil

Lys R.   Oct. 8

**Battle of
La Bassée**
Oct. 12-27

Lille

Oct. 4-8

La Bassee

Lens

Sept. 30

Mons

Charleroi

Namur

Maubeuge

Arras

Oct. 1

Oct. 5

Douai

Cambrai

**Captured
Sept. 8**

Abbeville

Somme River

Bapaume

Le Cateau

Sept. 27-28

Albert

Peronne

Amiens

St Quentin

Sept. 24

Guise

Sept. 22

Sept. 18

La Fere

Laon

FRANCE

Sept. 17-18

Battle of the Aisne

Aisne R.

*Front line
Sept. 14*

Soissons

Oise River

Chantilly

Ourcq R.

Reims

Seine
River

Chateau
Thierry

Marne River

Vesle R.

PARIS

Chalons

*This "Race to the Sea" map shows how each side tried to outmaneuver the other—the
Germans swinging to their right flank, the Allies swinging to their left flank—until
they reached the North Sea. All of which led ultimately to the establishment of a sta-
tionary front of trenches running from Switzerland to the North Sea. (Public domain;
Wikipedia sourced as "gsl-gsl origin.")*

SIX

The First Major Battles

E. E. Hunt Looks for a Good Story

On Tuesday, September 8, Edward Eyre Hunt arrived in Rotterdam aboard the *Nieuw Amsterdam*, which had sailed from New York fourteen days earlier. He came to Europe as a freelance war correspondent who planned to sell his stories to any magazines or newspapers that would buy them. He was a slight man, of average height and with dark hair, mustache, and deep-set, thoughtful eyes. At twenty-nine, he was a Harvard graduate who had stayed after graduation and worked in the English Department for two years, and then headed to New York City, where he worked on the editorial staff of *American Magazine* for a couple of years. He was a passionate, introspective, and sensitive young urbanite looking for something meaningful to write about.

Five months before the war started, Hunt wrote to a friend named Steff and in the process gave insight into himself and possibly his generation's college-educated elite. He referenced a discussion their group

Edward Eyre Hunt, also known as E. E. Hunt. (*One Generation*, Erskine Carmichael, M.D., self-published, 2013.)

of friends had had about the "conflict between their ideals and their conduct." He then wrote: "Anyway, here the bunch of us stands, young, impatient, and cruel. Our cruelty I am no apologist for, except to remark that we are as cruel to ourselves as we are to others. We are not satisfied to be human. We will neither comfort nor be comforted. 'Democracy' or any other of the categories, is an empty word to us. That you call a thing 'human' makes no appeal to us: it must be 'superhuman' to win us. We have no desire to reconcile our antagonisms and live happily ever after."

Hunt put his ideals and conduct on the line when he decided to go to Europe to see the war for himself. From Rotterdam he went to Germany, and for most of September he observed, interviewed, and reported on everything from German officials and their policies to children playing in the streets.

And when he got to Belgium in early October, he would live through the bombardment of Antwerp, walk with the fleeing refugees to Holland, grieve over the death of his fiancée back in the States, and find his passion amidst it all.

Invasion Moves Toward Trench Warfare

In the first few days of September, the German juggernaut still moved forward relentlessly. It wasn't from lack of trying to stop it. Throughout the nearly month-long invasion, the Belgians, French, and hastily assembled British Expeditionary Force had all tried at different times and places to make a stand and stop the invaders, but with no success. No matter what the Allies threw at them, the Germans just kept coming.

While half of Belgium was by then in German hands, the northern part of the country and the coast had been spared—primarily because those areas weren't in the prescribed arc of the Germans' attack plan. That would change by the end of September as the Germans turned to tackle Antwerp, with its impressive ring of fortresses.

But in the first week of September, the one thing on many people's minds was Paris and whether it would fall. A military governor, General Joseph Gallieni, had been appointed August 25 to defend the city. He began work immediately, gathering troops and building defensive fortifications. By September 3 it seemed inevitable that the Germans would reach the city, so the French government moved out to ensure the continuation of government if Paris fell.

With the Germans fewer than twenty-five miles (forty kilometers) from the city, Paris braced for attack.

And then something unexpected happened. As the First and Second German armies approached the city, their commanders decided Paris could wait. They sensed a bigger prize was possible—the encircling of the retreating Allies. They knew that if they could do that, the war on the western front would be over. It was a big gamble, but they were confident it was within reach. They turned their armies southeast, away from Paris, and headed for their prize.

As luck would have it, though, this major strategic movement was spotted by a British pilot and then confirmed by a captured order. When the Allies fully understood what the Germans were doing, they knew the Germans' right flank was vulnerable to attack. The French and English planned to attack that flank on the morning of September 6. Their plans were disrupted, though, by the commander of the German First Army, who detected the Allied approach on September 5 and began swinging his army back to the west to face the enemy.

It was the start of the First Battle of the Marne (so named for the Marne River), which would continue for seven bloody days.

During the conflict, on September 7, a major event occurred that would stir a nation and the world. It began because the French needed reinforcements at the front, so 10,000 reserves were brought up. Surprisingly, 6,000 of those troops were transported to the front by hundreds of Paris taxicabs, requisitioned by General Gallieni. These "taxis de la Marne" became a rallying cry, a symbol of national unity and solidarity with the soldiers. While the event's military impact was marginal, it had a huge effect on morale. According to one historian, "There is no more cherished episode than this in French military history."

By September 9 the tide of battle had turned, and it appeared as if both the First and Second German armies might themselves be encircled by the Allies. When news of this possibility reached the overall German commander, General Helmuth von Moltke, he suffered a nervous breakdown. His staff took over and ordered a retreat to the Aisne River.

The First Battle of the Marne was a huge victory for the Allies and one of the most significant battles of the war. It kept the Germans from a quick victory and began what they most feared, a prolonged, two-front war: France and England on the western front and Russia on the eastern front. It was also the first battle in which reconnaissance airplanes played a decisive role—by spotting the initial strategic German move and later by identifying weak spots in the German forces that the Allies then pursued.

The battle also had a huge psychological impact on both sides. As one American historian put it, the Allies, after a month of retreats, "knew at last that they could beat the Germans," while the Germans "began slowly to comprehend that they had suffered a great defeat by enemies whose fighting abilities they despised."

But two other important events came on the heels of the First Battle of the Marne.

First, the Germans had retreated across the Aisne River and dug in to make a stand on September 12. The following day the Allies engaged them in the First Battle of the Aisne, which was fought to a standstill, with major losses on both sides.

Second, that battle was followed by each side's attempt to outmaneuver each other's western flank in what's now known as the "Race to the Sea." If one army could only turn the corner on the other, it would gain a huge strategic advantage. So each kept throwing troops to the west, and each time they were met by troops of the other side also heading west. When they both reached the North Sea—which would not happen until late November/early December—the maneuvering would be over and both the Allied and German soldiers would begin to dig in, establishing the trench warfare that World War I is known for.

Long before the entrenchment was finalized, however, people began questioning the initial consensus that the war would be a quick conflict, over in no time. The kaiser had told his troops at the start, "You will be home before the leaves have fallen from the trees." One American wrote, "Even the most pessimistic hardly believed the war would last more than a few months." Others thought that the results of a conflict between the great powers of Europe would bring such devastating results that the war would not be allowed to last. They were right on the first part, but horribly wrong on the second.

The trench warfare that developed through the fall indicated it would be a long and deadly conflict. And the first major battles seemed to confirm that—more than 2 million men took part in the First Battle of the Marne and the First Battle of the Aisne, with nearly 500,000 killed or wounded.

The killing had just begun.

SEVEN

Antwerp

The City Braces for Attack

In September, Antwerp was a heavily fortified city filled with Belgian soldiers and preparing for a German assault.

Before the war the Flemish city was named by *Baedeker's Belgium and Holland* tour book as "one of the most interesting towns in Belgium" and was considered by most to be the unofficial capital of Flanders (the Flemish-speaking northern part of Belgium). Antwerp had started out as a walled medieval city with one side being the east bank of the River Scheldt and the other three sides being fortified ramparts built in the 1500s. By the mid-sixteenth century, the town was such a thriving port of commerce that some said it was the most prosperous and wealthy in Europe, even surpassing Venice.

By 1914, Antwerp was Belgium's second-largest city but still maintained its bustling, small-town feel. This was especially true in the medieval Old Town, which hugged the river and was a picturesque maze of narrow cobblestone streets, crooked alleys, and open squares accentuated by buildings with magnificent facades, ornate gables, and graceful spires. A reminder of the ancient past remained in the more than 300 Madonnas that graced numerous street corners. Placed high above the heads of many who never glanced up, these statues of the Virgin Mary had held candles and lighted the way for nighttime pedestrians hundreds of years before.

The heart of Old Town was the large market square, *grand place* (later known as *grote markt*). Ornate sixteenth- and seventeenth-century guild halls, owned by the associations of the major industries and professions that had built the city, stood proudly on two sides. Dominating the square and its guild halls was the 1561 *hôtel de ville* (city hall), with its Renaissance style and center section rising an impressive 184 feet high. In the square itself, a centerpiece fountain depicted the legendary Silvius Brabo, who brandished the severed hand of a giant. Legend had it that the name Antwerp had come from "handwerpen," meaning "to throw a hand," which Brabo had done after cutting off the hand of the giant because he would not let him pass.

A stone's throw from the square was the city's finest building, the Cathedral of Notre Dame (*Onze Lieve Vrouwekathedraal* in Flemish). By far the largest and most beautiful cathedral in Belgium, it was started in 1352 and took 169 years to build. Its graceful, soaring spire stretched more than 400 feet high and could be seen from practically anywhere in Antwerp.

The cathedral's old churchyard was by that time a major city square named Place Verte, which held the prominent bronze statue of the city's most famous son, Peter Paul Rubens, who had not only been a painter but also a diplomat and statesman. On the square was the Hotel St. Antoine, which boasted a restaurant, central heating, and 200 rooms, 50 with bathrooms. During this chaotic September, the hotel was a center of great activity, due in part to its being close to the royal palace and across the street from the Belgian general staff offices. Additionally, though, it had become temporary home of the Belgian ministers of state, a handful of foreign journalists, and various diplomatic corps, including the American, British, and Russian corps.

The edges of Antwerp's medieval Old Town—where the "new" parts of the city started—were marked by four broad, tree-lined avenues that had replaced the 1500s ramparts in the major city renewal of 1859.

Avenue du Commerce, Avenue des Arts, Avenue de l'Industrie, and Avenue du Sud created an artistic and practical semicircle around three sides of the city.

Just a few streets east of the Avenue des Arts was the modern heart of the city—the magnificent Central Station. Built in 1905 and featuring a stunning neo-Gothic facade, soaring main hall, and perfectly proportioned dome, the train station was already considered one of the most beautiful in Europe.

Altogether, the grace, beauty, and charm of Antwerp seemed to flow from every ornate window ledge and stately building, every cobblestone lane and finely wrought balcony.

In September 1914, however, most residents probably wondered what would survive the coming German invasion.

There was no talk of declaring the city an open one as Brussels had done. Antwerp would fight, and the Belgian Army would make its stand to show the Germans how tough the little Low Country was. Many residents felt the city, with its two outer concentric rings of fortresses, was nearly impregnable. One American journalist reported, "In fact, Antwerp was almost universally considered one of the three or four strongest fortified positions in Europe." Rumor had it that the city and its forts could hold out for months at the very least—plenty of time for the Allies to join the Belgian fight and push the Germans out of the country before winter.

Antwerp was worth such fortifications primarily because it was one of the largest commercial ports in the world. Even though it had a metropolitan population of only 400,000, its port was the third busiest in the world when it came to vessel tonnage in and out. (At the time, the busiest, in order, were New York, Hamburg, Antwerp, Rotterdam, and London.) As a 1910 *Baedeker's Belgium and Holland* tour book related, Antwerp, "situated on the broad and deep Scheldt [River], 55 [miles] from the sea, is one of the greatest seaports of Europe, serving as an outlet for the commerce of Germany as well as of Belgium."

The 1910 tour guide veered off tourism and eerily foreshadowed World War I when it stated, "Antwerp is the principal arsenal of the kingdom of Belgium, and since 1859 it has been made . . . one of the strongest fortresses in Europe. The city and river are defended by a circle of advanced forts. . . . Part of the environs can be placed under water. Antwerp is intended to serve as the rendezvous of the army, should it be compelled,

Belgian civilians with shovels rushing to the front to dig trenches. (Public domain; *A Journal From Our Legation in Belgium*, Hugh Gibson, Doubleday, Page & Co., 1917.)

in case of the violation of the neutrality of the country, to retire before an enemy of superior force."

That's exactly what had happened in August, as much of the Belgian Army not fighting the Germans' push to the south ended up in the Antwerp area. So, as the Germans roared toward Paris, everyone in Antwerp waited with growing tension to see what the invaders would do. When the First Battle of the Marne began on September 5, the city held its collective breath—everyone knew that, depending upon how that fight ended, Antwerp might be next.

Their worst fears were confirmed—although no Belgian knew it then—when on September 9, as the Germans began their retreat from the Marne River, the kaiser ordered Antwerp to be taken. The Germans no longer wanted such a fortress complex and its attendant army to be at its rear.

Erica Bunge—"The Days Pass and Are Never the Same"

Through September, Erica Bunge, her sisters, and her father moved with greater and greater difficulty between their townhouse in Antwerp and Chateau Oude Gracht, twenty miles northeast of the city. Erica's diary entries still reflected confusion and concern, but they were also clear-eyed in many of their assessments. No matter where the Bunge sisters lay their heads at night, Antwerp or Oude Gracht, Erica, Eva, and Hilda were volunteers at multiple facilities—from soup kitchens to hospitals—and spent much of each day helping out somewhere. Nightfall did not bring much relaxation, as reflected in Erica's diary entry from Antwerp on August 25: "We had gone to bed as usual and around 2 a.m. I woke up suddenly. We could hear very strong detonations and we all got up and dressed. A zeppelin had come over the city and was dropping bombs. Nine bombs caused tremendous damage."

Her first entry in September continued with yet another zeppelin attack.

Saturday, September 5: "I haven't written for a long time, it is September 5, 1914, today, and a great deal has been happening. . . . The zeppelin came back during the night of Tuesday and Wednesday. . . . The whole city is in darkness from eight in the evening on, but we have a full moon and it is as light as day. Five bombs were dropped today. . . . The Queen left [Antwerp] with the princes for England, but she is planning to return to be with the King. Her departure created quite a panic, and a number of Antwerp people fled to England . . . 17 people at the chateau. . . . Yesterday, Sept. 4, the Major called me on the telephone to announce their departure [from Hoogboom]. He regretted it and did not know where they were going. There is a battle around Termonde [southeast of Antwerp] and the Belgian division had to make a retreat."

Monday, September 7: "The days pass and are never the same. . . . The Russians are advancing still [on the eastern front], and of the French and the English we know nothing definite. . . . Here, Termonde was evacuated, it had been bombed and partly burned. A bridge on the Scheldt was destroyed, which makes it seem that the Germans are advancing to encircle Antwerp. Crazy rumors are all over the town. This afternoon we heard that the Russians had landed in Belgium and are marching toward Liège to cut off the German troops and crush them. A miracle is predicted for September 8. We are ever hopeful, and may we receive good news! I go to the soup canteen three times a week from 11 a.m. to 1 p.m. There are a great many men and also women. 230 to 260 wounded. I go to visit, and everything we bring them gives them pleasure."

Wednesday morning, September 9: "I went to Hoogboom in the dogcart of Mme. Schnitzler [who had to leave earlier because she and her family were German]. It was an interesting trip. From the Old Barrier to the Dock there was a lot of damage, all the small houses have disappeared, the pubs, Kaizerhoek. . . . At Hoogboom it was the same thing, and the same soldiers and officers. In Pereken's room, Major DeWalche (5th Regiment) with orderly. In Loke's room, Commandant Nyssens, Capt. Commander of the First Artillery Battery of the Fortress, Group 9. Very nice and a gentleman."

Wednesday, September 23: "We met Mr. [E. Alexander] Powell, an American war correspondent, at Friling's [house, a friend who lived near Chateau Oude Gracht]. Most interesting man and evening. He has been at seven wars. He dined with nine officers and [German General] von Boehn at Brussels and was received very well. His photographer, [Donald C.] Thompson (funny man) travels with him. (Swears always.)"

"The People Did Not Smile"

Within five short days of Erica's last diary entry, Antwerp and its rings of forts would come under siege. Antwerp's waiting was over; the war had arrived. And it was to bring with it an ugliness that would deeply scar the lovely city.

As thirty-five-year-old war correspondent E. Alexander Powell, who had recently dined with Erica Bunge, stated about prewar Antwerp: "No other city in Europe could boast of more beautiful suburbs than Antwerp. Hidden amid the foliage of great wooded parks were stately chateaux; splendid country houses rose from amid acres of green plush lawns and blazing gardens; the network of roads and avenues and bridle-paths were lined with venerable trees, whose branches, meeting overhead, formed leafy tunnels; scattered here and there were quaint old-world villages, with plaster walls and pottery roofs and lichen-covered church spires." It was an idyllic land of beauty.

But by the first days of September, all that had disappeared. Antwerp's outlying suburbs would never be the same—and the change started even before the first German shells began to fall. With the city hemmed in by the River Scheldt to the west and the Dutch border to the north, everyone knew that the main German invasion would come from the east and south. As such, the countryside in those directions was purposefully leveled so that Belgian guns could sight better on German invaders. According to Powell, "It is estimated that within a fortnight the

Belgian sappers [combat engineers] and engineers destroyed property to
the value of $80,000,000. Not San Francisco after the [1906] earthquake
. . . presented scenes of more complete desolation than did the suburbs of
Antwerp after the soldiers had finished with them."

For those who witnessed the destruction, it was a sad event, watching
"groups of Belgian soldiers tearing down their own walls and hedges and
applying match and gasoline to those which still stood. . . . This was a case
of self-inflicted destruction. Farmhouses, stores, churches, old Belgian
mansions, and windmills were either in flames or smouldering ruins.
Where burning had not been sufficient, powder and dynamite had been
applied to destroy landmarks which for centuries had been the country's
pride. As far as the eye could reach the countryside was flattened to a
desert," noted *New York Evening Post* war correspondent Horace Green.

For the people who had lived in those houses, Green wrote, it didn't
make much difference that "the devastation was for the defensive purpose
of giving an unobstructed view to the cannon of Antwerp's outer fortifications." Their homes were gone.

In their place, Powell observed, "acres and acres of barbed-wire entan-
glements were constructed, the wires being grounded and connected with
the city's lighting system so that a voltage could instantly be turned on
which would prove as deadly as the electric chair at Sing Sing. Thousands
of men were set to work sharpening stakes and driving these stakes, point
upward, in the ground, so as to impale any soldiers who fell upon them."
Canals around the city were fortified with parapets of sandbags, bridges
laid with dynamite, barricades erected on critical roads, and fields seeded
with land mines.

Within the city itself, martial law was imposed, with cafes and shops
shuttered by 8 p.m. and all streetlights extinguished and windows darkened by nightfall to protect against zeppelin bomb attacks. "The darkness
of London and Paris was a joke beside the darkness of Antwerp," said
Powell, who had to feel his way around the city's narrow, winding streets
with a cane, like a blind man. He remarked that the city "became about
as cheerful a place of residence as a country cemetery on a rainy evening."

Such conditions took their toll on the residents of Antwerp. "The people did not smile. They went about with grave and anxious faces. . . . One
rarely heard a laugh," Powell noted. And they became suspicious of everyone they did not know, as the city became "spy-mad. If a man ordered
sauerkraut and sausage for lunch he instantly fell under suspicion."

A thirteen-year-old Belgian Boy Scout who was attached to an officer (far right) and staff. (Public domain; *Fighting in Flanders*, E. Alexander Powell, Charles Scribner's Sons, 1914.)

During these very dark days, one good side of the city was found in a very unlikely organization—the Boy Scouts. Originally founded in England, the Boy Scouts officially launched in Belgium in 1910, and its membership had grown rapidly across the country by the start of the war. As Antwerp prepared for invasion in late September, these young boys were everywhere, sporting their distinctive broad-brimmed hats, short pants, and green leggings folded over at the top just below the knees. They didn't just help little ladies cross streets; they ran about as messengers, guides, and couriers for various governmental ministries and agencies. They operated lifts in hotels, worked at hospitals, and acted as door-keepers. Some were orderlies for army officers. They even "slept rolled up in blankets on the floors; they obtained their meals where and when they could and paid for them themselves, and made themselves extremely useful." Powell added, "I don't quite know how the city could have gotten along without them."

As the Boy Scouts and citizens of Antwerp prepared for invasion, the Belgian Army took the opportunity to harass the German flank after the

A Belgian machine-gun battery pulled by dogs ready to head to the front. (Public domain;
A Journal From Our Legation in Belgium, Hugh Gibson, Doubleday, Page & Co., 1917.)

main German force had moved south into France. The Belgian Army
ventured out from fortified Antwerp and made three attacks—one on
August 25–26 and two in September. And alongside the soldiers were
their ever-present companions—dogs. Green reported: "I watched the
long lines of Belgian hounds, pulling their rapid-fire guns out toward
the trenches. Many times later I was destined to see them. They made a
picturesque and stimulating sight—those faithful dogs of war—fettered
and harnessed, their tongues hanging out as they lay patiently beneath
the gun trucks awaiting the order to go into action, or, when the word had
been given, trotted along the dusty roads, each pair tugging to the battle
front a lean, gray engine of destruction."

While none of the three Belgian attacks from Antwerp was tremendously successful, each served a huge purpose—the Germans had to
maintain vigilance and troops on their flank rather than have those troops
on the main thrust into France. Antwerp and its troops were becoming a
major thorn in the side of the Germans.

On September 28 the Germans began extraction of that thorn—they
started shelling Antwerp's outer forts. Spotters in high-altitude balloons
helped guide the massive artillery guns. With the Germans' seventeen-
inch howitzers and one-ton projectiles, it would not be long before the
forts began to fall and the beautiful medieval city of Antwerp would
come under bombardment.

EIGHT

Brussels

German Occupation Starts the War of the Wills

Before Antwerp came under siege, and as the fighting still raged to the south, Brussels was learning what it was like to be an occupied city. German troops were everywhere, patrolling the streets, eating and drinking in the cafes, marching and singing up and down the wide avenues and boulevards, and commandeering park bridle paths for cavalry officers and their well-groomed mounts. Brand Whitlock, minister of the U.S. Legation in Brussels, saw foot soldiers "trudging by in those uncouth heavy boots, into which their trousers were so clumsily thrust. Huge motors would sweep by, flying the [German] imperial standard, followed by great auto-busses [filled with German soldiers]. . . . The hotels were turned over to German officers; in the dining-room of the Palace Hotel they were eating and drinking every evening."

Before the war, the city had had an air of gaiety and boasted magnificent architecture. The charming old section of town had crooked little streets and boasted the magnificent *grand place* (main square), which Baedeker's tour book proclaimed was "one of the finest medieval squares in existence and, whether seen by daylight, when lighted up at night, or by moonlight, produces a striking effect." The square was anchored by the city's magnificent *hôtel de ville*, "one of the noblest and most beautiful buildings of its kind in the [region]." Begun in 1402, the building's facade was in the Gothic style, and its 370-foot-tall tower was completed in 1454.

On a less grand scale, but nearly as famous a tourist attraction, was the nearby Manneken Pis (Little Man Pee), a small bronze sculpture of a naked little boy relieving himself in a fountain. As Baedeker explained with a slightly elevated nose, the statue "is a great favourite with the lower classes." He did admit, however, that "the figure is not without considerable artistic excellence." On the edges of the old part of town were beautiful, broad tree-lined boulevards where city walls used to stand.

For many visitors before the war, Brussels had always compared favorably to Paris. In September 1914 under German rule, however, the city was probably barely recognizable to its citizens. As one British woman still living in Brussels wrote, "We go to bed very early now—nothing to be done, and to save gas. All cafes are closed at nine, and it is like the city of the dead from that on—not a cat to be seen anywhere. There is no traffic in the streets even in daytime, as the Germans allow no motors of any description, or bicycles, and there are no horses, as they took them all away—only a stray old broken-down horse vehicle to be seen occasionally."

The Germans, famous for their precision and eye for detail, even went so far as to change the time in Brussels and throughout occupied Belgium. Before the war, Belgium had only one time zone, Greenwich Mean Time, while Germany had set its clocks one hour earlier. When the Germans took over, they insisted that the country convert to German time and that all town clocks be set to the new time. Immediately, towns all over Belgium reported faulty tower clocks that couldn't be repaired. Most Belgians began referring to all appointments in Belgian time, as opposed to German, or "hour of the clock," time.

Hugh Gibson of the U.S. Legation had an early run-in with the time differences. On September 19 he was to meet a German official at the man's office, but when Gibson showed up, no one was there. The next day, when Gibson talked with one of the minions of the official, he told Gibson: "Oh, I see, you came at half past six, Belgian time! Of course von der Lancken expected you at half past six, German time!" When

PROCLAMATION.

Inhabitants of both sexes are strictly forbidden to leave their houses so far as this is not absolutely necessary for making short rounds, in order to buy provisions or water their cattle. They are absolutely forbidden to leave their houses at night under any circumstances whatever.

Whoever attempts to leave the place, by night or day, upon any pretext whatever, will be shot.

Potatoes can only be dug with the Commandant's consent and under military supervision.

The German troops have orders to carry out these directions strictly, by sentinels and patrols, who are authorised to fire on anyone departing from these directions.

THE GENERAL COMMANDING.

A German affiche *(French for "poster") displayed in occupied Belgian territory. It reflects how completely the Germans wanted to control civilian life.* (Public domain; Joseph Green papers, Seeley G. Mudd Manuscript Library, Princeton University, New Jersey.)

Gibson was asked when he would like to reschedule, his sense of the absurd came through, at least mentally: "I felt inclined to set eleven in the morning and then wander over at three in the afternoon, with the statement that, of course, I did everything according to New York time."

Occupied Brussels was also adorned with a new sight, German *affiches* (French for "posters"). These posters were plastered daily around Brussels and all over occupied Belgium. Belgians were used to the occasional local government placards, which gave residents neighborhood information, but these German posters were new. They carried war news or rules and regulations of the occupation and, according to Whitlock, "played as large a part in the life of Brussels just then as had newspapers before the war. They might not always provide news, but they could provide sensation, and if written by the proper hand, send a thrill through the community."

On September 2, an *affiche* appeared that was the first proclamation of the new German governor general in Belgium, Field Marshal Baron Wilhelm Leopold Colmar von der Goltz. The placard stated that a new civil administration would be installed, and both it and the already-present military government in Belgium would be headquartered in Brussels.

"My task will be to preserve quiet and public order in Belgium," von der Goltz stated frankly in the *affiche*. "Every act of the population against the German military forces, every attempt to interfere with their communications with Germany, to trouble or cut railway, telegraph or telephone communications, will be punished severely. Any resistance or revolt against the German administration will be suppressed without pity."

If such sabotage did occur, von der Goltz warned, the innocent would be punished along with the guilty. This was the German doctrine that had been carried out with such brutality in Visé, Dinant, Louvain, and many other Belgian towns and villages. The German governor general called on Belgian citizens to help control their own as a way of preventing such incidents. "It is inevitable in war that the punishment of hostile acts falls not only upon the guilty but also on the innocent. It is the duty of all reasonable citizens to exercise their influence with the turbulent elements of the population to restrain them from any infraction of public order. Belgian citizens desiring to return peaceably to their occupations have nothing to fear from the German authorities or troops. So far as is possible, commerce should be resumed, factories should begin to work, and the crops harvested."

He finished the *affiche* with what he probably thought was a reasonable, compassionate note: "I do not ask any one to forego his patriotic sentiments, but I do expect from all of you a sensible submission and absolute obedience to the orders of the German Government."

The impact of this proclamation on residents of Brussels was significant. As Whitlock explained, the Belgians had felt since the start of the war that the Germans were only passing through. But here was a proclamation announcing the formation of a civilian government. Such a thing "had a somewhat too permanent, if not ominous, sound! There was a word on everybody's lips that no one dared to pronounce; did it mean—did it mean—annexation?"

Outwardly, Brussels—and Belgium—complied with von der Goltz's proclamation, but inwardly the story was quite different. The very nature of a people who had been continually invaded but never conquered in spirit was to fight back in creative ways that would not bring the wrath of retaliation. In short order, citizens everywhere began tactics such as subtle subterfuge, passive-aggressive compliance, and occasional outright defiance.

One way that residents of Brussels struck back was by the use of their own flag. Because von der Goltz had specifically stated in his first *affiche* that no one needed to "forego his patriotic sentiments," Belgians began displaying their country's flag wherever and whenever possible. From balconies, on doors, outside windows, hanging from carts, and as lapel pins, hat pins, and parcel wrappings—Belgian flags were practically everywhere the Germans looked.

On September 18, only three weeks after von der Goltz's statement, a new *affiche* appeared ordering the Belgians to take down their flags. Signed by Baron Arthur von Lüttwitz, the military governor of Brussels (different from von der Goltz, overall governor general in Belgium), it stated that the order had been made to protect residents because the display of Belgian flags was "regarded as a provocation by the German troops living in or passing through Brussels. Purely in order to avoid having our troops led to acting on their own initiative, I now call upon house owners to take down their Belgian flags. . . . It is intended solely to protect the citizens against harm."

As Gibson noted in his journal, the *affiche* "made everybody furious, and for a time we thought there might be trouble. If the flags had been ordered down the day the Germans came in there would not have been half as much resentment, but, on the contrary, they began by proclaiming that the patriotic feelings of the people would be scrupulously respected."

With a city tense and ready to release some of its resentment in violence, Burgomaster (Mayor) Adolphe Eugène Jean Henri Max stepped in.

The Brussels burgomaster was forty-four years old and had been a lifelong member of Belgium's liberal party. After attending law school at the Université Libre de Bruxelles, Max not only practiced law but also did a little work in journalism. He had always been politically active, and when he was twenty-five he was elected councillor for the province of Brabant, whose capital was Brussels. In 1903 he was elected a Brussels city councillor. Later he worked as a magistrate before being appointed mayor of Brussels in 1909.

In appearance, Max was slender with short-cropped hair and a majestic beard whose mustaches swept up with a flourish. In his official uniform of office, complete with sword, broad chest sash, medals, and gold-embroidered high collar and wide cuffs, Max was nearly as regal looking as the city's famous *grand place*.

His appearance reflected his inner resolve to take his job seriously and to work for the everyday citizens of his city. Generally, he was a popular

Adolphe Eugène Jean Henri Max was burgomaster (mayor) of Brussels and became famous for his passive resistance to the Germans. (Public domain; *A Journal From Our Legation in Belgium,* Hugh Gibson, Doubleday, Page & Co., 1917.)

mayor with a good Belgian dry, sarcastic sense of humor. When the Germans came to town, he fought them in his own way—constantly questioning their authority and striving to get every possible advantage for Belgians out of every interaction.

After Max read the German *affiche* prohibiting Belgian flags, it didn't take him long to get his own *affiche* plastered around the city. He called for calm and restraint in what appeared to be an appeasing turn to the Germans. But at the end of his *affiche* he showed his true feelings. "I ask the population of the town to give a fresh example of self-restraint and greatness of soul which it has already so often shown during these sad days. Let us provisionally accept the sacrifice which is imposed upon us; let us take down our flags in order to avoid conflicts, and patiently await the hour of redress."

There, in the last few words, was the wonderful possibility that this German occupation would not last, that someday Belgium would be a free country again.

Now it was the Germans who were furious. According to Gibson, within an hour of the posting of Max's *affiche*, von Lüttwitz's men were running around the city covering them up with white paper. In short order, Max was hauled in front of von Lüttwitz and told he would spend the rest of the war in a prison in Berlin. The little burgomaster reportedly said he was ready to accept the consequences of his actions, but, as recorded by Gibson, he added shyly that "he could not be held responsible for what might happen after his departure."

Those words were not lost on von Lüttwitz, who, according to Gibson, "rushed off to see von der Goltz. In ten minutes he came back and told Max that he was free and that the Field Marshal desired that he should continue to act as Burgomaster as though nothing had happened."

Max, who had been popular before, was becoming a hero.

Meanwhile, Belgians obediently took down their flags . . . then promptly began using the Belgian flag's colors (black, yellow, and red) as hair ribbons, parcel string, and other adornments.

The war of wills had just begun.

Van Doren and de Moor Team Up

There were some in Brussels who were not content to merely wear their country's colors. Eugene van Doren was a Belgian who hated inactivity, and after watching the Germans march into Brussels he was ready to do something, anything, to oppose the Germans. With his small cardboard business shuttered, thousands out of work, and the city in turmoil, he had the time and energy. But what to do?

Van Doren's newfound friend, the Abbé de Moor, was more than happy to accommodate this passionate, willing volunteer. He suggested that van Doren "assist him relieving the distress among his parishioners." Van Doren jumped at the chance, not caring what that might entail or where it might lead him.

He learned quickly that the abbé had a very liberal definition of parishioners. It included French and English soldiers caught behind enemy lines who desperately wanted to get to neutral Holland. An underground network was spontaneously springing up around the country to help such soldiers. Some called it the "Nurse Cavell organization" after British nurse Edith Cavell, who had a clinic in Brussels for years and was allowed to stay after the Germans invaded. She showed her compassion by treating the wounded of both sides and showed her patriotism by secretly helping Allied soldiers get to Holland. That would not last long.

For the stranded soldiers, it was a fugitive life of being smuggled from place to place until the time and circumstances were right for crossing the frontier into Holland. Many of them came through Brussels and were secretly boarded at homes around the city. They needed to be fed and clothed, given money, and ferried around until they were moved out of the city on their way to the border.

Van Doren took to the task like a duck to water. He seemed to enjoy the risk and the danger involved. It was so different from the quiet, restrained life of a bourgeois businessman with five children that he had led only months before.

Soon, the abbé surprised him with yet another activity that was just springing up—letter smuggling in the underground network Mot du Soldat ("Word of the Soldier"). Since the beginning of the war, communication between soldiers and loved ones had been nearly impossible. So, of course, attempts were made on both sides to get letters back and forth across the frontiers. Successful couriers could dictate whatever fee they wanted for delivery of a letter. In one of the poor sections of La Louvière, a town in southern Belgium, a woman named Madame Pol Boel witnessed a scene between an old woman and one such letter courier. He had come, she said, "with a letter from her son, who had joined up on the outbreak of the war and who she feared was dead. The man wanted five francs for bringing the letter. The woman was very poor; she offered all the money she had, two [German] marks. . . . The man sneered and tore her son's letter to shreds before her eyes. That day . . . I determined to organize a free postal service between the soldiers and their parents." And so Mot du Soldat was born.

Van Doren, as directed by the abbé, passed on letters through the network while wondering what other activities de Moor might be engaged in. He didn't have long to wait. Soon he found out his friend was also an agent working with the "Allied Intelligence Service." Van Doren felt "there was apparently no clandestine activity in which the Abbé had not a finger."

But van Doren longed to do more. What he was doing was good and important work, but according to a later book, *Underground News*, it just didn't "satisfy an urge he felt to strike some personal blow at the gigantic war machine that was crushing the life out of the nation and threatening to drive the last vestiges of the Belgian Army into the Channel."

He found his inspiration in a German *affiche*. The *Underground News* related that as van Doren walked through Brussels one day, he saw another poster touting the many German victories in battle. His frustration and rage were barely contained when suddenly he got an idea. He turned and immediately went to buy a "small hand duplicator."

His next stop was to see de Moor. "We're going to take it out on His Imperial Majesty and his confounded conquering armies. . . . You can try your hand at caricatures and I'll do the text."

Van Doren and the abbé were suddenly in the publishing business, albeit with equipment that made their bulletins extremely small and difficult to produce. The duplicator was what some called a "jelly press" because it transferred images and text to a master sheet that was laid onto a flat bed of firm chemical jelly, which absorbed the image. Multiple copies could then be made by pressing paper down on the imaged jelly. The process was slow and sometimes messy, but it was easily hidden from the Germans and didn't have the noise that came with regular printing presses.

The two men immediately began circulating their bulletins, which were "ironical little sheets illustrated with insulting caricatures pillorying the kaiser and his troops. These they slipped into letter-boxes as opportunity offered as they went about their more serious business."

The bulletins came out in a country where the free press had ceased to exist. When the Germans had marched into Brussels, Max requested newspaper editors stop publishing "to avoid the indignity of the inevitable enemy censorship." The Germans then called the newspaper proprietors together and tried to persuade them to continue publication with promises of a very lenient censorship. The owners and editors unanimously refused.

This refusal led the Germans to post an *affiche* on September 8 "prohibiting the bringing of newspapers to Brussels from the outside world, and announcing that any one who brings newspapers here or is found with papers in his possession will be severely punished. Two German papers will be distributed by the authorities, and everything else is taboo." The only newspapers legally for sale in Brussels and the rest of Belgium were German. The city could see beyond its streets only through the eyes of the conquerors.

That didn't mean non-German newspapers weren't available, but they could come at a high price, both literally and figuratively. As Whitlock explained, "No newspapers were published in Brussels, and none were allowed to enter unless they were German, but as one walked along the streets toward evening, furtive figures would approach and whisper: '[London] Times, monsieur?' And one might buy a copy . . . several days old for ten or twelve francs. Then we learned that these salesmen were being shot if they were discovered. So we bought their contraband papers no more, not caring to be even indirectly associated with such tragedies."

The news from these older papers held little interest, at least to Whitlock, because he felt "nothing so quickly evaporates, perhaps, as the interest of a newspaper, which, like waffles, must be hot from the iron to be worth while." Most Belgians probably didn't feel the same way; they would have loved to have had any objective news from the outside world, no matter how old.

While van Doren and the Catholic priest knew their little bulletins were more irritant than threat to the Germans, they also hoped theirs—along with the other anti-German missives popping up throughout Brussels and the rest of Belgium—would have an impact. They wouldn't have long to wait for a response. Less than a month after the first van Doren/Abbé de Moor bulletin was distributed, the German military governor issued a decree "threatening the direst penalties for duplicating, distributing or even reading uncensored pamphlets."

Success! But what to do next?

The priest and the businessman continued to circulate their bulletins and work in their others clandestine activities but wondered how they could strike a bigger blow to the Germans while boosting Belgian morale.

Whitlock and Gibson Tackle Neutrality

While life for most residents in Brussels in September settled down to a tense calm, Whitlock and his legation secretary, Gibson, continued to deal with a dwindling number of stranded American travelers and a growing number of Belgians seeking favors from one of the neutral countries still represented in Brussels (other neutrals with representation in the city were Spain and Holland).

When Whitlock had first come to his post in February 1914, he had chosen a quiet street and a modest house that could accommodate both his budget and the few official functions required. He had written a friend back in America about how difficult it was to secure housing and transportation, especially because he was responsible for picking up the tab for everything not covered by a small government stipend.

He and his wife finally decided on a furnished house at 74 Rue de Treves, eight blocks east of the royal palace and park, in the fashionable Quartier Leopold that, he wrote a friend, had "solid blocks of stately houses." Whitlock's choice, he wrote his friend, was "a house with four stories and a basement, a fine hall hung with tapestries, etc., etc. and the rent is 12,000 francs—$2,400 a year. The whole lower floor we use as a chancellery—all the legations have their chancelleries in the house—for which the [U.S.] Government pays. The government has been paying $1,600 for the chancellery, and the quarters were not as commodious or convenient or attractive as these. I presume the Government will continue the same arrangement. . . . Our only remaining problem is the kind of equipage we shall set up. I wish I could afford a motor, but we can not, and I think we can probably rent a brougham and pair [carriage and two horses]."

Whitlock also knew the necessity of his lesser diplomatic duties, which to him seemed tiresome at best and required more "equipage." Whitlock wrote his friend: "We also need a voiture [small carriage] because of the ceremony of calling and leaving cards, a dreadful task. For nearly a week after my presentation [to the king] I was rushing about leaving cards on all the King's household, the Ministers of State and my colleagues. Then after our presentation to the Queen of the Palace, last night, at the ball, we have to leave cards on her household. It is a great weariness."

Whitlock had a staff that included Gibson, a Miss Caroline Larner (an American who was probably a stenographer), a Belgian legal adviser, Maitre Gaston de Leval, and household servants Joseph, Colette, and Omer, who had been called up August 1 by the Belgian Army.

Before the war Whitlock's usual duties as the highest diplomatic American in Belgium were to represent the United States at all diplomatic functions, convey all relevant political information back to the State Department, and follow any instructions he might receive.

When the war started, those duties became increasingly more important because he was now the representative of the largest and most influential neutral country in the world and was physically in the middle of a major conflict. His position was further enhanced by the fact that he accepted responsibility to be representative of countries that had to leave Belgium—the German delegation before Brussels fell and then the British contingent after Brussels was occupied. The U.S. Legation even represented Belgium's own government after it relocated to France. By mid-September Whitlock, Gibson, and the U.S. Legation represented in total five legations that officially had left Belgium.

When the Germans marched into Brussels, one of the biggest problems Whitlock and the U.S. Legation faced was communication with the outside world. Telephone and telegraph operations were controlled by the Germans and were highly irregular. Mail service had been stopped and would not resume for months. The only way of getting secure messages to and from America was to use the diplomatic pouch. But that meant getting the pouch out of Belgium either through German lines to Antwerp or later, when Antwerp had fallen and Germany had nearly complete control of Belgium, through neutral Holland.

Hugh Gibson's motorcar. It was being stopped by the Germans, who placed a white flag on the car so he could make a dash through the active battle lines. The adventuresome Gibson carried U.S. diplomatic dispatches. (Public domain; *A Journal From Our Legation in Belgium,* Hugh Gibson, Doubleday, Page & Co., 1917.)

Gibson—the second in command and younger and much more adventurous than Whitlock—was given the task of carrying dispatches in the diplomatic pouch, which he gladly accepted. He and his volunteer chauffeur, American businessman D. L. Blount, made numerous forays in his borrowed automobile either northwest to Antwerp, while it still remained free, or north to Holland. His first trip was on Wednesday, September 9, when he took a "little jaunt to Antwerp." It was risky business, but Gibson, his driver, and a passenger had the protection of diplomatic neutrality, not to mention Gibson's own glib self-assurance that nothing would go wrong. On one motorcar expedition with dispatches and some passengers, Gibson went motoring off "bearing a napkin to use as a white flag." Friends joked that it was either Gibson's great naïveté or his overconfidence that led him on one trip to stuff a pillow in the window of his hotel room during a bombardment to protect himself, as if goose down would be much help against flying shrapnel.

One of the first messages Gibson relayed out of Belgium was Whitlock's request to the U.S. State Department for guidance on whether or not he and the staff should stay in Brussels. Because of America's neutrality, the

U.S. Legation was able to stay, but Whitlock wanted to make sure the decision was part of America's overall diplomatic strategy. And, because no one knew how the Germans were going to act ultimately toward neutrals, Whitlock was also worried about the safety of himself, his wife, and the other Americans working at the legation.

After long days of delays, the official response came through: You decide. Whitlock, to his credit, decided to stay and settled down in August with Gibson and the rest of the legation staff to do what they saw as their primary job, helping American tourists. By September, however, their efforts had shifted to focus more on the Belgians, who were facing not only numerous German occupation issues but also the real threat of running out of food.

"We began to note a new phenomenon," Whitlock wrote, "new at least to Brussels—women begging in the streets. Hunger, another of war's companions, had come to town."

Belgians Begin Organizing to Stave off Starvation

Before the war Belgium was the most industrialized country in Europe and with its 7.5 million residents boasted the highest density of any country—652 people per square mile (the United Kingdom had 374, Germany 310, France 189, and America 31). The country imported more than 75 percent of the food it consumed and more than 78 percent of the cereals necessary for making bread, which was a vital part of every Belgian's diet. One journalist wrote in the London *Times*: "To the Belgian, bread is not only the staff of life; it is the legs. At home in America, we think of bread as something that goes with the rest of the meal; to the poorer classes of Belgians the rest of the meal is something that goes with bread."

Prior to the start of hostilities, Belgium's high import rate of food was not a problem because of the country's well-developed industrialization. Belgian industries—from coal to armament plants to lace-making co-ops—exported enough to balance the tremendous amount of food imports the country needed.

That all changed when the Germans invaded. Suddenly the factories and mines were closed, thousands were out of work, and much of the harvest was destroyed or requisitioned by soldiers from both sides or rotted in the fields for lack of workers to harvest it. And there was never any question that the Germans would not provide food for the conquered Belgians. In fact, the invaders simply took food and material wherever and whenever they wanted, despite the world's shocked reaction to their lack of responsibility. With winter only a few months away, a food crisis was coming closer every day.

But as one observer noted, "Famine sweeps over a country like a blighting wind—yesterday even its approach was unsuspected; to-day it is everywhere." By September, food in Belgium was expensive and getting harder to find, but it was still in markets, restaurants, and unharvested fields that could be scavenged. Farmers retained at least some of their livestock and worked hard to produce whatever they could, no matter how small the quantity.

On the international stage, full alarm bells regarding a pending food crisis had not yet been sounded by the press—that would only happen in October, when it became a cacophony—but within Belgium, some people and organizations had begun taking action even before the war's first shots were fired. On August 1 the Belgian government had bought the entire wheat supply on the market in Antwerp and stored it for the coming need. Stockpiling by some began on a local level as well.

Overall, the country was better prepared than some for such a crisis. It boasted numerous wealthy individuals of the upper and merchant classes who traditionally helped out during tough times, a general population ready to sacrifice and volunteer if called upon, and an extensive network of canals used for mass distribution of goods. But by far the most important element to aid Belgium in this particular situation was the country's commune system of governance.

While there was a federal government in place, much of everyday life and everyday affairs was handled by the more than 2,600 local communes throughout Belgium. Each hamlet, village, and town had a commune that kept track of all residents; acted to represent, protect, and adjudicate when needed; and provided charity for those who could not provide for themselves. In larger cities there were multiple communes to handle different districts. The greater Brussels area alone had sixteen communes that dealt with its 700,000 residents.

These communes worked so independently from each other and from the higher levels of government that they continued to function relatively well even after the Belgian government fled to Le Havre, France. Additionally, the German occupation government dealt more with the larger cities and regional levels of government and usually did not meddle in local affairs. As one American historian told it, "The whole machinery of the Belgian central government had been broken down or swept away by the invader. . . . Only the communal administrations remained fairly intact and possessed the liberty of action to permit them to meet the crisis brought on by the shortage of food and the tremendous increase in destitution. It was a happy circumstance for the Belgian population that the local government was so well organized and so relatively independent in normal times."

Because of this, the communes were the perfect vehicles for massive food distribution—if only an adequate and steady supply could be found.

The first Belgians to feel the effects of the war and therefore require assistance were the August refugees. Those who had left their homes in advance of the German armies or had been forced out by the invaders sought food, clothing, and shelter from anyone who would give it. Many headed to Brussels. One American war correspondent reported: "Waves of refugees, many of them utterly destitute, all of them in a state of abject panic and demoralization, thronged into Brussels as the Germans advanced. Day by day their numbers and their distress increased. Relief measures were imperative unless the fugitives were to starve by the roadside or be driven in desperation to plunder right and left." Thousands had already made it into Holland and France, but many more were still on the move because the mobile fighting in Belgium would not be completely over until November.

By late August and early September, however, the writing was on the wall regarding the food situation for anyone who read the signs. According to one later history, "It was practically impossible to purchase more than a pound of flour or sugar at a time, and almost all stocks of tinned goods were sold out, bought by anxious people who besieged the shops in the desire to get hold of a private stock before all was gone. The price of food rose to exorbitant figures."

In accordance with a law passed on August 4 and a king's edict of August 14, the local communes took steps to prevent speculation and to fix maximum prices. They "began to establish soup kitchens, and attempted to cope with the problem as best they could with limited resources and with steadily diminishing food stocks." Some of them even sent "purchasing agents with dog-carts to buy a little flour and potatoes in the open market," according to one American journalist.

Additionally, local volunteer relief committees sprang up, "sometimes in place of [the communes], sometimes co-operating with them, sometimes subordinate to them. . . . Everywhere the natural leaders of the communities came together, and forgetting political, social, religious, and personal differences, devoted their time, money, and energy to the service of the homeless and the destitute. A marvelous variety and number of relief committees were organized in the chief towns of Belgium to collect funds, to care for the refugees, to feed the destitute, to centralize the existing stocks of food and to attempt to avert the threatened social disaster."

On this local level, relief was reaching many refugees and others already in need, but there were two major problems inherent in the situation: one, the coming food shortage would not be just local, it would be nationwide (although few saw that yet); and two, communication throughout Belgium was nearly nonexistent. As a later history told it, "No communication was possible between the localities, and all circulation was extremely limited. Any co-operation in relief work between various parts of the country at this time was materially impossible."

In this highly volatile, challenging, and chaotic situation, the communes in the various Belgian provinces tried to band together and determine how best to solve the problem. Limited success was found in such places as Liège, Charleroi, Namur, and to a lesser degree the mountainous Ardennes. By far the largest and most effective efforts were those implemented in Brussels, and they were outside the realm of the individual communes.

While Brussels politicians such as Max were doing as much as they could to provide relief to the needy, their hands were in many cases tied by the German authorities, who had little incentive to untie their bonds. Max did help to stockpile food, facilitate the coming together of important individuals, negotiate with the German authorities, and provide his offices for meetings of groups committed to aiding Brussels's citizens.

Outside the political spectrum, residents who accomplished the most were men from the wealthy upper and merchant classes. Many of them had business interests in multiple countries, could speak numerous languages, and were well respected by all European powers, so they were able to talk with the German authorities, deal with the city fathers, and have a little more freedom of action than the average Belgian.

Within this elite group, the major instigator of early relief efforts in Brussels was Ernest Solvay. He was at the time seventy-six years old, the country's richest man, a distinguished and respected businessman, and a world-renowned philanthropist. Never having attended university, he began to work at his uncle's chemical factory at twenty-one. In 1861 he had developed, and in 1872 further refined, the Solvay process, an improved way of manufacturing soda ash, a critical product that is still necessary for treating water and making items such as glass, paper, soap, and detergent.

Wealthy from his process and patents, Solvay turned to educating and involving the world on key issues. He established in Brussels the Institute for Sociology, the International Institutes for Physics and Chemistry, and the Solvay Business School. In 1911, he began the Solvay Conference on Physics, which included famous participants such as Albert Einstein and is still considered the turning point in the development of modern physics.

When faced with a war-torn Belgium in August 1914, Solvay had used his prominence and influence to bring together respected leaders in social, banking, and business circles to aid the thousands of refugees displaced by the war.

By September, however, Solvay and others saw that the real need was addressing the coming food crisis. Once again he consulted with a high-level group of distinguished Belgians, who agreed to help. On September 1 there was a preliminary meeting in Max's offices, on September 3 an executive committee meeting was held, and finally, on Saturday, September 5, the first official meeting took place of the newly created Comité Central de Secours et d'Alimentation ("Central Committee of Assistance and Provisioning"). Solvay was appointed chairman of the new Comité Central, while Émile Francqui was appointed president and instantly became the group's driving force.

Just as Solvay was the Comité Central's unofficial elder statesman, Francqui was its man of action. At fifty-one, he was a major force in the financial world and was director of the Societe Generale de Belgique, arguably the most important financial institution in Belgium. He had been a driven, ambitious man all his life and had literally come up through the ranks to achieve his fame, fortune, and power. An orphan at a young age, he was sent to military school at fifteen. When he was an officer of twenty-one, he was appointed by King Leopold to be one of a group to organize and run the Congo Free State. After that the king sent him to China to negotiate the awarding of a contract to Belgium for the large Hankow-Canton railway concession. While he was there from 1897 to 1902, his "main rival in these negotiations was Herbert Hoover,"

Émile Francqui was a major force in the Belgian financial world and a man who disliked Herbert Hoover intensely. Francqui became president of the Comité National, which was the Belgian counterpart to Hoover's CRB. (Public domain; CRB portrait book, Herbert Hoover Presidential Library Archives, West Branch, Iowa.)

according to a history provided by the Francqui Foundation.

As fate would have it, Francqui and Hoover—two powerful men of distinction—had met before, battled before, and disliked each other intensely. And yet they would soon be called upon to work side by side. Historians would probably agree that none but the highest cause could have convinced these two men to work with each other. Even then, it would be a marriage both of them would probably consider rocky at best and made-in-hell at worst. Their first face-to-face meeting since the China days would take place in October in London, and lives would hang in the balance as to how well they reacted to each other.

But in September in Brussels, Francqui was the man on center stage. He was known for running businesses and meetings as a dictator who brooked no questioning of his commands and took no prisoners if anyone dared to cross him. His physical appearance—big, burly, with mustache and cleft chin—was as imposing as his business methods. One man called him "the iron man of Belgium." E. E. Hunt described him as "a type familiar to Americans: a big-business man in the prime of life, self-made, brusque, bourgeois, sometimes intolerably rude, but always efficient, and the man of the hour in Belgian financial affairs. He resembles an American trust magnate, with more than a spice of Gallic salt in his composition. He has no small ambitions, no cheap ideas of glory, and no sentimentality or cant."

Francqui was also highly patriotic and felt, in many cases, that Belgium could take care of Belgium. That's why some might have found it surprising that at the organizational meeting of the Comité Central on September 1, there were Americans in the room: Hugh Gibson, Dannie Heineman, and William Hulse.

Americans in Belgium Get Involved

The Americans were at that Comité Central meeting for a critical purpose, but the story of their attendance began in August. That's when Whitlock had acted as patron and supervisor of a committee of American residents in Brussels aiding stranded American tourists. Included in the committee's members were electric company head Dannie Heineman, his associate William Hulse, and mining engineer Millard Shaler. As the food situation began to deteriorate, the committee also began working on how to provide supplies to the American colony in Brussels. After the Germans entered Brussels and the food situation worsened, Heineman heard about the Belgian committee that was being discussed but not yet formed, and he decided to act.

The forty-one-year-old Heineman had been born in North Carolina to an American father and German mother. His early education was in the United States, but after the death of his father he and his mother had moved to Europe, and in 1895 he received a degree in electrical engineering from the Technical University of Hanover in Germany. When the war broke out, he had ties to Germany, was multilingual, and had been living in Brussels for years and working as the head of a small but growing tram and energy-industry company, Sofina, which had been founded by a group of Belgian bankers and German industrialists.

Because of Sofina, Heineman knew Francqui and had heard of the proposed relief committee. He volunteered to help. He also "suggested to Francqui and others that it would be of great utility to the proposed [Comité Central] to invite the American and Spanish Ministers . . . to act as patrons; in this way the committee would be given a neutral character and protection against requisition of its stocks of supplies might be assured," according to one historian.

Francqui, ever the pragmatist, liked the idea and knew that in this case Belgian self-reliance could not achieve all that was needed. Additionally, Whitlock reported that Max asked him and Spanish Minister Villalobar to act as neutral patrons to the new group. In short order, the Comité Central had two neutral patrons: America and Spain. They would add the critical ingredient necessary, one historian stated, to form a "strong private body, possessing sufficient prestige and credit to carry on large operations, and enjoying a neutral character such as would induce the local officials, the German authorities, the national government, the neutral powers and public opinion to give it their confidence. At this first meeting the general scheme of organisation was sketched out and plans were made for beginning activities at once."

Francqui also saw the Comité Central as an overarching group working for the greater good of all sixteen communes of Greater Brussels—none of which alone would have been able to do what he was aspiring to do. The Comité Central was a "private body [that] would command greater resources and would enjoy a greater freedom of action than the communal administrations, hampered and harassed as they now were by their ordinary official duties and by the demand of the military authorities."

This did not necessarily mean that the communes fully embraced the concept of the Comité Central or of Francqui and what some perceived as his grab for power. Belgium's political situation before the war had always been highly charged, if not downright explosive. Factions included the Catholics, Protestants, those speaking French (Walloons) in the south, and those speaking Dutch-derived Flemish (Flemings) in the north, as well as socialists and every other usual political party. Outwardly, the Greater Brussels communes knew they didn't have the power the Comité Central did, and they couldn't even begin to achieve what the Comité Central wanted to do, but that didn't mean they had to like it. Those not solidly behind the Comité Central sat back and bided their time, hoping Francqui and his group would somehow slip up without jeopardizing the feeding of the city.

Meanwhile, through the course of the three foundational meetings, the Comité Central established a few practical principles and the mechanisms for carrying them out. "Soup-kitchens and canteens were to be established and subsidized in all the communes of Greater Brussels. A uniform daily ration of 200 grams (seven ounces) of bread and a half-litre (a pint) of soup was to be everywhere distributed. This ration was not to cost more than fifteen centimes (approximately 3 or 4 U.S. cents), and everyone was expected to pay five centimes for the ration he received. The commune would, however, issue free soup and bread tickets to those who were completely destitute."

To do this, the Comité Central would put in five centimes toward the cost of each ration, the balance to be paid by the communal charity office or by the communal administration. The Comité also decided on a central warehouse to handle the anticipated food supplies. A special subcommittee under the direction of Heineman and including Gibson, Hulse, Shaler, and another American mining engineer, Charles Macloskie, would take charge of the central warehouse and secure food.

But where to find the food?

With the country's food supplies dwindling rapidly and no possibility of international trade resuming while the war still raged, Heineman and his subcommittee realized they would somehow have to import the food themselves—a daunting venture that had a myriad of seemingly insurmountable obstacles:

- The Germans had to allow the importation of food.
- The Germans had to guarantee not to requisition any imported food.
- The British had to agree to allow food through the blockade it had established to cut off Germany from world trade.
- Processes had to be developed for determining how much food was needed to feed Brussels, then the food had to be bought, shipped, and transported into Belgium, and distributed to Greater Brussels's sixteen communes.
- Some entity had to be found to pay for such a giant undertaking.

There was nothing to be done but start and see how far the Comité Central could go toward achieving its to-do list. The first small step was taken the next day, September 6, when placards were placed all over Brussels announcing the new Comité Central, explaining what it hoped to do, and asking for donations from those who could afford to give.

The members of the Comité Central knew that asking for donations only within Belgium would not be enough. Francqui immediately contacted an official in the Canadian Branch of the Societe Generale, asking that he form a committee in Canada to gather contributions to be sent to Belgium. Francqui also sent a request on September 9 to the Belgian minister in London, asking that an appeal for donations be sent out to the world, as well as a request to all Belgian diplomatic and consular offices to have charitable committees formed for sustained giving. "This appeal was widely acted upon, especially in Great Britain, the self-governing dominions of the British Empire and in the United States, where dozens of Belgian relief committees were almost immediately formed under the patronage or direction of the Belgian Ministers and Consuls."

The next steps would be progressively harder, however, even with the power and influence of the two neutral patrons. While it was true that, compared with the Belgians, the representatives of America and Spain had greater freedom of movement, freedom of speech, and freedom to negotiate with Germany and the Allies, those freedoms didn't guarantee success. It still remained to be seen if the patrons and the Comité Central could overcome all the obstacles and feed the city of Brussels.

Meanwhile, the need was becoming greater. On September 19, Gibson wrote in his journal: "The food supply of the country is being rapidly exhausted and there is urgent need for importations. The public knows little about the situation, but a serious shortage threatens and we must have a considerable stock aboard. . . . [In Brussels] there is enough [flour] for only a few days now, and there will be trouble when the bread gives out."

The first major hurdle was Germany. If, miraculously, any food was brought into Belgium, what would stop the German Army from taking it? The Germans had already shown they were capable of taking it and willing to do so when they nearly picked Belgium clean during the invasion. One American journalist had declared after the invasion: "Belgium was gutted."

Those in a position of prominence began using their contacts and special avenues of influence to apply pressure to von der Goltz to formally guarantee the Germans would not requisition any imported food. The task was a little easier than some would have imagined. At this stage of the war, the German thought process was straightforward: The Germans would not feed the Belgians. There was little left to take from Belgium. They needed every man at the front. Peaceful Belgians did not require many soldiers to control. Belgians would remain peaceful if they were fed.

This logic dictated that a neutral effort to bring food to the Belgians would serve German interests. On September 17 a letter from von der Goltz to Whitlock served as a hands-off guarantee. It did agree "not to requisition the shipments of wheat and flour destined for the alimentation [the provision of nourishment] of the Belgian civil population." It did, however, have a stipulation that was not acceptable to any Belgian. Von der Goltz stated that the German civil administration "reserves to itself alone the right of decision as to the distribution of the wheat and flour in the different portions of the occupied territory, according to local needs, and to supervise this distribution." This meant the Germans—not Francqui and the Comité Central—would have final say over all distribution.

It was definitely not a perfect document, especially in the minds of the Comité Central's members and neutral patrons, but victories had to be taken when they came, even if they were less than ideal. There were so many other hurdles to overcome before food distribution in Belgium could happen that the group focused on what had been achieved—the Germans had agreed not to touch any imported food. That was a major concession and one that allowed the Comité Central to move forward to the next step.

With the guarantee in place and large sums of donated money already secured, it was time to go to the outside world for help. Millard K. Shaler, who had had experience in food purchasing for mining companies in the Congo, was chosen to take that next step.

Shaler, thirty-four, had been born and raised in Ellsworth, Kansas. He had studied at the University of Kansas, where he had earned a

Millard K. Shaler was a mining engineer living in Brussels when the war broke out. He volunteered in relief efforts and was the first to travel to London in an attempt to buy food for Brussels. (Public domain; CRB portrait book, Hoover Institution Archives, Stanford University, California.)

bachelor of arts degree in 1901 and an engineering degree in 1904. The university was where he met his wife, Mary Jane Johnson, who graduated with a bachelor of arts degree in 1904. Shaler then worked for the U.S. Geological Survey and the Guggenheim Exploration Company of New York before becoming a mining engineer for the Societe Internationale Forestiere et Miniere du Congo (a corporation formed by an earlier Belgian king to mine diamonds).

Even though he worked all over the world, Shaler was still the kind of man whose roots in the cowboy American West and Midwest ran deep. One photo of him during this time shows a man who seemed to be open, honest, direct, and not happy to be wearing a three-piece suit. He must have been cowboy tough, for when he was sent to Africa in 1906, he made several explorations and surveys in the wild and brutally rugged Belgian Congo, and he played a leading part in the development of a diamond field in South Africa and the Angolan oil field in West Africa— all difficult assignments at best. By 1914 he had earned the much more comfortable life that living in Brussels provided.

From the start Shaler took an active role in the relief efforts—not only of stranded American tourists but also of the Belgians, who were quickly running out of food. In fact, some said he was the one who came up with the idea of relief on a grand scale. As one U.S. historian stated, "An American engineer in Brussels named Millard Shaler conceived the idea of a large-scale relief effort under neutral management."

Regardless of who came up with the idea, Shaler had the responsibility for going out to Holland and buying food and shipping it back to Brussels. He had in hand von der Goltz's guarantee, a *passierschein* (a German safe-conduct pass), and a credit for £20,000 ($100,000) to buy wheat, flour, and other foods from anyone who would sell them to him.

On the afternoon of Saturday, September 19, Shaler had lunch with Gibson, who then saw him off on his journey, noting, "It is not an easy task he has ahead, but he went to it with a good heart." Shaler, accompanied by his assistant, Mr. Couchman, hurried off in a motorcar toward Liège and Holland with high hopes and the good wishes of an entire city.

He didn't get far. In Liège, sixty miles from Brussels, he was arrested and thrown in jail for being a spy.

Searching for Food in Belgium

Heineman and his subcommittee had known there was no single answer to the coming food crisis, so while they had made plans to send Shaler to London, they also sent agents into the countryside to find and buy as much food as possible. Heineman himself traveled to Louvain on Thursday, September 10, to determine what flour still remained in the mills and to arrange permission to buy and ship whatever he could back to Brussels.

Heineman did find a supply of flour that he purchased for Brussels. But how was he to get it the thirty miles by train from Louvain to Brussels when the country was still in major lockdown and no trains other than military transports were moving?

Heineman struck on "the brilliant idea" of using the motortrucks from the Brussels Fire Department. After discussions with the Belgian and German authorities, he obtained all the permissions necessary and, according to a later history, "one fine September morning these motortrucks came to Louvain to carry the flour to Tervueren, some ten miles out of Brussels. From Tervueren to Brussels ran a tramline of a company under Heineman's control, and this was utilized to carry the flour into the city."

While this flour was earmarked for Brussels only, Heineman's efforts regarding transportation ended up helping the entire country. After the fire truck event, he negotiated with the Germans to allow the restart of the vicinal railways—a network of narrow-gauge tramways throughout Belgium—so that further food shipments from the countryside could be brought to Brussels without the use of fire trucks. Permission was granted September 24, and the little tram railways began running through Belgium again.

Heineman and his group were making things happen. Most important, as one history related, "the Brussels [food] stocks would not have lasted until the end of September if they had not been largely supplemented by the quantities of food secured by this sub-committee." But the situation was getting worse. On September 22, Heineman told Max that there were only two days of flour left in the city's central depot—5,700 sacks remained, when the city normally consumed 3,000 sacks a day.

Somehow, the Comité Central and Brussels stumbled along, day by day through September, still meeting demand. But demand was growing. The committee soon realized that the one ration of 200 grams of bread and a half liter of soup per person per day that it had established was not enough for those who were completely destitute. It decided to distribute through the soup kitchens a second daily ration, financed exactly like the first. The second ration would be "composed of warm cooked foods, such as potatoes, rice, bacon, etc., when the facilities of the canteen permitted; otherwise the food supplies were distributed to be cooked at the home." By the end of the month, 120,000 daily rations were being distributed.

Such an increase could barely be covered by the buying and shipping of food from around the country by Heineman's subcommittee. There was only so much that such shifting around—this basic taking from Peter to pay Paul—could achieve. For some, it became evident that the entire nation, not just Brussels, needed assistance. It would remain to be seen how the city and the country would fare as September rolled to its end.

NINE

London

A Formidable American Force Emerges

Working in London to aid the stranded tourists, Hoover had organized, developed, and built the Committee of American Residents into an efficient, effective organization through August and early September. He had done it carefully and methodically like the engineering of a building or bridge. He started by constructing a foundation of core volunteers made up of mostly trusted friends and associates. They comprised the group's executive committee and were chosen not only because of their loyalty, knowledge, and expertise but also because they would serve as a mirror to reflect his beliefs, policies, rules, and regulations. He then recruited and inspired other volunteers to do the actual work since he spent much of his time in one-on-one meetings and in writing pointed correspondence to convince those in power of the rightness and necessity of the work. To build critical trust and respect for him and his organization, Hoover also released periodic reports that were highly detailed and scrupulously prepared. And finally, Hoover took the time and thought to use—some would say downright manipulate—the international press so that the citizens and governments of all countries concerned saw the situation, his organization, and himself in the way he wanted them to. Most surprising to many was the fact that Hoover's "structure" had generated only a tiny percentage of administrative overhead and no misuse of funds (unlike many traditional benevolent organizations).

Hoover probably didn't fully realize that he had just built a successful organizational template that he would use again very soon. For the time being, he could take pride in the fact that his work had paid off, as by the end of September more than 100,000 American tourists had been helped, and all of those who wanted to get home did so. While the work wouldn't fully wind down until early October, it was then obvious that the spontaneous relief effort had worked well and had achieved its stated goals. "Here was a team of citizen-volunteers, led by successful businessmen, operating under official patronage and distributing both its own and U.S. government funds. Even [Assistant Secretary of War] Breckinridge acknowledged that a 'paid organization' could not have accomplished what Hoover had done," according to one historian.

In late September, Hoover made a move to formalize what had been done through his informal Committee of American Residents: He officially changed the name to the American Committee, elected officers with himself as chairman, and drew up a constitution and bylaws. It was now official: Hoover was in the business of helping people—in this case, Americans still in Europe who he felt might need assistance throughout the course of the war, no matter how long that lasted. With the American Committee, Hoover had established a vehicle that he could take in any direction he felt was necessary.

August and September had been pivotal months in Hoover's life. During that time, the little-known mining engineer had won the day, emerged onto the world's stage, and thereby established himself as a formidable American force to be reckoned with. What happened in London also showed that Hoover was a can-do American businessman who brought engineering and business principles to the process of relief and charity (something that had not been done before). It also seemed to prove Hoover's belief that one strong man leading one organization could be much more efficient and effective when confronting a massive problem than numerous groups run by committees.

All the lessons he had learned and all his personal qualities and business skills would be sorely tried during the next four years. And yet, in early September, he probably would not have believed that a little more than a month later, he would utilize and improve upon all those newly learned lessons on a much larger, more consequential scale. The new venture would not involve a mere 200,000 people; it would encompass an entire nation. And the consequence of failure would not be just traveler inconvenience, but starvation and death for untold numbers of civilians.

Hoover was ready; his time had come. But would he be a match for the massive test that lay ahead?

Shaler's Mission Hits Roadblocks

On Friday, September 25, a very frustrated Shaler arrived in Rotterdam and began making inquiries regarding the purchasing and importing of food from Holland into Belgium. After talking to Dr. Henry van Dyke, the minister of the U.S. Legation, and various Dutch officials, Shaler was told that "in view of the shortage of available food even in Holland, the Netherlands Government would prefer to have him make the purchases in England."

And so on Saturday, September 26, a doubly frustrated Shaler finally arrived in London after having left Brussels on September 19. This had been a major setback when every day counted in securing food for Brussels.

His arrest as a spy in Liège had occurred because the Germans had found that he and his assistant were carrying private letters to be posted when they reached Holland or England. Because the letters were open and contained only information about the welfare of individuals in Brussels, Shaler had thought it would be okay to take them. But, as Gibson noted, "These are parlous times to be traveling with correspondence." It took nearly three days of telegrams and pressure by Whitlock, who went straight to the German authorities in Brussels, and the efforts of the U.S. consul in Liège to get Shaler moving again. It took an additional three days for him to get to Holland, then catch a ferry across the English Channel, and hop a train to London.

Shaler's time in London began in only a little less frustrating way than his time in jail. While he was able to buy 2,500 tons of wheat, rice, and beans, he discovered quickly that that was the easy part. It became downright difficult when he went to the Belgian Legation on September 29 to get assistance in securing permission to ship the supplies. Shaler was accompanied by some prominent Belgians, and yet the group was not able to speak directly with the Belgian minister. They outlined their problems and their hopes for help to an underling, who promised to talk with the minister. The next day, Shaler was told the minister was loathe to do anything without instructions from the Belgian government, which was then residing in Antwerp. The diplomatic wheels were barely turning.

But the Belgians, Shaler soon realized, weren't his biggest problem. "The British authorities feared that despite the written guarantee of the German command against requisition, these commodities might directly or indirectly benefit the army of occupation." Descriptions about a potential famine fell on deaf ears. There was a war on—who did Shaler think he was, trying to ship food right into German hands?

Such discussions were taking place at the highest level of the British government and were heightened by the fact that Britain had, at the outbreak of war, immediately established a blockade of German ports. Although it wouldn't be until early November that Britain would declare the North Sea a war zone, the point of the blockade, a part of Britain's war planning for many years, was clear: starve Germany as a way of shortening any war.

Further muddying the waters was the acknowledged fact that Britain and France owed Belgium a great debt of gratitude for slowing down the German invasion just enough that a quick victory had been avoided. As British Prime Minister Herbert Henry Asquith stated: "Belgium has deserved well of the world. She has placed us under an obligation which as a nation we shall not forget. We assure her today in the name of the United Kingdom and of the whole Empire that she may count to the end on our whole hearted and unfailing support."

Now, though, Shaler was discovering there was a chance these same courageous people might starve to death. Were not the Allies obligated by their debt to allow food shipments into Belgium?

Absolutely not, said Britain's most famous field marshal, Lord Kitchener, who was then secretary of war. He was joined by up-and-coming politician Winston Churchill, first lord of the admiralty. They led the group of mostly military men who were adamantly opposed to any food relief for the Belgians.

In favor of allowing humanitarian aid to the Belgians were such notables as Prime Minister Herbert Asquith; the Earl George Curzon of

Kedleston; Foreign Secretary Edward Grey; and diplomat Lord Eustace Percy.

The English and American public, unaware of a possible famine, had not yet had a chance to weigh in on the issue. But they would learn of it shortly, and the reaction would be strong and swift.

A political war in London was brewing, and in early October—a few short days away—it would come down to some hand-to-hand combat. But as September 1914 came to a close, Shaler still couldn't ship his food. He also found that there were others—Belgian representatives from such cities as Liège, Charleroi, and Namur—who wanted to petition the English government to allow food through the blockade. It was a somewhat disorganized mess, but each person in it was striving for the same thing—food relief to Belgium.

Back in German-occupied Belgium, more and more citizens had no choice but to join the soup-kitchen lines as the country quickly consumed its dwindling supplies.

TEN

Coming From America

On Wednesday, September 23, the SS *St. Paul* sailed out of New York City bound for Liverpool. The elegant vessel had been converted in 1910 to carry only second-class and steerage passengers on the busy transatlantic route. During this autumn sailing, the *St. Paul* had thirty-nine second-class passengers who probably could not have cared less that they were sailing on a second-tier vessel—they were newly minted U.S. Rhodes scholars bound for their year of academic studies at one of the numerous colleges within renowned Oxford University. They ranged in age from nineteen-year-old Bennett Harvie Branscomb, who was born and raised in Alabama and was the second son of a Methodist minister, to twenty-four-year-old Charles Russell Clason, who was born and raised in Maine, had attended Bates College and Georgetown University, and was the second son of an attorney.

David T. Nelson was another student on board. He had turned twenty-three on September 10 and had been born and raised in North Dakota

In September a group of American Rhodes scholars sailed on the SS St. Paul, *heading for a year at Oxford University. Less than three months later, some of these young men would find themselves in German-occupied Belgium as CRB delegates, with the youngest being only nineteen years old.* (Public domain; The David Th. Nelson papers, Luther College Archives, Decorah, Iowa.)

by parents who had emigrated from Norway. He was about five feet ten inches with a full head of hair and a face that at rest was as unreadable as the prairies he had grown up around. But his smile was open and straight-forward, and no doubt, people could tell instantly that he was trustworthy and hardworking.

After graduating in 1912 from Luther College in Decorah, Iowa, Nelson spent the next year as principal and teacher at the high school in Hannaford, North Dakota. He then moved to Bisbee, North Dakota, and taught in a one-room school while studying Greek in his spare time to prepare for his year as a Rhodes scholar. During the summer of 1914, as the world braced for war, Nelson rode around North Dakota on his new Indian Motorcycle, saying his good-byes to relatives and friends.

He was the first North Dakotan of Scandinavian descent to be awarded a Rhodes scholarship, and as such, he was important enough to merit a column in the *Mayville Tribune*. The newspaper also agreed to publish any of Nelson's letters home that he wished to share. It was a job that came easily to him because, as a family book later stated, he was a good letter writer, enjoyed recording his thoughts, and had "a lifetime habit of making notes, copying quotations, poetry and the like in his pocket jour-nal which he always had with him."

On board the *St. Paul*, everyday life during the eight days at sea was much like that before the war, complete with chess, golf, and tennis tournaments. Nelson and his partner won second place in the golf tournament, losing out to an Englishman and a Spaniard. According to Nelson, passengers also "gave the usual ship concert, the proceeds of which go to the Seamen's Orphan Home, [but] the star number of the program was a demonstration of 'Thought Transference' by Dr. Herman Schmitz, a bluff old Englishman despite his German name. To those who were in on the game, it was amusing to see how well he played it, and how easily he fooled the majority of the crowd."

David T. Nelson had just turned twenty-three when he started at Oxford University as a Rhodes scholar. He would be in the first wave of Oxford students who would go into Belgium in early December 1914. (Public domain; John P. Nelson.)

Although the ship was carrying only about a fourth of its normal complement of 1,370 passengers due to the war's inhibition of international travel, the European conflict intruded only slightly on the trip. Two English warships had been sighted as the *St. Paul* left New York, and another British warship came close and signaled the *St. Paul* two days before reaching landfall. The last event was recorded by Nelson, who wrote: "Everyone cheered and waved as we swept by, but not a sound was heard from the warship, which rested lazily until well astern, and then steamed suddenly across our wake and off into the darkness. I stood next to an English naval officer returning for service, but like all the English I have so far met, his enthusiasm was of a very sober kind, even though it was clearly genuine."

As for Nelson's fellow Rhodes scholars, they ate, drank, smoked, and played games together on many occasions. "I eat at the same table with the men from Washington, South Dakota, Kentucky, Virginia and South Carolina. It is almost amusing to hear the three southerners talk—especially [twenty-two-year-old John L.] Glenn from South Carolina. He has the southern accent and southern drawl to perfection. 'Yes, suh,' is a regular thing with him."

Those who had crossed before remarked that it was the finest, calmest transatlantic trip they had ever experienced. The ship finally dropped anchor in sight of Liverpool at 10:30 p.m. Wednesday, September 30, but "as it was late, we were not allowed to land, so the best we could do was to gather on deck and watch the hurrying tugs on the river, and beyond them the lights of Liverpool."

The students would have to wait one last night for their big adventure to begin. And just as those thirty-nine young men could have little guessed what lay ahead in the next months at Oxford, a select group of them had no idea that by early December they would be far from the hallowed halls of learning, experiencing totally different lessons of life—and death—that would change their lives forever.

ELEVEN

Resistance Is Futile

Burgomaster Max Gets Arrested

By the end of September, Max had become a bigger and bigger problem for the Germans. Every time he got away with another little slight or joke against the Germans, his popularity grew. The Germans had to acknowledge that Brussels residents were relatively peaceful and reserved, but that would carry Max only so far in the face of his growing impertinence. His famous repartee was about to get him removed from office, and worse.

Max's final hurrah began around two German actions: one, the demand for payment of a *contribution de guerre*, or war tax, and two, the lack of payment when soldiers requisitioned anything from civilians. The Germans were in the habit—as other countries had been as well—of demanding cash as a war tax from conquered towns and cities. Additionally, any food or material that was requisitioned (in other words, taken) by German troops was traditionally not paid for at the time, but a receipt was usually issued by the soldiers that supposedly would be settled for cash at the end of the war.

When the Germans had marched into Brussels, Max had agreed to pay the war tax, but he had asked that the Germans pay in cash when taking anything from civilians. They had agreed.

By September 24 the Germans had not gotten their tax money, so von Lüttwitz posted an *affiche* that reiterated the previous agreement and said it was no longer in force because the Germans had not received their war tax. The placard ended with "Inasmuch as the city administration of Brussels refuses to settle the remainder of the forced payment, from this day forward no requisition will be settled in cash by the Government treasury."

Max couldn't let that sit. He wrote a letter to the city's banks, saying that they were not to pay anything on the war tax unless and until the Germans kept their part of the bargain and went back to paying in cash for all requisitioning by their troops.

Additionally, Max put up his own *affiche*, calling out as a lie a proclamation that appeared in Liège that had used his name and implied that he had said the French were falling back against the German invasion. His placard read: "The German Governor of the town of Liège, Lieutenant-General von Kolewe, caused the following notice to be posted yesterday:

"To the inhabitants of the town of Liège.

"The Burgomaster of Brussels has informed the German Commander that the French Government has declared to the Belgian Government the impossibility of giving them any offensive assistance whatever, as they themselves are forced to adopt the defensive.

"I absolutely deny this assertion. Signed Adolphe Max, Burgomaster."

This was simply too much for von Lüttwitz, who promptly stripped Max of his office and threw him in jail. This time there was nothing to be done. Despite the efforts of Whitlock and Villalobar as neutral diplomats, Max was "spirited away to Namur" during the night and locked up. Brussels residents were left to read a posted notice of September 26 that read: "Burgomaster Max having failed to fulfil the engagements entered into with the German Government, I am forced to suspend him from his position. Monsieur Max will be held in honourable detention in a fortress. The Military Governor, Baron von Lüttwitz, General."

Max would not get out of jail for nearly four years.

"We Shall Never Forgive!"

As September came to a close, Max was not the only Belgian in jail. All Belgians under German occupation rule had become "prisoners in their own land," according to reporter Arthur L. Humphreys in the *Times* of London. "They may not go from one town to another; they may not use the telephone or the telegraph; they may write letters only through the German military post; they may not use their own railroad system as passengers or for parcel transport. Belgians seen walking across the fields are hailed by a Landsturm guard. They may walk only in the streets and go to their shops and offices within the radius of their own communities. The psychological effect of this is appreciable only after it is endured."

Humphreys also recorded a conversation he had had with a Belgian: "We know how to suffer in Belgium. . . . Our ability to suffer and to hold fast to our hearths has kept us going through the centuries. Now a ruffian has come into our house and taken us by the throat. He can choke us to death, or he can slowly starve us to death, but he cannot make us yield. No, we shall never forgive!"

When asked if the Belgian hated the Germans, he replied: "Of course I hate. For the first time in my life I know what it is to hate; and so do my countrymen. I begin to enjoy my hate. It is one of the privileges of our present existence. We cannot stand on chairs and tables as they do in Berlin cafes and sing our hate, but no one can stop our hating in secret."

That hate would grow stronger through four long years and become less and less secret.

The flight from Antwerp before the bombardment began. In the upper left corner is the pontoon bridge across the Scheldt River—the only way out of Antwerp at the time.
(Public domain; *The Track of the War*, R. Scotland Liddell, Simpkin, Marshall, 1915.)

OCTOBER 1914

STUMBLING TOWARD ORGANIZATION

A baby being handed down into one of the last boats to leave Antwerp. (Public domain; *The Track of the War*, R. Scotland Liddell, Simpkin, Marshall, 1915.)

TWELVE

The Fall of Antwerp

As October began, the weather seemed to mock the mood of Antwerp's residents. Gone were the biting rains of September, and in their place were chilly nights and dry, sunny days. American journalist Will Irwin reported it was an "October blessed, in this year of dread, with clear, cool, bracing weather, much like our own Indian summer." Few in Antwerp were cheered as they hunkered down to await their fate.

While there was a continuing trickle of those leaving the city and heading north for Holland or west to the coast and a ferry to England, most people stayed because they were sure the city's two rings of forts would hold back the invader. The entire region contained "54 fortresses, forts and redoubts forming, together with the ramparts, the fortified place of Antwerp." This giant defensive complex would surely hold against the Germans.

Taking the place of those leaving Antwerp were those coming into the city. Before the German siege of late September had sealed off Antwerp from much of Belgium, the city had been a magnet drawing thousands of refugees from the countryside. They had fled either to escape the advancing German troops or because their homes and villages had been destroyed. Also coming into the city were the wounded—both Belgian and German. While the city's hospitals tried to cope, makeshift hospitals and recovery centers were established in various parts of the city. The German school that Erica Bunge had said was vandalized by angry Belgian crowds back in August had been converted to just such a hospital and had a steady stream of wounded coming through its doors. To tend to them, there was a full complement of doctors, nurses, orderlies, and volunteers.

Numerous soup kitchens had sprung up to try to handle the needs of all the refugees and an ever-increasing number of residents who could no longer find or afford food. Started by the local communes and managed mostly by volunteers, the soup kitchens opened every day to what seemed to be longer and longer lines of people waiting patiently for a meal, no matter how meager.

On the battlefront, by October 1 the German siege guns had devastated two of the outer forts, and German soldiers were moving up into the breach while Belgian troops, who had been fighting continuously for days, were trying to hold them back. The battle line was barely a half-dozen miles outside of town. King Albert wired England for help, knowing his 150,000 troops couldn't hold the outer forts against the Germans and their big guns. Everyone wondered when the English would come and rescue them.

In the city, American war correspondent E. Alexander Powell reported that "the hospitals were swamped by the streams of wounded which for days past had been pouring in; over the city hung a cloud of despondency and gloom, for the people, though kept in complete ignorance of the true state of affairs, seemed oppressed with a sense of impending disaster."

Even though city and government officials had not provided any news, residents needed only to listen to know which way the battle was going. From anywhere in the city, people could hear the thundering of the big German guns pounding the forts and the lighter pops of the smaller Belgian guns answering as best they could. But like a prizefighter with shorter arms than his opponent, the Belgian guns were no match for the German artillery that stayed out of reach and yet continued to send massive shells into the Belgian defenses. And as the forts continued to fall one by one, the German guns moved closer to the city, and the cannonade got louder and more distinct.

The Belgian government, which had moved from Brussels to Antwerp, met on Saturday, October 3, and decided it should leave the city the next morning to avoid capture when Antwerp inevitably fell. Officials immediately changed their plans, however, when they received a telegram from England saying that Winston Churchill, the first lord of the admiralty, had started for Antwerp and wanted them to stay until they heard what he had to say.

The English were finally coming! After weeks of waiting, Belgium's ally was rushing to the rescue. And who better than the dashing young Englishman Churchill, famous for his battlefield exploits during the Boer War. It was just what the doctor ordered for Antwerp. No official news was posted, but rumors spread rapidly around the city that the English were on the way and all was not lost.

The next day, Sunday, October 4, at around 1 p.m., a big touring car filled with British naval officers "tore up the Place de Meir, its horn sounding a hoarse warning, took the turn into the narrow Marche aux Souliers on two wheels, and drew up in front of the hotel [St. Antoine]," according to Powell.

Hardly waiting for the car to stop, a youthful, clean-shaven man with sandy hair literally hurtled himself out of the car and dashed into the crowded hotel lobby, flinging his arms wide to the startled onlookers as if to say, "I'm here." Winston Churchill had arrived!

Powell, who watched him come in, remarked that it was "a most spectacular entrance and reminded me for all the world of a scene in a melodrama where the hero dashes up, bareheaded, on a foam-flecked horse, and saves the heroine or the old homestead or the family fortune, as the case may be."

Churchill was not alone. He had brought approximately 2,000 British Royal Marines with him. During the next two days, approximately 6,000–8,000 British troops of the Volunteer Naval Reserve also arrived. Another American war correspondent, Horace Green, noted the troops' entrance into town: "At sundown a mist crept up from the river, and through it we heard a roar of welcome and the rumble of heavy artillery [wheels on cobblestones]. Charging down the Avenue de Keyser came a hundred London motor-busses, Piccadilly signs and all, some filled, some half-filled, with a wet-looking bunch of Tommies [British soldiers], followed by armored mitrailleuses [wheeled, multiple-barrel guns], a few 6.7 [inch] naval guns, officers' machines, commissary and ammunition carriages—the first brigade of Winston Churchill's army of relief."

When the troops marched through town to the city's outer defenses, Powell noted, "[A]s they tramped down the tree-bordered, cobblepaved highroad, we heard for the first time in Belgium, the lilting refrain of that music-hall ballad which had become the English soldier's marching song:

> *It's a long way to Tipperary,*
> *It's a long way to go;*
> *It's a long way to Tipperary—*
> *To the sweetest girl I know!*
> *Good-by, Piccadilly!*
> *Farewell, Leicester Square!*
> *It's a long, long way to Tipperary;*
> *But my heart's right there!"*

It was the song that spoke longingly of a town in Ireland and would quickly become synonymous with marching Allied troops of World War I.

Back at the Hotel St. Antoine, which had by then become unofficial British staff headquarters, the smoking room had been requisitioned by Churchill, and a sign on the door stated, "Reservee pour la Gouvernement Anglaise."

Even with his bluster and his troops—which were a fraction of what was really needed—Churchill didn't have much to say to the Belgian government or its king. There were no more troops coming, and he knew it. The Germans would soon succeed in pounding the forts to rubble, and he knew it. Belgium was already all but lost, and he knew it.

What Churchill also knew, however, was that every day Antwerp held out against the Germans was a day that kept critical numbers of German troops and artillery away from the front in France. This gave England and France another day to find a way to stop the German invasion. The siege of Antwerp also kept the Germans from taking the critical English Channel ports that were necessary for resupplying the Allies. The fall of those ports into Germans hands could turn the tide of the war.

With so much riding on Antwerp's outcome, Churchill's job was two-fold: to show the Belgians that Britain had not totally forgotten them and to convince the Belgians to hold out until the very last second.

That second was rapidly approaching. On October 5, with more forts blasted to ruin, it was only a matter of time before the German artillery trained their sights on the city itself. The Belgian government decided to leave Antwerp for safer ground across the Scheldt River in East Flanders. It would make its new home at the port town of Ostend. Belgian Queen Elisabeth—who had left the city in late September to take her two children to England and had promised she would return to stand by her husband—had returned to the city. At this point, she and her husband contemplated leaving Antwerp one last time but decided to stay a little longer.

That morning the city's military commander, General Victor Deguise, finally posted placards around the city that told everyone the truth: The situation was grave, the city was about to fall, and all noncombatants should immediately flee north to neutral Holland. Those who were not able to flee were told in the placard to retire to their basements, disconnect gas and water lines, stuff the staircases with mattresses as protection, and, "having taken these precautions, the population can await the bombardment in calm."

Deguise neglected to tell the whole truth, however, omitting the fact that the Germans had given the city a forty-eight-hour ultimatum: If you don't surrender, we will start bombarding the city at exactly 12:01 a.m. Wednesday morning, October 7.

In the end, knowledge of the ultimatum would probably not have made much difference. After Deguise's proclamation was posted, the city turned from relative calm to panic in a heartbeat. "Hundreds, thousands of terrified fugitives filled the streets," wrote Antwerp merchant Edouard Bunge. "Trains were made up to run to Esschen [Holland], the only line still in operation. As fast as they were filled—and God knows they filled quickly—people fought for their places. Vehicles that were still left in the city were appropriated by force. One would see hacks, market wagon trucks, push-carts, dog-carts, and all sorts of vans laden with people. One noticed especially the throngs of the poor, those who could not afford the luxury of a vehicle, walking with their eyes straight before them, a mixture of men, women and children, burdened with their poor belongings—a pitiful crowd driven by fear, and whose only desire was to gain the Dutch frontier at the price of no matter how much suffering."

Down at the city's docks on the Scheldt River, the scene was frightening, chaotic, and close to total pandemonium. Every boat and canal

barge, no matter how small, was so packed with people and their meager belongings that they verged on swamping. Thousands more refugees
jammed themselves from the wide docks onto a narrow pontoon bridge
like wet sand in a giant funnel. All the permanent bridges had been destroyed previously to prohibit the Germans from using them, so every
Antwerp resident knew the pontoon bridge was one of the last ways out
of town into still-free East Flanders.

Meanwhile, the Germans, showing a small measure of compassion,
offered through the U.S. Legation in Brussels to spare the historic monuments and hospitals of Antwerp in their bombardment if the Belgians
would provide maps of the city with all critical sites marked. The stouthearted and adventuresome secretary of the U.S. Legation, Gibson, who
was already in Antwerp with dispatches needing to be telegraphed, agreed
to carry the maps back through the fighting and deliver them to the
German authorities in Brussels. He and Harold Fowler, private secretary
to Ambassador Page in London, took on the task bravely. After a long
day of traveling through Holland and back into Brussels, they succeeded
in their mission. It would remain to be seen whether or not the German
gunners followed those maps.

In Antwerp, events continued to escalate during the evening of Tuesday,
October 6. The water was shut off throughout town. People continued to
fill the streets and crowd across the pontoon bridge. The king and queen
finally decided it was time to leave the city.

At the Hotel St. Antoine, according to Gibson, Churchill left with
no fanfare or dramatic gestures: "Winston Churchill came down with
his party, got into motors, and made off for Bruges." It should be noted,
however, that Churchill did send a wire back to England volunteering to
take command of the British forces already there, but he was turned down.
He also left with a profound appreciation of the Belgian royal family. He
wrote, "The King and Queen through these tense and tragic days [were]
magnificent. The impression of the grave, calm soldier King presiding at
Council, sustaining his troops and commanders, preserving an unconquerable majesty amid the ruins of his kingdom, will never pass from my mind."

The king had also made a profound impact on Gibson, who had talked
with him before taking the maps to Brussels. Gibson wrote that during
their conversation, the king had asked about conditions in occupied
Brussels: "His interest was not only for his own friends, but he showed
particular interest in learning how the poorer quarters of the town were

being treated—whether the poorer quarters of the town were keeping calm and avoiding trouble with the Germans. He was most anxious that they should avoid doing anything that would arouse the Germans against them. He spoke simply and touchingly of his confidence in the loyalty and patriotism of all his people, and his certainty that they would come through the war with an even greater love of country. . . . I have seldom felt so sorry for anyone, partly perhaps because all of his sympathy was for others."

The same evening that the king left, so did the Belgian Army. Under the cover of darkness, the troops began an orderly retreat over the pontoon bridge that would continue through the next day. Ultimately, only a small band of Belgian and English soldiers would be left in Antwerp to hold off the Germans for as long as they could. It was a sound strategic move that would save tens of thousands of soldiers from capture.

Right on time, at 12:01 a.m. on Wednesday, October 7, the Germans began hurtling 1,000-pound projectiles into Antwerp.

The Bunges and E. E. Hunt

Since late September, Erica, Eva, Hilda, and their father, Edouard Bunge, had been living in their Antwerp townhouse at 21 Rue Marie-Therese. With them, and always working in the background, were their servants. Some of them lived there permanently, while others, such as the sisters' personal maids and Edouard's valet, came to the townhouse when their charges did. The servants lived on the top floor while the Bunges lived on the second and third floors.

The townhouse was in the fashionable part of the newer city, just east of the broad, tree-lined thoroughfares that had replaced the medieval ramparts. Rue Marie-Therese was at the apex of a large triangle that outlined the city's major park, and the Bunge townhouse overlooked the greenery of the park and a large statue of Quinten Matsys, the renowned Flemish painter who had founded the Antwerp School of painters. The townhouse location was very desirable in the city, for the Bunges needed to walk only a few blocks northeast to reach Antwerp's magnificent Central Station, or they could take a leisurely fifteen-minute stroll northwest down the wide Place de Meir, which was the city's business avenue, to reach a major square, Place de Verte, and the city's main square, *grand place*, in the heart of the medieval Old Town.

Erica Bunge, at upper right, stands with four other nurses and a male orderly or driver. (The author's family archives.)

By late September, Erica and her sisters were going every day to tend to the wounded at the makeshift hospital that had taken over the German school. They also volunteered at local soup kitchens that were feeding more and more people who could not pay for food.

Edouard Bunge, who had his business offices in downtown Antwerp, kept walking to them every day even though most businesses—especially the Bunge company's international shipping, grain, and rubber operations—were nearly impossible to manage from a city under siege. He worked five and a half days a week at a clerk's high-chair desk, standing because he was very nearsighted. He was never far from his worn leather dispatch case that kept the most pressing business papers of his worldwide business affairs. Those who knew him said he was a gentle, thoughtful man who rarely spoke, but when he did, people listened. He had turned down a barony offered by King Leopold II, preferring the simple title of merchant.

He was a distinguished-looking gentleman with a snow-white, well-trimmed beard, close-cropped hair, and high forehead. He would turn sixty-three on October 16. Large pince-nez sat firmly on his nose and accented startling blue eyes that still retained some of the sadness from losing his wife many years before. Always dressed impeccably, if not traditionally, he wore a starched high collar and a precisely tied tie in suitably dark colors. On chilly autumn days like the ones Antwerp was experiencing, he wore a broad-brimmed business hat and a thick wool cape that fell below his knees. When at Chateau Oude Gracht, he always tried to have classical music playing. In the evenings he would have a billiards game with Erica and then retire to his study with his full dispatch case.

On October 5, with Antwerp businesses nearly shut down, Bunge was called into action. As one of Antwerp's most prominent citizens, he was asked by Burgomaster Jan de Vos and prominent lawyer Louis Franck to come to the *hôtel de ville.* There, in the city hall's ornate conference room, they told Bunge that the king had sanctioned a committee to act as advisers to the local commune council in this hour of need. This committee would informally be taking the place of the Belgian government, which was leaving the city. De Vos and Franck asked Bunge to be a member of this thirty-man committee; Bunge immediately agreed. He was told he would be one of only four committee members who would also sit on the city council—the others being Franck, Monsieur Carlier, and Senator Pierre Ryckmans.

Bunge was also informed just how bad Antwerp's situation was.

Edouard Bunge at Chateau Oude Gracht. (The author's family archives.)

As he walked home that night, he was worried about many things. Would he be able to help his beloved city? Would he do so with honor? Would he live through the coming bombardment? Coming up to his sixty-third birthday, he knew he was nearing the end of his life, and yet he also knew the war could be his greatest challenge. He hoped he would have the strength and stamina—both physically and mentally—to do his best to bring his country, his city, and his businesses safely through. Most of all, though, he thought of the three precious daughters who were with him, and the other two daughters who had their own lives and families.

The moment Bunge arrived at the townhouse, he called the three daughters together. He quietly and calmly told Erica, Eva, and Hilda all the military details he had heard from de Vos and Franck, including the prediction that the bombardment might start within a day or so. No one knew how long it would last, where it would be targeted, and how intense it would be. He also talked about the rumors that had been Belgium's constant companions for weeks. Most notably, he had heard how brutal the Germans could be toward towns and villages that resisted. The pillage and destruction of Louvain was very much on Bunge's mind when he suggested there was still time for his three daughters to get out of the city and home to the relative safety of Chateau Oude Gracht. Because he had to stay, he told them he could find a companion to travel with them.

"The three without hesitating replied that they would not dream of it," Bunge wrote, "that it was impossible to leave their wounded without care in this dangerous condition. I did not insist, and from this time on between us there was never a question of leaving the city."

He had never been prouder of Erica, Eva, and Hilda.

By October 6, American war correspondent Hunt had found his way from Germany into Antwerp. It had not been an easy journey, and at one point he was arrested by the Belgians for being a spy, but the trip would later seem like a joyride compared to what he was about to experience.

As with most foreign journalists, Hunt immediately headed for the city's unofficial rendezvous spot, the Hotel St. Antoine. There in the spacious lobby, occupying the comfortable high-backed chairs, settees, and couches, was a menagerie of foreign diplomats, army officers, and British and American reporters. According to Hunt, "Horace Green of the New York *Evening Post* was there; gentle-voiced, observant, and calm as a *Harvard Crimson* scribe writing a collegiate lecture. Julian Arthur Jones dropped in, eager as a cub reporter on his first assignment, and explaining to all of us what was going on." Later, a "thin-faced Westerner in immaculate riding-breeches and puttees [lower-leg coverings] came into the lobby and slouched down wearily in a chair." It was Donald C. Thompson, the photographer for the *New York World*, who had dined with Erica Bunge in September and had been accompanying E. Alexander Powell on some of his travels.

As Powell described him, Thompson was "a little man . . . physically as well as sartorially, as though he had been born on horseback. . . . He reached Europe on a tramp steamer with an overcoat, a toothbrush, two clean handkerchiefs, and three large cameras." He used large equipment because, as he would say, "By using a big camera no one can possibly accuse me of being a spy." In photos, he appeared to be a pixie of a man with a devilish smile who was looking for any kind of trouble that he could capture on film.

Thompson and Hunt had never met, but they struck up a conversation. They both determined they would stay through the bombardment—which everyone knew was coming—and therefore be able to witness the conquering Germans marching in. But what would the invaders do when the city was conquered? Would they march in with bands playing? Or creep in like villains wary of *franc-tireur* attacks? Would they burn, loot, and kill as they did in Visé, Dinant, Liège, and Louvain?

The questions were simply too provocative to ignore, and both Hunt and Thompson wanted to learn the answers firsthand. They knew they each had three small shields to protect themselves during the coming days—they were neutral, they were Americans, and they were journalists. They hoped that would be enough to keep them alive.

But where should they make their stand? At the Hotel St. Antoine?

Thompson invited Hunt to share the house he had been given by some Belgian friends who had already escaped to Holland. He promised it was comfortable and stocked with plenty of food and drink. Hunt jumped at the chance to trade a hotel room for a house because "a hotel always seemed to me a poor place to die in."

They took off through the city to get to 74 Rue du Peage, a townhouse just off of the Avenue du Sud, which was the southernmost broad boulevard that had replaced the city's old ramparts. A block or so east was the Palais de Justice and a few blocks south was the Musée Royal des Beaux-Arts d'Anvers (Royal Museum of Fine Arts of Antwerp).

Other companions in the house were Edwin F. Weigle, a photographer for the *Chicago Tribune*, and Mynheer de Meester, the Dutch vice-consul. A large American flag hung over the front door as a reminder to Belgians and Germans alike that the occupants were neutrals and should not be fired upon. Before the siege was over, the house would become known as Thompson's Fort.

As Hunt drifted off to sleep that Tuesday night, October 6, he had no idea the bombardment was only hours away and that the neighborhood he was in would be one of the first ones hit by the Germans' giant shells.

Erica and her sisters helped the servants rearrange the townhouse in preparation for the bombardment. They carried beds and mattresses down into the cellar so anyone could quickly get to safety when the shelling started. The sisters arranged their beds, the bed for their father, and a

Left to right, Donald C. Thompson, photographer for the New York World, *and E. Alexander Powell, a well-known war correspondent.* (Public domain; *Fighting in Flanders,* E. Alexander Powell, Charles Scribner's Sons, 1914.)

bed for a visiting friend, nurse Rimmel, in the area before the wine cellar. Their father's bed was discreetly behind a screen. Sleeping arrangements for the servants were made near the Bunges in the small rooms, storage closets, and passages toward the street. "We had kept the servants' quarters for our meals," Edouard wrote, "and the servants were to stay in the kitchen during the day."

The Bunges each prepared a small valise with necessary items so that they could make a hurried exit in case of fire or destruction. "Further," Edouard said, "I gave to each of my daughters the sum of 500 francs in case we should not be able to return, they remaining during the greater part of the time in their hospital and I at the *hôtel de ville*, and promising each other in any case to meet at our house, whether it was destroyed or not."

Late on October 6, the shelling of the forts seemed to increase considerably. Eva came back late from the hospital and told the group that she had seen a flash accompanying each shot fired, which seemed to indicate that the siege batteries were getting closer. Just after midnight, a few minutes into October 7, Erica wrote, "We heard distinctly the scream of the first shells passing over the house followed by the roar of their explosion in the city."

———————————————

Hunt was ripped from his sleep by a blast that was so ferocious it felt as if the house had been lifted from its foundation. Two more shells came screaming through in quick succession; then the fourth hit, and "every pane of glass in the house blew out in the chaos which followed the bursting of that fourth bomb. It had hit directly across the street, less than 35 feet from where I was hurrying into my clothes. I could hear screams and sobs; then the sound of people rushing by the house, and the crash of glass which littered the sidewalks, splintering to bits as the people ran."

The bombardment of Antwerp had commenced, just minutes into October 7, as the Germans had promised.

"'Everybody all right?' I yelled, strapping on my belt of gold-pieces and flinging on my clothes.

"'All right!' answered Thompson shrilly from the next room. 'Y-yes,' called Weigle from upstairs."

They dashed to the basement as more shells screamed into the city. They found de Meester already in the basement in a small coal closet. They joined him.

"To my astonishment, the cannonade gave me an intense feeling of exaltation. It was like the exhilaration of fever. I was convinced that we should all be killed, so I wrote on the walls of our cyclone-cellar the names and addresses of Thompson, de Meester, Weigle and myself. My senses were keenly alive to danger, but there was a strange joy in the thought that life was to be obliterated in a mad chaos of flame and steel and thunder. Death seemed suddenly the great adventure; the supreme experience. And there was something splendid, like music, in the incessant insane snarl of shells and the blasts of explosions."

Hunt and Thompson ran upstairs and brought down mattresses and blankets. They tried to sleep, with intermittent success, as the pounding continued above.

At four in the morning, Hunt and Thompson, ever searching for stories and photos, went out onto the Avenue du Sud. Hunt wrote: "Refugees, most of them women, were hurrying by in every direction, half-dressed, only half sane, and horribly afraid. Many, no doubt, were crouching in the cellars, but most of the people ran. Old and young, in little coveys of fours, fives, half-dozens, dozens, ran along the sidewalks, slipping and crashing over the broken glass, making a terrifying and unearthly racket as they ran."

One shell smashed into the corner of Avenue du Sud and Rue du Peage, ripping through the cobblestones and the curb and carving a hole three feet deep and seven feet across. People screamed and scurried for cover. Another shell hit the house across the street and blew out the whole hallway; another took out the third story of a house four doors down. In the pre-dawn, a thick column of black smoke from the ignited fuel storage facilities near the Rempart d'Hoboken rose like some evil presence above the southern part of the city. Some said the Belgians had set them on fire so the petrol wouldn't fall into German hands; others reported they had been bombed by German "Taubes"—the German word for "doves," used because the single-wing airplanes had silhouettes from below that looked like birds.

Hunt wasn't far from the blown tanks and could smell the acrid smell of petrol, but his mind was elsewhere. "I stood in the middle of the street and watched the gray sky in the hope of seeing a shell. The idea was absurd, yet I felt an odd sense of being cheated of part of the spectacle. The air seemed full of steel. I counted three explosions a minute: I wanted to see something. One could hear the shells so easily, it seemed ridiculous not to see them."

Daylight brought only light, not comfort. A dark, overcast sky seemed at times the source of the three to four shells a minute that continued to rain down on the city. The exodus Hunt had seen earlier continued unabated. All means of transportation, from milk wagons and dogcarts to handcarts and wheelbarrows, were being used by "all classes of the population: well-to-do burghers, dock-dwellers, servants, and peasants." They were all trudging toward the docks and the one last place of escape, the pontoon bridge.

The air was thick with ash and the bitter smell of powder, occasionally accented by the sharp smell of kerosene and gasoline.

The noise was at times deafening, with shell detonations and explosions from the fires that raged around the city. At other times, all that was heard was the sound of thousands shuffling with leaden feet through rubble and debris. People rarely talked, but there was much moaning and groaning, and startled screams mirrored every explosion. There was also the incessant howling of dogs—honored and loved in Belgium, but forgotten in the rush to save family, friends, and selves.

With morning came the realization that the Germans paused every hour or so to let the guns cool, while at noon they stopped for nearly half an hour for what residents presumed was their lunch. But right after that, the shelling started up again, with approximately three a minute screaming into the city.

When each landed, it was devastating. As Powell described it, "When one of these big shells—the soldiers dubbed them 'Antwerp expresses'—struck in a field it would send up a geyser of earth 200 feet in height. When they dropped in a river or canal, as sometimes happened, there was a waterspout. And when they dropped in a village, that village disappeared from the map."

During that first day, Horace Green came by the house and told Hunt and the others that so far the center of the city had not been shelled. It seemed as if their neighborhood was the one being targeted.

Even so, Hunt and the rest decided to ride out the bombardment down in the cellar. That decision changed quickly the moment the townhouse took a direct hit. "It seemed to bring down half the house about our ears." While it didn't trap the men in the cellar, when they came up they found that the shell had blasted through three thick brick walls and taken out two floors and part of a third. Altogether, five rooms and a hall were gone. No fire had started, but Hunt knew it was time to move on. He decided to follow the crowds of refugees as they headed into the Old Town and down to the docks.

It was already late afternoon, and dusk was coming. Hunt arrived down at the docks and found massive crowds. Just then the military shut down the pontoon bridge for the night, and "thousands of unfortunates who had stood in line for hours, hoping to cross, were driven back into the city again." That was necessary because the bridge was needed to begin evacuating the wounded to the relative safety of East Flanders. As many as possible had been rounded up from the hospitals and the front and brought down to the docks by any means available. The Piccadilly double-decker buses that only a few short days before had brought hope and the British Royal Marines were now stuffed with the wounded. They inched their way through the crowds that milled around in hopes of using the pontoon bridge later. After the wounded were carried over, soldiers started across, using the cover of darkness to hide their early retreat from the Germans. Tired, ragged, and beaten, they trudged across as if every step were their last.

Hunt found refuge in the Queen's Hotel, which overlooked the main harbor street, Quai van Dyck, and the pontoon bridge. From the upper stories he could see that the bridge was supported in large part by a string of boats that had been strung together across the wide river. He wondered how long the bridge would stay intact.

For the Bunges, on the morning of October 7, as the shells "continued to rain into the city, whistling over our heads, and filling the air with the roar of frightful explosions . . . it needed a good deal of will-power to go into the street . . . my daughters to return to the hospital established in the old German school, and I to repair to the Hotel de Ville." The three sisters kissed their father good-bye and hoped they would all still be alive by nightfall.

When Erica and her sisters reached their hospital, they were shocked at what they found. In the hospitals all around the city, many of the wounded had been evacuated. Unfortunately, the most severely wounded were left behind because moving them might have killed them, and it would have slowed down the retreat. But this meant that those who remained were left to the mercy of the Germans. Every Belgian had heard stories of German "mercy," so it was understandable that some of those left behind became extremely agitated. "There was panic in some of the wards. Mutilated men dragged themselves from their beds and pulled on what garments they could; they screamed and implored the nurses not to let them fall into the hands of the Germans. Some begged revolvers so they might shoot themselves."

At the hospital where the Bunge sisters worked, fifty severely wounded men had been left behind. The Bunges weren't too surprised by that. What they were shocked about was the fact that all "the regular nurses, the stretcher-bearers, the director, even the doctor . . . the entire male personnel of the hospital had fled." The only staff left were the directress, one Belgian nurse, and two English nurses who had refused to go with the retreating English soldiers.

With shells still flying overhead, the seven women got to work calming the patients, cleaning festering wounds, rebandaging where necessary, making comfortable where possible, and tidying up from the hurried exit of the others. Most importantly, though, they wanted to find the best place for the wounded to ride out the bombardment. They agreed

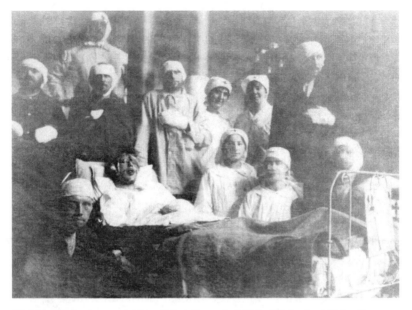

Unidentified nurses and wounded at the makeshift hospital where Erica Bunge worked. (The author's family archives.)

upon the basement. It took tremendous effort and no small amount of brute strength, but they somehow managed to get all fifty badly wounded men—twenty of whom were British soldiers—down to the relative safety of the cellar.

That night, as Edouard walked home warily, "everywhere that one looked one saw the flames appearing above the house-tops; one heard the shells come whistling over, and the roar of their explosions together with the crash of the falling walls made a great and terrible combination; one felt powerless, at the mercy of some irresistible force let loose." At one intersection he saw "two women lying dead on the side-walk; one of them struck in the side by an exploded shell, the other without any apparent wound, but from beneath whose skirts blood was flowing."

In a different, somewhat comical moment, a friend whom Edouard was walking with spotted a canary flying about, obviously escaped from its cage. The friend "momentarily forgot the shells and started to pursue the little bird, making long passes at it with his hat." The bird easily avoided capture and quickly flew away.

When Edouard reached the townhouse, he had news—good news, he thought. A friend knew that the Bunge townhouse was on the Avenue

Marie-Therese next to the city park. Because the shells were coming over the park into the city, the townhouse was not protected in any way by other buildings. The friend offered space for the Bunge family in the large cellars of the Banque Nationale, which provided greater safety than the townhouse's cellars.

Once again, Erica and her sisters turned down their father's offer. This time, they did not "wish to abandon our servants, leaving them alone in the house, and the distance between the hospital and the Banque seemed to them too great."

The second night of the bombardment, Thursday, October 8, was "especially terrible," according to Edouard. "The number of shells coming into the city was estimated at four per minute, and the city was constantly in flames. It was burning in 17 different places, no one attempting to put out the fires; the fire-department was no longer working, and the fire-men could not work because of the shells."

As Bunge and a friend walked cautiously toward the *hôtel de ville*, he saw Belgian soldiers passing them on the run. "They told us that they had received orders to abandon their positions and to try to cross the Scheldt. They told us that the gates of the city and the fortifications were no longer held by our troops and that the forts had stopped firing."

All that was confirmed when Bunge attended a city council meeting in the great council room of the *hôtel de ville* on Friday morning, October 9. The burgomaster, numerous aldermen, several councilmen, and the four appointed from the special committee all heard that the Belgian Army and its artillery had gotten safely away, and the pontoon bridge had been blown up behind them so no Germans could follow. Most disconcerting was that city military commander General Deguise and his staff had left without communicating with the civilian government or leaving word as to how to communicate with them.

As Bunge later wrote, "The only authority which could surrender this fortified place of Antwerp had disappeared without leaving any traces, so there was no reason for the bombardment's not continuing until the city had been completely destroyed. In face of this frightful situation, which was apparently inevitable, Monsieur Franck [the lawyer] took the only possible initiative." He told the group that they should send a delegation to the Germans and outline the situation so "there remains nothing to justify the further continuation of the bombardment of the city which has ceased to defend itself."

In short order a car and two motorcycle policemen carrying white flags had been arranged, and Franck, dressed in frock coat and top hat, was accompanied by the burgomaster, Senator Ryckmans, and the Spanish consul. They took off heading southeast out of the Porte de Malines. As Bunge noted drily, "It was an adventurous departure, for the headquarters of the German General Staff was not known."

At noon, the shelling suddenly stopped. When it didn't resume after a decent interval for the gunners' lunch, Bunge and the group at the *hôtel de ville* realized the bombardment was over. They erroneously assumed it was because their envoys had reached their destination.

No one knew, or would have guessed, that at approximately the same time Franck's group was leaving to find the Germans, the Germans had dispatched their own delegation to go into the city and find a military man who would negotiate Antwerp's surrender. While the two sets of envoys did not meet on the road, they surely passed each other somewhere along the way.

Franck's party found an advanced German outpost near Contich, a village little more than five miles from the city. The Germans told the envoys that the General Staff headquarters was further south, near Louvain in the little town of Thildonck (now Tildonk). It would take them long hours before they stood in front of the Antwerp siege commander, General Hans Hartwig von Beseler.

Von Beseler was an old-school Prussian officer who at sixty-four had been pulled out of retirement to lead part of the invasion and then was given the assignment to take Antwerp. When he saw the Antwerp envoys, he was shocked. According to Hunt, "It was a common story in Antwerp afterward that the German General, Hans von Beseler, could not believe his eyes when the deputation appeared before him, for there was not a man in uniform among them! 'I will not receive them,' he stormed. 'I will not treat with civilians. I have conquered one of the great fortresses of the world,' he burst out, turning to Mr. Franck, 'and a civilian comes to render it up! You come to render it up!—a man in a top hat!'"

Once the situation was explained and confirmed by the Spanish consul, he calmed down and agreed to work with them.

Earlier, the four German envoys arrived at the *hôtel de ville* and were probably just as surprised as their general to find only civilians to greet them. After reassurances by the council group that there were no military officers in Antwerp, coupled with a quick trip to the last known command post of the Belgian Army, where no officers were found, the four frustrated Germans left to go back and report the failure of their mission.

In all this confusion, with no surrender terms yet discussed or signed, German soldiers began walking into Antwerp. According to Bunge, the actual entry of German troops into the city took place quite independent of all negotiations. It seems one of their commanding officers had noticed that the forts were no longer firing and that his advance posts had lost contact with the Belgian advanced posts. He stopped the bombardment and gave the order for his men to advance. Finding the road into the city free of troops and seeing not a living soul because the civilian population had fled, he pushed forward and so made his entry into Antwerp.

Earlier the same day, at 6 a.m. on Friday, October 9, Hunt watched the "magnificent and terrifying spectacle" of the Belgian Army blowing up the pontoon bridge behind it so the Germans couldn't follow. Belgian gunboats then began firing on all remaining empty vessels along the docks that could be used by the enemy to get across the Scheldt. The noise and bedlam were heightened by the terror on the faces of all those civilians and soldiers who had not made it across the bridge to safety. As the dockside crowds turned away from the river, frantically searching for other ways out of town, Hunt and Thompson went to the American Consulate, which overlooked the broad commercial avenue Place de Meir. The American Consul and staff had left Antwerp earlier, so the consulate was empty, but as the bombardment continued, it began to fill up with Americans and Belgians seeking help.

In the afternoon, after the bombardment had stopped, Hunt took a walk through the city. "The streets were deserted and the city silent, except for the snapping of flames in the burning houses. Suddenly, I heard a new sound—low, insistent, measured—the sound of men marching. I turned a corner and looked. . . . There, coming down the avenue in absolute silence, were the Germans.

"The troops were advancing cautiously," Hunt continued, "like men who fear a trap. There was no music, there were no flags. First came some of the bicycle corps, then masses of infantrymen and a few cavalrymen, then came floods of soldiers. Column after column they rolled past, all in the gray-green service uniform which is the most remarkable disguise

According to journalist Powell, flames ignited by the German bombardment of Antwerp destroyed one entire side of the Marché aux Souliers. In the background, at left, is the Hotel St. Antoine, rendezvous spot for many diplomats, British Army staff, and journalists. (Public domain; *Fighting in Flanders*, E. Alexander Powell, Charles Scribner's Sons, 1914.)

ever invented by mortal men. Line after line they tramped by, anonymous as swarming bees, indistinguishable from the mass at fifty yards, stamping the cobble-stones in perfect time, with the remarkable springy march-step of the German recruit."

Nearby, Edouard Bunge had just returned to the townhouse from the *hôtel de ville* to "take the second daily meal with my dear daughters when the servant came to announce the arrival of the Germans. We ran out of the house, going as far as the boulevard, where they were already marching past in good order." By this time, the Germans had decided there was no need for caution or silence. "The infantry came first, the soldiers singing patriotic airs, then the field artillery. They appeared to us well fed, well clothed and not at all as soldiers who had passed weeks in the trenches. I learned later that as a matter of fact these were fresh troops who had come only a few days before from somewhere near Brussels."

Bunge hurried down to the *hôtel de ville* and found the Germans had already arrived. "Their artillery filled the Grand' Place, the guns trained on each street leading into it [in case of *franc-tireur* attacks]."

Antwerp was now occupied, while officially still not surrendered, and so far all was calm. The Germans had been true to their word, either by effort or by luck: The principal architectural treasures of the city had been spared, with only slight damage to the Cathedral of Notre Dame and the *hôtel de ville*. While troops were now in the streets, it would not be until Saturday, October 10, that a parade of 60,000 troops would come marching in as conquerors, filing past in review in front of the royal palace. When the Belgian flag that had fluttered from the cathedral spire throughout the bombardment was replaced with the German black-white-and-red flag, soldiers all around the city began singing the song "Deutschland, Deutschland uber alles" ["Germany, Germany, over all."]

Many Belgians refused to come out and watch, so the troops marched, sang, and played fifes and drums down nearly empty corridors of buildings. Powell noted, "I think that even the Germans were a little awed by the deathly silence that greeted them." The massive army took more than five hours to pass.

Erica Bunge spent the day at the hospital, relieved that the shelling was over and working with the other staff to bring the wounded back up to the wards. When the tiring work was done, she went out into the hospital's little courtyard to take some air even though it was a chilly, clammy October day. Heavy, rain-laden clouds hung low and seemed to match her mood and the mood of the city she loved. As tired as she was, she suddenly noticed something that seemed even more so. A tiny yellow canary stood on the sidewalk as if dazed and unsure of what to do next. Erica, moving slowly and with great purpose, inched closer, murmuring to the little bird. She then gently and carefully captured it with little fuss—the canary did not seem to mind at all. Cradling it in her hands, she thought of all the soldiers she had tended, all the young men who had died, and all those who were still fighting.

She vowed to always take care of this little life for as long as she lived.

For many Belgians, when Antwerp fell, the saddest part might have been all the destruction that had been wrought in preparation for the invasion. The Germans had not attacked in the traditional way, with troops storming the fortresses and city; they had simply sat back six to eight miles and pounded the forts with their big guns until there was nearly nothing left to defend. They used artillery spotters in balloons to give the guns deadly accuracy. Then they turned the big guns on Antwerp and bombarded the city until it surrendered.

As Powell wrote, "In fact, when the Germans entered Antwerp not a strand of barbed wire had been cut, not a barricade defended, not a mine exploded. This, mind you, was not due to any lack of bravery on the part of the Belgians . . . but to the fact that the Germans never gave them a chance to make use of these elaborate and ingenious devices." As Edouard Bunge put it, "All this costly work, and as a result all this devastation for nothing, absolutely useless."

There was another aspect to the invasion, and now the occupation, that few outside of Antwerp would have thought of. It concerned how accepting and open Antwerp had been before the war to Germans. Powell wrote about it. "The citizens of Antwerp [now] hated the Germans with a deeper and more bitter hatred, if such a thing were possible, than the people of any other part of Belgium. This was due to the fact that in no foreign city where Germans dwelt and did business were they treated with such marked hospitality and consideration as in Antwerp. They had been given franchises and concessions and privileges of every description; they had been showered with honors and decorations; they were welcome guests on every occasion; city streets had been named after leading German residents; time and time again, both at private dinners and public banquets, they had asserted, wine-glass in hand, their loyalty and devotion to the city which was their home. Yet, the moment opportunity offered, they did not scruple to betray it."

Belgian refugees fleeing the German invasion, somewhere in the Belgian countryside. (Public domain; multiple sources.)

THIRTEEN

The Refugees

For days they simply walked. Bundles in hand, cold, exhausted, frightened. Pushing carts, leading children, helping the elderly. The Antwerp refugees had little idea of where they were going, other than toward Holland, and no idea of what they would do when they got there. They only knew they had to get out of the way of the inhuman creatures who, they had heard, wanted to burn, loot, rape, and murder. This massive flight northward had started in earnest on Wednesday, October 7, and continued unchecked through Saturday, October 10.

Edouard Bunge got an unasked-for front-row seat to the refugees' flight. Just after the bombardment stopped and the Germans entered Antwerp, they demanded that the city council choose six prominent men for a critical task. These men would each be accompanied by two German officers to the forts in their assigned area to make sure the forts had surrendered. If the forts hadn't, or refused to, the Germans would retire from the city, and the bombardment would begin again. Bunge was one of the six who volunteered.

On Saturday at 6 a.m. Bunge and two German officers, Major von Stresow and Lieutenant Stockhausen, took off for their assigned area. "Chance, or perhaps the Germans' information, willed that the sector which they assigned to me should be ground on which I was at home: Merxem, Schooten, Brasschaet and Cappellen."

As they drove out through the city, Bunge wrote later: "Shortly before and during the bombardment of the city an enormous wave of [refugees] made its way steadily towards the Dutch border. Thousands and thousands of people fleeing from the city as well as from the surrounding communes had saved themselves as best they might. . . . The great majority were poor people without any resources, wanting food, blankets and shelter. There were women at the point of childbirth, little children who were sick and old men who could scarcely stand alone. All this pitiable crowd walked and walked some 10, some 14 hours until their strength deserted them and they stopped completely exhausted. Some stayed in the fields, others were more fortunate, in the pine groves."

As the refugees trudged north through the countryside, German soldiers were seen in the act of confirming the rumors. "Pillage had already commenced," Bunge stated. "The scoundrels could be seen coming out of the houses loaded down with objects of all kinds, and others were in the act of forcing doors, not in the least disturbed by our passage. The inhabitants had fled and we saw no policemen in these outlying districts. A desolate picture of war."

Bunge and the two officers found the forts they had been assigned were deserted and in most cases destroyed. At one that had been hit especially hard by the Germans' big guns, Bunge wrote: "It is the exact truth that not one stone remained on another. The entire fort was reduced to dust, a vast mass of shapeless ruins; what was formerly a small hill had become a hole."

Because they were in the area, Bunge asked if they could stop by the Bunge property of Hoogboom and Chateau Oude Gracht. What they found surprised them. Refugees covered the land like floodwaters from an overflowing river. "A great crowd was surging around the farm, the cattle barns, the sheep barns, the superintendent's house and even the Chateau Oude Gracht. They had come in hundreds. The superintendent had all the buildings opened; all had served as shelters during the night for these unfortunates. Even so, the larger part of them had been obliged to pass the night in the pine groves. Our farm tenants, the superintendent, Verheyen, and his wife Jo, Pier and Louise, the farmers, Phil, the gamekeeper and his wife, all had stayed at their posts. Under the direction of the superintendent these brave people, refusing to become panic-stricken, had helped the refugees to the best of their ability and had maintained order so that no depredations had been committed; they had done their duty."

Bunge was touched by their courage, compassion, and loyalty to him, the property, and the refugees. When they saw he was in the approaching car, they surrounded the vehicle and told him how happy they were to see him. "I confess to never having shaken hands with such sincere emotion, so great was my pleasure at seeing again all these kind faces."

Even the accompanying German officer, Major von Stresow, was touched by the plight of the refugees and wanted them to know there was no need to take flight and that it was safe to go back to their homes despite the isolated pillaging they had seen. "Speak to them," he told Bunge. "I do not know their language."

As many of the refugees gathered around the car, Bunge stood up, and in the loudest voice he could muster, he spoke to them in Flemish. "Gaat allemaal naar huis, gij zijt overall beter dan hier. Het bombardment is gedaan, er is geen gevaar meer. Als gij in Uw huzen zijt, zal U geen kwaad gebeuren." ("Go home, all of you, this isn't the right place for you to be. The bombardment is over, the danger has passed. When you will be in your homes, all will be fine.")

American Journalists Join the Refugees

The few journalists and photographers who had stayed in Antwerp through the invasion now had a very difficult task ahead. They had to get to a place where they could transmit their stories to their home publications. German-occupied territory was out: The authorities would never allow them use of the telegraph lines. The best hope was to go north with the refugees to Holland.

Horace Green wrangled his way onto a nearly swamped canal barge for a trip north down the Scheldt. "I managed to clamber on a river barge laden nearly to the sinking point with Antwerp's peaceful burghers and their dumb-looking women and children. Slowly—very slowly—we steamed out of the haze of powder and oil-laden smoke, through long lines of gunboats and a flotilla of drifting scows packed to the gunwales like our own, and past Fort St. Philippe, whose garrison was at the

According to journalist Powell, this was the only known photo of the Germans marching triumphantly into Antwerp, down the Place de Meir. (Public domain; *Fighting in Flanders,* E. Alexander Powell, Charles Scribner's Sons, 1914.)

moment heaving tons of [gun]powder into the river" so the Germans wouldn't get it. Later, he hopped off the barge and walked the last few miles into Holland.

Hunt, Thompson, and Powell, still not yet ready to leave, headed to the American Consulate, which overlooked the Place de Meir. They found it still empty, but they stayed and had ringside seats as more than 60,000 German troops paraded by on Saturday, October 10. Additionally, many Belgians and Americans residing in Antwerp came to the consulate, and each journalist tried to help in whatever way he could.

By Saturday afternoon, Hunt was ready to leave. It was time to find a working telegraph and get Antwerp's story out to the world. But would the Germans allow him out of Antwerp?

For the Germans, there was no desire to stop anyone from fleeing Antwerp as long as they weren't young men of fighting age. Let the women, the children, and the old go. To the German empire they were nothing more than burdens to be controlled. The fewer of them the better. And besides, whether they were refugees or civilians staying at home, the German stance was that they were not the responsibility of the Germans to feed, clothe, or shelter. The German Army was there to fight and conquer, and it officially maintained to the world no sense of responsibility for the civilian population, especially when many of the civilians, in their minds, were *franc-tireurs* who had brutally attacked them at every opportunity.

So the steady stream of Belgians fleeing Antwerp kept flowing, and Hunt joined that flow. Ever the journalist, he recorded what he saw, heard, and felt as he walked the long twenty miles to the Holland border that Saturday.

He had no choice but to walk. All the boats on the Scheldt River had by then been commandeered. Most of the canals had been wrecked with sabotaged locks or sunken boats and damaged barges. Trams and trains sat still on their tracks, and no motorcars moved except those of the military. Walking was the only option.

Hunt headed north, not knowing which way to go. At first, he traveled a route out through the city's by-then destroyed and deserted fortifications; he hardly saw a soul, with the notable exception of an old man who agreed to show him the road to Holland. As they walked, the old man took a philosophical approach to the situation. "The war? Ah, monsieur, the war it is a curse," he told Hunt. "But then, much in life is a curse, and we must bear it tranquilly. To live, that is the important thing. Men fight each other, cheat each other, steal each other's land, lust for one another's wives—yes, monsieur, it is true—but we must live. We must bear all tranquilly. It is war. It is life, *n'ces-ce pas* [isn't it]?"

As he came to the road to Holland, he found the crowds of *vluchtelingen* ("refugees" in Flemish). There were young men on bicycles, "pedaling as if for dear life," and an old woman carried along in a wheelbarrow. There were women and children; horses, dogs and farm animals; and carts of every kind, shape, and size. Hunt was surprised by one aspect of the refugees. "I never before realized how many old people there are in the world. Half of these refugees seemed over sixty years old and practically helpless. War kills the old like flies. Life owed them a warm chimney corner, a friend or two, a pipe and a bottle; instead of these, it had hurled them out into the center of one of the most terrible cataclysms of history and had chased them in panic from their homes and native land."

Because many Belgian soldiers had been on this route earlier, the ditches beside the road were filled with all that they had cast off, from uniforms, caps, and helmets to rifles, pistols, bayonets, and ammunition. They had either dropped them because they didn't want to carry them anymore, or they were purposefully leaving all signs of military life behind. They knew that once they entered Holland, the country would be obligated by its strict neutrality to intern soldiers from any other nations until the end of the war. Some young Belgian soldiers hoped to enter Holland as civilians and somehow get to France or Britain so they could ultimately rejoin King Albert and the Belgian Army in their continued fight. Few soldiers looked forward to internment until the end of the war.

Back on the road, the valuable military items did not stay in the culverts very long. The farmers in the area were salvaging many of the military supplies, while "little peasant boys, their trousers rolled high, waded thigh-deep in ooze and ditch water, fishing out clips of cartridges and arms, and quarreling over their finds."

As the crowd moved along, people would pull over, exhausted, and stop in the fields or in the little towns to rest. In late afternoon it started to rain, but most refugees keep plodding along, since, as Hunt wrote, "absolute terror still was upon them. No one thought of stopping for rest, for the Germans were somewhere behind."

Later, after the rain had stopped, panic reared up in a surprising place— far ahead on the narrow, tree-lined road. A "huge" German military car was speeding toward Antwerp, not stopping or even honking to warn people out of the way. "I saw people run out of the road, jump the ditches, flatten themselves against hedges," Hunt wrote. "The car came thundering along, a great white flag flapping from its wind-shield, and when it got nearer I saw that two German officers and a civilian sat in the tonneau [back seat]. . . . The eyes of all in the automobile were fixed on the straight road ahead. I do not think they noticed the panic their passing caused. They flew by without giving us a glance, speeding back toward Antwerp."

Hunt didn't know it at the time, but the Belgian in the car was very likely Edouard Bunge, and after Hunt came to know the Belgian merchant well, he would know that Bunge might have appeared uncaring while sitting in that car at the same time as his heart ached for every person who was pushed off that road.

It wasn't long after the car passed that word spread through the refugees from those in front: The Dutch border was just ahead. A small wooden sentry box was decked out with the red, white, and blue flag of Holland. They had made it!

There were no bands playing, no choirs singing; just a few Dutch soldiers who looked rather stunned at the endless stream of people walking into their country. Near the sentry box was a pile of rifles and military equipment that the Belgian soldiers had had to give up to enter Holland. As Hunt recorded it, "Most of the fugitives crossed the line and plodded on mechanically as if they were blind and dumb. Some sank exhausted to the ground and lay with faces buried in the grass. A few prayed. Scarcely any smiled. Panic still was upon them—panic which they would feel for days, and dream of for years."

Hunt went immediately to the nearby tiny station in hopes of getting on a train to the closest town, Bergen op Zoom. The station was packed with hundreds of Belgians who had been waiting hours for the same thing. After nightfall Hunt finally boarded a train. As he traveled through the Dutch countryside, he saw little villages ablaze with lights to welcome the refugees, who were accepted into most homes and fed as if they were family. Schools were turned into emergency hospitals and churches into lodging houses. Factories became refugee camps and "in every imaginable way the Dutch tried to cope with the awful situation which the war had thrust on their neighbors."

Hunt also noticed something that became a common sight in the weeks ahead—refugee directories. Along major thoroughfares and village main streets, the Belgian refugees quickly filled any unadorned fence, house wall, or side of a building with their names and addresses to show where they had been and how they might be contacted. In the chaotic panic of fleeing, family members and friends had become separated from each other. For weeks, the Dutch newspapers would be filled with ads for those lost as the impromptu countryside directories tried to bring people back together.

Most of all, though, the Dutch forgot their animosity toward the Belgians and simply became good neighbors. As Hunt described it, the Dutch "forgot the Revolution of 1830, which resulted in a final separation of the Belgian Provinces from those we call Holland. They forgot that it is a Dutchman's patriotic duty to dislike his Belgian neighbor. And it is to their eternal honor and glory that they opened their country . . . to the disinherited hordes that overwhelmed them."

From Bergen op Zoom, Hunt finally caught a Rotterdam express train after midnight. Disheveled, with "tousled hair, soft collar and coatless shoulders," Hunt considered himself "half-dressed and half-frozen," but alive and heading for a major city that was not under siege.

At 3 a.m. on Sunday, October 11, Hunt cabled from Rotterdam to New York the story of Antwerp's fall. Tired beyond imagining, he wondered what he would be doing next.

FOURTEEN

Battle of the Yser and the First Battle of Ypres

As most of the Belgian Army and the British soldiers escaped west from Antwerp, they headed to the coast and south. The plan was to link up with arriving English forces as well as troops already on the continent who were moving up from France. All these forces together would try to keep the Germans from the important English Channel ports of Dunkirk and Calais, which were main junctions for material and troops between the British Isles and France, as well as portals to the rest of the world.

The Germans who fought in the Antwerp siege weren't long in pursuing. In fact, in a matter of only hours after the first Germans marched into the city, German artillery batteries were set up along the docks near the picturesque tenth-century Castle Steen and began lobbing shells onto the retreating troops and refugees on the west side of the Scheldt River. German engineers were also hard at work repairing the bridge. According to Hunt, those Germans who weren't working on the bridge were sifting through what the fleeing Belgians and British had cast aside. There were "uniforms, rifles, bayonets, cartridge boxes, cartridge clips, camp knives and forks, swords, and scabbards which lay scattered in disorder for more than 150 feet along the edge of the quay."

It wasn't long before the Germans were over the Scheldt and on the march again. Days later, the cities of Ghent and Bruges fell swiftly as the Germans advanced and the Belgians fell back.

On October 16 the Germans attacked Dixmude. According to *Baedeker's Belgium and Holland* tour book, it was a "quiet little town on the Yser River . . . [where] dairy-farming is practiced with great success in this neighborhood, and a brisk trade in butter is carried on with England." Through fierce fighting and heavy losses, the Belgian and French troops under Colonel Alphonse Jacques held the town. It was a fight that would later be praised by many as heroic.

But only two days later, the full German offensive began and hit the Belgian forces head-on as they stood their ground along the Yser River. One military history stated, "Belgian units had become scrambled during the retreat from Antwerp and the army was scarcely more than a mob when the attack hit; even so, it lost 35 percent of its strength to enemy fire in the fight along the Yser and did not break."

The Germans had problems of their own. The surrounding countryside was flat and swampy—so much so that roads and rail lines crossed it on causeways that were sometimes ten feet high. It was not good country for an invading army. The Germans "wallowed through the muck," and "the marshes turned red, but the German reservists persisted," according to one historian.

King Albert, who had taken command of the Belgian Army long before, assessed the situation. After numerous days of fierce fighting, the line was holding. But his troops were battered and nearly beaten, and he wasn't sure how long they could hold out. There was one way of guaranteeing a German halt and the freedom of a thin slice of Belgium: flood the countryside with seawater. Under pressure from the Allies to take such action, the king made the decision. The sluice gates at the seaside town of Nieuwpoort were opened during high tides, October 26–29, creating an impassable barrier two miles wide and shoulder deep from the sea inland to Dixmude.

The Germans were effectively shut out of a coastal march south.

But a little farther inland and to the southeast, the little town of Ypres would lend its name to one of the most massive battles of the war.

Before the war, the town of 22,000 inhabitants had boasted "broad and clean streets" and was known for the manufacture of Valenciennes lace, which had been produced there since 1073. On October 20 a German drive opened the First Battle of Ypres against British forces. The fighting would rage for ten days, take a small break, then begin again and last until the third week of November, with hardly a movement of the line either way. Altogether, nearly a quarter of a million men lost their lives, and the battle resulted in the establishment of trench warfare that extended from the Alps to the North Sea.

From then on, for nearly four years, "every supreme effort that aimed to break the deadlock produced the opposite effect, intensifying the paralysis. Soldiers no more understood the war than did the politicians," noted one historian.

With the belligerents locked in an unbreakable death grip and a small sliver of Belgium safely beyond an unconquerable barrier of seawater, people in the rest of Belgium grappled with the fact that they were now in German-occupied territory.

FIFTEEN

London, October 1–17

During the last days of September and the opening days of October, a stymied Millard Shaler was telling practically anyone in London who would listen that he had bought 2,500 tons of wheat, rice, and beans for Brussels but couldn't get permission to ship it through the English blockade. He had tried to work through the Belgian Legation with little success. While many of his conversations fell on deaf ears, Shaler's words did have an impact on fellow American and friend Edgar Rickard.

Rickard was the son of mining engineer Reuben Rickard and brother of Thomas Rickard, another mining engineer who was at one time mayor of Berkeley, California. In 1914, Edgar was forty years old and living with his wife in London as the publisher/editor of a monthly technical publication called *The Mining Magazine*. He was above average in height, lean and clean shaven, with a long, thin nose and a strong jaw. Overall, his face radiated compassion and empathy.

Edgar Rickard was a friend of Hoover,
a mining engineer, and an editor of
a mining magazine who volunteered
to help Hoover with Belgian relief.
(Public domain; *Fighting Starvation in*
Belgium, Vernon Kellogg, George H.
Doran Co., 1918.)

Rickard was also Herbert Hoover's closest friend and confidant. He had known Hoover in California, and the two men had shared mining experiences in Australia and Burma. They were such good friends that they and their wives had vacationed together and saw each other frequently now that both couples were living in London. While he had achieved individual success in his mining engineer career, Rickard seemed content, when it to came to any business relations with Hoover, to remain behind the scenes and serve in the role of loyal confidant and volunteer associate. This was true when Hoover had asked him in August to serve as a volunteer on the Residents' Committee to help stranded American travelers. Rickard had, of course, said yes.

At this point, in the last days of September and first days of October, as the Residents' Committee was wrapping up its work, Rickard was approached by Shaler, who told him what was happening in Belgium and what he had been assigned to do by the Comité Central. Shaler also told Rickard that he had heard of Hoover's work with stranded tourists and wanted an introduction, in hopes Hoover might be helpful. Rickard was more than happy to oblige as he knew that Hoover had a way of making things happen.

Hoover met with Shaler and was, as a later history book states, "immediately impressed by the seriousness of the Belgian situation." He "promised to help if any means could be devised to send in relief." Hoover took the next few days to work the project over in his head while also consulting with many of his close associates who were still part of the Residents' Committee. They included Rickard, Colonel Millard Hunsiker, Clarence Graff, and John Beaver White, all of whom agreed that something had to be done to help the Belgians avert a major crisis.

While this was happening, on Wednesday evening, September 30, a tired Hugh Gibson arrived in London after a long and eventful diplomatic trip that would ultimately cross multiple battle lines: Brussels-to-Rotterdam-to-Antwerp-to-London-to-Antwerp-to-Brussels. Even though Gibson considered London a respite from the rigors of the trip, he would get little rest during his time there. The next morning, October 1, when Gibson arrived at the U.S. Embassy to deliver messages from Whitlock to Ambassador Page and to fully brief the ambassador on the critical food situation in Belgium, he found Shaler and his assistant, Couchman, waiting for him.

The engineer, who had last seen Gibson when they had shared lunch in Brussels nearly two weeks before, told Gibson of the difficulties he had been having and that he had had "some talk on the general problems that confront us with Herbert Hoover, an American mining engineer, who has given some very helpful ideas and may do more still." Shaler also told Gibson of his less-than-successful visit to the Belgian Legation.

Even though Gibson was a career diplomat, with the attendant perception that his obligation was to do everything slowly, deliberately, and through the proper channels, he was, in fact, "a most energetic and capable diplomat, and one who does not permit red tape to stand in the way of needed action," according to one contemporary. He and Shaler marched back to the Belgian Legation, where Shaler had previously been unable to gain an audience with the minister. In short order they were seated before the Belgian minister, Count de Lalaing, telling him what was needed. The minister reiterated what he had passed on through an assistant to Shaler the day before: He could do nothing without being first instructed by the Belgian government, which was then residing in Antwerp. He was a diplomat; his hands were tied.

Undaunted, Gibson quickly sent some lengthy telegrams to the appropriate Belgian government officials in Antwerp, asking that they direct de Lalaing to act and adding for emphasis, "Food supplies in Brussels are practically exhausted and immediate action is imperative." Telegrams flashed to the minister in London to proceed with all haste in supporting the Shaler mission.

Now that he had been authorized to act, the Belgian minister did so. Because the food was earmarked for the civilian residents of Brussels, de Lalaing knew he would have to secure permission from Britain's Foreign Office. The next day, he made multiple calls to various officials at the

Foreign Office, putting in his official request for permission. The process had finally begun.

While Gibson headed toward Belgium on Saturday, October 3, feeling good about getting things moving, Shaler was still left with the uncertainty of whether or not the British would give their approval to ship the food.

Meanwhile, Hoover had not been idle, engaging in a constant stream of meetings and discussions. He had also spoken with Page. The two men had already formed a good relationship and respected each other from the work they had done together helping stranded American tourists. Page, especially after his conversations with Gibson and Shaler, was enthusiastic about helping the Belgians.

Throughout this time, it became apparent to most of those involved that the food crisis was not just in Brussels, but throughout Belgium, and it was not a temporary issue but one that would last as long as the war. Most people felt the war would be over soon, but there were enough unknown factors to the war that those working on the Belgian problem began seeing it on a longer time frame than first imagined. Overall, the scope, magnitude, and duration of the project began to grow with every conversation and every day that went by.

No matter what their thoughts, the first hurdle to be overcome was the approval to ship what Shaler had already bought.

It was no small task. Arguments in the highest levels of Britain's government were still raging. Even though Shaler's request seemed to be of limited scope, it was nevertheless probably also seen as setting a precedent that appeared humanitarian to some British officials but to be aiding the enemy to others. An added element was legitimacy. A few days earlier, the shipping request had been a request from an individual, representing a nongovernmental Comité Central. Now the request was from an official representing the Belgian government—the same government that had stood and fought the Germans and in so doing had given the British and French enough time to marshal their own forces.

But how far would the debt of honor and treaty obligations take this shipment request?

On Monday, October 5, a break came. The British Board of Trade informed the Belgian minister that approval for the shipment was given. But, as historian George Nash explained, "At this point a misunderstanding occurred that was to shape the entire outcome of the relief mission and, indeed, the course of world history." The English made a "procedural suggestion" that the food be sent from the American Embassy in London to the U.S. Legation in Brussels. But the Belgian minister told Ambassador Page that this was a *condition*, not a suggestion, and asked if America would accept this responsibility.

Why was this of such major importance?

As Nash states, "It was an extraordinary, probably unprecedented, request in the history of warfare: that a neutral government, far from the scene of battle, oversee the provision of foodstuffs to the capital of a belligerent country under enemy occupation."

Page had no idea how to reply. He had been moved by personal accounts from Gibson and Shaler of the pending food crisis and Hoover's thoughtful points, but faced with the British demand for direct U.S. patronage, he felt he could not officially act without instructions from Washington. With Hoover's help, Page immediately wrote a cable to the State Department outlining the situation and asking that he be allowed to participate in such a necessary shipment to Brussels. He also added that if the State Department agreed to this, it should also seek additional guarantees from the German government in Berlin to reinforce the guarantee from Governor General von der Goltz in Brussels.

A long two days later, working slightly faster than its usual snail's pace, the State Department contacted James W. Gerard, the U.S. Ambassador in Berlin, and outlined the situation, asking that Gerard get the imperial German government to approve the plan and confirm von der Goltz's guarantees.

Meanwhile, Hoover was in nearly constant discussions with Shaler and others. He had met with Page again on Saturday, October 10. At this meeting, according to one historian, "the idea of the Commission for Relief in Belgium first took tangible form." Page later told others that this was the meeting at which Hoover asked if the ambassador would support him and his associates if they needed diplomatic assistance once they took up relief work for Belgium. The ambassador "approved heartily of the plan and promised to render all possible assistance." He also told Hoover that representatives from other Belgian cities, such as Liège and Charleroi, had come to see him asking for assistance to cut through British red tape and gain American support. Page told Hoover that from then on he would refer all Belgian delegations to him. Hoover would ultimately meet with representatives of multiple Belgian cities.

Two days later, on October 12, Hoover once again sat down with Page, this time with a more concrete plan that dealt with the entire country of Belgium, not just individual cities. There was still no reply from the State Department to Page's October 6 cablegram, so what Hoover suggested was all predicated on the ultimate U.S. acceptance of responsibility for the Shaler shipment. If that happened, other shipments would have to follow immediately if Belgium was to be saved. It was assumed these additional shipments would also fall under the protection and patronage of America.

To organize these relief efforts, Hoover recommended that a central American committee be formed and authorized with the patronage of America to administer the entire program. That program would include everything from handling and spending all funds raised worldwide (which was already starting) to the purchasing, shipping, and distribution of all food in Belgium. Hoover also recommended that the new committee absorb the American committee then in Brussels and that Dannie Heineman be asked to take charge of the work of distributing of food in Belgium as vice-chairman of the new committee. Page immediately approved the plan although his hands continued to be tied by the lack of news from the State Department.

Hoover Stimulates Public Opinion

People in the growing circle involved with Belgian relief were not very patient waiting for the American and German governments to make decisions. This went doubly for Herbert Hoover. He couldn't abide government bureaucracies and proper diplomatic channels, especially when people's lives were at stake. He wasn't going to sit and let others decide Belgium's fate: He would bring as much influence and pressure as possible to bear on the governments to take action quickly. By the time he was done, those governments would know where he stood, what morally needed to be done, and that action was demanded immediately.

Hoover's primary method was simple and straightforward and had been successfully tested in his mining career and in the more recent work with stranded Americans. He would engage the power of public opinion, not only in Britain and America, but all over the world. He would do this by using the press to tell the Belgians' food story in a compelling way. That story, he knew, would garner major public support for Belgium. He hoped that that support would force the governments to move faster in accepting their roles in the relief of Belgium.

He immediately went to those in the press whom he knew and trusted. For years he had cultivated strong relationships with journalists in and out of the mining field because he knew and valued the power of the press. Rickard was his strongest contact in the mining industry.

Hoover knew many journalists outside the mining industry and trusted a few, most notably Ben S. Allen, a fellow Stanford graduate and reporter for the Associated Press; Melville Stone, general manager of the AP; and Will Irwin, another Stanford grad and personal friend who had become famous for his coverage of the 1906 San Francisco earthquake and numerous investigative pieces. Hoover had such a good relationship with the thirty-one-year-old Allen that the reporter had volunteered for Hoover's tourist relief effort since August, editing a bulletin for the stranded travelers, writing press releases, and advising Hoover and the committee on the best ways of utilizing the press for maximum benefit.

While it was true that Belgium had been in the news all over the world since the war began, that news consisted of the broken treaty; heroic stands by the small, determined army led by courageous King Albert; the occupation of Brussels; the impending fall of Antwerp; and the heartbreaking stories of refugees fleeing the German onslaught.

Here was a new story, just as compelling as the others but with a surefire way for readers to become actively involved. Previous Belgian stories had generated great sympathy and empathy, but there was little that saddened, frustrated readers could do. This was something different: They could put pressure on their government to support relief efforts or give money or donate food. And the stories, as the journalists knew, would fall on fertile ground. A history of the CRB stated: "Already America had shown in no uncertain way her sympathy for Belgium's sufferings. Americans were ready and willing to hear the story of Belgium. Any items about Belgians made good copy for the press." As historian Richard Norton Smith put it, "Starving Belgium was on its way to becoming an international cause célèbre."

The press offensive began on October 6, with a dispatch sent to America by Philip S. Patchin, the London correspondent of the *New York Tribune*. Shaler had talked with him, and the resulting urgent cablegram detailed the desperation of the food situation in Brussels. It also told of the approval of the British government to ship food, provided it was consigned to the United States. Another dispatch went out October 10 describing the frustrating wait for the American and German governments to give their approvals. Both dispatches were relatively reserved, while still trying to convey a sense of urgency.

Things changed on October 12, when Hoover, immediately after his major meeting with Page, issued a much more confrontational press release. No doubt co-written by Allen and Irwin, Hoover's release was fashioned as an interview with Shaler regarding his mission. It called for quick action by the U.S. State Department—with or without German approval—to save Belgian lives. Hoover's name was never mentioned, but his style, tactics, and even phraseology were obvious throughout the piece.

Papers picked up the press release immediately. The *New York Tribune* declared "U.S. Red Tape Starves Brussels," and the October 13 *New York Times* proclaimed: "Immediate action by the State Department at Washington is urged to save many thousands of persons in Brussels from starvation."

The *Times*, which ran the press release nearly verbatim, quoted Shaler as saying the situation in Brussels had "grown positively desperate" and "positively dangerous. It is not only a matter of feeding a certain number of hungry people running into scores of thousands, but it is also a question of keeping the population from consequences which usually accompany starvation, for it is quite possible that the hungry mad people will commit some overt act which will cause the German authorities to take severe action."

In words that sounded very similar to what Hoover might have said, Shaler seemed to throw down the gauntlet when he stated: "Nearly a week ago ... the embassy here presented the matter to the State Department ... [which] awaits an answer from Germany.... Either the State Department should take action on its own initiative or should insist on Germany giving a speedy, definite answer. It is no exaggeration to say that thousands of lives actually depend on immediate action." These words were supposedly from Shaler but were in classic Hoover style, complete with a demand to act or face dire consequences.

While public opinion might have been swayed to the cause, it didn't seem to have much impact on the U.S. government at the time. Hoover had anticipated that possibility, so on the same day he sent out the Shaler story he also sent word to Whitlock at the U.S. Legation in Brussels that it would be helpful if the minister would appeal directly to President

Wilson. Whitlock took days to do so, but on Friday, October 16, his cable went out to the president stating boldly, "In two weeks the civil population of Belgium, already in misery, will face starvation." Whitlock hoped Wilson's "great heart will find some way by which America may help to provide food for these hungry ones in the dark days of the terrible winter that is coming on."

The next day the big break came. Ambassador Gerard in Berlin cabled Page that the German government had approved the plan to supply the population of Belgium with food. Two days later, October 19, the State Department informed Page that he could act as the neutral consignor, shipping Shaler's food to Whitlock in Brussels.

Major hurdles had been overcome, and as a result, "the diplomatic framework for the work of relief in Belgium was thus erected," according to one history of the CRB.

Hoover didn't wait for the formalities to be completed. He knew the key had been German approval, so once that came in he was off and running. On October 17, the same day the Germans agreed not to touch food shipments, a Hoover-generated story went out over the wires. This one announced "a comprehensive scheme for the organization of an American committee with the purpose of taking over the entire task of furnishing food and other supplies to the civil population of Belgium, so far as American relief measures are concerned, under the official supervision of the American Government." This committee would also "concentrate and systematize" all funds and food donated to Belgian relief, and Page had "consulted" with Hoover, who "would be one of the leading members of the committee, which would also include leading Americans in Brussels." While the release did mention the committee was a "proposal," there was little doubt that creation of the entire committee was a fait accompli.

Once again, Hoover was putting the cart before the horse, just as he had with his tourist committee a few months before. In this case, the news had not yet come that the U.S. government had approved Shaler's initial shipment to one city, and the government had certainly not yet agreed to forming a committee for relief of an entire country. But those were, no doubt, just inconvenient details as far as the driven man of action was concerned.

Hoover was going to save Belgium, and no one was going to stop him.

SIXTEEN

Brussels

At this stage, Belgium certainly needed saving. Nearly a month had passed since Shaler had left Brussels on his mission. When he left, 200,000 people were receiving rations in Brussels alone. That number had grown every day. Additionally, numerous cities, towns, and villages—including Liège, Charleroi, Mons, and Namur—had sent representatives to the Comité Central and to Whitlock and Villalobar asking for assistance to avert starvation in their areas.

Those delegations usually talked to Heineman because it was his Comité Central subcommittee that was charged with getting food for Brussels. He heard the same story over and over again: Supplies were running low, especially of the all-important cereals for making bread, and soon there would be nothing. Heineman's work had also led him to fully understand the city's current supplies and the daily growing needs of its residents. He quickly came to realize Shaler's 2,500 tons of food would barely dent what would ultimately be needed throughout Belgium.

Belgians wait patiently outside a Brussels soup kitchen for their daily ration of bread and soup. (Public domain; *War Bread*, E.E. Hunt, Henry Holt & Co., 1916.)

Convinced the Comité Central had to be expanded to take on nation-wide relief, Heineman went to Francqui and the executive committee to recommend, as one historian said, that the group "extend its services to all Belgium and assume the responsibility of finding, importing and distributing food for the whole country." He put forth a bold plan not just for one or two shipments but for "a regular monthly supply sufficiently important to provide the whole population with bread and other staple foods." He was talking about importing nearly 100,000 tons a month.

Francqui wasn't convinced. If Shaler, as far as Francqui knew, couldn't secure 2,500 tons of food in nearly a month, how were they expected to secure more than thirty times that? And how would such an undertaking be financed? Neither the German nor British government would agree to such a plan. "Francqui therefore, at first consideration, condemned Heineman's idea as unrealizable and energetically discountenanced it," noted one historian.

On October 11 Heineman went to Whitlock and sought the U.S. minister's support for the plan, asking him to approach the Germans with the idea. He also recommended that Hugh Gibson go to London to help a delegation of prominent Belgians lay the case before the British government. Villalobar was also consulted as the other neutral patron of the

Comité Central. Both the American and Spanish ministers wholeheart-edly agreed with Heineman's idea.

The support of Whitlock and Villalobar led Francqui to rethink his po-sition, and on Thursday, October 15, Solvay, Francqui, Heineman, Gibson, and the rest of the Comité Central met in Brussels and decided to extend their operations to the entire country. The need was there, both for action and for a central administrative body to coordinate the work on a national scale. Additionally, in a move to begin nationalizing internal relief, the Comité invited all the heads of provincial committees already in existence to become members of the Comité Central.

Even with such actions, the relief picture looked bleak. Because no one in Brussels knew exactly what was going on in London, and what Hoover was cooking up, nearly every part of the relief effort was uncertain. As far as the Comité Central knew, in the diplomatic realm there were three major hurdles that had yet to be overcome.

German approval. Von der Goltz had given his approval to Shaler's shipment, but that didn't mean he would approve a massive escalation of relief. Additionally, now that America had asked the German govern-ment in Berlin for its approval, denial would override anything von der Goltz did.

British approval. The English had approved Shaler's shipment, but the discussion of relief to Belgium was still raging in parliament, with strong opposition being voiced, which could adversely impact a governmental decision on more shipments.

American acceptance. So far there was no word on whether or not America would accept the unprecedented responsibility of food ship-ments into Belgium.

With such uncertainty, the Comité Central first tackled the one item it felt it could directly influence: German approval. It had a surprising ally—the fall of Antwerp. While the Germans had been still actively fighting over a substantial portion of Belgium, they were reluctant to make any deals regarding the country. But "now that Antwerp was in their hands, their military position in Belgium was much more secure, and they could afford to be more generous in their attitude toward food importation," according to one historian.

On Friday, October 16, the Comité formally asked Whitlock for his official help in approaching the German government in Belgium to agree to the expanded plan. Whitlock met that day with Baron Oscar von der

Lancken, who represented von der Goltz, and officially brought up the issue. Von der Lancken was agreeable, and later that day the Comité Central received a statement signed by von der Goltz saying that the German government in Belgium would honor all foodstuffs imported by the Comité, and that they would be exempt from requisition.

That was a huge step forward. But what of the British, the Americans, and the German government in Berlin?

That same day, it was decided by all that Gibson should head for London at once to try and influence the British to accept continual shipments. As Gibson described in his journal, the job given to him was to "lay the situation before the Belgian Minister, the Spanish and American Ambassadors and, under their chaperonage, before the British Government."

It was also suggested that a group of fifteen prominent Belgians accompany Gibson to lend weight to his appeal. Gibson probably turned away and rolled his eyes; he had no desire, as he put it, to "carry the weight of 15 speech makers" to London. Much to his relief, Whitlock and Villalobar, as the committee's patrons, said no. It was finally decided, however, that two members from the Comité Central should go. Francqui and Baron Léon Lambert would add their voices to the expanded relief appeals and approach the Belgian government in exile for financial assistance for the massive effort.

After securing all the proper German permits for travel to and from London, Gibson recorded in his journal that at 4:30 a.m. on Saturday, October 17, the three men set off "in three motors—one filled with servants and mountains of small baggage." There might have been a war on, but that was no excuse to let slip upper-class standards of dress and servant support!

It was, however, a mission that set off with low expectations. The group still thought the German government in Berlin had not given its approval and that America had not agreed to act in any capacity. Additionally, the earlier reluctance on the part of the British regarding approval for Shaler's shipment did not bode well for permission for future shipments.

The servants were probably more excited about getting to London than Gibson, Francqui, and Lambert.

SEVENTEEN

London, October 18–22

When the Brussels delegation arrived in London late on the evening of October 18, it found a landscape much altered from what Gibson had seen three weeks before.

Shaler was no longer a lone supplicant begging for help. He was now part of an established American committee that had already drawn up a rough plan of action, was issuing press releases and meeting with officials, and, for all intents and purposes, was sanctioned by the United States.

Even more impressive was the news that Ambassador Page had received the cable the day before that said the German government in Berlin had agreed to allow all food shipments into Belgium for the sole purpose of feeding Belgian civilians.

Still unknown was America's response, but Hoover's actions in moving forward after the German agreement led to a great sense of confidence that American approval was close at hand and relief might truly go forward.

Hoover and Francqui Meet Again

The major players—Hoover, Shaler, Gibson, Lambert, and Francqui—gathered the next day, Monday, October 19, in Page's office to discuss the situation and determine the best way to organize and coordinate all actions for maximum efficiency and effectiveness. Joining them was the Spanish ambassador to Great Britain, Señor Alfonso Merry del Val, representative of one of the two neutral patrons of the Comité Central and now patron for the much larger relief effort that was developing.

There was one other critical player in the room who was never verbally acknowledged. It was the 800-pound gorilla of animosity that existed between Francqui and Hoover.

In some ways the two men of industry were surprisingly alike. Both had been orphaned at a young age. They each had carved out impressive careers, often by sheer force of will. Both worked best as dictators (Hoover generally benign, Francqui ruthless) surrounded by loyal associates, and both brooked little dissension after decisions were made. They each had a strong temper, but Francqui's was more flamboyant, Hoover's more restrained.

Their differences were apparent: Francqui, at fifty-one, was eleven years older and was so short and portly that Whitlock noted he was a rather poor symbol of Belgium's poor. His domineering personality was such that he commanded notice when he walked into a room. He would stare down his opponents with his dark brown eyes and military bearing. Francqui, according to one American observer, "impressed men by his ability, led them or drove them to follow him." He appreciated and enjoyed recognition by others.

As for Hoover, even at five foot eleven inches tall, he could sometimes enter a room with few noticing. He would normally avert his eyes when in conversation, but his practical, straightforward logic and no-nonsense approach to discussion led few to best him. "Hoover, with his odd persuasiveness, drew men to him, and won their love and friendship and confidence," noted one contemporary. He also had a habit, when talking, of jiggling the coins in his pocket and, when space and situation allowed, liked to pace. He abhorred praise of any kind from anyone, so much so that on one occasion as he stood listening to Whitlock praise him to a small group, he literally began wrapping himself up in a heavy doorway curtain. Hoover was generally quiet and reserved. As E.E. Hunt put it, "He can be so silent that it hurts."

Reportedly, when Francqui was told before the London meeting that Hoover was the man leading the American relief for Belgium, he had shouted: "What! That man Hoover who was in China? He is a crude, vulgar sort of individual." Those were some of the worst insults a Belgian of prominence could toss at any man. While it's true that the recorder of that scene did not personally witness it, the words sound so Francqui-esque that it's more than likely they accurately reflected the Belgian's re-action, if not his exact words.

As for Hoover's personal reaction when he first saw Francqui again, there is no record of how he really felt. A hint of what took place be-tween the two men came from Whitlock. Even though the minister was in Brussels, he later picked up the story from the famous Belgian rumor mill. Belgians were then known for their love of sharing rumors and their love of the dramatic. In this case, the story of the two giants meeting was low-key and understated, which certainly fit Hoover's personal style.

As Whitlock wrote, "The gossips said . . . when fate brought them together again after so many years, they met at the American Embassy in London to organize the largest humanitarian enterprise the world had ever seen, and the only international institution then existing on the un-happy planet; they looked each other in the eye a moment—and shook hands. Such a scene and such a situation was one the gossips could not resist, so much of romanticism is there in all of us, and the story had not deteriorated in its engaging qualities by the time it reached occupied Brussels."

Whitlock continued in his usual literary way and ended the story by paraphrasing Rudyard Kipling: "I do not pretend to know the details; all I know is that M. Francqui was a strong man who came from Belgium and spoke one language, and that Mr. Hoover was a strong man who came from California and spoke another, and that

There is neither East nor West,
    Border, nor breed, nor birth,
When two strong men stand face to face
    Tho' they come from the ends of the earth."

Officially, the record shows that they got along and accepted each other somewhat graciously. Probably this was a classic case of necessity being the mother of setting aside differences. Simply stated—they needed each other to achieve their individual goals.

While Francqui was on the way to becoming head of an excellent nationwide distribution network inside Belgium, he did not, as a Belgian, have the freedom of movement nor the diplomatic influence that came only from being a neutral among belligerents. All of which meant he had no access or ability to secure massive quantities of food; he had to face the fact that a great distribution network was nothing without something to distribute.

On the other hand, Hoover had a neutral's freedom and diplomatic influence to possibly obtain the food, but he lacked a practical way of distributing it once it entered Belgium. In his earlier meeting with Page, when he had roughed out what the American committee would do, Hoover had mentioned distribution but only to suggest that his friend Dannie Heineman and Heineman's Brussels American committee handle distribution.

So, in this major meeting of the two headstrong men, each had to know that what one lacked, the other had, and the solution to the deficiency was being offered up on a silver plate. Each saw the person holding the silver plate as an adversary, but for now it was just too good a situation to pass up. There would be plenty of time to fight for dominance later. The two men simply silently shook hands, sat down, and got on with the difficult task of pounding out the details of relief and how best to approach the British for full-fledged approval.

Before the details, though, came the conceptual theory. Both Hoover and Francqui agreed that relief would have two prongs: Provide food at a slight profit for those who could pay; and provide outright charity for those who couldn't. The profit from one should pay for the other.

In essence, both men wanted to reestablish commerce in a country where it had died. They wanted to restimulate the food chain so that it could become self-perpetuating while also providing funds for the charity portion of relief. Taking the most important commodity—wheat—as an example, this meant that the wheat imported by the CRB for Belgian mills would be paid for by the millers, who would pay Francqui's group. The millers would be paid for the flour by the bakers, who would pay a portion of all sales to Francqui's group. The bakers would be paid for the bread by those who could afford to pay. Francqui's proposed Comité National would collect the funds from various points of Belgian sales, provide subsidies for certain portions of relief, and ultimately pay, through complicated transfers not yet agreed to, the CRB for the original imported wheat. Prices for everything would be set to provide a small profit, and the whole system would be primed by the operating capital that came from donations and governmental subsidies.

Working with this concept, and a high degree of focus—feed starving Belgium now—the first Hoover/Francqui meeting quickly outlined the two organizations to be established. Francqui and Lambert would transform the Brussels Comité Central into a national organization, the Comité National de Secours et d'Alimentation (National Committee of Assistance and Provisioning) once they returned to Belgium. Acceptance and coordination would have to be developed between the newly minted Comité National (CN) and the regional and local commune committees. Before leaving London, however, the two Belgians would approach both the Belgian and British governments to secure as much financial assistance for relief as possible.

Outlining the American Organization

Hoover's task would be to organize the American committee. Its duties were roughed out to be extensive:

- Centralize and expand worldwide giving of gifts, cash, and supplies
- Purchase food from markets around the world
- Arrange shipping and permits to Rotterdam
- Establish a Rotterdam operation for trans-shipping the relief from ocean-going vessels to canal barges and, where possible, trains for distribution into Belgium
- Supervise the distribution within Belgium
- Enforce all the conditions imposed on the relief effort by the various governments

For the Americans and Belgians in London, the next four days, October 19–22, were filled with numerous meetings, later termed the "October conferences," to pound out the details of relief, to decide on the approach to the British government for more approvals and assistance, and to refine the relationship between the American committee and the Comité Central (soon to be Comité National). It was at this time that Hoover brought in many of his associates who had worked with him on the stranded-tourists committee.

But this new American committee was not a temporary group to help a relatively small, limited number of tourists. What Hoover was proposing was relief for an entire nation for as long as the war lasted. What had started as Shaler's single shipment of 2,500 tons of food was rapidly growing into relief that the organizers would later estimate needed to be 80,000 tons a month.

As the members of the group confronted the magnitude and scope of what they were trying to achieve and the fact it had never been tried before, they realized the relief effort would take monumental commitments from each of them. A surprised Gibson wrote at the time: "There is something splendid about the way Hoover and his associates have abandoned their own affairs and all thought of themselves in order to turn their entire attention to feeding the Belgians. They have absolutely cut loose from their businesses, and are to give their whole time to the work of the Committee. This is done without heroics. I should hardly have known it was done, but for the fact that Hoover remarked in a matter of fact way:

"'Of course everybody will have to be prepared to let business go and give their whole time.'

"And it was so completely taken for granted that there is nothing but a murmur of assent."

For Hoover, personally, the decision had probably been made internally more than a week before. He was too astute a businessman to not have known by the first few meetings with Shaler and Ambassador Page that this would take a total and complete commitment of time and effort.

But numerous sources say that Page officially asked Hoover to head up the relief only in the October 19 meeting. Gibson wrote that Hoover's answer was: "Yes, I'll take over the work. I have about finished what I have in hand. Now we can take up this." Hoover's personal account, recorded in the section of his memoirs titled *Years of Adventure*, said that he waited a day to give Page his answer and then said he would do it only if he had "absolute command" because such a massive project could not be run by a "knitting bee."

Another account says that when Ambassador Page asked him, Hoover said he needed a few days to think about it and how it would impact his life and businesses. Then, "on the morning of the twenty-first he remarked to Will Irwin over breakfast, 'Let the fortune go to Hell.'"

This last story certainly has the stamp of journalist Irwin conveying good drama about a close friend, and the other stories also have a flair for the dramatic. While the words sound like Hoover, his reported doubt and uncertainty until October 19 or 20 don't. It's probably true that Page did officially ask Hoover in front of Francqui and Lambert on October 19. But that could easily have been set up by Hoover to make sure the Belgians knew who was boss. Much more telling are Hoover's actions prior to the meeting, not what was said later.

The amount of time and energy Hoover had already invested in meetings, organizational thinking, and the strategic outreach to the press bespoke a man who had made up his mind long before October 19. Additionally, the stories' portrayals of doubt and indecision regarding this monumental task simply hang like a poorly tailored suit on such a consistently decisive man.

There was no uncertainty in Hoover a day later, October 20. He cabled Whitlock and outlined the idea of a "purely American relief committee" made up of Whitlock, Page, and "leading Americans" in Brussels and London. Such a committee "properly recognized by the various governments concerned would put matters on permanent systematic neutral basis." Hoover ended by asking that Whitlock convey his views on the matter to Page.

That same day, Hoover crafted a major memorandum that turned out to be the founding "constitution" of the American committee, soon to be the Commission for Relief in Belgium (CRB). Laid out logically in concise language, the document outlined the problems, the present situation, and, item by item, what it would take to solve the problems identified. It was an engineer's blueprint for something the world had never seen: a privately run enterprise, sanctioned by belligerents and neutral governments alike, that would step into a war zone and feed an occupied nation. The document was only a few pages long and contained only eight numbered items, but it described what would become the largest food and relief effort the world had ever known. It was classic, straight-shooting Hoover at his best.

The document started by stating that Belgium, in normal times, was dependent on imports for 75–80 percent of its breadstuffs and for large portions of other commodities. A "considerable proportion of the population have resources with which to pay for their food, if some economic rehabilitation can be effected." But the war had also created "unparalleled destitution" that needed to be addressed with outright charity. Unstated was the fact that the longer the war dragged on, the number of those who could pay would dwindle as the number of destitute people grew.

Acknowledging that numerous small relief committees had already sprung up throughout Belgium to solve local problems, the document stated that for "proper distribution of foodstuffs and relief there must be a consolidation of organization in Belgium on national lines with sub-committees in the provinces and communes, under strong centralized control." In a nod to Francqui and his group, the memorandum went on to state, "The Brussels Committee embraces the strongest financial and administrative element in the country, and had already . . . considered the question of expansion to the leadership in the creation of this national organization."

But Hoover felt it was critical that Americans be officially involved in this Belgian group: "To assist in the extension of an organization, and to provide an element of cohesion, additional American membership to that of Messrs. Heineman, Hulse, and Gibson must be recruited at once."

As for the American participation, Hoover's document explained that an American committee would be established "in order to provide for the purchase and shipment of foodstuffs abroad, for the mobilization of charity through the world, and for the guardianship of the supplies in Belgium and the supply of American members to Belgian committees."

Hoover called for the two committees to "co-operate intimately" and "interlock by membership and support." Additionally, Hoover, no doubt remembering the past conflicts with multiple groups helping the stranded tourists, stated clearly in the memorandum that no one else would be allowed to participate in the relief effort: "Furthermore, it is impossible to handle the situation except with the strongest centralization and effective monopoly, and therefore the two organizations will refuse to recognize any element except themselves alone."

If Hoover had had his way completely—as reflected in the first rough ideas of relief discussed with Page—the CRB would have been the only team on the playing field. But Francqui's control of distribution was too important to ignore. That said, Hoover would make sure that the CRB and CN were the only ones involved in Belgian relief.

To pay for such a huge program, Hoover had written that it was "absolutely necessary, in order to solve the financial situation outside of charity, to obtain from the belligerent governments permits for exchange transactions in and out of Belgium." Because Hoover knew none of the governments would agree to currency being transferred across borders, an accounting arrangement had to be made so that the outside world and the Belgian world could function together. Additionally, the relief would require a lot of working capital to buy and ship the food, so "an endeavor should be made to effect a loan in England, guaranteed by the Belgian banks, for this purpose."

The fledging group had recently received £100,000 from the existing Belgian Relief Fund in France, and "an assurance" of a contribution of £100,000 from the British government. But this kind of charitable giving was, as Hoover wrote, "wholly inadequate, and as the flow of public charity, no matter how great, will be irregular and of uncertain quantity, it is absolutely necessary to secure positive subventions [grants of money] from the Allied Governments in some form or other." Charity was fine, but what was really needed was government subsidies on a huge scale.

Money wasn't the only thing the relief effort needed from the governments. It needed permits to ship food on a continual, much larger basis than Shaler's one-time permits, which were then in hand. Those permits also were limited in that they allowed shipping only through the American ambassador in London to the American minister in Brussels. One person to one person. Hoover's memorandum explained, "Such an arrangement is impracticable for the provision of the entire country, and it is therefore necessary to seek an arrangement with the Allied Governments whereby this guarantee can be carried out by the American Committee and its delegates in various centers in substitution of the Minister." If this was allowed by the belligerents, the CRB could delegate Americans to be in occupied Belgium and act as Whitlock's representatives to receive the food.

There, in one sentence, was born the CRB delegate, an ultimately fascinating and multi-faced category of volunteer who would become, to most Belgians, the true heart and soul of the CRB. The first few delegates would appear in November.

Lastly, the document dealt with the highly controversial issue of basic relief to Belgium and the German refusal to feed those they had conquered. Here the writing showed Hoover's belief that the way around belligerent governments' objections to the entire relief effort was the power of public opinion, driven by the press.

"It appears that there was a great deal of antagonism on the Part of the Allies to the introduction of foodstuffs into Belgium, as in their view it was the duty of the occupying army to feed the civilian Population. On the other hand, it was certain that the occupying army would do nothing of the kind and that in order to maintain open a gateway into Belgium and at the same time protect the native food supply from further absorption by the occupying army, it would be necessary to create the widest possible feeling, both in the belligerent and in neutral countries, as to the rights of the Belgian population in this unparalleled case of an entire country, under practical siege, which was dependent normally upon importation for its food supply, that, therefore, one of the first duties of the American organization would be to create such public opinion as widely as possible, through the Press."

With such a comprehensive document in place, the CRB was formally founded at a meeting on October 22 in Hoover's offices at No. 1 London Wall Buildings. The sole attendees were eight Americans: Hoover, Gibson, Shaler, Rickard, John F. Lucey, Millard Hunsiker, John Beaver White, and Clarence Graff. Ben Allen, the journalist and Hoover's friend, was supposedly there as well, according to a later statement by his wife, but no record exists to corroborate her assertion. Most of the eight men were engineers, and most had worked with Hoover on his tourist relief work. They were a committed bunch, dedicated to helping Belgium and, in most cases, supporting whatever Hoover wanted to do.

Hoover officially opened the meeting by telling the men that Page had asked him to "set up an organization to carry into execution the engagements undertaken by the American Ambassadors in London and Brussels with regard to the importation of foodstuffs and relief generally for Belgium."

At that time, the organization envisioned was to be "purely American," as Hoover had cabled Whitlock. This was Hoover's first instinct, and it came from a few factors. Even though he had lived much of the last twenty years overseas, Hoover still spoke only English, so language could be a barrier in meetings. He worked best when he was the unquestioned leader, which usually meant being surrounded by loyal friends and associates. He was also definitely a product of American times. As the United States had grown and expanded both externally and industrially/technologically, many Americans, especially businesspeople, became supremely confident in their own abilities. There was a hands-on, can-do attitude that Americans could achieve practically anything better than others. Hoover had demonstrated that feeling and that ability many times during his mining career. At that point, no doubt, he was sure a small group of highly motivated and committed American businessmen, led by him, could do much more than any European counterpart.

So the group chose a name that reflected all that in its straightforward simplicity: the American Commission for Relief in Belgium. The only governmental patrons, or honorary chairmen, would be the American ambassadors in England, Belgium, and Holland.

Necessity would change the Americans-only concept quickly. The proposed relief effort was just too big, the international agreements too complex, for America to go it alone. The additional influence and power Spain could bring to the table as a neutral country would be necessary in securing agreements from the belligerents, both in and out of Belgium. And Holland's participation was needed to allow massive quantities of food to pass through Rotterdam into occupied Belgium.

Whitlock, when informed of the U.S. name and members, replied in a telegram to Page that the Spanish ambassador in Brussels should not be omitted from the commission. Villalobar deserved to be a member, Whitlock wrote, because he had "worked earnestly and efficiently" for relief. But then, true to Whitlock's egocentric self, he brought the issue back to himself, saying it would also be "embarrassing to me if he were to be made to suffer in his feelings by anything that might be interpreted as a slight."

Later that same day, long before Whitlock's cable was received, the decision was made to add the Spanish ambassadors in London and Brussels as honorary chairmen. Either Hoover had changed his mind or others had helped him adjust his thinking. The name, however, would not be changed for four days, and then it would simply be the Commission for Relief in Belgium (CRB) to better reflect its expanded membership.

The next step at the October 22 meeting was to assign positions and responsibilities. Hoover, of course, was named chairman. Heineman, living in Brussels, was named vice-chairman. Graff became treasurer. Shaler and Hulse became honorary secretaries. White was placed in charge of the purchase and transportation of foodstuffs in England. Rickard took charge of publicity. Lucey was given the job of creating a Rotterdam office through which all food would be received and reloaded into canal barges for shipment into Belgium.

That evening the last of the October conferences took place at the U.S. Embassy with Francqui and Lambert in attendance. This meeting was to formalize the cooperation between the new American Commission for

Relief in Belgium (the name had not yet been changed) and the Comité Central, which soon would be transformed into the Comité National, if Francqui had his way when he returned to Brussels.

The CRB was now officially a living, breathing entity with a purpose—at least in the minds of its creators.

Hoover didn't seem to stop to take a breath as he immediately turned from being a man of memos and meetings to a man of action. That same long Thursday, October 22, he and Rickard put out a press release that was picked up in America, England, and many other countries. Without actually giving the group an official title, the release stated that "the organization of the American commission was completed." Using nearly the exact words from the minutes of the all-American meeting, the press release described who was involved and what they would be doing, but it then included this line: "The Spanish Ambassadors at Brussels and London joined the commission as honorary chairmen."

London would be the location of the main office of the CRB, a Rotterdam office would handle shipping into Belgium, and a Brussels location would be the main supervisory office within Belgium. Satellite Belgian offices would be set up where America already had consulates: Antwerp, Ostend, Liège, and Ghent. There was no mention of the need or desire for an American office (that would change quickly).

The commission's purpose was simply to "assist in provisioning all Belgium. It will co-operate fully with the Belgian committee." The need was great, as shown by the Belgian city of Charleroi, where the food "is exhausted and . . . the people are subsisting entirely on potato soup." In Brussels, the world was told, the food would run out in just four days.

In no uncertain terms, but without using the exact words, the release conveyed the thought that America was the key to saving Belgium. Because of Holland's own food shortage and England's wartime needs, "supplies from America are even more imperatively needed than was originally expected." Which meant "a stream of supplies must be started from America if the Belgians are to be saved from famine."

A start had been made, however, as the press release declared $250,000 of food had been bought, and the commission had received "considerable sums in addition to the various Belgian funds." The plan was to begin distribution on Monday, October 26, in Belgium, only four days away.

The food had yet to leave Britain—and would not make that deadline.

EIGHTEEN

Rotterdam

Lucey Begins Building a Trans-shipping Business

On Sunday, October 25, with the first two shipments of food already loading in the Thames, Hoover sent Shaler and Lucey to Rotterdam to begin the arduous task of setting up the main CRB shipping office between the outside world and German-occupied Belgium. Shaler would stay in Rotterdam for a few days and then go back into Belgium, but Lucey remained to spearhead the initial operations.

Hoover couldn't have picked a better, more resourceful, and hardworking man than Lucey. Born in County Kerry, Ireland, he and his family had moved to America when he was very young and settled in New York City. From a young age Lucey was independent. He first took a job as a newsboy and left home in 1888 when he was only fourteen, heading west and becoming a news agent for the Santa Fe Railroad between Albuquerque and Los Angeles. At eighteen he joined the army and served for nearly four years before joining the National Guard in Sacramento and becoming a captain.

During the Spanish American War (1898), he went to the Philippines as part of a heavy artillery unit. It was there that his life changed. When his health deteriorated, he resigned from the service and went back to California. While recuperating, he started studying to be a lawyer, but something didn't feel right. Lawyering had too much "being" and not enough "doing."

Captain John F. Lucey. Hoover sent him to Rotterdam to establish a trans-shipping operation for Belgian relief. (Public domain; *Fighting Starvation in Belgium*, Vernon Kellogg, George H. Doran Co., 1918.)

Soon, Lucey was off again; this time he headed north with thousands of others to try to make his fortune in the Alaska gold rush. As with most, he came back much poorer but a bit wiser. It was then that he abandoned vain pursuits in gold fields and turned instead to oil. First working in the California oil fields as a roustabout, he then moved into management before starting his own firm, Lucey Manufacturing Corporation. With hard work and a lot of traveling, both in America and overseas, he was able to turn his company into the second-largest oil-well supply company in the world in twelve short years.

In August 1914, when the Germans invaded Belgium, Lucey was just another American businessman in Europe trying to expand his business. He was still in London in October when Hoover asked him to be part of the CRB.

A good-looking, clean-shaven man with a prominent nose and dark hair swept back and tight to the head, Lucey stood over six feet tall and had the erect posture of a military man. He liked being addressed as Captain Lucey. An outdoorsman who loved golf, he was in perfect health at forty years old and was "endowed with an enthusiastic and optimistic nature" that had never left him through his various experiences. He had slogged through Alaskan snow, wrestled with drilling pipes and roughnecks, and survived boardroom brawls in the cutthroat business world. Successful and financially independent, Lucey probably felt there was nothing he couldn't do, and if he did fail, he knew it would be simply a matter of trying again until he found a way to succeed. And he shared an important trait with Hoover: impatience.

Altogether, Lucey was the perfect volunteer for Hoover and the CRB because, as one associate noted, he "possessed the requisite experience, energy and force of character."

When Lucey and Shaler arrived in Rotterdam, they hit the ground running, setting up a temporary office in their living quarters. With the help of U.S. Minister Henry van Dyke, who was just returning from a two-day diplomatic trip into Belgium, and his U.S. Legation Secretary Marshall Langhorne, permission was secured from the Dutch government to import all the supplies needed for Belgian relief. The Dutch government also provided free use of the state telegraph lines to the CRB and even agreed to carry free of charge a definite amount of food per day from Rotterdam south to Liège once the system was set up. The two Americans conferred with the German Consulate in Rotterdam and found waiting there 150 safe-conduct passes for the first shipments, already signed and stamped by the German authorities in Brussels.

Lucey and Shaler also secured the services of the local office of the British Furness shipping company to "handle, for the time being, the supplies received and to provide transportation through to Brussels." Stevedores, cranes, and modern floating elevators would transfer the cargoes from the oceangoing vessels to either trains or canal barges that would take the supplies throughout Belgium. Lucey and Shaler started searching for clerical staff for what they envisioned would be a blizzard of paperwork necessary to ensure Hoover's demand for scrupulous accounting of all transactions and activities.

After the two men learned that transporting the food by train would be out of the question—rail service in Belgium for civilians had not been restarted and any running of trains was for the exclusive use of the military—they began to map out the best routes of canal entry into Belgium. They didn't need to worry about finding barges, or lighters, for the work. Since the start of the war and the disruption of commerce, hundreds of Dutch lightermen and their craft were sitting idle. Added to that were the hundreds of Belgian lighters that had been taken into Holland to evade seizure by the Germans.

But where to send what to whom once the food began arriving in Rotterdam?

Lucey knew he needed more information about the situation in Belgium: Who needed what, how soon, and who would handle distribution. But that information was nearly impossible to get. Cut off from the outside world, Belgium was a great unknown, with only diplomats and a handful of men allowed out by the Germans. There were, of course, countless Belgian refugees, but they had only seen their small slice of the situation. Lucey spent a great deal of time conferring with as many people as he could. His problem was that information was "abundant but conflicting." So much so, in fact, that he had "neither definite information regarding the internal relief organization nor specific recommendations as to where to direct the first shipments of food." That wasn't from lack of people asking, begging, and pleading. "Appeals, rumors, orders, suggestions came in showers from local [Belgian] committees, refugees, American consuls in Belgian cities, from the American Legation in Brussels and the Comité Central," according to a CRB history.

What was needed was better information. Shaler departed Rotterdam on October 27 to obtain it. Heading back to Brussels via Ostend, Ghent, and Antwerp, he was accompanied by the Dutch consul at Ghent and Henry Albert Johnson, the U.S. consul at Ostend. They would all try to get word back to Lucey about the situation in each area and inform the Belgians that help was coming.

On the same day, Monsieur Van den Branden, a Belgian associated with the Solvay Company, was allowed out of Belgium to be the Comité Central's representative in Rotterdam and work with Lucey and the CRB. But Lucey found out that "he brought no definite instructions as to shipping . . . nor as to destinations to which the first shipments should be directed."

Lucey was not happy. He "began almost at once to be discouraged and irritated by the lack of such definite instructions from Brussels," one historian related. He knew that before he could ship anything he would have to have "detailed information about the way the food should be divided between the various regions, about the size of [canal barges] that could be used on each canal, and about the condition of the various canals."

The overall situation wasn't helped by the fact that the Dutch government had commandeered all the country's flour and wheat for its own citizens and was reluctant to sell any of it to the CRB for Belgium. For the near future—before the CRB's worldwide efforts could take effect and the newly formed Comité National could organize the country's communes into a cohesive whole—there would be limited supplies available to an ever-growing number of people.

Solomon would have had a difficult time deciding what to do.

Lucey turned to Hoover. On Sunday, October 29, Lucey sent an extensive cable to Hoover giving him an overview of the situation. He wasted no time in getting to the point: "As near as we can ascertain there are approximately four millions of people to be fed. Provisions must be provided whether the people have money or not." Not mincing words, Lucey stated clearly, "We have all underestimated the desperate condition of the Belgian people." Dire consequences were close at hand: "The people are so hungry and so desperate that the sight of every German incites them, and in their desperate frame of mind, seeing their children and families without food or clothes, they are liable to attack the German soldiers at any moment, which would mean another terrible and useless sacrifice of the Belgian people."

Stating the obvious to one who already knew, Lucey told Hoover: "I would urge you to resort to any measures to relieve these districts. Could you not obtain a fast cruiser from the American Government to deliver the first cargo of flour?"

Knowing that was a long shot, and that the Belgians had been anticipating a faster delivery of food, Lucey suggested a stopgap measure. If Hoover could cable him that flour was en route, Lucey would personally go—"or any member of our Commission could do so"—into the districts of Liège, Charleroi, Namur, and Dinant and, accompanied by Belgian officials, "satisfy the people and restrain them from resorting to any violence until we can deliver the flour."

Lucey said in his second-to-last sentence, "We again repeat: the necessity of the Belgian people is very great; they are in a desperate frame of mind, and if we are to accomplish anything we must act, and act at once."

His last sentence showed how he knew what was also important to Hoover: "If there is any statement which you wish to publish in the Dutch press, please forward same and we will have it attended to."

NINETEEN

London, October 23-31

During these early days of CRB organization, relief was a heartbeat away from being stopped before it properly began. Months and years later, this October time would become great fodder for legends about Hoover's abilities and how he accomplished what many thought was impossible.

A story that was supposedly well known in later CRB circles was about Hoover in one of the early October meetings with Ambassador Page. Hoover was watching the clock and suddenly got up and left without saying a word. When he returned a significant time later, Page said rather pointedly that he had missed some good information. Hoover said he had noticed the New York market was about to close, so he had gone to call in an order for a shipload of flour. The surprised group had not the slightest idea of how it would be paid for and asked Hoover for his thoughts on it. Hoover replied, "Well, there was the flour and here was the need, let's put them together and talk about it later."

The same storyteller also related that when the first shipment was ready to leave England for Rotterdam, Hoover went to the British Board of Trade to get the clearance papers approved.

The man at the window asked, "What's in the ship?"

"Flour," Hoover replied.

"Where's it going?"

"To Belgium."

"But Belgium's under German occupation," the man said.

"That's why it's going there."

"Well, that's just why it's not," the clerk stated.

The next day Hoover was back at the same window with the same papers, and the same clerk was there.

"What did we tell you yesterday about this flour shipment?"

"There's no use making a fuss about it," Hoover explained. "The ship's now unloading at Rotterdam."

Another story about Hoover is slightly more credible but was never verified by other sources. Journalist Lewis R. Freeman related it in a magazine article written nearly a year after it supposedly happened. The tale takes place at the critical moment when the ships in the Thames containing the first food shipment were ready to sail, but clearance had not yet been granted by the British. Freeman explained that Hoover went in person to the one cabinet minister able to arrange for the only things he could not provide himself—clearance papers.

Freeman then reported that Hoover stated, "If I do not get four cargoes of food to Belgium by the end of the week, thousands are going to die from starvation, and many more may be shot in food riots."

"Out of the question," the minister told Hoover. "There is no time, in the first place, and if there was there are no good wagons to be spared by the railways, no dock hands, and no steamers; moreover, the Channel is closed for a week to merchant vessels while troops are being transported to the Continent."

Hoover replied simply: "I have managed to get all of these things, and am now through with them all except the steamers. This wire tells me that these are now loaded and ready to sail, and I have come to have you arrange for their clearance."

As Freeman then reported, the minister "gasped, and said: "There have been—there are even now—men in the Tower for less than you have done. If it was for anything but Belgian Relief—if it was anybody but you, young man—I should hate to think of what might happen. As it is—er—I suppose there is nothing to do but congratulate you on a jolly clever coup. I'll see about the clearance at once.'"

Hoover's reputation for being straightforward was expressed by British Lord Curzon, who stated that "Mr. Hoover is the bluntest man in Europe." But that directness, combined with his tremendous focus, got things done—even if it was many times at the expense of irritating people. "Once Hoover has set his heart on a thing, that thing will come to pass," wrote one associate later. "He will squarely meet every obstacle in his path, and overcome it, and forge ahead. . . . Whenever, in the old days, the case of the Belgians brought only discouragement to others, a certain face would harden and a certain face would say, 'Those people are going to be fed.'"

The Work Starts Having an Impact

That resolve and purpose are what helped make the CRB an immediate success on some fronts in the waning days of October 1914. The official CRB record shows that once the CRB was formed, Shaler's 2,500 tons were increased to nearly 10,000 tons of food by more buying of food in London. Loading of the first ship, the small Dutch freighter *Coblenz,* began on Tuesday, October 27, in the Thames and, thanks to Hoover's press efforts, made many of the British papers: "All day . . . the *Coblenz* . . . strained at her moorings as food stuff, which is to save the lives of Belgian heroes and heroines who have remained in their devastated country, was poured into her holds." The steamer carried 600 tons of wheat, 300 tons of rice, 75 tons of peas, and 25 tons of beans, for a total of 1,000 tons of provisions. It sailed the next evening and arrived in Rotterdam at 3 a.m. on November 1. Three other ships from England followed in quick succession, the four of them helping to carry the initial 10,000 tons to Rotterdam, where Lucey's stevedores enthusiastically unloaded the ships.

Relief was starting to trickle toward Belgium.

Additionally, Hoover's press campaign to mobilize worldwide public support was gearing up, with weekly press releases and numerous items of information given to the press as they were received. This included letters the CRB received from multiple sources that came from Belgian officials begging for help, statements from Whitlock and Page, and telegrams back and forth between Hoover and Lucey in Rotterdam describing what was being done and what still needed doing. Hoover knew he had to keep Belgium and the CRB in front of the press constantly.

Hoover even secured an appeal to the American people from King Albert, who had become in the eyes of the world a dashingly courageous king and soldier of quiet strength and fortitude. The king's statement appeared in American newspapers on Sunday, November 1, and read in part: "It is a great comfort to me in this hour of sorrow and misfortune to feel that a great-hearted and disinterested people is directing its efforts to relieving the distress of the unoffending civilian population of my country. Despite all that can be done, the suffering of the present winter will be terrible, but the burden we must bear will be lightened if my people can be spared the pangs of hunger, with its frightful consequence of disease and violence. I confidently hope that the appeal of the American Commission will meet with a generous response."

Many newspapers that ran the king's appeal also ran what Hoover and the PR team had written: "Accompanying this message is an appeal from the American Commission for Relief in Belgium stating that it is the only channel through which food can be introduced and distributed in that country." The critical word in that statement was "only." Hoover was already sending a message to those in America who were currently involved in Belgian relief, or who were thinking of getting into it, that his group was the only authorized entity that claimed neutrality. (Some Belgian relief groups were affiliated with the Belgian government.)

Overall, Hoover and his publicity team were relentless in their efforts to inform the press of what was being done, including everything from the purchasing of food to the loading of ships and the ongoing negotiations of agreements with the various governments. "We have worked up a sentiment in the United States, Canada, Australia and other countries," Hoover wrote, "in favor of the feeding of the Belgian people to such an extent that it became a worldwide movement of interest, second only to the war itself. We carried on the most active campaign of publicity by every device we could invent in England as well as in these countries. We demonstrated our capacity as a business concern and our ability to distribute the foodstuffs to the civil population without interference."

The publicity campaign was complemented by a drive to establish committees around the world that would gather donations. Hoover knew that individual giving could never be sustained in the large amounts needed to fund the CRB, but he also knew that engaging people in their own regions and hometowns would serve two critical functions. First, people would be more prone to giving something—food or cash—if they were approached by someone from their area. And second, if engaged in that way, they would become a stronger part of the critical court of public opinion that Hoover would need to keep numerous governments supportive of Belgian relief in general and the CRB's efforts in particular.

So the CRB immediately set out to build a network of local Belgian relief committees around the United States and the world. Hoover and his team contacted every prominent person they knew, from businessmen to politicians, and asked if each would start a local Belgian relief fund. With Lou Hoover's input, prominent women were also targeted for such requests, focusing on the idea of women's groups to help the Belgian women and children. The governors of large agricultural states like Kansas were asked to throw their support behind funding entire shiploads of food. Because of Lou and Herbert's connections in California, the outreach was even greater to that state's individuals and organizations, including businesses, universities, and social and religious groups.

The combination of this kind of outreach and the relentless publicity campaign showed surprisingly quick results. In an extensive report on the first full week of CRB operations, Hoover detailed what had been achieved. The CRB had bought 4,000 tons of food in New York and an additional 4,000 tons in a joint purchase with the New York–based Belgian Relief Committee, which had been established a few weeks before the CRB came into existence. The CRB also had promises of 4,000 tons of foodstuffs by the newly created Rockefeller Foundation in New York City and whole ships of food sponsored by Nova Scotia, San Francisco, Chicago, and the Minnesota-based magazine *Northwestern Miller*. The San Francisco ship was a direct result of Hoover sending Lou back home to raise awareness and organize local committees to gather donations. She was as good a motivator and organizer as her husband, and the ship that San Francisco sponsored was one of the first pledged from America—although it would not reach Rotterdam until December.

All the promised food would take weeks, if not months, to get to Rotterdam, but it showed that the world was becoming engaged in Belgian relief. Altogether, supplies committed for November equaled

22,800 tons valued at £199,000, and December had 25,000 tons valued at £60,000 committed. (The significant difference in price between the two months was primarily the difference between initial emergency buying in England and less-expensive long-range buying in America.)

While those figures might have seemed large to some, they weren't much when the goal was feeding an entire nation. Once Francqui had returned to Brussels, the Comité National had informed Hoover that starting December 1, the minimum foodstuffs required would be 60,000 tons of grains, 15,000 tons of maize, and 3,000 tons of rice and dried peas, or a total of nearly 80,000 tons a month. A significant amount, but as Hoover was quick to say, Belgium normally imported more than 250,000 tons a month. The estimated 80,000 tons per month would translate to approximately ten ounces of food per person per day, or, according to Hoover, "considerably less than one-half of a soldier's ration."

Hoover needed more food—a lot more food.

But first he had to tackle the problem of financing. The balance sheet from the first week of operations showed that the November and December shipments—which were then woefully less than the 80,000 tons per month necessary—would cost a total of £259,000; the CRB had collected only £220,000. While Hoover hoped that charitable giving would increase and continue, he knew he could never count on it as a steady source of operating capital. Subsidies were what he needed—large monthly subsidies. In his first week's report, Hoover stated, "It has now become necessary and positively critical for us to have some sort of definite financial backing."

Britain Gets Behind Belgian Relief

As quickly as Hoover flooded the world press with Belgian and CRB stories, the British newspapers picked them up and ran with them. Every day, in multiple papers around the United Kingdom, the story of potential famine and the CRB's efforts to head off starvation were big news. Each individual ship was followed, the loads were detailed, the routes and methods of transfer into Belgium were explained, and cables supplied by the CRB were regularly published.

All these stories were riding on the momentum that had already been built up by months of tales about Belgian refugees fleeing the battlefields, wounded Belgian soldiers brought to England for treatment, and the tens of thousands of Belgians who sought sanctuary in Britain.

On October 24, English newspapers announced that the government had taken over the buildings of Earls Court in London to house Belgian refugees until homes could be found for them. More than 1,500 refugees were already there, with space for an additional 4,000. A card index of every refugee was being compiled at Somerset House in London. A depot on Kean Street in Aldwych, London, was collecting clothes for the refugees, and it was recommended by one newspaper that "generous hearted readers who cannot afford to give much should note that handkerchiefs, not necessarily new, are badly needed. Hair brushes and razors would also be very welcome." The paper also stated, "There were crowds of refugees patiently waiting for clothes, and it was pitiable to see the gratitude with which warm coats and underclothes were received."

That same charitable giving was going on all over the United Kingdom and was, by many accounts, amazing. Money was given, but more importantly, personal items and valuable heirlooms were donated. Even though it was October, one newspaper was collecting donations on behalf of the "Belgian Christmas Fund." Mrs. Bayliss of Yorkford gave "a pair of antique fretted silver coasters," but she stated they were "not to be sold for less than £8 8s." A "Grateful and Sympathetic English Woman, K," donated "old fashioned gold and silver brooches and locket," while a "Hater of War and a Lover of Peace" gave "two gold rings (one diamond and turquoise)."

The British people were practically unanimous in their initial appreciation and support of everything Belgian.

Such public sympathy and support did not go unnoticed by the British government. Regardless of any politician's moral feelings about Belgian relief, it was simply good politics to show support for the courageous little country. Those who did oppose food shipments to Belgium had to tread lightly and couch their opposition in sensitive ways, especially in light of editorials such as the one in the *Westminster Gazette* on October 24, which stated clearly that even if food to Belgium could give some advantage to the enemy, it was still the right thing to do: "A whole people is threatened by starvation. Food can only be obtained if it is admitted by England, and adequate precautions seem to have been taken to see that it shall reach only those for whom it is intended. That arrangement might, in conceivable circumstances, be of some slight advantage to our enemies, but we must take the risk for the sake of the Belgian people."

That didn't mean, however, that all those in the British government would roll over on the issue, especially when the discussions took place behind closed doors.

Initially, Prime Minister Asquith and Foreign Secretary Edward Grey approved of Belgian relief by neutral America as long as Germany did not seize the food. But others in the cabinet did not. Lord Kitchener, David Lloyd George, Winston Churchill, and Reginald McKenna all disapproved of direct aid to Belgium. They believed that it was the duty of Germany to feed Belgium. If the Germans did not do so—as they had already proclaimed—then they would have to suffer the consequences, which would probably mean world condemnation, Belgian food riots, and a full-fledged civilian uprising that would take critical numbers of men from the front lines to subdue. Whether the Belgian situation would drain German troops from the front or suck money and food from German coffers, the result would be the same in the minds of the British military: an earlier end to the war.

But how to say that without sounding incredibly callous?

"In an effort to sound less cynical, the British cabinet maintained that relief in Belgium would prolong the war and lead to more suffering in the long run," according to one historian.

The Germans maintained that they had no obligation to feed the Belgians and that the threat of famine was due to the English blockade, which prohibited food imports to Belgium and Germany.

Hoover had little patience for British opponents of relief. He used every argument he could to convince the British government that Belgian relief was something to support—in permits, diplomatic negotiations with the Germans, and direct financial backing. One of Hoover's "favorite expressions," as he himself explained, was "You, the English, have pointed out that your entire object in this war was the preservation of the independence of Belgium and thus the obligation rests on you to preserve the lives of the civil population."

TWENTY

Brussels

Arriving back in Brussels, Francqui got right to work. One of his most pressing priorities was how to pay for the relief that he and Hoover envisioned. The estimated 80,000 tons of food per month would take approximately £1 million in working capital. But there needed to be two months of working capital "since the time required for transport to and inside Belgium was such that at least two months' supplies would always be on the seas or at the warehouses." Francqui, in coordination with Hoover, needed to bring pressure to bear on the Belgian government and secure German and Allied permissions. The two men would be able to secure relatively good financial footing only in early November.

Nearly as important as the money, though, was the Belgian centralization of all the relief efforts that had spontaneously sprung up and the creation of a national distribution chain that would cover the entire process, from unloading canal barges of wheat to selling or handing out individual loaves of bread.

On October 29 the Comité Central held a major meeting in Brussels. In attendance were the invited heads of all the established provincial committees and delegations from those areas that were not yet organized.

Francqui opened the meeting by giving a report on his recent trip to London and his attendance at the October conferences. He outlined what had been discussed and decided. He even acknowledged and praised the American and Spanish diplomats in London and Brussels and the men of the newly formed CRB: "As you perceive," he said, "the devoted intervention of these men, and especially of Hoover, Gibson and Shaler, has greatly facilitated the accomplishment of our task."

Francqui's words were as carefully chosen as Hoover's. The "our task" phrase could be interpreted to imply that Francqui felt Hoover and the CRB were working for the Comité Central. In many ways, Francqui saw the CRB merely as the purchasing arm of his organization rather than his organization being the distribution arm of the CRB. But as Hugh Gibson stated, "The members of the Belgian organization are, of course, prisoners of the Germans and unable to give any effective guarantees as to the disposal of the supplies. The British Government has, therefore, stipulated that all authority and responsibility are to be vested in the American Committee, and that the Belgians are to be regarded simply as a distributing agency."

Francqui never mentioned that during the October 29 meeting. It was a time to celebrate the arrival of the Americans. The president of the group, Ernest Solvay, expressed his country's sense of relief that people were out there helping them. "The Belgian population was on the verge of famine and the inquietude was general, because we foresaw dimly terrible days, frightful and perhaps irreparable events. Thanks to the precious and devoted intervention of the neutral diplomats and of the American Commission we are free, at least for the moment, from the threat of the fresh calamities which hung over our heads."

Solvay also "emphasized the necessity of putting aside all political activities, and of insisting upon absolute impartiality in the distribution of food and of relief." This was no time for partisan politics or local disputes. It was a time to come together and organize local distribution procedures before regular imports could begin.

A follow-up meeting was held on Saturday, October 31, when delegates were appointed by the Comité Central to represent the committee in the provinces and ensure that national instructions were followed at local levels. By November 5, the reorganization plans were final, and the Comité National de Secours et d'Alimentation officially came into being.

Now all that was needed was a steady supply of food.

Van Doren Gains Another Partner

Food was not usually on the mind of Eugene van Doren in October; anger and frustration at the German occupation was. He and the Abbé de Moor continued to put out their jelly-press bulletins while also smuggling Allied troops out of Belgium and letters to and from soldiers in the underground network Mot du Soldat. The abbé even recruited some Belgian Boy Scouts to help circulate their bulletins and any other underground material they wanted spread around the city.

As van Doren, de Moor, and the Boy Scouts did their clandestine work, the German government came up with an idea for trying to win over the belligerent Belgians. Since the occupation of Brussels, the only newspapers officially allowed in the city were German papers, and the only news in French was on the German *affiches* that were posted nearly every day all over the city. Neither the newspapers nor the *affiches* garnered any respect, although the *affiches* were read simply because there was no other news source except smuggled Allied papers.

So it was, in this news-starved city, that von der Goltz decided to finance and publish a French-language newspaper. Titled simply *Bruxellois*, the publication "made a great show of impartiality in its presentation of war news and of independence in regard to the German government. With its homely title and its Belgian-named contributors it promised to be a valuable medium of subversive propaganda.

"It probably would have been but for Victor Jourdain," according to the later book *Underground News*, which told the story of van Doren, de Moor, and Jourdain.

As the book noted, Jourdain was a seventy-four-year-old, heavyset man with blue eyes and "an expression of permanent irritation and a gruff voice that often reached the listener as an indistinct mumble through the bushy white moustache that drooped over his mouth onto his clipped beard." He had an air of "grandfatherly grumpiness."

But he was also a talented and highly skilled writer and newspaper editor. For thirty years he had captained the *Patriote*, "the most influential organ of the Catholic press." He was followed by 100,000 readers

Victor Jourdain was a renowned Belgian journalist who secretly became a partner of Eugene van Doren in the underground. (Underground News: The Complete Story of the Secret Newspaper That Made War History, Oscar E. Millard, Robert M. McBride and Co., 1938.)

who generally respected and admired him. On one point, though, he had few friends. Contrary to so many other Belgians, he opposed armaments in Belgium and had even fought against preparing for war. His cause was pacifism, and he maintained a strong faith in the treaties guaranteeing Belgium's neutrality. As a neutral country, he believed, Belgium should do nothing to show otherwise.

So, when the Germans had invaded, it was "more than a national disaster to him. It was a deep personal tragedy. It shattered a belief clung to in face of fierce opposition, and irrefutably demonstrated to the 100,000 readers of his paper the tragic fallacy of his policy."

He was nearly inconsolable; his personal integrity had been shattered, and he actually felt a "personal responsibility for the helplessness of the nation under the heel of the invader." He went into a depression that was not helped by the fact that he had closed down the *Patriote* in concert with all other Belgian publications. Unfortunately, he was reminded every day of his stance against war preparations because he, his ill wife, and his daughter lived above the by-then-shuttered newspaper offices.

All would probably have been lost for the elderly man if not for the appearance of the *Bruxellois* newspaper and its subtle preaching of pacifism to keep the citizens calm. Here was a real slap in the face—his ideals, "torn and twisted, were now being used by the enemy for defeatist propaganda," according to *Underground News.*

While that might not have been the last straw for others, it was to Jourdain "like the proverbial red rag." He was mad and wasn't going to go quietly into the night. "For the first time since he had closed down the *Patriote,* Victor Jourdain took up his pen and wrote a scathing denunciation of the *Bruxellois,* pouring into it all the suppressed bitterness that had been gnawing at his heart."

When he was finished, "it was a new man who sat back and glowered with savage satisfaction at the scrawled sheets in which the perfidy of the enemy *Bruxellois* lay exposed for all to know."

But how to get his words out to the 700,000 residents of Brussels?

He needed help. He thought he would approach the brother-in-law of his son, Joseph. The man might be able to help. His name was Eugene van Doren.

TWENTY-ONE

At Oxford

The large group of American Rhodes scholars just off the SS *St. Paul* pulled into the Oxford train station on Thursday, October 1, and were immediately reminded of the war—a troop train was also in the station. David Nelson wrote his mother that the soldiers "stared at us in a curious manner. They knew by our hats that we were Americans, and such a large party as ours attracted attention."

Two Rhodes men met the group and hustled everyone into horse-drawn hansom cabs for the clattering ride to Wellington Square and their rooms. The young men found that they each had a bedroom and sitting room, although in the first few days many of them gathered in the common lounge around the fireplace because, as Nelson noted, "we are not quite English enough yet to stay each one in his separate sitting-room."

Nelson's quarters had a fireplace in each room and heavy rugs to keep out the chill. Besides a bed, he had several chairs, a sofa, an easy chair, desk, table, bookcase, and cupboard. The dormitory's floor had six servants who were known as "scouts." Nelson wrote that the scout "builds your fires in the morning, looks after your rooms, calls you in the morning, takes your order for breakfast and lunch, and serves it in your rooms if you wish, runs your errands, and answers all questions you may ask. Mine is quite talkative. He generally gives me the war news before I get out of bed in the morning."

It was a far cry from the life of a North Dakota boy used to tooling around the country on his motorcycle, sleeping under the stars, and studying in a one-room schoolhouse.

The Americans had a week before the term started so they could settle in and explore their new surroundings. They found Oxford's lovely broad thoroughfares, its narrow streets with overhanging houses, the little lanes and the "devious alleys" all filled with bicycles because "everyone seems to ride a wheel." For the motorcycle-loving Nelson, it was truly exciting to see the occasional motorcar go by, and he "felt like cheering" when he saw during one afternoon "two Fords, an Overland, and a Hupmobile."

The school term began on Thursday, October 8, and Nelson was a bit surprised how slow the initial process was. First, he had to meet with his tutors and instructors. "All you need to do is make yourself comfortable before your fire and presently a messenger raps, enters, and hands you a slip of paper informing you that Mr. So and So would like to see Mr. Nelson in his rooms at such and such a time. You ask your scout how to find Mr. So and So's room, and at the appointed hour put on your gown and go over. You are told to come in and have a chair, and then for ten or fifteen minutes you have a little talk with him in which he advises you as to the work you should do. That is all there is to it."

When it came to lectures, Nelson had two each on Mondays and Tuesdays, one on Wednesdays, two on Thursdays, two on Fridays, and one on Saturdays. "After lunch I go down to the river and row until about 3:30 or 4:00—when I get back it is tea-time, then an hour or two till dinner—after dinner an hour at the Junior Common Room on most evenings, after that two hours study, if no one drops in to visit, or no one invites you out. We breakfast at eight and read the morning papers after that an hour or two till lectures. As you see, it does not leave a great deal of time for hard study."

Socially, he and all the other new American students were brought together by the American Club, an organization of Oxford's U.S. students that had clubrooms downtown. They first gathered on Saturday night, October 10, and then again the next Saturday, when they heard two "very interesting and exceedingly humorous talks" by two Oxford students who had been arrested in Germany as spies while they were on a bicycling trip during summer break.

One of the speakers was twenty-three-year-old Tracy B. Kittredge, who was an Oxford man but not a Rhodes scholar. Two other non-Rhodes men were Laurence C. Wellington (better known as "Duke") and Perrin Comstock Galpin. Nelson, no doubt, met all three of them that night. From sailing on the *St. Paul*, Nelson probably would have already known the first-year men: Emil F. Hollmann, Ridley Richard Lytle Jr., John L. Glenn, Bennett H. Branscomb, Oliver C. Carmichael, and Carleton G. Bowden.

None of these men had any idea during that festive American Club evening how important each would become to the others starting in early December, when they suddenly would become CRB delegates and head into the great unknown that was German-occupied Belgium.

They did know, though, on that October night that a war was raging. They merely had to look around. Portions of Oxford's New College were being used as a hospital for wounded soldiers. The night the new American students had arrived, a nine-car Red Cross train pulled in Oxford station and unloaded many more wounded. There were fewer students on campus because a large proportion had already left school and joined up. Total fall-term attendance at Oxford was down about 30 percent while New College, one of Oxford's colleges, saw only 80 students instead of the usual 210. The English students who had remained on campus weren't sure how long they would stay because "many of them have applied for commissions [in the armed services], but have not received them yet."

The town was filled with British troops, with some officers billeted in college rooms. Belgian refugees, who by then numbered 100,000 in Britain, were housed throughout the city, and some professors from the destroyed University of Louvain were working at Oxford.

"One feels the grimness of war," Nelson wrote his mother, "when one gets out in our beautiful College garden and walks about with many wounded soldiers, some with bandaged heads, others with arms in slings, still others with canes or on crutches. One of our college men was brought here with twenty-eight wounds, but is now recovering and hopes soon to return to the front. It is all very pathetic."

Nelson finished another letter by stating simply, "War is a reality here."

By December, it would become a far greater reality for Nelson and a handful of his fellow students.

TWENTY-TWO

Speeding Toward the Belgian Coastal Border

Nearly two weeks after Hunt had cabled his Antwerp story to America, he was hot on the trail of another. This time he was speeding in a private yacht from Rotterdam toward the Belgian coastal border. Dr. M. P. Rooseboom, a Dutchman and one of the secretaries of the International Court of Arbitration at The Hague, had borrowed the motor launch from a friend and filled it with food and clothes he had collected for Belgian refugees. Hunt was along for the ride as his guest.

While no accurate count was possible of how many Belgians had fled before the Germans, all estimates indicated that there were well more than 100,000 refugees in Holland. Camps of 25,000 civilian refugees each were in the towns of Bergen op Zoom and Roosendaal. The people in those camps, according to one British newspaper, were "mostly women, many with tiny babes and children. Their condition is pitiful. They are terrified. They have no money. There are various kinds of illness, but no epidemics."

Dr. Rooseboom had borrowed the launch because he wanted to deliver the supplies where he felt they were needed most—to the small villages along the frontier that had been overwhelmed by panicked and frightened Belgians. Onboard, "all available space on the yacht was piled with bags of rice, beans, coffee, tubs of lard and butter, cheese big as cartwheels, packages of underclothing for women and children, and more than eight hundred loaves of bread."

As the two negotiated the extensive network of rivers and canals, they came across lots of refugees packed into barges that were tied to the banks. They spent the night at Hansweert, where the Dutch customs house was located. The next day in Sas van Gent, the last Dutch village before Belgium, they found 5,000 refugees. The village officials told them that 2,000 were living in the ships along the canals and could pay for their needs while 600 were destitute. "For a week the town authorities had been passing fugitives along to the less crowded ports farther north at a rate of several thousand a day."

When the refugees had first begun appearing in Sas van Gent, someone had come up with the brilliant idea to turn the idled phosphate factory (owned by Belgians) into a sanctuary. "They filled the store-rooms and offices with straw, collected all the blankets in town, set doctors promptly to work, and had the situation well in hand from the start."

Hunt described a building in the middle of the plant facilities that was as large "as a circus, where the Belgians camped by the thousands." The entire plant was organized, well kept, and the refugees were in relatively good shape. Altogether, it was "paradise compared with camps in some other towns along the Belgian-Dutch border."

From Sas van Gent they took the boat to Hulst, where conditions were a lot worse. In the square before the town hall, a huge tent had been raised, and "civilian refugees were camped on straw under its thin shelter, in a hideous, beast-like commonwealth." The town's schools had become makeshift hospitals where the sick lay on pallets in the classrooms.

Bread was no longer to be found, and "most of the fugitives lived on boiled beans, cooked in ten great cauldrons in an open courtyard. There were crowds of Belgians jammed about the enclosure, waiting to be allowed their turn inside, and they were ravenous as beasts. No dishes or spoons were to be had. Men, women, and little children brought empty tins, bowls, or fragments of old crockery to hold their share of the pre-

Belgian refugees somewhere in Holland. (Public domain; *Back From Belgium*, Father Jean B. DeVille, H. K. Fly Co., 1918.)

cious food, and they ate from little wooden shovels which they had whittled out for themselves."

To add to these people's miseries, it poured rain all day long. And as Hunt so vividly described it, the rain didn't just come down; it "sluiced and spotched and oozed from the atmosphere, as if the air were a cold, wet sponge. It crawled down necks and up trouser-legs. It sopped cheeks and beaded eyebrows. It snuggled into the roots of the hair, and churned up mud that clung like cottage-cheese."

In such conditions, and seeing the thousands upon thousands of tired, frightened, hungry people, Dr. Rooseboom and his guest handed out supplies until there were no more to give. Then the men turned the motor launch north and headed back to Rotterdam.

It was sometime during October, in this transformative period between summer and winter, that Hunt received news from America that his fiancée had suddenly died. He would grieve privately. So privately, in fact, that he recorded nothing of the tragedy—who she was, what had happened—in his book or any journals available to the public. Within all that material, there is only one comment he wrote at the end of a letter to one of his magazine agents: "My fiancée's death leaves me still pretty ragged. Your letter helped."

With Hunt's generally heightened sensibilities and sensitivity, it's not too surprising that as he went about gathering, experiencing, and writing each new war story, he began changing. He was becoming more involved, more emotionally affected by what he saw happening around him. Hunt was moving, consciously or unconsciously, from objective journalist to passive observer to budding participant. He would make his final transformation in November when he joined the CRB and became an active relief worker.

NOVEMBER 1914

COMING TOGETHER

Rotterdam harbor: A U.S. cargo ship in the process of off-loading sacks marked "Kansas Sun Wheat Flour" into a canal barge. (Public domain; Herbert Hoover Presidential Library Archives, West Branch, Iowa.)

TWENTY-THREE

Rotterdam

"Nothing that has been written could exaggerate the misery of Belgium," Jarvis E. Bell told the press after his first trip into Belgium on November 2. He called it "a country without a smile" and described what he had seen. "We drove for miles through graveyards. Stakes, on some of them a soldier's tattered coat and helmet, were the tombstones; deserted fields the cemeteries. As we entered villages, women and children sought refuge in the ruins of their roofless homes, terrified lest we were some fresh visitation of war. Their faces were drawn and lined. If you could only see the gruesome surroundings in which they are struggling for existence you could not wonder that they do not smile. The Belgian peasant, in many districts, has no home in which to sleep, no seed to sow, no implements to work with, no transport with which to reach a market, and no heart to struggle against the impossible."

Bell went on to comment that it was "inconceivable that any war ever produced such complete and tragic paralysis as we saw in many parts of

Belgium. It cannot be attributed to lack of courage on the part of the conquered civil population or to the inhumanity of the conqueror. It is simply war—up-to-date, civilized, Christian war."

———————————

Bell was one of Hoover's American volunteers, and he had been sent in late October from London to Rotterdam to help wherever he could. Lucey had told Bell that he would be the CRB representative in the three-man critical job of escorting the first barges of food into Belgium. But before they could do their job, the food had to get to Rotterdam. The world press had reported that the *Coblenz* had sailed from London on October 28, but no one was sure when it would arrive.

Finally, in the pre-dawn hour of 3 a.m., on Sunday, November 1, the small steamship *Coblenz* pulled into Rotterdam harbor with its precious cargo earmarked for Belgium. According to one CRB history, the Dutch government, "with great kindness, made an exception to their rigid rule against work being done on Sunday, and the Labour Union also allowed their men to unload" so that the 1,000 tons of supplies could be handled as quickly as possible. All through the day the sacks of beans, rice, and flour were hauled by hand and by cranes out of the *Coblenz* and into barges that hugged each side of the ship.

Lucey, no doubt, was there directing, supervising, and urging on any who didn't have the right sense of urgency. He knew that this food had been needed weeks ago. Throughout the day, onlookers watched from shore as this historic event unfolded—the Dutch knew this was the first ship to arrive with Belgian relief supplies.

Lucey was also desperate for information regarding what was happening in Belgium—everything from the organization of distribution and a determination of what areas needed what supplies the most to the condition of the canal network that would carry the cargoes. That Sunday, November 1, he sent Edward D. Curtis from Rotterdam south to Brussels with a letter to Whitlock and an urgent request for reports on the organization of distribution within Belgium.

Curtis's trip represented a momentous occasion that no one had time or interest in marking. It was the first trip into Belgium of the first CRB courier—a critically important job when there was no telegraph or postal service out of occupied Belgium. The Germans had agreed to allow the CRB to send mail to and from Belgium by special courier, similar to the permission they had given Whitlock and Gibson as neutral diplomats. Years later, it was realized that "this first trip of Curtis marked the beginning of the organization of communication by the Commission." As the first courier, Curtis could also lay claim, as E. E. Hunt later said, to being the first CRB delegate to enter Belgium who was not part of the executive committee or a U.S. diplomat. He beat Jarvis Bell by one day.

Curtis was one of a handful of young Americans who had been swept up by Hoover to help with the stranded tourists in August, and then he naturally followed along as those efforts transformed into the CRB. He had been born

Edward Curtis was a mature-looking twenty-one-year-old who was the first CRB courier to travel into Belgium. (Public domain; CRB portrait book, Herbert Hoover Presidential Library Archives, West Branch, Iowa.)

and raised in Boston, and his father, Francis George Curtis, was a well-respected and well-to-do physician. Edward was the third born of four children and had two brothers and a sister. He had gone to Harvard and then been accepted into Cambridge. On March 18, 1914, he had sailed for England not realizing he would be quickly swallowed up by the war and by Herbert Hoover.

Curtis was a mature-looking twenty-one-year-old who stood five feet eleven inches and had a square and slightly dimpled chin, blue-gray eyes, high forehead, and brown hair slicked tightly to his head and parted near the center. Well-dressed with appropriate starched white collars, dark ties, and suits, he was a dapper man who was the epitome of the young American go-getter. Gibson wrote that Curtis "exudes silence and discretion, but does not miss any fun or any chance to advance the general cause." Edgar Rickard, who had gotten to know Curtis during the stranded-tourist days in London, called him an "earnest and well-equipped man."

Curtis's skills would have undoubtedly included speaking French and German—probably well—although no record has been found that he did.

Even though the CRB at this early stage accepted some men with limited or no language skills beyond English, the courier's job was demanding in a special way. Traveling in and out of Belgium numerous times a week, he would constantly be in contact with German officers and sentries and Belgian officials and citizens. This would have demanded at least competency, if not fluency, in both French and German, with a bonus for knowledge of Dutch and Flemish. Curtis's ability with language would definitely have come in handy during the numerous times in those early days when he was harassed and sometimes thrown in jail by German sentries convinced he was a spy.

On that first Sunday in November, as Curtis and his chauffeur and motorcar were stopped at numerous German checkpoints on his trip to Brussels, Dutch stevedores kept laboring to unload the *Coblenz*. By Monday morning the ship was empty, and eight barges, or lighters, were ready to go. Towed by four tugs, they slowly made their way out of Rotterdam harbor bound for Brussels. The holds of each barge were sealed, and a large sign stated in English, "Consigned to the American Minister in Brussels for the Comité National de Secours d'Alimentation." On the door of each lighter captain's cabin was a copy of von der Goltz's guarantee and his request that German officials give the shipment safe conduct. The crews were all neutral Dutchmen who carried with them individual German passes allowing them to travel to Brussels and back.

This "Flotilla of Mercy," as one English newspaper christened it, was shadowed by a motorcar that contained three men. Marshall Langhorne was the secretary of the U.S. Legation in Holland, and he represented Whitlock as the neutral diplomatic patron of the shipment. Bell was the newly designated CRB delegate and was destined to play a much larger role in the Brussels operations in December. Mr. Wyman was the European manager of the American Express Company and presumably along as an observer. They carried with them the German guarantee, signed by von der Goltz, and the Berlin government's agreement not to requisition the food.

TWENTY-FOUR

Into Occupied Belgium

"Staring at Our Flotilla as If It Was Some Mirage"

The first barges from Rotterdam were towed to the Dutch border town of Hansweert before heading up the Scheldt River to Antwerp, where they branched off to the southeast into a major canal that went to Malines (Mechelen in Flemish) and Brussels. All of these sections of canal were cleared of enough war debris to allow passage. The trip took two days, during which time Bell made his observation that nothing yet written had exaggerated Belgium's misery.

Notwithstanding Bell's comments, it was an uneventful trip in terms of German interference. As for the Belgians' perspective, the barges were something of a miracle, according to Bell. "All the way to Antwerp, to Malines, and to Brussels the country people came running to the canal banks staring at our flotilla as if it was some mirage. For weeks not a single barge had passed where formerly there were a thousand craft within an hour. To the Belgian country folk it was at first just a

The serene look of a Belgian prewar canal, this one through the city of Tournai southwest of Brussels. The canal-barge tugboat is waiting for the footbridge to be raised. (Public domain; multiple sources.)

God sent dream to remind them of the peaceful days that preceded the nightmare of war."

On Wednesday morning, November 4, Langhorne, Wyman, and Bell pulled up in front of the U.S. Legation in Brussels and announced to Whitlock that the barges were safely tied up at the city's main canal terminal waiting to be unloaded. Belgium's informal communications network proved its worth that day because, as Bell said, "in an hour all Brussels knew and rejoiced." Best of all, this first shipment had confirmed one thought Belgians had been clinging to: Help was on the way. Bell admitted to the press that "many people feared we should never manage to obtain permission to get the relief into Belgium, and that if we got it in we should never get it through the wall of soldiers that surrounds Brussels."

Initially, there had even been a question of whether or not the barges could get through the canals. Belgium, like Holland, had a vast network of canals that covered practically the entire country. There were three main arteries from Holland into Belgium, with some continuing into France.

The first major canal was from the Dutch towns of Terneuzen and Sas van Gent (where Hunt had unloaded relief supplies in late October) to the Belgian city of Ghent. This was a large canal that could handle big barges carrying 1,200 tons. At Ghent, the cargos from the larger barges

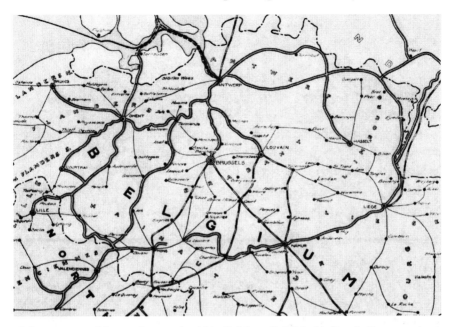

A closeup view of the canal network within Belgium. Solid double lines indicate canals, smaller two-toned double lines are railways, and single lines are roads. (Public domain; CRB map in the author's archives.)

had to be reloaded into 300- and 400-ton lighters to go north to Ostend and Bruges, or south to Courtrai (Kortrijk in Flemish), Tournai, Mons, or Charleroi, with branches leading to the French cities of Lille and Valenciennes.

The second major canal ran from the Dutch town of Roosendaal to Antwerp and from there to Brussels or Louvain. It was also large enough to handle 1,000-ton barges. At Antwerp, small canals led to Mons and the surrounding area. This second major canal was doubly important because most of Belgium's chief flour mills were around Brussels or Louvain. If the CRB was successful and wheat shipments began coming into Belgium, much of the wheat would head down this canal to the flour mills for processing before leaving again as flour in smaller lighters along smaller canals.

The third major canal came from Rotterdam to the Dutch town of Weert and into the Belgian province of Limbourg (now spelled Limburg). It branched west to Turnhout and Antwerp, south into Holland again at Maastricht, and then back into Belgium to Liège and Namur. "If the water was neither too high nor too low, lighters could be sent from Namur along the Sambre [River] to Charleroi, or south on the Meuse [River] to Dinant, and ultimately Charleville [France]."

This waterway network meant that "all the chief centres of Belgium and all the provinces, save Luxembourg, could therefore be provided with food directly from Rotterdam via the canals."

But that was only if they were clear. Before and during the invasion, many of the canals had been blocked by sunken barges or remnants of bridges that had been destroyed either by the retreating Belgians or by the advancing Germans.

Liège—"We Are Now Threatened by Famine"

While the canals had been passable for the first shipment of food to Brussels, they simply could not be trusted yet for clear passage to the rest of the country, especially when it came to the critical second shipment of food for the hard-hit city of Liège. Because Lucey in Rotterdam had no good information on the condition of the canals, he arranged approval from the Dutch and German authorities to ship the supplies to Liège by train.

As with many efforts during these early CRB days, the actual event didn't go as smoothly as the planning and approvals would have suggested.

Liège was a large urban center of 117,000 in eastern Belgium near the Dutch and German borders. The city anchored the eastern side of Belgium's industrial backbone, which ran roughly west to the Belgian cities of Namur, Charleroi, and Mons along the valleys of the two largest rivers in the area, the Meuse and the Sambre. When war had come, tens of thousands of industrial workers had been thrown out of work. Additionally, Liège had borne the brunt of major fighting in the invasion's earliest days because its ring of fortresses made it a primary objective of the German Army.

Since late October, the city's desperation had become well known as its plight was reported by numerous British newspapers. The press was constantly supplied with information by Hoover, his PR team, and others. Through their efforts it became well publicized that during the last three weeks of October Liège residents had received only three ounces of flour per day and, according to one British newspaper, "a small portion of salt. These are the only supplies available."

At the end of October, two members of the Liège town council, Émile Digneffe and Paul Staes, had received permission from the Germans to go to Holland and had made a statement to the CRB about the city and its need. Hoover made sure the statement found its way to the British press, and on November 7 it was published in the *Morning Post*. The Liège officials said in their statement: "To sum up the situation, an industrial population of high efficiency is entirely out of work and cannot earn its food. It has no reserves any more in food or savings and a rescue is immediately and urgently needed, for fear that a catastrophe would be brought about by the impending starvation. Food for relief is only the beginning of all kind of relief up to the time when the population is allowed to organize its work again. You may rest assured, dear sirs, that in spite of circumstances our population is full of courage and worthy of all the sympathy that the American and other nations can show to the Belgians."

The same newspaper edition also ran another statement, given on November 1 by other Liège and Namur officials. "We have rudely suffered. After the atrocities and horrors of the war we are now threatened by famine. The German armies, since the beginning of the invasion, have lived on our soil by requisitioning to the death for victuals of all nature. Our production of grain normally is hardly sufficient for a fifth of the consumption. . . . Solely for Liège and its environs 1,500 bags of grain are necessary per day. At the moment of writing we have hardly grain for a few days. Without the generous assistance of the United States, it would mean for us famine with its unavoidable consequences of riots and plundering. We have suffered enough; at least let this misfortune be spared us. . . . In the country of Liège the City has first been compelled to pay a war contribution of 30,000,000 francs, while the requisitions which have been made so far exceed 29,000,000 francs. Liège has a population of 117,000 inhabitants, and its ordinary annual budget hardly reaches 14,000,000 francs!"

Lucey had met with the Liège and Namur representatives in late October and later telegraphed Hoover. "Their description of the conditions of the people in and around Liège is pitiable. You are justified in making any appeal or resorting to any measures, however extreme, to provide instant relief for these districts. It is feared that in their desperation the hungry people will attack the authorities. This would cause serious loss of life." Hoover once again released Lucey's telegram to the press as part of his media campaign to keep the world informed of what was happening inside Belgium and to help build support for his relief efforts.

When food was finally ready to be sent to Liège, two train shipments were loaded with supplies. The specially authorized trains would be hauled by Dutch engines to the border town of Eijsden (not to be confused with the nearby Belgian town of Eisden). The Germans had agreed to have their engines pull the loads from the Dutch border into Belgium and Liège. To ensure everything went smoothly, Henry van Dyke, U.S. minister to the Netherlands, sent Captain A. H. Sunderland to accompany the first train.

Sunderland, a captain in the Coast Artillery Corps, had originally been one of the twenty officers assigned to the U.S. government's tourist relief expedition aboard the USS *Tennessee* at the start of the war. Sunderland had worked extensively in Holland with van Dyke and the legation staff in aiding frantic American tourists trying to get home. Later, he transitioned into working for van Dyke as the U.S. military attaché at The Hague.

He would be the sole guardian of the first shipment of food into Liège. At around 4 a.m. on Tuesday, November 10, the train and its American protector pulled out of Rotterdam heading for the Dutch town of Eijsden and its rendezvous with a German locomotive. Under normal conditions the journey of roughly 140 miles would have taken only half a day, meaning the cargo would have reached Liège, and the unloading begun, around lunch time. Dinner came and went with no news of the train.

Meanwhile, that morning in the U.S. Legation in Brussels, a concern had arisen about the Germans' fanatical adherence to rules and regulations. Officially, the only people in Belgium who could receive any relief shipments were Whitlock and Gibson or those to whom they delegated their authority through a power of attorney. (That's why CRB representatives became known as CRB delegates.) In this case, the concern was that no power of attorney had been sent to the U.S. consul in Liège, so the Germans might not allow the shipment to be received. Gibson, the ever-present problem-solver, was immediately dispatched—as he said, "on an hour's notice without any lunch"—to Liège to find the train and Sunderland and make sure both were properly received in Liège.

When Gibson and his driver reached the city, they went straight to the consulate "without pausing to set ourselves up at a hotel, but found that nothing was known of Captain Sunderland or his food trains. Then to the German headquarters where we inquired at all the offices in turn and found that the gentleman had not been heard from. By the time we got through our inquiries it was dark; and, as we had no [German] *laisser-passer* to be out after dark, we had to scuttle back to the hotel and stay."

As Gibson was searching for Sunderland, the captain surfaced, but not in Gibson's sight. Sunderland contacted Lucey and told him that the shipment had been held up at the Dutch town of Eijsden because the German military authorities in the Belgian town of Eisden had received no instructions about the train and refused to provide an engine to go to Eijsden. Lucey called van Dyke "quite late" and told him of the situation.

In the end, according to one American journalist, Sunderland got into Belgium somehow and commandeered the only automobile in Eisden and headed for Liège. There, not knowing that Gibson was looking for him, Sunderland went straight to the German commander's office and received the necessary written approvals for the German engine. It was then back to Eisden to convince the German station master that everything had been properly authorized and that he should send an engine to the Dutch town of Eijsden to pick up the train cars of food and haul them to Liège.

A day later, Gibson and Sunderland finally joined forces, and the train arrived in Liège.

But then another problem arose. As the two men met with the Belgian provincial governor, the mayor, and other Liège committee members, Gibson remembered, "I had to collect a part of the cost of the food before I could turn it over." The Belgians explained it was not possible—the chairman of the local committee had gone to Brussels to arrange a loan for the food. He would not be back for four or five days.

"That did not please me," Gibson wrote, "so I suggested in my usual simple and direct way that the Governor rob the safe and pay me with provincial funds, trusting to be paid later by the committee. It took some little argument to convince him, but he had good nerve, and by half-past twelve he brought forth 275,000 francs in bank-notes [a substantial $44,000] and handed them over to me for a receipt."

Gibson stuffed the money in his pockets and was ready to run when he was caught by one last Belgian problem—ceremonial protocol. Belgians loved to acknowledge important events with meals, toasting, and speech making. Even with this life-and-death situation of food relief, the Belgians insisted Gibson "must lunch with them all."

Gibson was not one for such formal proceedings, but he "accepted, on the understanding that it would be short and that I could get away immediately afterward." Yes, yes, of course, they assured him.

Four hours later, they were still at it. "When we got down the home stretch, the Governor arose and made a very neat little speech, thanking us for what we had done to get food to the people of Liège, and expressing gratitude to the American Government and people, etc. I responded in remarks of almost record shortness, and as soon as possible afterward, we got away through the rain to Brussels."

Stuffed with food, drink, and money, Gibson departed Liège. More importantly, though, the city had its food.

Still, as Sunderland headed back to Rotterdam, he was disturbed by what he had seen—not with the Germans holding up the train, but with what had happened after the train arrived in Liège. In his written report to Lucey on November 14, he stated, "There seemed to me a great lack of organization in the relief work in Liège." The overall problem, in his opinion, was that "there seemed too many persons involved in this work of relief in Liège, and no man seemed to have sufficient authority to obtain any tangible results."

Sunderland would not just complain; he would offer a solution. Well aware of the strained relations between Belgians and Germans, he felt "it would greatly facilitate the operations of the Commission were all the work in connection with the relief, short of the actual distribution, put in the hands of an American to be stationed at Liège to represent the Relief Commission. Such a man could investigate the needs of the different localities, and communicate this to the Rotterdam office, could meet shipments coming and pre-arrange payment of freight or any other details, and thus prevent confusion similar to that which attended the arrival of the shipment I accompanied and which will attend, in my estimation, every shipment under the present regime."

Sunderland probably had no idea that he had hit on what Hoover and Lucey would very soon be advocating: CRB delegates scattered all around Belgium and running the show until the final act of distribution.

Refugees Begin Returning Home

As Sunderland escorted the first food shipment via train to Liège, and canal barges brought the first food to Brussels, they passed thousands of refugees, but this time the Belgians were walking back into their country, not leaving it. It was like some gigantic tidal flow that had moved one way and then, after a lull, was moving back the other way.

During the invasion and the months of heavy fighting that had followed, tens, if not hundreds, of thousands of refugees had fled south to France or north to Holland (any accurate count was impossible). But after Antwerp fell and the fighting was confined to the coast, many of those who had fled north began to trickle back into Belgium. By the end of October, British newspapers were reporting that thousands were returning home. The *Yorkshire Post* reported, "14,500 Belgian refugees returned on Tuesday [October 27] and 12,850 yesterday [October 28] to Antwerp."

All over Holland, the refugees were weighing the choice between staying in a neutral country, where conditions in many of the refugee camps were not ideal, or taking a chance on going home and possibly finding nothing left and no food to eat. One important incentive was the fact that the Germans were maintaining a rather porous one-way border, permitting people back into Belgium while not letting many out. There was a good chance this would not be the case for too much longer.

Even King Albert weighed in on the issue. A Central News dispatch reported in late October that some Antwerp "municipal officials and workmen who had taken refuge in Holland telegraphed to King Albert that their civil authorities had threatened them with dismissal if they did not at once return to Antwerp. The King, whose intervention had been requested, replied from the Belgian General Headquarters, 'Return to Belgium and resume your duties.—Albert.'"

Many Belgians decided to walk home.

On November 7, the *Daily Telegram* reported that Shaler, on a trip from Holland into Belgium on October 27, had seen "a stream of poor people pouring back into Antwerp in every conceivable kind of conveyance and on foot. They carried their babies and other belongings."

A month after Shaler's trip into Belgium, Lucey took his own trip on November 28 from Rotterdam to the Belgian border. He reported in a telegram to the London CRB office that "the main influx of refugees into Holland has practically ceased, and that great numbers have made and are making their way back to Belgium. Those remaining say that some returned on account of German assurances, others because they were anxious to see what is left of their homes, and also hoped to secure work and food."

Lucey continued: "The majority of these belong to the agricultural element. This means that the population of Belgium requiring food during
the winter is likely to be largely increased by those who appeared likely to
settle in Holland for a considerable time.

"The principal impression on my mind as a result of the trip is that
those physically capable or sufficiently unhampered by circumstances
have preferred or will prefer to return to Belgium rather than endure the
camps, and that the population in Belgium requiring feeding during the
winter is likely to be many thousands more than seemed probable a short
time ago."

That's not exactly what Hoover had wanted to hear.

Lucey Finds Some Food

Despite Lucey's own trip into Belgium, he still had little concrete
knowledge of which Belgian canals were cleared and usable and which
ones were blocked. According to a CRB history, "Days and even weeks
passed before this information was forthcoming and Lucey became very
impatient. The reports that came out of Belgium made him feel that
thousands of people might be starving in Belgium, while food was being
held at Rotterdam because of the lack of instructions from Brussels."

This didn't mean he was sitting on his hands. On November 2 he had
attended to the second Hoover shipment from London that came into
Rotterdam aboard the *Iris*. But Lucey, much aware of the stated goal
of 80,000 tons per month, was also "very busy searching Holland for
food-supplies available for immediate shipment to Belgium."

A somewhat surprising development was the discovery that 8,000 tons
of wheat, much of it owned by the Belgian government, was lying in the
holds of some of the Belgian barges that had fled to Holland during the invasion. After negotiations with the German authorities, it was agreed that
this wheat could be returned to Belgium for use by civilians. Additionally,
while the Dutch government had taken charge of all its country's cereals
for its own citizens, it did agree to loan 10,000 tons of wheat to the CRB
to be replaced as soon as a steady stream of supplies was established.

Things were moving, but moving at glacial speed as far as Lucey was
concerned. For the moment, though, he had to be content with the
knowledge that the first eight barges had made it to Brussels and had
delivered much more than food; they had delivered hope.

But with no telegraph or postal service between Rotterdam and Belgium, Lucey was flying blind. That's why he had sent in Curtis on November 1 and why he spoke to every Belgian dignitary whom the Germans had allowed out. Unfortunately, they "could give Lucey neither definite information regarding the internal relief organization nor specific recommendations as to where to direct the first food shipments."

Lucey could only wonder what the devil was up with the Brussels CRB office. He needed information about the canals and where he should ship what to whom—and he needed it yesterday.

TWENTY-FIVE

Brussels

When Bell, Langhorne, and Wyman arrived in Brussels the morning of Wednesday, November 4, their job had changed from protecting the barges to collecting as much useful information as possible for Lucey. So they, according to one historian, "endeavored to get more definite information about conditions in Belgium, but found the Comité National not yet fully organized, and the Heineman [sub]Committee swamped in the details of the difficult and delicate work of trying to arrange with the Germans a satisfactory basis for the successful execution of the work."

The obstacles to establishing a CRB office and fully developing the Comité National were formidable. The German occupation created "constant frictions between the population and their rulers"; then there were the suspicions from both sides, all of which "made the Germans slow to grant any concessions from their rigid military regime."

Additionally, from a practical standpoint, there were numerous other hurdles to overcome. As noted by a CRB history, "The absence of a means of communication, the great restriction of circulation—passports being at that time required even to go from one region to another—the breakdown of the credit system, the paralysis of industry, the spiritual and physical shock that still weighed heavily upon the people, made any attempt at organization a slow and difficult process."

So, even though Francqui and his team had converted the Comité Central (CC) into the Comité National (CN) on November 5, that didn't mean nationwide distribution was suddenly organized and ready for foodstuffs—as evidenced by Sunderland's experience in Liège. Inventories of available foodstuffs were still being laboriously conducted all over Belgium to get a statistical grasp on the issue. Francqui still had a lot of work to do.

Francqui Begins Building the CN

The Belgian financier and his executive team, which remained the same from the CC to the CN, began to implement an organizational plan. Ten committees would be set up, one to correspond roughly to each of the country's nine provinces and an additional one for Brussels. These provincial committees would become the middlemen between the CN on the top floor and the local communes' committees on the ground. The member of each provincial committee, as a CRB history explained, "should be impartially chosen, and the committee should include representatives of each political party, and from each arrondissement [administrative district] so that the needs of all sections and districts would be known to the committees. They should assume the responsibility of an equitable distribution of food and a wise administration of charity."

The CN would assign its own delegates to each provincial committee, and each committee would assign one delegate to sit on the CN. The provincial committees would "enjoy entire independence of action except for the general measures prescribed by the Committee National," but they needed to stay in constant communication with the CN. Each of the committees would be required to maintain a bank account at the Societe Generale (Francqui's bank) to ensure timely payments for food.

With dedication and determination to overcome the hardships of German occupation—restricted communications, limited movements, and myriad regulations—the Belgians were able to make all the provincial committees operational by the end of November.

Another part of Francqui's CN organizational plan involved the CRB. As required by both Hoover and the British, he included CRB delegates. "The Commission was to have offices in each of the provinces under the charge of delegates of American nationality, who should be assigned to work with the provincial committees. These delegates should act in co-operation with the delegates of the Comité National: they should reside in the chief place of the province, and should visit even the smallest hamlet to ensure the efficient working of the organization."

Francqui had to make such a statement to get British approval for relief, but just as Hoover had wanted a purely American relief program, Francqui wanted a purely Belgian-run program within Belgium. He would have preferred no CRB delegates in his country. He admitted publicly that the CRB was able to provide the critical services of organizing world charity, gaining diplomatic agreements from the belligerents, and buying and shipping food into Rotterdam, but he and a number of his associates were privately convinced that Belgians—and only Belgians—should do the work from the moment the food touched Belgian soil. There was no need for Americans in the country.

But being a military man who thought strategically, Francqui knew the tenuous position he and his country were in during this embryonic stage of relief, so he sat back and waited. The issue would not go away, however, and "this attitude of the Belgians in the Comité National who felt that the work, as a purely Belgian institution, should be carried on altogether by Belgians, was to lead to many complications and much difficulty later on," according to one CRB history. In fact, after the difficult year of 1914 had passed, Francqui would make an incredibly audacious move to remove the CRB from Belgium. It would be an action that nearly cost the country its collective life.

In early November 1914, however, with the CN organization mapped out and the Americans forced upon him, Francqui turned to the problem of securing some kind of financial backing that would keep the relief effort going. The economic system of relief established earlier in Brussels with the Comité Central would be expanded to all of Belgium—ration cards would be used to provide a uniform daily ration delivered through soup kitchens (also known as "canteens") to those who could pay and to those who needed complete charity. Everyone (except for the destitute) along the chain, from millers to bakers to consumers, would pay a price slightly over cost. Additionally, the CN and the local communes would subsidize a portion of the total costs. All of that meant the charitable portion of the work would be covered. And, through a complicated financial transaction system, the CRB outside of Belgium would be paid for the food it was importing.

But this system needed major funding to prime the pump. After considerable efforts, Francqui was able to get Brussels bankers to put up a loan of £600,000 to add to the £100,000 from the British government and the £100,000 from the Belgian Relief Fund in France. But what he really needed was money to cover the necessary working capital for the CRB. Using his connections, he began to put pressure on the Belgian government, which was operating from Le Havre, France, to provide those funds. In

Dannie Heineman was an American engineer living and working in Brussels when the war broke out. He helped start Belgian relief and was the first director of the CRB's Brussels office. (Public domain; multiple sources.)

early November, the Belgian government agreed to advance £1 million to the CRB as "working capital and as a transportation fund."

It would remain to be seen whether or not the Allies and the Germans would agree to the complex and unprecedented financial arrangements Francqui and Hoover were developing.

A Weak CRB Office in Brussels Causes Problems

Like Francqui, American Dannie Heineman—by then director of the newly formed CRB office in Brussels and still a member of the CN—had his hands full. That was true not only with his ongoing tedious work securing permits and guarantees from the German authorities but also in determining just how the new CRB office would operate. How would the CRB work be different from his work as Francqui's subcommittee chair—especially when Heineman would still work out of his office at 48 Rue de Naples?

According to one historian of the CRB, Heineman "had been engaged for two months in gathering together food for Greater Brussels, and he went on now from the same offices with hardly more than a change in name. He was now director of the Commission for Relief in Belgium and not, as before, chairman of a subcommittee under Francqui's direction. Many of the chief men of the Comité National probably failed to realize the significance of this change in name. They continued to regard the Commission as a subordinate agent of the Comité National, just as Heineman's food-supply subcommittee had previously been. They were consequently inclined at times to object to any interference on the part of the Commission in the control of food distribution."

With no real CRB staff support yet, and his loyalties mixed between his CN friends and CRB associates, Heineman just kept doing what he had been doing: finding food for those in the greatest need. Hoover's first shipment to Brussels would help, Heineman knew, but more was needed immediately.

An interesting twist on the concept of give-and-take helped solve the immediate crisis. It was common knowledge at the start of the war that the Belgian government had requisitioned much of the stored wheat within Belgium and kept it for future use in what was thought to be impregnable Antwerp. Also well known was the fact that after the city fell, the wheat had become part of the Germans' spoils of war.

From those sad bits of knowledge, a somewhat audacious plan was conceived. Heineman approached the Germans with the idea of borrowing 50,000 sacks of grain, or 5,000 tons, for immediate relief, with the understanding that the grain would be replaced by the CRB when regular shipments began flowing into Belgium. The Germans agreed and were so goodhearted that they "offered to provide further quantities on a similar basis if such should be needed." It seems they were happy to loan the Belgians what they had stolen; or another way of saying it is that the Belgians were allowed to borrow what was rightfully theirs.

Such finer points, of course, were irrelevant when it came to a possible famine. The 5,000 tons were quickly distributed by the CN to those in critical need.

Because most of this activity in Brussels was unknown to Lucey, on Saturday, November 7, Heineman made a trip to Rotterdam to talk personally to the Rotterdam director. He told the captain of the newly created Comité National and the borrowing of wheat from the Germans. Lucey filled Heineman in on what he had been up to. Together they agreed to establish better communication between cities and their respective groups.

According to a CRB history, "During these first weeks there developed at times considerable irritation between Captain Lucey and his office in Rotterdam and the committee in Brussels, but as soon as each office understood better the difficulties of the other the early irritation wore off, and the work was soon running more smoothly."

Looking deeper into the communication and organizational issues, though, it became obvious to Lucey, Hoover, and others that what was needed most was a greater CRB presence in Brussels and throughout Belgium. A strong CRB office in Brussels was critical for smooth working relations with the CN, Whitlock, and the Germans. And, as Hoover thought privately, to keep Francqui in check.

Heineman, heading back to Brussels after his meeting with Lucey, was somewhat unconvinced of the need for strong communication between Belgium and the outside world. He and his associates in Brussels, according to one CRB history, "hardly realized the urgent necessity of closer co-operation with their colleagues in London and Rotterdam, so absorbed were they in daily negotiations with the German authorities about passes, transportation guarantees and permissions of various kinds. The Commission was really not yet established in Brussels, and there were as yet no delegates to supervise distribution, to maintain communications, and to collect the information so badly needed by the Commission." Additionally, "Heineman himself probably did not realize to the full the importance attached by the Allied governments to the direct control of the relief operations by the Commission."

Lucey and Hoover knew that to comply with the Allies requirements and to follow Hoover's plan, they had to extend the CRB reach and influence in Brussels and throughout the country. That would take CRB delegates—the same delegates that the British and Hoover had demanded from the beginning and the ones suggested by Sunderland in his report to Lucey. The same delegates that both Francqui and the Germans probably would have preferred not to see entering Belgium.

As Heineman motored back to Brussels, Hoover—probably pacing back and forth and jiggling his pocket change (as he was famously known to do) in London—was thinking not only about who those future delegates might be and where they might come from but also of the numerous other issues and problems that were arising inside Belgium, many of them created not by Germans but by Belgians. He would not tolerate for long a weak and ineffective Brussels office; a strong Brussels office was critical to CRB success. Soon he would start taking decisive action.

Where Did the Germans Stand on Relief?

Inside Belgium, no matter what Heineman and the CRB, or Francqui and the CN, did—or planned to do—none of it would work if the German military and civilian authorities in Belgium did not agree to their plans. One historian declared, "The success of the whole work depended to a very great degree upon the attitude of the military power toward the work." While it was true that Governor General von der Goltz had given his guarantees, "many details had yet to be arranged before the organization of the shipping service inside Belgium and of the system of distribution could be effectively completed."

Negotiations with the Germans fell mainly to the relief effort's neutral patrons—Whitlock, Gibson, and Villalobar—and two of the CRB executives in Brussels—Heineman and his associate Hulse. Numerous meetings and informal discussions led to a letter, sent on November 10, to the Germans by Whitlock and Villalobar, "explaining the situation and outlining the concessions that must be made by the Germans before the relief work could be permanently established."

The following day, the CN sent its own memorandum to Whitlock detailing what it felt the Germans needed to agree to before the CN could do its job. Multiple points were boldly and clearly stated.

The first part of the CN's memorandum involved requisitioning. The Belgian committee requested that the Germans stop all requisitions of cereals until the countrywide inventory had been completed. And if that count showed the total food stores "were not sufficient to permit the distribution of 350 grams [slightly more than twelve ounces] of flour per day to the civil population for a period of 100 days, the German Government should be asked to relinquish any further requisitions."

The second section was about freedoms. The CN requested freedom of movement of all material imported by the CRB and instructions to all German officers in Belgium explaining the situation and making sure such supplies would be off-limits to them. Tied to that request was the CN's plea to have the Germans "free the canals and rivers from obstructions, and . . . permit the use of railroads in the areas which could not be served by canal." The CN also requested that the "greatest possible freedom of communication must be permitted to the various committees inside Belgium to enable them to carry on their business." Additionally, the CRB should be allowed unrestricted use of telegraph service, "especially to Holland."

And, finally, Francqui and the CN brought up the financial situation. The memorandum stated that the sums needed for long-term food relief would be substantial, much more then the governor general had previously agreed to. "It was pointed out also that if subsidies from the Belgian Government could be obtained for the Commission in London, much of the financial difficulty would disappear. But these subsidies could only be obtained if the Germans would permit the equivalent sums to be paid out in Belgium by the Comité National in the interest of the Belgian Government from the money obtained from the sale of foodstuffs in Belgium. The Comité National would make payments to the communes and to functionaries and the employees of the Belgian Government."

Whitlock and Villalobar forwarded the CN's memorandum to Governor General von der Goltz with a letter that included "an appeal for favorable action."

They all waited impatiently for an answer. They would hear nothing for more than a week.

Van Doren Takes Precautions

Eugene van Doren was happy to help the elderly newspaper editor, Victor Jourdain, distribute the essay Jourdain had written raging against the German-sponsored *Bruxellois* newspaper. Jourdain was not only a relative by marriage but someone van Doren admired and adored. He had been worried, like other friends and associates, about Jourdain's reaction to the German invasion. However, when van Doren read Jourdain's editorial raging against the recently created German-controlled newspaper, he knew the old Jourdain was back and ready to fling some fire and brimstone at the occupiers.

With Jourdain's editorial in hand, van Doren spent many long hours in November working with his jelly duplicator, creating "pale, violet-inked sheets" that became Jourdain's pamphlet. Then, after his children had gone to bed, van Doren and his wife would lock themselves in their bedroom and quietly fold and stuff the pamphlets into envelopes. Most of the distribution to individual homes was done by van Doren himself during long evenings of surreptitious wanderings through the city.

With the fire lit within Jourdain, he not only contributed to the van Doren and the Abbé de Moor bulletins, but he also launched a major project to reveal to the world the atrocities the Germans had committed during the invasion. Working in an attic room in a wing of the *Patriote* offices just above his living quarters, the newspaper editor began to write in earnest. Through priests he knew, he "collected a number of eye-witness accounts of the atrocities committed during the German advance across Belgium." Jourdain was building not only a book but a "formidable indictment of Germany's terrorist campaign in Belgium." And every day, van Doren would drop by, collect the manuscript pages, hide them on his body, and then stroll home. Later, in the evenings, he would "type them onto the thinnest of paper," according to the book *Underground News*.

The tall and lanky Belgian cardboard manufacturer was getting deeper into clandestine activities. While they were still like a game to van Doren, he did begin to take some precautions, a few of which would later save his life and those of others.

At his home, he found a good hiding place to store his bulletins and other anti-German work. In the home's loft was a disused chimney that had an inspection plate on it. When it was time to hide things, van Doren would carefully remove the plate, tie all his papers together, lower the bundle on a long rope down the chimney hole, and replace the inspection plate.

For Jourdain, van Doren drilled three deep holes in the top of the editor's thick attic room door so he could roll up his papers at a moment's notice, insert them in the holes, and tap into place a wooden plug for nearly perfect hiding. Van Doren also installed a "discreet buzzer" in the attic that could be set off by someone in the living quarters below to warn Jourdain of any German raid.

While van Doren was learning, he had a long way to go to become as professional a clandestine operative as his abbé friend. The Catholic priest was a Belgian patriot who "never did things by halves," according to *Underground News*. When the Germans had invaded, he had wanted to give up his cassock and join the army, but others persuaded him he would be much more useful staying where he was. He was a healthy young adult male allowed by the Germans to stay in Brussels because of his calling. As a man of the cloth, he was given a little more freedom of movement than most—not to mention the fact that the heavy folds of his cassock could hide quite a number of items.

Soon, de Moor became "a member of a group of men acting on instructions from the Belgian Government at Le Havre [France]. . . . On the recommendation of Belgian Headquarters, he was also an agent for British Intelligence Service and a vital link in one of the chains of information that led from occupied territory via Flushing and Folkestone [two English Channel ports] to a little room in Whitehall [the center of the British government]."

As if that wasn't enough, he was also a letter drop for the Mot du Soldat and aided Allied soldiers to the border as a member of a group named after English nurse Edith Cavell. He told only his closest friends that he engaged in these two somewhat smaller clandestine activities because, as he put it, "I can only be shot once."

Those who did not know him would never have guessed the breadth of the Catholic priest's anti-German activities or that he possessed "half-a-dozen identity cards under different names," according to *Underground News*.

Van Doren knew of some his friend's activities and guessed of others, but he would probably have been surprised at just how deeply involved the Catholic priest was in the complex world of the underground. With de Moor on his side, though, van Doren had a fighting chance of staying alive.

Even with de Moor's knowledge and expertise, van Doren's chance of capture grew every day, as did those of any who engaged in underground activities. That was primarily because the Germans were not remaining idle. German *agents provocateurs* were all over Belgium, "posing as super-patriots" to lure people into divulging information or names related to clandestine activities. When they were successful, the Germans would make arrests, hold trials, and send their quarry to prison. Even though it had only been a few months since the invasion, these agents had, according to *Underground News*, "already made numerous victims, and people were not so ready as formerly to listen to strangers with patriotic schemes." People in Brussels and throughout the country were becoming much less trusting of those they did not know and were "anxious at all costs to avoid running foul of the German authorities, even to the extent of reading an uncensored paper."

One of the major targets for these German agents was the author of the pamphlet that had attacked the *Bruxellois* newspaper. During November, van Doren, de Moor, and Jourdain did not realize Jourdain's words had "struck a new and graver note among the publications of van Doren's secret 'jelly press,' [and] marked the beginning of a collaboration that was to culminate a few months later in the foundation of *La Libre Belgique* [*The Free Belgium*]."

In November, however, the idea of creating, printing, and distributing an underground newspaper called *La Libre Belgique* was only a spark of anger and frustration in the heart of Jourdain. It would take another month before that spark grew into a flame.

The German Occupation Gets Tougher

The Brussels that van Doren, Jourdain, and the abbé had known before the war was quickly disappearing as the Germans began exerting their control over the city and its citizens.

On Sunday, November 15, a day that Gibson recorded as the king's Saint's Day (currently Dynasty Day), word had gone around the city that there would be a special mass at the city's magnificent Cathedral of Saint Michael and Saint Gudula. Just before it was to begin, the German military authorities sent soldiers to the church and forbade the service.

Even the smallest gestures of patriotism or dissent were punished. In mid-November, according to Gibson, the little boy of the Countess de Buisseret was playing in the street when German troops passed by. He had imitated the soldiers' goose step and was promptly arrested. When the U.S. Legation's Belgian lawyer, Gaston de Leval, petitioned for his release, pointing out that he was just a child, the Germans replied that he "must be punished and would be left in jail for some days."

As for British subjects living in Brussels, they had initially been allowed their freedom. By November the Germans were arresting them, no matter their age or circumstances. Because the U.S. Legation had agreed to handle the affairs of the British Legation in Brussels once war had been declared, Whitlock and Gibson felt morally responsible for any British subject still in the city. Gibson wrote about the British: "We have our hands full dealing with poor people who don't want to be arrested and kept in prison until the end of the war and can't quite understand why *they* have to put up with it. It is pretty tough, but just another of the hardships of war, and while we are doing our best to have the treatment of these people made as lenient as possible, we can't save them."

On Wednesday, November 18, the Germans struck at one of Whitlock and Gibson's favorite places, the Brussels Golf Club. That morning, a servant from the club appeared at the legation and informed Gibson that there were fifty soldiers looting the place. Gibson went out that afternoon, not only to see if it was true but also to "get my golf clubs." He found "a lot of soldiers under the command of a corporal." They had already done their damage. "They had cleaned the place out of food, wine, linen, silver, and goodness knows what else." The poor steward, Florimont, had been arrested "because he would not tell them which of the English members of the club had gone away and where the others were staying."

The Germans were also getting tougher on permissions to travel, even for U.S. Legation staff. Gibson complained in his journal, "They want to limit us in all sorts of ways that make no difference to them, but cut down on our comfort." On November 19, Gibson continued: "[The Germans] announced to the Dutch Chargé [d'affaires; a diplomatic official] that our courier could no longer go—that everything would have to be sent by German field post. You would think that after the amount of hard work we have done for the protection of German interests and the scrupulous way in which we have used any privileges we have been accorded, they would exert themselves to make our task as easy as possible and show us some confidence. On the contrary, they treat us as we would be ashamed to treat our enemies."

That same day, November 19, snow began to fall in Brussels. Gibson recorded that it was a "light, dry snow" that turned the city into a "lovely sight." After that day, however, the weather turned "terribly cold," and the forecasters were saying "this will be one of the coldest winters ever known."

The weather was a portent of things to come for the legation, the CRB, Brussels, and Belgium. The American Thanksgiving came and went with hardly any acknowledgment from the U.S. Legation staff; all worked that day just as hard as they had any other. But during that week, Gibson got wind of some shake-ups in the German command of Belgium. "Both von der Goltz and von Luttwitz have gone and have been replaced—the first by [Baron Moritz Ferdinand] von Bissing, and the latter by General von Kraewel. There are several explanations for the changes, but we don't know what they mean."

Gibson wouldn't have believed it—especially with how he was currently feeling about the Germans—but the command changes meant the occupation was about to get much rougher and tougher.

TWENTY-SIX

London

As November dawned, the London CRB office was making great strides. John Beaver White was in charge of purchasing foodstuffs from around the world. He, Hunsiker, and Hoover "soon worked out advantageous arrangements for making food purchases in the various markets of the world, and for securing ships to carry the purchases to Belgium."

When it came to the number of ships alone, the need was staggering. The 80,000 tons of supplies needed in Belgium every month would necessitate approximately twenty oceangoing vessels arriving in Rotterdam every month. To sustain that arrival rate in port, the CRB would need more than double that number somewhere along the line—waiting in other ports, in the process of loading, or on the high seas heading for Rotterdam.

During normal times, without a war going on, securing such a number of ship charters would be impressive. To do so during the world's first global conflict would be unprecedented.

To make matters even more difficult, the English had thrown a monkey wrench into the shipping gears when they had initially agreed to allow the CRB to ship food to Rotterdam. The British permission had been for neutral ships only; no Allied ships could be used.

The first few cargoes that had left English ports in English ships had been allowed to do so as an exception. The CRB had been able to obtain the exceptions only after Hoover explained that the ships had already been loaded and ready to sail before the neutrality ship rule had been fully understood. The British govern-

Walter H. Page was U.S. ambassador to the United Kingdom and helped Hoover immensely in his quest to feed Belgium. (Public domain; multiple sources.)

ment granted the exceptions only because it felt the CRB had acted in good faith without realizing the restriction.

But after that minicrisis had passed, the British stipulation remained in place. And it was quickly realized by the CRB London office that "it was very difficult to obtain sufficient [ship] bottoms to carry the food needed. . . . If English ships could be used it would greatly lessen the difficulty and expense of securing ships."

What was needed was for the British government to reverse its policy. But the British had no interest in allowing its ships to be used if it meant they might be sunk by German U-boats, either as they carried their cargo to Rotterdam or as they returned with empty cargo holds to British ports.

Hoover immediately went to Page to approach the British to see if they would yield on this issue. After "considerable discussion on the matter," the British did agree to allow English ships to be used, but only if the German government agreed to extend the same protection it was giving the CRB's neutral ships.

Hoover immediately cabled Ambassador Gerard in Berlin to ask that he approach the Germans with such an extension of their protection guarantee. He then waited. And waited.

The British and the CRB

Meanwhile, some officials in the British government were questioning the entire Belgian relief program. On Wednesday, November 18, the Earl of Ronaldshay, representing those who did not fully support Belgian relief, stood up in the House of Commons and addressed the assembly. Through a series of questions he posed to Prime Minister Asquith, he asked if the government had "given its consent to large shipments of flour and food being sent to Belgium by an American Committee; whether some of these foodstuffs are being shipped from the Port of London; whether, seeing that Belgium is in German occupation and requisitions of food and money are constantly levied upon the inhabitants, [the prime minister] will say what steps are being taken to secure that these shipments shall not benefit the enemy?"

The issue of Belgian relief was now in the official record and awaited a reply to the Earl of Ronaldshay's multi-faceted question.

On behalf of the prime minister and the government, F. D. Acland, the British under-secretary of state for foreign affairs, responded. He first outlined the October 16 guarantee from von der Goltz that any foodstuffs brought into Belgium by the CRB would not be requisitioned "but would remain at the sole disposal of the committee." Acland went on to state that at the "request of the United States, Spanish, and Belgian governments, His Majesty's Government have undertaken not to interfere with shipments of foodstuffs from neutral countries in neutral bottoms consigned to the United States and Spanish Ministers at Brussels, or to the United States Consul at Rotterdam."

It was lucky for Hoover that Acland stated the U.S. government was officially behind the request and the work, because President Wilson had not yet determined if that would be the case. As it stood when Acland made the statement, the requests for British approval were being proffered by Page and Whitlock, who were technically speaking more as private American citizens than as representatives of the U.S. government on a fully sanctioned project.

Acland went on to say that "His Majesty's Government have made a Grant of £100,000 to the Belgian Government for the purchase of foodstuffs towards the cost of these supplies. This undertaking does not apply to general shipments of foodstuffs from this country. Any application for permission to export foodstuffs to Belgium from the United Kingdom is, therefore, considered by the Board of Trade in each individual case in the same way and on the same principles as are held to govern other applications for permission to export articles the export of which is restricted or prohibited."

The under-secretary did admit that permits had already been issued for the first few shipments of food out of London, but they were "consigned to the United States and Spanish Ministers at Brussels" and protected by the German guarantees. He finished by saying that he believed "a great deal of the food supplies are purchased by money subscribed in the United States to relieve distress of the Belgians, and the greatest care is taken that it should go to that and to no other object."

By the time Acland spoke, the entire issue of Belgian relief had become a major issue in the minds of the British public, due in part to Hoover and his associates and their diligent work with the media.

Nearly every day in the British press there were stories of local Belgian relief groups springing up to raise money. The Glasgow Belgian Relief Committee gave £10,000 and promised to give another £10,000 soon. And numerous stories were told of charitable giving from British citizens. The *Daily Citizen* reported on November 9 that "the following letter has been received by the Commission from a little girl at Edingthorpe Schools, North Walsham, Norfolk. 'We are sending from our school 16s. 6d. We collected it among ourselves, and not one of the teachers helped us. Governess thought of the idea and we did not spend any of the money on sweets that week. We English people ought to be very thankful we have not been treated like the Belgians.'" Even faraway Australia, despite its small population, had gathered together £100,000 pounds and in the first week of November had given it to the CRB. The country would continue throughout the war to send more money and supplies for Belgian relief.

Such public support was critical to Hoover's diplomatic efforts because few British politicians would have the stomach to publicly oppose, or even question, Belgian relief that had been thoroughly embraced by so many British subjects.

It was not until Monday, November 23, that Hoover finally received the cable he was hoping for from Gerard in Berlin. It gave "official approval to the CRB, and guaranteeing freedom from seizure to non-neutral vessels carrying supplies of the CRB to Dutch ports." Gerard's wire said:

A ship filled with food donated by the state of Virginia displayed large banners—standard on all CRB ships—to alert German U-boats that it was not an enemy vessel. (Public domain; *A Journal From Our Legation in Belgium,* Hugh Gibson, Doubleday, Page & Co., 1917.)

"The German Government is entirely in sympathy with the laudable work of the American Commission for Belgian relief. Germany will not interfere with any neutral ships bound for Holland with food from the United States, if the food is destined for Belgium. Subject to later revocation, the German Government agrees to permit unneutral ships also to carry food for the Belgians to Dutch ports, and will give the same guarantee as for neutral ships."

The cable went on to say that the Germans recommended that each non-neutral ship carry a certificate from American authorities testifying that the food was being shipped via the CRB to Belgium, and that a pass should be issued to every such ship by the German ambassador in Washington.

It was a laborious process, but from then on each ship received from U.S. customs a certificate stating the cargo and destination, which led the German ambassador in Washington to issue a permit, which led to a safe-conduct pass by the German Consulate at the U.S. port of departure, which led—finally—to a certificate from the British Consulate.

Not only did the CRB ships carry a wealth of documentation, they were all—neutral and non-neutral—supplied with large banners to hang over the sides that proclaimed, "Commission for Relief in Belgium, Rotterdam." Unlike Allied ships, they also ran with their lights on during night steaming so that U-boats could see that they were CRB ships doing relief work.

This entire shipping situation not only resulted in a long-term process for approvals, but it also helped pave the way for a long-term solution to Hoover's working relationship with the British. The problems and challenges he had seen in the first shipments to Rotterdam made Hoover realize that he needed a way either through or around the tremendous bureaucracy and red tape that ensnarled those who petitioned the British government.

He once again went to Ambassador Page for help. This time, Hoover suggested that Page request of the British government that Hoover be allowed to go straight to those in charge of what he needed rather than going through diplomatic channels. Hoover also asked that one person be assigned to CRB matters to help facilitate movement through the system.

In short order, the British agreed. "The Foreign Office assigned Lord Eustace Percy to the work of co-operating with the Commission, and the members of the Commission were permitted to go directly to the officials concerned in any matter of Commission business, instead of having to go the circuitous diplomatic route. This ready and friendly co-operation on the part of the British authorities made the work of the Commission in London infinitely easier," according to one historian.

Hoover Comes out Swinging at Francqui

Shipping was far from Hoover's only concern. During the first weeks of November, he kept receiving nearly daily reports from Lucey that reflected the Rotterdam director's frustrations at the lack of communications and general difficulties with the Brussels office.

On Saturday, November 14, Hoover sent a long letter to Francqui "outlining the relation of the CRB Rotterdam office to the offices in London and Brussels, the methods of accounting, and the relief campaign inaugurated in America." Reading between the lines, anyone could see that the letter was a strong statement that Hoover and the Americans were running the show and if Francqui wanted the show to continue, he'd have to play by Hoover's rules.

The letter's first sentence was uncharacteristically subtle for the American mining engineer and did not reflect the substantial multipage letter to come: "It seems desirable that we should get a little more system in the relations of this office and the Rotterdam office with the head committee in Brussels."

The straightforward Hoover came out swinging right after that, though, on the subject of who was to control the critical Rotterdam office. Francqui felt that because he and his CN would be sending orders to Lucey as to what shipments should go where, the entire office should be controlled from Brussels. Hoover had a slightly different point of view. He wrote Francqui that it was "entirely impossible" to run the Rotterdam office from Brussels simply because of the slow communications in and out of Belgium. Hoover stated that because the London office was "in hourly communication" with the Rotterdam office, the "Rotterdam office should be a branch of the London [office]."

And because the CRB was consigning all food to the Rotterdam office, Hoover wanted a representative of the "Brussels committee, who should be a substantial business man, who will remain there at all times and put himself generally at the disposal of the head of this office, whom we should select."

Hoover did acknowledge that Rotterdam's allocation of foodstuffs—where to send what to whom—"must absolutely rest with you in Brussels." But even here, Hoover added an American twist for greater accountability. He reminded Francqui that all the supplies were only allowed into Belgium because they were officially consigned to the American minister, Whitlock. Therefore, Hoover suggested that Whitlock should be asked to approve all allocation orders.

Knowing full well Whitlock's heavy workload at the time, Hoover innocently wrote, "I do not know whether this will be placing an unnecessarily large amount of detail on Mr. Whitlock, but I feel that in view of the political situation and the clearness with which this will define matters so far as our end of the business is concerned, it is a labor which he will be willing to undertake." Those who knew Whitlock would have probably agreed that the minister's heavy sigh at reading Hoover's words would have been heard clear across the channel.

Using the lack of communications within Belgium as leverage, Hoover reinforced the need for what he really wanted, CRB delegates in Belgium. "We have the feeling that if a corps of our Americans can be recruited (in which we are now actively engaged) so that some of these gentlemen may be established as guardians at different centers, these communications will thereby be facilitated, as they can possibly move more freely through the country than your own countrymen."

To possibly justify or soften all that he was saying, Hoover then gave an extensive rundown on the successful efforts in America for Belgian relief. He prefaced them with the statement: "We have carried on, with the assistance of practically the whole of the American press, an enormous propaganda on the subject of the Belgian people. We have cabled to all associations of whom we could hear, stimulating them as to position. We have cabled to the governors of every state asking them to see that such an association was set up in their territory."

Hoover noted several highlights. The San Francisco Chamber of Commerce, "at the instance of my wife," purchased 5,000 tons of food and chartered the ship *Camino*, which would sail November 30; the Seattle Chamber of Commerce and the state of Idaho were combining to secure a ship's cargo of food; ex-governor Walter R. Stubbs of Kansas had begun "an efficient committee" to collect donations; David S. Chamberlain of Iowa was "organizing a complete cargo of maize"; in Minnesota, William C. Edgar, the editor of the trade publication *Northwestern Miller*, was putting together a ship of donated flour from millers in the northern part of the Mississippi Valley; the Philadelphia Belgian Relief Committee, working with the *Ladies Home Journal*, which had run the queen's letter of appeal, had already sent the SS *Thelma* with 2,900 tons of cereals; the Rockefeller Foundation sent 4,000 tons aboard the SS *Massapequa*; the people of Nova Scotia, having already sent 2,100 tons, were going to be sending 3,000 tons more on November 13; the people of Ottawa were soon sending 4,000 tons.

Hoover also announced that Belgian relief organizations were getting started in Spain, Italy, British Columbia, North Carolina, Maine, and Virginia. Almost as an afterthought, Hoover wrote that a CRB office had been opened in New York City to "undertake the free transportation of foodstuffs into Belgium," but there was much more to the opening of the CRB New York City office than Hoover would ever admit to Francqui.

Not forgetting the power of women—his wife, Lou, wouldn't let that happen—Hoover told Francqui that the CRB had organized a women's division in New York and had "the cooperation of all of the women's clubs and societies in the United States."

To handle the ever-increasing donations and purchases of foodstuffs, the CRB had also taken on "some steamers on time charter for regular trips across the Atlantic," which were expected to "supplement the irregular supplies of gift food by purchases to keep these steamers employed." The CRB had even secured the "two largest shipping firms in England, and they have agreed to handle the whole of our shipping problems for absolutely no cost whatever for commissions or agency charges or anything of that nature, and they have placed one of their most expert men in our office and at our elbow." The CRB was on its way to becoming a massive shipping operation.

Nearing the end of the letter, Hoover outlined once again what the CRB really was and how the CN fit into the CRB operation: "In our London office we are conducting three commissions: i.e., the American Commission, the Spanish Commission, and the Comité National de Secours et d'Alimentation. . . . We combine representatives of all of these commissions into the general organization which we style simply 'The Commission for Relief in Belgium,' which is dealing with all of the minor points of international complexity."

One can only imagine Francqui's reaction to this direct letter and its commanding tone.

TWENTY-SEVEN

Hoover Fights for U.S. Dominance

While Hoover, from London, was fighting for supremacy with Francqui in Belgium, he was also waging a similar war with others in America. The U.S. conflict revolved around which group was going to be the one major American organization representing the Belgian relief effort. Hoover's firm belief was that such a vast undertaking as feeding an entire nation, which required multiple international agreements during the waging of a world war, needed one organization to lead it. He had already been forced to accept a partnership with the Comité National. He wasn't about to accept any others, especially within his own country.

When the Germans had first invaded and stories of Belgian devastation and refugees had filled newspapers and magazines, spontaneous relief groups had sprung up all around the world—most notably in Britain and America. The Belgian ministers within these two countries had tried to aid and stimulate as much charitable activity as possible.

There was a problem with this situation, though. According to one CRB history, "All these efforts, however, had been scattered and uncentralised. The various activities often overlapped. There was no common object to which the various committees were devoted. There even existed invidious jealousy and competition between the various committees."

When the CRB was formed October 22, Hoover had immediately set out to establish his own branches around America, but he had also wanted to bring all the existing relief efforts under his umbrella, even if some of the parties objected. "During the first few months embarrassing complications were occasionally encountered before the Commission's position was recognized, but ultimately the difficulties were overcome and the work of centralising charitable efforts was put on a harmonious basis."

Two Major Competitors

Most of the spontaneous, early American relief efforts and groups were small and localized, but two in particular, both headquartered in New York City, were substantial and had grown bigger every day: the Belgian Relief Committee and the Rockefeller Foundation.

The Belgian Relief Committee had been founded in the late summer by a "few modest Belgians and their sympathizers," according to one magazine article. At its head was Rev. J. F. Stillemans, a Catholic priest of Belgian birth who had recently moved from Oklahoma to New York City to take charge of a bureau for aiding Belgian immigrants. With that job no longer viable because of the war, Stillemans got involved in trying to help the Belgian refugees and became the president of the Belgian Relief Committee.

The chairman of the executive committee, and the real power behind the group, was Robert W. de Forest, the vice president of the American Red Cross. During a vacation in Europe that was interrupted by the start of the war, he had seen the Belgian devastation. When he returned home he started the group outside the confines of the Red Cross.

The Belgian members of de Forest's organization included the Belgian consul in New York, the Belgian minister to the United States, and a well-to-do patron, Madame Vandervelde. Her husband, Emile Vandervelde, was a member of the Belgian Commission that had been sent to America in September to appeal for American condemnation of Germany's alleged violations of international law. She had become a darling of New

York City, and the country, when she announced she would not go home until she had collected $1 million to aid her country.

Another prominent member of the Belgian Relief Committee was Thomas Fortune Ryan, a tobacco, insurance, and transportation mogul who had turned philanthropist. He was also a sore spot for Hoover. While Hoover had not known Ryan previously, Shaler had talked with him in London in early October. Ryan's prominence, business acumen, and philanthropy had made him a perfect candidate for CRB executive in New York. At the founding meeting of the CRB on October 22, item ten on Hoover's memorandum of the meeting had been "a telegraph to be drafted to Mr. Thomas J.[*sic*] Ryan of New York and ordered to be dispatched." Ryan had not responded immediately to Hoover's invitation and then surprised the CRB executive committee in London by joining the Belgian Relief Committee instead.

The Belgian Relief Committee's influential members were a potent combination of representatives of religion, professional charity, business, and politics. And they were a fundraising force to be reckoned with, having amassed nearly $200,000 by the end of October. On Friday, October 23, a day after the official founding of the CRB, but probably before most Americans had heard the news, the Belgian Relief Committee cabled $50,000 to Ambassador Page, asking that he put it to good use for Belgian relief.

In addition to the Belgian Relief Committee, there was the Rockefeller Foundation. Established in 1913 by thirty-nine-year-old John D. Rockefeller Jr., the foundation's mission was to "promote the well-being of mankind throughout the world." The foundation's first grant of $100,000 was given to the American Red Cross to purchase property for its headquarters in Washington, D.C. When Rockefeller learned of the Belgian plight, he was ready to throw the financial resources of his new organization behind the relief effort. On Sunday, November 1, he issued a statement declaring his foundation would "give millions of dollars, if necessary, for the relief of non-combatants in countries involved in this war." It had already chartered the steamship *Massapequa* to take 4,000 tons of supplies to Belgium.

With the previous Rockefeller Foundation grant to the American Red Cross, and de Forest's position as Red Cross vice president and chairman of the Belgian Relief Committee, it was natural that the two organizations would join forces. It also appears that de Forest thought the CRB could be a European satellite, or distribution arm, of his Belgian Relief Committee.

A November 3 *New York Times* article, "Plan Co-Operation in Belgian Relief," said that Belgian Minister Emmanuel Havenith and de Forest had had a meeting "in regard to co-operation between the Belgian Relief Committee and the Rockefeller Foundation." De Forest said after the meeting that while the Rockefeller Foundation's statement on November 1 about spending millions on Belgian relief was "on its own initiative . . . there is complete co-operation between it and the New York Committee."

De Forest also said that "complete international co-operation" was taking place among his Belgian Relief Committee, the Belgian minister, and the "American Committee in London, in which our Ambassador in London, Mr. Page; our Minister in Belgian [*sic*], Brand Whitlock, and our Minister in The Hague, Dr. Henry van Dyke, are members, and of which Herbert Hoover is Chairman."

While de Forest did acknowledge Hoover and his group, it was only as a piece in de Forest's organization, not the other way around. He told the *Times* that "all American contributions for the immediate relief of Belgians in Belgium, whether received by the Belgian Minister or the New York Committee, or any other Belgian Relief Committee, so far as the Belgian Minister and the New York Committee can control the same, will be placed in the hands of a supply committee, consisting of Thomas F. Ryan and Robert W. de Forest. This supply committee will purchase supplies and forward them direct by the steamer load as soon as they have sufficient amounts from time to time to make up a cargo."

In de Forest's organizational chart, it seemed as if Hoover and the CRB would be relegated to mere middlemen in the chain of distribution between de Forest's group and Francqui's group. Not exactly what Hoover had in mind.

De Forest finished his statement to the *Times* with a call to rally American relief efforts around him and his organization: "There are undoubtedly many committees organized and organizing in different parts of the country for Belgian relief. It is earnestly requested that these committees forward the amounts collected by them as promptly as possible."

Less than a week later, de Forest and the Rockefeller Foundation were back in the *Times*. The Rockefeller Foundation announced it had "arranged to provide a steamship pier, to charter ships, and to convey free of charge from New York to Belgium such supplies as the public may wish to contribute." This plan was "in co-operation with the Belgian Relief Committee of New York, of which Mr. Robert W. de Forest is Chairman."

Hoover was not happy to hear the news for multiple reasons. For one, according to a CRB history, "In these arrangements the Commission had no part, and indeed was hardly even consulted, as the New York committee and the Rockefeller Foundation regarded it merely as a distributing agency, and proposed to organise themselves the collecting end in America." More importantly, though, free shipping was a huge PR move that would go a long way in establishing dominance in the minds of the public.

The article also reported that the Rockefeller Foundation was preparing to send a "War Relief Commission" of experts to Europe "to advise as to time, place and means whereby relief can be best provided for needy non-combatants in all the warring countries." Three experts would sail for Europe on November 11. The chairman of the group was Wickliffe Rose, director general of the Rockefeller Foundation's International Health Commission. He would be accompanied by Henry James Jr., manager of the Rockefeller Institute for Medical Research, and Ernest P. Bicknell, national director of the American Red Cross.

Accompanying the article was another appeal to the American public to give money or supplies, and it was signed by Rockefeller, de Forest, and members of the Belgian Relief Committee. Lastly, the article made only one slight mention of the "American Committee": "The arrangements for distribution have been made by the American Committee in London, of which Ambassador Page is Chairman, and provide for distributing stations in Belgium under the immediate supervision of the American Consuls in the afflicted region." There was no mention of Hoover, the chairman of the committee, and the article erroneously assigned that position to Page. The newspaper had probably simply printed what had been stated or provided by de Forest.

Even worse, a four-page article that was probably written in early November and later published in a prestigious monthly journal, *American Review of Reviews*, featured de Forest and the Belgian Relief Committee. Only one sentence mentioned "the committee in London of which Ambassador Page is at the head," while another mentioned Brand Whitlock. Nowhere was Hoover's name to be found.

All of this media coverage had an impact. One CRB historian noted, "the impression prevailed in America at this time that the Commission was only a London committee under Page's direction to forward supplies to Belgium. Hence the New York and other committees went on

making independent appeals and arranging independent shipments vari-
ously consigned to the American Ambassador to London, the Minister at
The Hague, the Consul in Rotterdam, or to the Commission."

"We Must Centralise Efforts"

None of this—from minor slights and major omissions to the fact that
the two New York groups were gathering serious momentum—was lost
on Hoover. In a telegram to New York at the time, Hoover's frustration
is clear, to the point where he let slip a highly unusual use of the word
"myself": "To the embarrassment of the Ambassadors, people in America
insist on cabling them instead of myself in these matters. We must cen-
tralise efforts and get people to recognize the Commission as the only
channel for relief in Belgium."

But how was Hoover to get de Forest and the Belgian Relief Committee
into the backseat—not only in the minds of the public but in the minds
of U.S. government officials—when de Forest wanted to drive?

Hoover would need some time to marshal his forces to deal with this
threat to his organizational chart. That was especially true considering
there was a major war raging, communications technology was limited to
overseas cables, and it took an average of ten days to two weeks to cross
more than 3,000 miles of ocean.

In the meantime, he knew he had to cooperate as best he could—if
nothing else, for good PR. He, no doubt, reminded himself that nothing
really mattered except getting food into Belgium. A way of publicly showing cooperation and helping the Belgians, while privately planning how
to deal with de Forest, came at the end of October. During the CRB's
first official week of operations, Hoover committed to match funds with
de Forest to buy a shipload of food. The *New York Times* reported October
31 that each group had put in $150,000, and Hoover's first week's report
of CRB activity showed £35,000 (the equivalent sum) as a joint purchase
with the de Forest committee.

To gain his own momentum, Hoover knew he needed a strong CRB
presence in New York. He turned to one of his closest friends and associates, Lindon W. Bates, an internationally known civil engineer.

When Bates had first read that Hoover was organizing a relief effort,
he had cabled his friend on October 19: "It's a fine idea; you were always
a born consolidator, and would consolidate the solar system if there was

a chance to make a needed fundamental change in this wicked world." On October 28, Hoover had cabled Bates to see if he would be interested in working with the CRB. Bates had immediately replied that he would, and that his wife would try to organize all the women's organizations in America to aid Belgium.

On October 30, Hoover cabled Bates and stated: "Stronger action than that proposed by Ryan is necessary. . . . We are asking [for] the formation of a committee of leading New York men who will recognise that the situation requires a strong and important body in New York to control the expenditure of the various relief funds already raised and see that they reach Belgium in the shape of food, instead of being given independent application. . . . Under the various international agreements it is utterly impossible for any relief or foodstuffs to reach Belgium except through this Commission."

There, in the last sentence, was a major key to Hoover's taking complete command. The multiple and complex agreements and guarantees that the CRB and CN—working with diplomats Page, Whitlock, Gibson, and Villalobar—had secured from Germany, England, and Belgium were proof, at least in Hoover's mind, that the CRB was the only authorized agent to bring relief into Belgium.

Hoover began to work on multiple fronts to counteract de Forest and the Rockefeller Foundation. He knew that the Belgian minister in Washington was a supporter of the Belgian Relief Committee and had not responded well to the CRB's direct appeals for cooperation. So Hoover went to the minister's bosses, Belgian officials in London and Le Havre, and "arranged to have positive and definite instructions sent to the Belgian Minister in Washington that all committees organised under this patronage should work through the Commission." While the minister was not so quick to roll over, he ultimately did after additional pressure was applied.

Hoover also added to all media releases a statement that read, "The Commission for Relief in Belgium is the official body recognized by the various governments for the transmission of food-shipments into Belgium; it is the only channel through which food can be introduced into Belgium; and has by its association with a committee in Belgium the only efficient agency for the distribution of food within the country."

Hoover also turned to his ally Page, who always seemed ready to go in any direction Hoover suggested. According to one CRB man, Page once remarked, "Mr. Hoover never did me the unkindness to accept my advice." This time, Page probably didn't need much convincing of Hoover's consolidation plan, for he had received numerous cables from various relief organizations asking the same questions about how they could help Belgium. He probably wouldn't have minded if they all went to Hoover rather than himself.

At Hoover's prompting, Page sent a request to the U.S. State Department for official recognition of the CRB. Hoover wanted President Wilson to tell the American public that his organization, the CRB, was the only official, authorized group to handle Belgian relief.

On November 7, an indirect, but nonetheless critical, answer came when Robert Lansing, the legal adviser to the U.S. secretary of state, replied to a request for information from the governor of Iowa. Lansing's reply, which was published in the *New York Times*, had included: "The Commission for Relief in Belgium is the only agency that has machinery for the distribution of food in Belgium. It has the benefit of complete diplomatic arrangements with all the belligerent governments. It works with the only committee in Belgium that has machinery for local distribution in every community. No cargo is safe unless it is properly shipped and consigned. All shipping directions are given by Herbert Hoover, chairman of the Commission in London."

While not official presidential recognition, Lansing's statement was an important acknowledgment of preeminence. Despite Hoover's and Page's appeals, though, President Wilson would not go further. In fact, Wilson actually viewed U.S. diplomats such as Page, Whitlock, and Gibson as acting as private citizens when working for Belgian relief—a finer point that was never fully publicized nor brought to the complete attention of the belligerents. While there is little doubt that Wilson morally supported the CRB's plan, full endorsement might have jeopardized his stand on neutrality, especially when considering the myriad international agreements that were required for relief to proceed. Personal support, in this case, did not translate into official approval.

Some might have contended that an added benefit to this lack of official recognition was potential legal defense—albeit flimsy—of the U.S. government if anything went horribly wrong: "What! You thought these men were acting officially on America's behalf? Why they were only private citizens."

In an ironic twist, Hoover was almost undone by his desire for official recognition and quest for dominance. The back-and-forth in the press between Hoover and de Forest and the Rockefeller Foundation was perceived by some as creating confusion in the minds of the general public and the government. Additionally, since October there had been discussion within the U.S. government about establishing an overarching committee for relief. On November 12 the *Washington Post* ran a front-page article that said President Wilson was going to form a "central committee" to oversee the Belgian relief.

If Hoover had been frustrated and angry before with two NYC relief groups in the picture, he was probably apoplectic at the thought of U.S. bureaucrats mucking up his show. He scrambled through multiple levels of emissaries to get the message to Wilson that such governmental intervention was not necessary and would, in fact, hurt the cause.

In a rare show of solidarity, most of those already in Belgian relief agreed with Hoover. "Nobody, it seemed, wanted a single national committee," according to Nash. The common thought was that such a move by the American government might be considered a breach of America's neutral stand (similar to officially recognizing one relief group over the others). Hoover agreed with that, but he also drove home to anyone who would listen the notion that the Midwest and the West would not give to Belgian relief through an East-Coast-based governmental committee. This somewhat parochial argument, hitting two beloved targets of Westerners (East Coast elites and the federal government) was a bit weak, but enough people felt it held some truth that it helped do the trick. The idea of a national relief committee died a quick death.

During this period of media battles, Hoover decided it was not enough to have a NYC-based committee led by Bates. He felt it had become critical to open a New York City office of the CRB. In the initial October press release announcing the CRB, there had been no mention of a New York office. But it was a logical move and one that had probably been discussed since the beginning. The charitable donations of literally hundreds of CRB-inspired relief groups could be collected with greater ease from New York than London. And, of course, a side benefit was that a NYC office established an American base from which the CRB presence could become better known and, it was hoped, put into proper Hoover-perspective de Forest's Belgian Relief Committee.

On November 13, with pressure building from the Belgian Relief Committee's media campaign, Hoover asked Bates if he would open a New York City office and serve as vice chairman of the CRB. Hoover's

first choice had been Ryan—as it had been with the American committee—but Ryan had surprised Hoover and joined the competition. Bates
agreed. Joining him was Robert D. MacCarter, a well-known electrical
engineer who had volunteered his services to Hoover.

Shipping Becomes the Key to Preeminence

Through all these machinations, the general public would have wondered, no doubt, what all the fuss was about. Why was Hoover so opposed
to de Forest and the Rockefeller Foundation when they were raising
money, gathering food, and shipping it to Rotterdam?

To Hoover, it all came down to control over shipping. He would be
happy if the two other NYC groups simply collected money and supplies.
The shipping, which would ultimately be massive, was a different matter. Hoover believed that the organization that controlled the shipping
would be perceived by the public and government officials as the preeminent relief organization. And taking charge of shipping would complete
Hoover's chain of control for getting relief into Belgium. There was a very
practical consideration for that. According to one CRB history, "If the
various Belgian relief bodies in different parts of the world each sought to
charter ships for their own cargoes, the result would be very unsatisfactory.
The committees would be competing with each other for bottoms, and
would certainly have to pay a bigger price than would be the case if all
shipping matters were to be taken over by the Commission."

For Hoover and the CRB, the biggest hurdle to the control of shipping
had come when the Rockefeller Foundation and de Forest had announced
they would provide free shipping from American shores to Rotterdam.

At first, there didn't seem to be much Hoover could do to counteract
such a tremendous move. The generosity was overwhelming, and the tide
of American support for de Forest and the Rockefeller Foundation surely
swelled.

Hoover was near his wit's end as to how to counteract such a move
when salvation arrived from a highly unlikely source: Émile Francqui.
Hoover received word of Francqui's securing of the Belgian bank loans of
£600,000 ($3 million) for the relief efforts. Finally, Hoover had something
concrete to work with.

In a huge strategic gamble, Hoover checkmated de Forest and Rockefeller by saying that Francqui's money was strictly for transportation

costs and if the NYC groups continued with their plan, their actions would jeopardize the $3 million. Hoover maintained they needed to back away from shipping to guarantee that this money would go toward helping the Belgians.

The only problem with Hoover's statement was that there was no such stipulation on Francqui's money. In fact, on November 12, as historian Nash wrote, "Hoover informed Francqui that he and his colleagues had *decided* to apply the fund for this purpose and to announce that it had been given with this proviso, lest (he said) the loan discourage charitable giving."

To sweeten the pot, Hoover added that all shipping of gifts via rail within the United States would be covered for free—an offer not made by the two other groups.

When Hoover made that announcement, he had nothing to back it up. The Belgian minister in America had already secured free rail services for Belgian relief, but he had so far refused to transfer that gift to the CRB. By the end of November, though, Hoover was able to honor his commitment because the minister finally relented under serious pressure from his government.

How did de Forest and the Rockefeller Foundation take the news? They did not call Hoover's bluff. They begrudgingly backed away from providing shipping. With great understatement, a history of the CRB stated: "The New York Belgian Relief Committee and the Rockefeller Foundation were at first loath to abandon the scheme they had devised for collecting and shipping themselves the food to be contributed in America, but they were soon convinced of the wisdom of leaving all such matters to the expert services of the Commission, and of devoting their efforts to the collecting of funds."

By November 20, a meeting of Bates, de Forest, and the Rockefeller Foundation determined that de Forest's group would be the preeminent relief agency for New York and the surrounding area only. The Rockefeller Foundation would continue to provide funds but back away from shipping.

From this point on, "The Commission would, therefore, take over the entire control of all food from the time of shipment. This measure gave to the Commission immediately the necessary control of shipments and made it possible to effectively manage the collecting and shipping of the food supplies contributed throughout the United States."

In the coming months, there would be a few bumps that would need smoothing out, but basically, from late November forward, the Rockefeller

Foundation and the Belgian Relief Committee would play just fund-raising and supply-gathering roles for Belgium relief.

Once again, Hoover had somehow miraculously cleared away obstacles that had threatened his exclusive control of Belgian relief. As Nash put it, "With the securing of the Rockefeller Foundation's seal of approval, the principal challenge—real or imagined—thus far to Hoover's preeminence in Belgian relief work disappeared. But what a wearying struggle it had been."

Tired or not, Hoover was forever the tough pragmatist. He outlined what happened and the CRB's success in correspondence to Bates: "I do not wonder at all that the de Forest line contingent are sore, as they thought they could treat us like school-children, and have found that here has grown up the one organization which is pointed to with satisfaction by all of the belligerent Powers, and with pride by all good-feeling Americans. They might have enjoyed considerable participation in it if they had played the game with us, but they themselves, by their own acts, put themselves out of court, and I am not at all sorry."

Hoover followed with a strong summary to Bates: "You can always bear in mind that the people who are going to control this Commission are the people who control the money and the people who control the international agreements, and that we have both of these things in our grip."

Hoover Turns to Finding Delegates

After such a battle, Hoover didn't even pause for rest or celebration (at least not publicly). The time had come to find volunteers to enter Belgium as CRB delegates.

By middle to late November, ten to fifteen men had floated into the organization like flotsam onto a beach and for the most part informally had become CRB delegates. Bell was in Rotterdam working with Lucey; Edward Curtis was courier between Rotterdam and Brussels; Frederick W. Meert, who had attended universities in Brussels and Louvain before the war, took charge of the Brabant Province on November 12; Robinson Smith, a writer whose book, *The Life of Cervantes*, had just been published, seemed to appear one November day in Brussels and was put to work as the chief delegate of the Hainaut Province; James Dangerfield, who had worked two years in Ghent, became a delegate in Flanders in early

December; and E. E. Hunt, the wandering journalist, would soon join the group through contacts in Holland.

Others would join them in a similarly random fashion through the next month, with most of them young, adventuresome, and usually from good universities. They included George S. Jackson (Harvard), Amos D. Johnson Jr. (University of Kansas), T. Harwood Stacy (University of Texas), Carleton B. Gibson (University of Alabama), Floyd S. Bryant (University of Nevada and Oxford), William M. Sullivan (Brown and Oxford), Frank H. Gailor (University of the South and Oxford), and William H. Sperry.

The men had found the CRB by following various paths. Some had had earlier associations with Hoover or one of the founding members. Others had come through word-of-mouth. Still others had been living in Belgium for school or business and had offered to help when the war broke out.

While each one of them was critical at the time for helping the organization move forward, they represented a haphazard way of recruiting that was not practical or reliable for the huge relief program on the horizon.

The big question was a tough one: Where could Hoover find some reliable volunteers? It could take weeks if not months to recruit volunteers from America. By middle to late November, the need was immediate.

"It occurred to Hoover to apply for volunteers among the American students at Oxford University," recalled Oxford student George Spaulding. It made practical sense. Here was a large group of relatively responsible Americans with no business obligations and, with fall term ending soon, six weeks off for winter break. It just might be the stopgap measure needed until permanent staff could be recruited from back home.

But would young students looking forward to winter break be willing to give up their plans for the unknown in German-occupied Belgium? And more importantly, would they be capable of handling the job, which was still not fully understood or defined?

TWENTY-EIGHT

At Oxford

By the middle of November, most of the American Rhodes scholars had settled into campus life and were adjusting to the English weather. David Nelson wrote home November 20 that he kept gaining weight and, at 161 pounds, was the heaviest he had ever been. "It's a chronic disease here they say. The climate is so damp and heavy that one has to exercise quite strenuously to keep in shape."

Each morning from 7:30 to 7:40, students had roll call in the main quad, where each name was checked off a list by the Don (a head tutor or fellow at Oxford) in charge. "Before the war, 'rollers' were held at eight, which was more reasonable." Nelson and the rest of his classmates were getting ready for their end-of-term exams. Nelson had an exam called a "Divvers," which was "mainly Greek Testament, the 'Divinity Exam' — hence 'divvers.'" School would be out for six weeks, from December 6 until late January.

When not in class or studying, Nelson kept a sharp eye out for the school's proctors, who patrolled the campus and the town as the "official guardians of the peace of the University." They could reprimand and fine any student for misdeeds or inappropriate behavior they witnessed. "They march about the streets at night with full paraphernalia of robes and caps and whatnot, while two Bobbies—policemen—march on before." As such, they were relatively easy to spot from a distance. "The main thing is to see them first; then if they are not too close you run. If they are quite near, however, it is not considered good form to run. And so you wait, are told to report next morning, and are then fined ten bob, one or two quid, or whatever the offense demands."

Even with such a normal academic life as Nelson and the others were experiencing, they were still not far from war, with wounded soldiers convalescing in and around them all the time. The students also had to contend with the Order of the White Feather. Founded at the start of the war by Admiral Charles Fitzgerald and supported by prominent people such as author Mrs. Humphry Ward, the order's purpose was to shame young men into enlisting by persuading young women to present men not in uniform with a white feather. The white feather as a symbol of cowardice came from cockfighting, in which a cock with a white tail feather was believed to be a poor fighter. Even though America was neutral, it was still difficult for these American students at Oxford to receive such a feather from a young woman. No amount of explaining helped the feeling many of them had when it happened.

Belgium was also on the minds of the students. Oxford, like many other British cities, hosted a Belgian Day in November that raised money for Belgian refugees in England. The Oxford students took the event to heart as only enthusiastic young students could. Nelson wrote home: "They sold little flags in Belgian colors and little bows of tissue paper. . . . The whole town took on a very gala appearance, for flags were everywhere in evidence, and everyone wore a Belgian bow. Some of the undergrads would buy enough to cover the fronts of their coats; some wore them on their hats, at their knees, and on their shoes. Two wore them on their gowns, covering them so thickly that you couldn't tell they had gowns on, and were 'progged,' that is arrested by the Proctors of the U. for 'unseemly conduct' and fined two quid each." The event raised £1,750, or about $8,750.

———————————————

Oliver C. Carmichael, who had just turned twenty-three on October 3, was in the second year of his Rhodes scholarship. The eighth child and fifth

Twenty-three-year-old Rhodes scholar Oliver C. Carmichael was one of the second wave of Oxford students to become a CRB delegate. (Carmichael family archives.)

son of Daniel Carmichael, a farmer in the small agricultural community of Brownsville, Alabama, Oliver had picked cotton and plowed fields behind a mule when he was growing up. The pursuit of education and knowledge began early with Carmichael and led him to a degree from the University of Alabama and acceptance in the Rhodes scholarship program in 1913. For leisure he would box, play tennis, and bike ride.

Striving always for academic excellence, Carmichael was an intense young man who could at times be focused on internal reflection and concerns—as many other young people have been for generations. A few days after his birthday, on an outing with friends, he took some moments to be alone and wrote: "I was disgusted with the stupid chattering and would be jokes of our party, so I remained by this stream alone. I was, to tell the truth, almost disgusted with life, itself, everything seemed so vain and nothing really worthwhile."

A few weeks later, as a young man searching for purpose, he admitted: "I have felt particularly down today. I wonder over and over again what life means, what my life is intended to mean. What ambition is, that horrible monster within that won't leave you alone when you would be quiet and peaceful. It must mean that there is something for me to do. O' that I could see that something, could decide on it."

By early November, Carmichael "felt a sort of indescribable mental depression which denied, in spite of me, the value of life. I prayed with unusual earnestness for guidance into usefulness." On November 22, he wrote: "Have felt a distinct restlessness, uneasiness and discontent for some reason. I wish sometimes that I didn't care, that the fires of ambition would stop. It does make one awfully uncomfortable."

These were the serious reflections of a young man wanting to find purpose and to feel that he was accomplishing something with his life.

He wanted and needed time away from the cloistered life of an Oxford student so that he could see and experience more of the world. He and new friend Harvie Branscomb, a first-year Rhodes scholar, made plans to vacation in Scotland during winter break. With reservations made and train tickets to Edinburgh in hand, they needed only to get through the last week or so of exams, and then they'd be off.

They never made the trip to Scotland.

Perrin Galpin Hears From Hoover

Like Carmichael, twenty-five-year-old Perrin C. Galpin was a second-year Oxford man, but not a Rhodes scholar. Born and raised in New Haven, Connecticut, with his older brother Harry, Galpin had lost his father years before. With a narrow, long face, mustache, glasses, and slicked hair parted down the middle, he was an earnest, sincere man and looked the part. He was also quite active in the American Club, knew Carmichael, and had met Nelson and the other new American students in October.

On Tuesday, November 24, Galpin received a telegram that would change his life and the lives of numerous other American students at Oxford. Signed by Herbert Hoover, the message was short and to the point, with no introductory words.

"Dear Sir, We are badly in need of Americans to take charge of our work in various Relief Stations in Belgium. We want people with some experience of roughing it, who speak French, have tact, and can get on with the Germans.

"If some of the American Rhodes scholars are disposed to fill this bill we should be grateful for their help.

"We are able to pay out-of-pocket expenses but the work is of volunteer order and we cannot go further than that.

"I should be glad to hear from you further in this matter.

"Yours Faithfully, HC Hoover, Chairman."

There is some question as to why Hoover contacted Galpin. In an interview forty-three years later, Galpin said he approached the CRB after seeing a newspaper notice saying men were needed. No such notice with this early date has been found. Conversely, the initial telegram from Hoover to Galpin and Galpin's own correspondence at the time to his brother, Harry, indicate Hoover made the first approach.

The passport photo of twenty-five-year-old Perrin Galpin, who was at Oxford when Hoover asked him to find students willing to spend their December break in Belgium. (Public domain; Perrin Galpin papers, Hoover Institution Archives, Stanford University, California.)

What is known is that John Beaver White, who was involved with Hoover and the founding of the CRB in London, had known Galpin the year before. It's probable that when the CRB executive committee was wondering where they could find Americans ready to volunteer immediately to work in Belgium, White could have brought up Oxford and Galpin. The CRB executive committee would have been interested in Galpin because he was a second-year man; slightly more mature than "freshers," as first-year Oxford students were called; and was active in the American Club, so he had the ability to reach a large group of Americans at one time.

When Galpin received the first telegraph from Hoover, he was immediately interested in helping the CRB find the right men and wanted to volunteer himself. During the following week and a half, a flurry of telephone calls, letters, and telegrams went back and forth between Galpin and the CRB London office trying to clarify what was needed, both as to the men and as to the job.

On Thursday, November 26, Galpin received a second telegram, this one containing only two sentences: "Would be glad if you would call and see Mr. Edgar Rickard and Colonel Hunsiker Friday [November 27] afternoon at four o'clock and bring any other men with you who would be willing to entertain going to Belgium. I myself am leaving for Brussels tonight. Hoover."

The next day Galpin took the train down to London. He wrote to his brother: "I am going to London to-day to see two men on the Executive Committee of the [CRB]. They have made an appointment with me so that I can learn what is required of volunteers for their work of distributing food in Belgium, for there are a number of Rhodes Scholars who might wish to do that sort of work, and I will act as a kind of advanced agent for the American Committee. Whether I will accept the job myself or not I do not know. The work should be intensely interesting and the opportunity of a lifetime." There is a strong probability that Galpin was accompanied by two first-year Rhodes scholars: Emil F. Hollmann (later changed to Hollman, then Holman), who was president of the American Club, and C. G. Bowden.

The next day, Saturday, November 28, Galpin received another telegram, this time from Millard Hunsiker: "Hoover telegraphs from Rotterdam is no use send any boys over for less than six weeks. If any of these can go for that period can use at least ten. Their duties would be living in provincial towns receive goods guard them dealing them out to the local committees. Please let us know Monday how many if any can go for six weeks with brief note of their respective qualifications and names."

What Would the Students Do in Belgium?

That same Saturday Galpin, Hollmann, and Bowden presided over an informal meeting of about forty American students at Oxford interested in hearing about the possibility of spending the six-week school break in Belgium with the CRB. At the meeting, there were more questions than answers, primarily because neither Hoover nor anyone else could say exactly what the work would entail. The CRB was—by the necessity of attempting such massive relief for the first time—making it up as it went along. And because conditions within sealed-off Belgium were sketchy at best, especially when it came to infrastructure, few outside the country knew what to expect within the country.

Shaler, in a statement that had been widely circulated in the British press nearly a month before, had said that each delegate "will see that the shipments of food supplies arrive intact, and who must be informed of any infraction by German troops of the guarantee given by Baron von der Goltz. When this delegate, covered by the American flag, learns of such infraction, he will verify it, and immediately call attention to it, when the Ministers of Spain and America will make the proper representations to the German authorities."

It was not much to go on. Galpin told the group there was a chance they would be camping. Generally speaking, their job would be to "collect information on the location and nature of the remaining food supplies, thus preparing for the distribution of large supplies which would soon be arriving from the United States and other countries." He related what Hunsiker's telegram had said about living in provincial towns, receiving and guarding the shipments of food, and ensuring they got to the local committees.

An important fact never mentioned in the telegrams was that any of these early to mid-twenties students who did go into Belgium would have to deal with middle-aged bureaucratic Belgians and tough German officers and officials. It would be hard for the young American men to do, and even harder for the many of the Belgians and Germans to accept.

What was mentioned by Hoover and his representatives was that those who did go into Belgium had to remain absolutely neutral, no matter what they saw and no matter what was said to them. They were to be neutral in actions at all times and, if Hoover had his way, neutral in thought as well.

Adding to this complex equation was the fact that no one could tell these Oxford boys what conditions were really like in Belgium, what the job would actually entail, and what kind of reaction they would get from either the Belgians or the Germans. The only certainty was uncertainty.

While such a lack of information might have scared off career-oriented applicants, it spoke deeply to adventure-seeking students. Before Galpin learned that Hoover had set a minimum of six weeks, twenty-five men offered to go. As the honest-speaking Galpin later recalled the event, his fellow students volunteered "more in a spirit of adventure and desire for active work than with a certain knowledge of their capacities to fill the bill."

The day after the meeting, Sunday, November 29, Galpin sent a long letter to CRB headquarters in London with an initial list of eighteen men (including himself, Hollmann, and Bowden) who were "passed by ourselves, subject to your approval, as regards their ability to do hard work and to keep their heads in Belgium." He knew that Hoover was only requesting ten men, but he had thought it was "worth while to send these extra names so that any unexpected vacancy could be filled and also should there be immediate and urgent need for more than ten men."

Galpin wrote that all but two (himself and Tracy B. Kittredge) were Rhodes scholars. For each man he gave a short description of his language qualifications and any characteristics he felt inclined to mention. Two had no language competence beyond English, while others had only basic or reading-only skills in French or German. All in their early to mid-twenties, they lacked many usual job skills, and Galpin felt the necessity to add to some men's names comments such as "excellent," "very reliable," "safe and sure," and "an excellent man." Honest to nearly a fault, Galpin wrote of one man, "Perhaps too nervous but otherwise very good and eager to go. Safe on the whole and used to camping. 2nd year." (He never went.) For another man he simply wrote, "Quiet almost to a fault." (He did go.) Galpin listed himself as a possible candidate, stating, "French and some German. Second year man. Cannot be away from London more than three weeks. Will pay own expenses."

He ended the letter with a list of questions that had been raised but not yet answered. They included how much cash each man should carry with him, and "whether the men will be stationed, singly or together[;] if the latter there would be a preference as to the pairings," and whether or not they could receive mail "through your office via courier or some traveller."

Included on Galpin's list was David Nelson, the motorcycle-riding North Dakotan. Not included were Carmichael and Branscomb, who may not have attended the Saturday meeting or were uncertain whether they should cancel their trip to Scotland to join the CRB.

Hunsiker in London telegraphed the next day, Monday, November 30, that he had received Galpin's letter and needed the men by the coming Friday, December 4. He reiterated that the men needed to stay not less than six weeks and asked for all passport details. He also told Galpin, "All men should report this office Friday morning where money will be provided and changed." In later correspondence, Galpin was told each man should carry £20–£30.

It still remained to be seen who the ten men would be.

The Possibility of Bad Seeds in the CRB

Before Galpin identified the final list of ten men in a letter to the CRB on Wednesday, December 2, he and Hoover had multiple communications regarding one man. It all started when Hoover telegraphed Galpin, "Tyler Dernett Fifteen Museum Rd. [Oxford] called here today offering his services Belgium makes excellent impression if you know nothing against will engage him additional your lot please wire."

Hoover also added to another telegram to Galpin that same day: "We telegraphed you to-day in reference to Mr. Tyler Denett [*sic*], who seems to us to be a particularly desirable man, and we will add him to your party if you have nothing against him."

Galpin shot back: "Know nothing of Dernett. If you can still use additional men can send at least two others. Please answer."

Hoover's one sentence reply: "Have decided limit number of men to ten you have chosen."

But the subject was not dropped, and a December 2 letter to Galpin from Edgar Rickard for Hoover stated: "We are rather surprised that you know nothing of Tyler Dennett [sic] as he impressed Colonel Hunsiker and me as being an excellent man when he called on us yesterday afternoon. . . . Would you be good enough to let us know by wire tomorrow morning if there is anything against him which would prevent his being chosen or does your wire merely indicate that you know nothing about him."

Wednesday, December 3, Galpin was obviously getting a little tired of the subject and put the issue to rest with two communications. The first was a to-the-point telegraph—"Do not think Dennett [sic] is a member of the University. stop. Have never met him and know nothing about him." Later that same day in a letter, he took a little more time to explain: "I could not find his name on the official list of members of the university or the temporary list of American students here. Of course, as I do not know him and have not heard of him in any way, I have no opinion on his case one way or the other. In any case I am glad that he came in person to your office and that he seemed to you an excellent man."

The fact that Tyler Dernett never reappeared in the CRB story tends to indicate he was not who he portrayed himself to be to Hoover and the CRB London executive committee. The situation also brings up the topics of CRB hiring and bad hires.

Historically, Hoover has a reputation for being a good judge of character and of picking the right men for the right jobs. Some accounts say that he personally picked the first groups of Rhodes scholars who served as CRB delegates. One later CRB delegate, Joe Green, even said that Hoover had to personally approve everyone who became a CRB delegate in Belgium and that he, Green, was the first exception to that rule.

In the case of the first ten Oxford men—and another fifteen right on their heels—Hoover did not pick them; they were chosen by Perrin Galpin. As Hoover telegraphed Galpin on November 30, "We propose to leave the selection of the ten men entirely in your hands as we have confidence in your ability and, furthermore after our conversation on Friday you are aware of the conditions which we impose."

Practically speaking, Hoover simply didn't have the time to choose delegates as he dealt with much larger issues and crises. He knew these young men weren't the ideal candidates for such a job, but he had no real choice. The time and distance from America made it impossible to wait for the perfect CRB delegates. For that matter, the concept of what constituted a "perfect" delegate was still unknown.

All of which meant that the efforts to find the right volunteers had the built-in probability that not all CRB delegates would work out. Numerous CRB delegates admitted later there were some bad seeds, but they always maintained the bad seeds were few and far between. In reality, they were more than some would imagine, but it's difficult to get an accurate count because the successful delegates rarely referred by name to those who had washed out, and CRB histories simply never mentioned them.

What is known is that at least six of the first twenty-five Oxford students to enter Belgium were never listed by the CRB as having served as delegates. The assumption is that they either did not complete their agreed-upon service or did so to such an unsatisfactory level that the CRB did not want to include them in official records.

The First Ten Chosen

In later times, there would be others who failed to make the CRB grade, and the stories of one or two have been tracked down, but at that critical moment in CRB history, when Galpin sent his final list to the CRB on Wednesday, December 2, no one could have known who of the first ten Oxford men would work out and who wouldn't. He explained that some of the names were new from his previous list of eighteen but that was because, "owing to family reasons," some had to withdraw their names. But Galpin was "sure that these substitutions have not lowered the standard." Besides Hollmann, Bowden, Nelson, and Kittredge, the list included Scott H. Paradise, Walter C. Lowdermilk, Laurence C. "Duke" Wellington, Richard H. Simpson, William W. Stratton, and George F. Spaulding.

Spaulding, a second-year Rhodes scholar who had attended the University of Arizona and was from Los Angeles, was one of those who had not been listed as one of the original eighteen. He probably was not at the initial meeting, for he later remembered being recruited directly by Hollmann. "I was gazing out my window in St. John's College into the President's garden. It was still a beautiful sight with a few flowers and much greenery, but the leaves were falling from the trees; there was a damp chill in the air; winter was approaching and the outlook seemed pretty dismal.

"While thus contemplating," Spaulding continued, "there was a knock at my door. Almost before I could shout, 'Come in!' the door opened to admit Emil Holman, a California Rhodes Scholar from Stanford University who was also a St. John's man. He was quite excited and eager to report an assignment he had been given by one, Herbert Hoover, in London, a trustee of Stanford University, to recruit ten American Rhodes Scholars to go to Belgium behind the German line! . . . Holman had little difficulty in persuading me."

Being one of the first ten, Spaulding had received instructions from Galpin. As Galpin explained in his letter to Hoover, "I have given the men your instructions about money and all of them will have between £20 and £30 each except Kittredge, who will require an advance as his check from home did not arrive as expected. I took the liberty of promising him that he could rely on you for an advance. He is one of the very best men on the list."

Galpin had taken himself off the list because he felt he could not commit to the six weeks. He did finish the letter by stating, "I trust that these men will prove satisfactory to you and that I may hear of any objections or omissions."

The ten were supposed to report on Friday, December 4, to the CRB London office at 3 Wall Buildings, where they would meet with Hoover before heading out for Rotterdam and ultimately Belgium.

Just when Galpin thought all details were wrapped up, Hoover and the CRB threw a little more uncertainty into the mix. On Thursday, December 3, Galpin received a telegram from London asking, "What time will the boys be here tomorrow morning have arranged for press interview."

Such a human-interest story—Oxford students taking their winter break to help out starving Belgium—was too great a tale to escape the Hoover publicity machine.

To Galpin, a press conference appeared a bit unseemly, as evidenced by his comment in a follow-up letter the same day: "I hope the press interview will tend to put the stress on the need for the work that the men are going to do rather than their past and present careers as Rhodes scholars or Oxford men but I feel sure that you will see to the accuracy of the reporting." After such a statement, he worried about how that might be taken by those reading it, so he added immediately, "Pardon this ill expressed and personal opinion."

The Friday press conference went well, and many newspapers in Britain had at least a mention of the occasion the next day. The *Evening Standard* declared the ten would "undertake the difficult work of supervising the distribution of relief supplies to the suffering people in Belgium." The *Daily Telegraph* headlined the story "Rhodes Scholars' Mission" and reported: "These young men come from eight different American States, and therefore eight States will have a selected and well-educated representative of their own who can see for himself and them what war means. Several

This photo of twenty-three-year-old Scott Paradise, one of the Rhodes scholars who became a CRB delegate, shows just how young looking many of these men were. (Public domain; Phillip and William H. Chadbourn papers, box 2, Hoover Institution Archives, Stanford University, California.)

of the undergraduates are likely to apply for leave to remain in Belgium longer than the six weeks' vacation, and, as the operations of the commission are now on a vast scale, more Rhodes scholars will probably be given the opportunity to educate themselves in the stern realities of war and its terrible effects."

For the Oxford students, the press conference wasn't the only notable event that day. They also met with Hoover. Rickard wrote Galpin that Friday that "Mr. Hoover gave them a nice little talk." He also added, "We think these chaps are going to prove quite adequate for the work."

As reported by journalist and CRB member Ben Allen, Hoover told the young men, "When this war is over, the thing that will stand out will not be the number of dead and wounded, but the record of those efforts which went to save life. Therefore you should in your daily service remember that in this duty you have not only a service to render to these people, but that you have a duty to this Commission, and above all have a duty to your own country.

"You must forget that the greatest war in history is being waged. You have no interest in it other than the feeding of the Belgian people, and you must school yourselves to a realisation that you have to us and to your country a sacred obligation of absolute neutrality in every word and every deed."

Hoover, according to Allen, also went on to explain that the work that was about to be embarked upon "not only demonstrated the positive neutrality of the American people, but has contributed to demonstrate that neutrality can have beneficence as well as reticence."

It was probably a typically short, direct Hoover speech, with the men either sitting or standing around him in the CRB office. His words, though, were no doubt inspiring and landed on the fertile ground of the young students' minds. While Hoover was never a great public speaker, in small groups he could be intense and compelling. This informal speech and many others that the CRB delegates would hear from him, coupled with what he achieved, imbued most of them with a profound respect and admiration for the man. No one knew where or how the practice started, but early in the life of the CRB, most of the men began calling Hoover "the chief" as a sign of respect, affection, and loyalty. "Hoover, to us," one delegate related, "was always 'the chief.' We had tremendous admiration for him. There was a good bit of hero worship involved which is natural among younger men, and he *was* our chief, of course. We were very much impressed, and properly so, by the ability that he displayed, and by the complete personal disinterestedness which he displayed throughout the entire operation of the CRB work."

Properly inspired by Hoover and ego-stimulated by the press, the ten Oxford students were ready for their great adventure to begin. The next day, Saturday, December 5, less than two weeks since Hoover's initial telegram to Galpin, they crossed the channel to Rotterdam and their final destination, German-occupied Belgium. All in their early to mid-twenties, they each carried a small suitcase, some cash (probably including some English pounds, Belgian or French francs, and German marks), and little clue as to what they were getting into.

Nelson wrote his mother: "Just at what place I shall be is a different question, and one I can't answer. We shall not learn anything of that until we get to Rotterdam and are given orders by Capt. Lucey. . . . They say we will have to be within doors with lights out at eight p.m.; that will be a rather startling change for one now fairly accustomed to Oxford hours."

They weren't even assured of a smooth sailing to Rotterdam because there had been "fearful gales" for the previous three days in England. Nelson noted in his diary, "I hope the sea is smooth so that I won't get sea-sick."

What did remain constant was the state of confusion over the work and what they would find in Belgium. "What we were to do, no one exactly knew," said Hollmann. "We had visions of sitting on the top of box cars or sleeping on the decks of small canal barges in their long journeys from Rotterdam into Belgium. . . . We expected to see German savages prowling around ready at the slightest provocation to scalp women and children and perhaps provoke a quarrel with us for the same purpose!"

Even before the ten had left London, though, Galpin, back at Oxford, received a terse, unsigned telegram from the London CRB office: "Hoover just returned from Belgium we must have more men send along at once."

It was time for Galpin, Carmichael, Branscomb, and another group of students to join the December party. Branscomb was only nineteen years old and would celebrate his twentieth birthday in German-occupied Belgium.

TWENTY-NINE

E. E. Hunt Joins the CRB

After Hunt's October adventures walking with the refugees from Antwerp to Holland and delivering food supplies by motor launch to refugees on the Dutch border, he spent much of the rest of October and November writing articles on what he had seen and done in Belgium and Holland. Even though he had visited Germany in September and early October before going into Belgium, his German articles had to wait. On October 31, he had written to one of his two agents, Mr. Forman, that "I hate like the devil to hold up the German articles for so long, but this Belgian stuff has been the most amazing thing I've ever seen in my life, and it clamored to be done. . . . I have some wonderful little human-interest sketches which may go to you from time to time. Treat them tenderly: you may find unmitigated Hell in them—for I've seen it and been scorched by it."

Hunt insisted to Forman, "I believe I am the only real flesh-and-blood Neutral left in Europe. Everybody here is wildly anti-German, or insanely pro, you can take your choice. But the 'campaign of lies' is international, and I am ashamed to say some of our newspaper correspondents have helped the bad work along."

Such neutrality, though, did not preclude him from feeling the emotional impact of war. On November 23 he wrote his other agent, Miss Holly: "I could write you endless 'human interest' things if I had the strength. The war is bedlam and takes life from all of us over here." On the same day, he wrote Forman, "I've so much to say, and so little mental or emotional vim behind it just now, that sometimes it all looks very dark."

As he worked on his articles and continued researching and interviewing people about the war, the Belgian refugees, and life in Holland, he naturally came into contact with the U.S. minister to Holland, Henry van Dyke, and through him Lucey, who was just then setting up the CRB's Rotterdam operations. The story they told Hunt of the CRB struck a chord within him, not only as a journalist, but as a person. "As an American citizen I was deeply interested in the budding work of the Commission for Relief in Belgium. . . . I learned that Americans were urgently needed in Belgium to oversee the distribution of food in each of the provinces and to certify that all of it went to the Belgians. Men were wanted who knew both French and German and who had business training, and they were wanted at once."

The more he learned, the more he was intrigued. But he was not yet prepared to commit completely to joining the CRB. There was a way around that hesitancy, though: "It was suggested that I go into Belgium and help in whatever way I could." He could visit various cities and talk with those already involved in the CRB, as well as meet Belgians and Germans. Even if he didn't join the CRB, it was a great opportunity for him as a freelance war correspondent to enter and travel around German-occupied Belgium.

He was probably more willing to join than he consciously wanted to admit, for "the suggestion was made to me at four o'clock in the afternoon of November twenty-third. I left for Brussels next morning at eight o'clock, by way of Bergen op Zoom and Antwerp."

The night before he left, he wrote both his agents. To Holly he stated, "Tomorrow morning I shall be on my way to Antwerp and Brussels on work for the American Relief Commission which is at present taking care of the food sent here for the Belgians." Emotionally he had already joined the CRB cause without realizing it when he also told her, "Incidentally, let me say that America must give and give and keep giving, if these people are to be kept from starvation." Always the journalist, he dangled a possibly interesting article idea without saying it by evoking a name that had become synonymous with Belgian relief: "I'm hoping to spend Thanksgiving with (or near) Brand Whitlock."

To Forman he stated, "The Relief Commission of Americans here is 'doing nobly,' and I have the honor to be sort of semi-officially-officially historian to the work." He added another reason why linking up with the CRB was a good idea: "As perhaps you know, it is now practically impossible to get into or out of Belgium; hence I value my privileges."

It was on these travels in Belgium—accompanied by neutral observer Lieutenant Victor Daniel Herbster, U.S. Navy, and G. Evans Hubbard, a staffer from the U.S. Legation in Holland—that Hunt was told by a German cavalry officer in the Brussels Hotel Astoria, "There once was a nice little town in that place."

During Hunt's November in Belgium, he and his companions were invited one day by German Lieutenant Sperling, aide to Baron von Huhne, the German governor of Antwerp city and province, to join him on a trip from Antwerp to Brussels.

They left at eight a.m. on a dreary, bleak day. "It was mercilessly cold and black as ink. A drizzle of icy rain fell, and the streets were dark and dead as a buried city." With no heat in the Mercedes motorcar, they bundled up "to the chin under fur rugs and lap robes." Even being in a military car, the group was stopped seven times at sentry posts during the hour's ride, and each time a red lantern or red flag was used to signal them to stop.

As they drove along, the Americans probably got colder as they saw what lay before them. In the misty rain, "the landscape lay blurred and drenched—a vista of burned villages and muddy roads. It was a country seen through tears." When the rain turned to drizzle, they could see better, "but our depression grew." Hunt, writing later, stated: "I was fated to travel that Antwerp-Brussels highway for a year, but always with the same feeling of sadness which I felt on first seeing it. Innumerable trees were scarred by shells. Huge holes, half full of mud and ice, were gouged in roads and fields. Farm-house after farm-house had been burned or else destroyed by shell-fire. And once we noticed a broken cradle beside what had been a doorway in the murdered village of Waelhem."

When they got to the Nethe River, there was a Belgian standing on the bridge with a collection box, "begging for contributions for the poor of Waelhem." When they drove through the village, "it was a living grave." Hunt said. "Of its two thousand inhabitants, twelve hundred had already returned. Not a house in the village had been spared, yet the refugees came back to their hearthsides, and were living in huts constructed against the empty rock walls, with curtains of bed-clothing to keep out the beating rain."

Reaching Brussels was somewhat of a relief because the city had been spared the war's ravages. As they pulled up to the German-requisitioned Hotel Astoria, Hunt noticed a line of German Boy Scouts in front of the hotel and in front of the other hotels lining the city's magnificent park. "They looked pathetically tired and lonely so far from home, but kept eyes front and shoulders back like mature servants of the Kaiser. Lieutenant Sperling smiled as we drew up before them, but he returned their salute gravely. *'Jung Deutschland*! Young Germany,' he whispered to us."

Walking around Brussels, Hunt felt that the city, "the proud Paris of the north, clung desperately to her self-respect and tried to ignore the Germans." Meanwhile, he saw beggars wandering the streets: "Women holding young babies in their arms stood on all the curbs, begging openly, or selling matches and shoestrings." On the streetcars, which had resumed service, the Belgians did the only thing they could do in protest: they "proudly turned their backs, or refused to sit beside the hated uniforms." It was the same in the cafes, where many residents preferred to leave "rather than sip beer or coffee beside the enemy."

Thousands of other Belgians "besieged the Pass Bureau for permits to travel. The soup kitchens and bread lines were thronged. There was no work to do. The rust of idleness was on everything. An occasional aeroplane from the Allies dropped little celluloid tubes containing encouraging news, but the Germans, waging a successful war, insolently published all the news, even the official reports of the Allies."

Hunt was caught up in the plight of the Belgians and the arrogance of their masters. "Above the prostrate Belgians, like another race or another caste, roared and flashed the brilliant, careless, militaristic Teutons, their lives hedged about with glory and sudden death."

Hunt's journey into Belgium had a profound impact. He returned to Holland, but not for long. "On December eleventh I was again in Antwerp, this time holding Mr. Brand Whitlock's power-of-attorney as chief delegate of the Commission for Relief in Belgium in charge of the fortress and province—a territory as large as the State of Rhode Island, and with a population of more than a million."

To hell with freelance journalism; Hunt was now in the volunteer relief business.

THIRTY

Brussels

On Saturday, November 21, more than a week after Whitlock and Villalobar had sent their letter and forwarded the CN letter to the German authorities asking for concessions that would allow the relief to move forward, an answer came back.

The reply came from Dr. von Sandt, the German civil administrator in Belgium, who started by saying that the governor general wanted to assure everyone that the relief work had his full cooperation. The Germans agreed not to requisition any more food at least until December 10, when the nationwide inventory should be complete. While they could not give full assurance that the railroads could be used, as the military had control of them, they would try to accommodate requests for rail use. As for greater communication between the relief offices in and out of Belgium, von Sandt offered to personally receive and transmit to the German consul in Rotterdam all the telegrams of the CRB—not exactly what the CN and CRB wanted. Von Sandt had even issued on November 16 a special army order outlining the relief work and the guarantees that the governor general had signed. "This order recapitulated the guarantees against any form of requisition of imported food, and stated that the committees were operating under the patronage of the neutral Ministers . . . that the forwarding of supplies from Rotterdam was directed by Captain Lucey of the American Committee; that all storehouses would be under American protection and administration by an American."

Overall, the Germans agreed to everything that had been requested. "The German authorities at this time were favourably disposed toward the relief, and were inclined to make every concession possibly compatible with the military situation," according to one CRB history. Von der Goltz had "from the first favoured a policy of conciliation, and had tried to restore so far as possible the normal life of the country." Responsible for occupied Belgium and its people, the governor general simply did not want to see food riots. Whatever could be done to prevent them, while not disturbing military operations, von der Goltz would do.

Von der Goltz had gone so far as to write Whitlock a week before to acknowledge that the first consignment of food would only temporarily relieve the situation and that "in the interest of all concerned, an effort must be made to effect some permanent arrangement whereby foodstuffs purchased abroad may be brought for an indefinite period into Belgium upon the distinct understanding that they shall be devoted exclusively to the use of the civil population." He said he was speaking on behalf of the imperial government, which would agree to a permanent arrangement if the British did so.

Such German willingness to work with and accept the CRB and CN seemed too good to be true. Everyone involved jumped at the opportunity and began working with the Germans to develop better relations and guarantees, but time would reveal that the devil was in the details.

A test of the Germans' official stand toward the relief work came quickly in the form of an incident that, "for the moment, seemed to seriously threaten the relief work." The incident also revealed that the media, which Hoover relied on so heavily to create public opinion to support his efforts, was a double-edged sword.

On November 22, the *New York Times* ran a story that shocked many. The article was written by Cyril Brown, a staff correspondent in Europe, and it quoted two Germans: "His Excellency von Frankenburg and Ludwigsdorf, personal adjutant to the military governor in Antwerp." According to them, Belgians were not "on the brink of starvation as a result of the German occupation. . . . The very contrary was the case." The two Germans agreed that Belgium was not a self-sustaining country, but imports had been secured, and the Germans had developed an idea to have an "inter-communistic commission" handle the imports to the localities that needed food. The commission the Germans referred to was the Comité National.

Making sure not to leave out Hoover and the Americans, von Frankenburg then stated rather starkly, "If America had not been so tender-hearted as to send foodstuffs, and if the food-supply had not run out, we should certainly have considered it our duty to bring food from Germany, for we are for the time being the government here and it is our duty to see that the people do not starve."

Francqui undoubtedly objected strenuously to the Germans' claiming the credit for the founding of what he considered his organization.

Hoover was furious. In a telegram to Whitlock on November 23, he declared, "If it is true that the Germans intend to feed Belgium, America will withdraw instantly."

Whitlock immediately sought out the German authorities in Brussels for an answer. The same day Hoover telegraphed him, Whitlock sent a reply: "It seems that a Captain von Frankenburg, a staff-officer, not authorized to speak, made statements to some person, claiming to be a newspaper man, relating to conditions in Germany, in which he said that there was no danger of starvation in Germany, and that Germany wanted no assistance in feeding its population. His remarks were therefore evidently entirely misunderstood. The German Government renews its official declaration that conditions in Belgium are as they have been represented, and views with great gratification the generous efforts of the American people to relieve the starving population here."

Once again, the issue of who truly was responsible or should be responsible for feeding the Belgians was in the open. Ever since the invasion, the Germans had officially said it was not their responsibility. The German argument went that if they were annexing the country, it would be their job to feed the populace, but they were merely conquering Belgium, so they had no legal or moral responsibility to do so. Additionally, the Germans officially maintained that the conditions within Belgium were due solely to the English blockade.

Because of views expressed in the *Times* article, the Germans took the opportunity to state their case. The imperial German government issued an official statement on November 25, "declaring that the starvation of Belgium would be due to the action of the Allies in cutting off Belgium's normal imports and that Germany could not and would not feed Belgium in view of the character of the Allied blockade." The Germans also reaffirmed the statements by von der Goltz that "the German Government is entirely in sympathy with the laudable work of the American Commission for Relief in Belgium."

Hoover Decides It's Time to Visit Brussels

Despite that one incident, relations with the Germans seemed to be going relatively well.

The same could not be said for the relationship between the CRB Rotterdam office and the CRB Brussels office, which appeared at times to be acting more like an extension of Francqui's CN than an independent CRB operation.

Hoover decided it was time to visit Brussels and get things back on track. He wanted to "see for himself the exact conditions in Belgium and to hasten the organization of the Brussels office." Whitlock explained that Hoover came to Brussels because the CRB "had already been functioning, but there were many defects in the C.R.B. and it was to remedy these that Mr. Hoover had crossed the North Sea and come to Belgium."

Leaving London on the evening of Thursday, November 26, he quickly and personally experienced some of the harsh realities of being in a war zone. He was strip-searched twice, once as he was leaving England by "British intelligence agents" and once at the Belgian border by German sentries. In great understatement, Hoover said later that his first trip to Belgium felt like entering a prison and that "possibly the rather rough search of my person by the German guards strengthened that impression."

Hoover's first impressions of Belgium and Brussels stayed with him the rest of his life. "German soldiers stood at every crossroads and every street corner. The depressed, unsmiling faces of the Belgians matched the mood of the dreary winter landscape. There were no children at play. The empty streets, the gaunt destroyed houses, the ruins of the fine old church

of St. Pierre and the Library at Louvain, intensified the sense of suspended animation in the life of a people."

He traveled with Shaler and the three Rockefeller Foundation War
Relief Commission men: Rose, James, and Bicknell. They would be observing not only Belgium but also Hoover and how he handled the relief
efforts. Much of what they reported would dictate how the Rockefeller
Foundation ultimately responded to the CRB.

Arriving on Sunday afternoon, Hoover entered into a series of meetings and conferences that would last for much of the next two days. Most
of the meetings were held at the legation offices and, at various times,
included Whitlock, Gibson, Francqui, Shaler, and Heineman. From the
meetings, Hoover was "more impressed than ever of the need for the
immediate extension of the Commission's services in Belgium. . . . No
effective office service had been organized and Hoover urged that this
should be created as quickly as possible."

Hoover's trip was also the occasion of the first meeting of Whitlock and
Hoover. Whitlock was impressed, and he wrote in his journal that Hoover
was "very direct, positive, able, speaks little but everything he says counts."
Whitlock was also a bit in awe and trepidation as to how quickly and force-
fully Hoover could make decisions and take action. Whitlock was used to
the leisurely, almost laconic pace of formal diplomatic processes that sometimes ran to the absurd: A diplomat would present a calling card at a person's office, write a note, decide to hold a meeting, write out possible dates,
wait for a reply, etc. As Whitlock himself wrote about his first meeting with
Hoover at the U.S. Legation office, Whitlock had only come down from his
chambers to meet Hoover "in response to the card that had been sent up."

Hoover had no patience for what he would have probably called such
silliness. If he had described his perfect meeting, he would have outlined
something simpler: Sit down with all interested parties, identify the problems, develop solutions, decide who is to do what, then go do what you've
been assigned.

While Heineman and Hulse had established a CRB office in Brussels
after returning from London in late October, it was more an office in
name than in operation. The two mining engineers were still working
out of Heineman's offices at 48 Rue de Naples and had been "too busily
occupied in conferences and meetings with the German and Belgian authorities or with their private affairs to give much time to the details of
the Commission organization," according to a CRB history.

Besides Heineman and Hulse, other early CRB staffers in Brussels included Charles H. Macloskie, a late-forties friend and associate of Heineman, and Amos Johnson Jr., who had reached Brussels around November 20 and had recently turned twenty-two. These two men were rapidly overwhelmed by the ever-increasing volume of correspondence, bills of lading, and other documents necessary for efficient operations.

Arguably the most important person in the newly created CRB Brussels office was not even an American. His name was Fernand Baetens. Independently wealthy and possessing experience in banking and shipping, Baetens had appeared at the Brussels office and volunteered his services the moment he heard about the founding of the CRB. He quickly became the head of the shipping department and was to "render invaluable services because of his ability, his local knowledge and his American-like directness and efficiency." He also had the distinction of being "the only Belgian ever to become formally a member of the American Commission, which jealously maintained its character as a neutral body," according to one CRB history (although some CRB rosters do not list him).

Hoover knew after reviewing the Brussels operation that what was needed was a strong, independent CRB office in Brussels, and he was not sure Heineman was the best person to head such an office. Hoover felt that Heineman was at times more focused on helping and working with Francqui and the CN than on guarding and nurturing the CRB. Whitlock related in his journal that at a conference with Hoover and Francqui, where they talked about possibly replacing Heineman, the three "agreed that we had great need of him since he has influence with the Germans." Francqui might like having allies around, but only if they managed their responsibilities appropriately.

Whitlock, disliking confrontation and trying to keep the peace among all parties, suggested that he take over personally all matters tied to shipping and distribution of the foodstuffs. He had Lucey in Rotterdam send all relief-related mail and telegrams to him. But good intentions don't necessarily translate to good ideas: "The work, however, soon developed into too great a burden to be carried by Whitlock and his staff."

As Hoover's first trip to Brussels was winding down, he knew he wanted Heineman out, but he needed the man's good German relationships too much to simply remove him. And he knew it would take some time to find the right kind of individual to be director of the strong Brussels operation he envisioned. Being a man of action, however, Hoover had to do something, even if it was incomplete or untested. He brought in Bell from Rotterdam to take charge of the CRB's administrative side of the Brussels office, while Heineman stayed on handling German relations. The idea, no doubt, was to let nature take its course between Bell and Heineman and see who came out on top.

Within weeks, the matchup would show that nature could get ugly at times.

Hoover left Brussels on Wednesday, December 2, with not much changed in Brussels but knowing change was in the wind. He would not get away, however, without first enduring what he disliked most: ceremonial gratitude.

The day before, the entire CN had been convened in a session at the ornate offices of Francqui's bank, Societe Generale. Ernest Solvay stood and made a heartfelt speech praising the ministers of Spain and America, Hoover, and the American people for coming to Belgium's aid. "From the bottom of our hearts we thank you for your indispensable support in our work, and we assure you in advance of the historic gratitude of a country which knows its duty."

Francqui even praised Hoover as "a man of great heart and a man of great activity also, who has succeeded in the course of a few weeks in assuring to Belgium three months' food-supplies."

Hoover in response warned that great difficulties lay ahead before a steady supply of foodstuffs would be available. He knew that most of the people in the room felt that they only needed to get through the winter and spring before the war would probably end.

What moved Hoover much more than the pomp and ceremony within the gloriously gilded conference room was the trip he had taken earlier that day into Brussels to see the relief work in action.

By that time, more than 400,000 meals a day were being served to Brussels residents from more than 130 canteens (also known as soup kitchens) throughout the city. That meant approximately 200,000 people—a third of the city's population—were receiving a ration of bread, soup, and coffee every day from their local soup kitchen. Brussels was divided into twenty-one districts and each had a local committee that organized its own distribution. Bread and soup were delivered directly to those committees before ten o'clock every morning. These facilities were

*Fourteen huge munici-
pal kitchens in Brussels
prepared the daily ration
of soup.* (Public domain;
*The Millers' Belgian Relief
Movement, Final Report,
1914–1915,* William C.
Edgar, Miller Publishing
Co., 1916.)

*The soup was transported
from the municipal kitch-
ens to one of 130 canteens
(also known as soup
kitchens) via carts pulled
by dogs, oxen, or humans.*
(Public domain; Herbert
Hoover Presidential
Library Archives, West
Branch, Iowa.)

supplied by fourteen huge municipal kitchens that were run by many of
the city's out-of-work chefs.

As reported by one British newspaper, "At the Central Kitchen 36
cooks and 50 assistants start at 2:30 every morning to make the soup. The
cooks are divided into two squads and are supervised by a special committee, which includes Senator Catteau, and the President of the Hotel and
Restaurant Society of Brussels. While delivery is being made, by means
of 14 trolleys, the cooks bone the meat and cut up the potatoes for the
next day's soup."

On the morning of Hoover's trip around Brussels, it was cold and
there was a "dismal rain." According to Whitlock, the entourage included
Hoover, Bell (probably as a way of confirming his new position), Dr.
Rose, Bicknell, Francqui, Shaler, Gibson, and two others. They took a trip
through the city on a journey that followed the food through to distribution. The group first visited one of the municipal kitchens, which was in a
large hangar of an express company that no longer existed. It was a bustle
of activity as cooks prepared the food and attended to gigantic cauldrons

A line of people in Brussels waiting for the daily ration of bread and soup. (Public domain; Herbert Hoover Presidential Library Archives, West Branch, Iowa.)

where the soup was cooking. The soup itself contained potatoes, meat, rice, onion, and leeks. Once the soup was ready, it would be transferred to manageable containers that were then carried by dog carts or horse carts to nearby canteens.

The next stop for the group was a soup kitchen. The one they visited was located in an old concert hall on the Rue Blaes, in the Quartier des Marolles. When the motorcars pulled up out front, Hoover and the group saw hundreds of people standing in line. As Whitlock reported the scene, "They stood with the divine patience of the poor, there in the cold rain, shivering in shawls and old coats and wooden shoes, with bowls or pitchers and each with his number and his card, issued by his commune."

Hoover seemed touched by the quietly spoken "merci" as each person received a bowl of soup, loaf of bread, and a little coffee and chicory. Whitlock wrote that each thank-you "somehow stabbed one to the heart, and brought an ache to the throat, and almost an annoying moisture to the eyes. One felt very humble in those human presences. . . . I knew what was going on in Mr. Hoover's heart when he turned away and fixed his gaze on something far down the street."

What struck an even stronger emotional chord were the canteens where the children and babies were fed. Before the war, children and babies of the poor had been fed at a few canteens operated by Les Petites Abeilles, or Little Bees. When Francqui and the CN were developing their soup kitchen organization in September, they decided to simply subsidize and expand the Little Bees operation. By the time Hoover showed up in Brussels, there were thirty-two such canteens feeding children and babies every day.

Children waiting for their daily ration of food. (Public domain; *In Occupied Belgium*, Robert Withington, The Cornhill Co., 1921.)

Hoover left Brussels with a new, even stronger resolve, if that was possible. He had seen the human side of the suffering. It was a picture that would stay with him forever. Whitlock wrote that when Hoover came to say good-bye: "He was very much moved by the sight of suffering he saw today, and very cordial and very fine. A remarkable man indeed."

Hoover also had a clearer understanding of how desperate the situation was. He knew that after December, relatively regular shipments of foodstuffs would be arriving—he and his team had been working on filling the pipeline continually since October—but time was against those shipments. It took time to buy the supplies, charter the ships, get the supplies to the ships, load the ships, gather all the permissions necessary, and then cross the Atlantic Ocean.

If something wasn't done quickly, December would shape up to be the month Belgians began to starve.

The Bunges in Antwerp—If the Germans Would Only Agree

The Bunges had survived the October bombardment and surrender of Antwerp and had quickly returned to a seminormal life. Edouard walked every day to the company office that he shared with his business partner, George Born. During the bombardment, a shell had passed through the wall of their office on the Rue Arenberg side and exploded in Born's office. It had destroyed much of the furniture and went through the vault of the rubber cellar, where they stored samples from their rubber plantations. Every day, the elder Bunge still walked to his office, where he, Born, and their staffs tried to piece together their office space and their worldwide empire.

At the same time, Edouard had been part of Antwerp relief efforts since the war started. He had offered his services and money not only to the city officials but also to the local communes in Antwerp and around Hoogboom and Chateau Oude Gracht. He was on numerous committees and rarely said no to a plea for his time, guidance, or assistance. He had also offered his Antwerp shipping warehouses as collection points for any foodstuffs that needed to be stockpiled.

On the national front, Bunge had kept an interested eye on the progress of Francqui and the Comité National. He knew that relief started locally but must be coordinated and operated nationally. While Bunge had known Francqui for many years and had been on occasion a business associate, he never considered Francqui a close friend. He certainly respected him and acknowledged his achievements, but he could not always abide the ruthless methods that Francqui sometimes used. They both had known and worked with King Leopold. Bunge had been offered a barony by the king, but he had turned it down because he felt the only title that should accompany his name was "merchant."

A major difference between Francqui and Bunge was their style of leadership. Francqui's was demanding and autocratic, and he rarely sought the counsel of subordinates or the socially inferior. He had been raised and trained in the military, and for him that style worked. Bunge preferred to hear what others had to say, regardless of their rank or social position. He would ask them countless questions so that he could fully probe their understanding of an issue before he would make a decision. It was not that he was an indecisive man—quite the contrary—but he preferred to tap into the knowledge and wisdom of those around him before he made his decision. Among his advisers he even counted his daughter Erica, who he felt had more of a business mind than many of his male associates.

When Francqui's Comité National passed the word around Belgium that it would be running a national program and that there would be ten provincial committees created, it was natural that Bunge would join the Antwerp provincial committee. He was immediately named vice president and, as such, sat on the Comité National along with the other provincial vice presidents and presidents.

One of Bunge's early actions on behalf of the Comité National was the purchase of a large stock of coffee that was in Antwerp warehouses. The coffee was owned by the Brazilian state of São Paulo. Bunge approached the German authorities and received permission to work with a representative of Brazil to buy the entire stock of coffee. Once that was arranged, Bunge also persuaded the Germans to agree to allow distribution to the provincial committees.

Bunge continued to look for ways to help the relief program, not only in his own area but nationwide.

As he did so, Erica and her sisters, Eva and Hilda, continued to work at the temporary hospital. After the city surrendered and the German occupation began, however, all the British soldiers they had been tending were transferred to the military hospital in the city. The three had been sorry to see them go and worried what would become of them. Either the British wounded would stay under the supposed care of German hospital staff, or, if they got better, they would be transferred by rail to a military prison camp in Germany. Neither option held much promise of a bright future. As for the Belgian soldiers the Bunges had cared for, they had died, stayed on as long-term wounded, or gotten better and were allowed to go back to their homes. While that meant fewer patients and less demanding days, it was still grueling work emotionally, for the men who remained behind had horrible burns or disfiguring injuries that refused to heal.

The Bunge sisters agreed that they needed to know more to be of greater service. In November they began taking a course from one of the Antwerp hospitals on how to tend to the wounded and assist the doctors. This they did while they still worked individually, whenever possible, in the soup kitchens or the canteens for infants.

The three young women would also travel back and forth—only after obtaining permissions from the German pass bureau—from Antwerp to Chateau Oude Gracht. Erica wanted to help out with her beloved farm, to make sure that all the farmers and their wives, children, and animals were doing as best as they could. With the farm manager, Verheyen, Erica organized and created distribution plans for what had been stored for winter, accounted for all that had been given out to refugees, estimated

what could be expected from the limited winter growing season, and projected what might be done in the spring if the Germans allowed it.

The Chateau Oude Gracht and its staff meant nearly as much to her
as her own family. Every day or night when Erica walked back to the
chateau, Isidore always seemed to be there waiting to take her coat, hat,
and gloves in the vestibule.

Isidore was the chateau's *maitré de hôtel*, or head butler. He had run
the household of servants and been Edouard's personal valet since before
Erica was born. He had a hooked nose and long, dour face that never
showed emotion. At every meal served in the dining hall he stood absolutely still against one wall, a towering giant, hands placed behind his
back, watching the other servants and the Bunges. When Erica and her
sisters had been much younger, they would try unsuccessfully to get him
to smile or react in some way. They made faces or played with their food
in hopes of a response. Most times they were caught and scolded by their
parents. She had rarely seen him smile. But as she grew older she had became quite fond of this stoic man who faithfully served her father and
ruled the servants with ominous silences and devastating stares.

Erica also had become attached to the little yellow canary she had
found so miraculously after the bombardment stopped. She kept him in a
large cage in her bedroom. There she would talk to it in the mornings and
evenings, telling it her hopes and dreams and her hatred of the Boches
(a derogatory word for Germans, especially German soldiers) who had
brought this horrible war down upon Belgium.

One evening in late November, Edouard asked her to come with him
to his study rather than go upstairs and play their usual game of billiards.
To get to the study in the left front tower, she and her father, whom she
lovingly called Pereken, walked through the library. Many people thought
the library was the prettiest room in the chateau. Erica agreed.

As they walked arm-in-arm, the two entered the library through massive wooden doors laboriously carved with numerous figures that climbed
up both sides. Along the walls, dark-wooded built-in cupboards came
to waist level. Above these were bookshelves, also built-in, that nearly
reached the twenty-foot ceiling. Hundreds of colorful leather-bound
books could be seen on the shelves behind the leaded glass doors. The fireplace was big enough to walk into and was fronted by two spiral marble
columns and a marble mantle. A brown leather upholstered lounge chair
was on either side of the fireplace. Beside one was a three-step library

stool. In front of the fireplace was a plush couch with side tables and two Flemish side chairs. Behind the couch was a French-carved oak refectory table with a lamp on each end. A window behind the couch looked out on the front lawn.

Walking through the single wooden door on the far side of the library, the two entered Edouard's study. Smaller than most rooms in Oude Gracht, it was still able to seat five or six comfortably. The room, Erica knew, held Pereken's heart. Here he had worked countless hours, pulling papers from his worn dispatch case. Here he had smoked and taken brandy with many friends and busi-

The fireplace in the library of Chateau Oude Gracht. (Author's archives.)

ness associates. The room was circular, conforming to the shape of the tower, with a ceiling that rose to a high conical point. Windows surrounded the room, bringing in what light the cloudy Belgian weather would give up. A partners desk with a hand-tooled leather writing surface dominated one side of the room. Behind it was a large fireplace, and in front were numerous chairs arranged in a semicircle around a low table.

When they were seated, each facing the other from their familiar chairs at the partners desk, Edouard began. He told her all that he had learned from the reports given to the Antwerp provincial committee. The food stores were dwindling. The Americans and Francqui's group were trying to arrange a steady stream of relief through Rotterdam and the canal barges. The soup kitchens in the city were serving more and more who could not afford to pay. Much of what he said Erica already knew or had guessed.

What concerned both of them the most, however, were the infants. Little babies and their young mothers were the critical recipients of relief and needed the best possible nutrition. And yet supplies could barely keep up with demand, and the one item most needed, fresh milk, was getting harder to find. The Little Bees organization was doing all it could to provide milk for its thirty-two infant canteens in Antwerp, but dairy cows had been prime targets of German requisition, and as meat had grown more difficult to find, the cows' milk production was sometimes sacrificed for the slaughterhouse.

During that night's discussion, the two Bunges decided that they needed to do something. A plan was slowly developed. If the Germans agreed, Edouard would arrange to buy cows from Holland and import them to Hoogboom. Erica would set up a dairy and arrange for men, horses, and carts to carry milk every day to the Little Bees canteens in Antwerp.

Erica had never run a dairy but she was sure that she, Verheyen, and the others on Hoogboom would be able to do it.

If only the Germans would agree.

THIRTY-ONE

Rotterdam

Approximately three weeks after first arriving in Rotterdam, Captain Lucey was able to secure CRB offices at 98 Haringvliet. They were "commodious quarters" on "a tree bordered street beside a busy canal in the heart of the city." From the window, Lucey and his staff could see the Meuse River and countless canal barges of the working harbor.

By the end of November, the Rotterdam office had received and unloaded 26,431 tons of foodstuffs. It was a far cry from the 80,000 tons that were the minimum needed to sustain more than 7 million Belgians. Would the CRB be able to obtain such a huge amount of foodstuffs?

Only time would tell—and time was running out for the Belgians.

From the start of the war through December 1914, many Belgians were uncertain where or when their next meal would come. (Public domain; Herbert Hoover Presidential Library Archives, West Branch, Iowa.)

DECEMBER 1914

UNCERTAINTY PREVAILS

The CRB delegates and their Belgian drivers were the only civilians allowed to use motorcars in Belgium. When the delegates first went into Belgium in 1914, they put CRB signs on the engine covers. Later, as this photo taken after 1914 shows, CRB banners were created and flown from the vehicles. (Public domain; Herbert Hoover Presidential Library Archives, West Branch, Iowa.)

THIRTY-TWO

The Students Head Into Belgium

Rotterdam Greeting

The first ten newly minted CRB delegates arrived in Rotterdam on Saturday evening, December 5. Their crossing had been somewhat challenging. Twenty-three-year-old David Nelson wrote his parents that "the sea was rough, but I was fortunate enough to retain everything I ate, although at one time Father Neptune came within an ace of scoring." The ship, according to some, came close to hitting a mine, but "after several frantic signals by the lookouts we veered off sharply and just passed by an object about the size and shape of a barrel; but whether it was a mine or not no one could say."

When they reached the Dutch port of Flushing (Vlissingen in Dutch), they were met by a "very polite Dutchman, who spoke excellent English." He escorted them on a walk around the town before they boarded a train that arrived in Rotterdam at 8:30 p.m. Nelson wrote, "We were all tired and hungry, and so when we got down to dinner it was the most agreeable experience of the trip, for my part at least, to sit down to a meal of the best cooking I have tasted since I left home. I make no exceptions. May the Fates smile kindly on the chef at this hotel!"

They stayed at the Maas Hotel, a sixty-room "first class with lift" establishment situated at 19 Boompjes Street. It was an international hotel that did business with Germans, English, Americans, and Dutch. Nelson was surprised by the country's mix of nationalities, which one British correspondent told him made Holland "the most interesting spot in Europe at present." The Oxford student was also surprised by a conversation in the hotel's lounge he had with "an old German and his wife." He wrote to his parents: "It was remarkable to see how strongly they trusted in Germany. The husband told me in all seriousness that he believed Germany would win; and being a well-trained business man, his representations are entitled to some consideration, even though a German victory seems now impossible."

The hotel not only served an international clientele; it overlooked the Maas River. The Dutch name did not fool the ten Americans, who knew that the water flowing by was part of the mighty 975-mile-long Meuse River, which was born in France, grew wide and deep as it flowed north through Belgium, then settled into the lowlands of Holland before emptying into the North Sea. If the Germans allowed them into Belgium— the German Consulate in Rotterdam still needed to approve their passports before entry—the Americans knew they would probably, at some point, travel along the river's course and see what was left of towns such as Visé and Dinant, which had been devastated in the German invasion.

Each of the ten Americans carried with him only a small valise, something they were not accustomed to as young Oxford men. In England, they would have been expected to be properly attired for any social or public event, dress formally for dinner, and during the day wear a laundered shirt, stiff collar with tie, and a jacket or suit. Because they had no idea what to expect in Belgium and had been told to travel light, they had packed little. Twenty-four-year-old George Spaulding wrote: "We had been warned before leaving Oxford that we might have to ride canal boats to guard food shipments and to be prepared for hardships. So we had not taken our best clothes, not to mention dinner jackets which were de rigueur in those days whenever asked out for dinner."

Spaulding's suitcase contained only his toiletries, "a couple of ties, handkerchiefs and socks," some shirts, "extra underwear and a sweater . . . extra trousers and my College blazer—a scanty wardrobe, indeed."

Regardless of such clothing limitations, these early CRB delegates were rarely, if ever, seen in public without the proper day attire of a businessman: jacket or suit, stiff collar, and tie. They would try to maintain that standard even in Belgium, with the added benefit of a long, thick overcoat to combat the weather, which was always uncertain at any time of the year. They might work hard while in Belgium, but they would not be inappropriately dressed.

Even though Hoover was not a clothes-conscious man, the chief, as the delegates referred to him, would never abide his men being out of form. That went double for most of the other CRB executives, and especially the Belgian men of industry who sat on the provincial committees and the Comité National. Most of them were men of the times and felt that a man dressed inappropriately could not be taken seriously.

That first night in Rotterdam, though, clothes were the least of the young men's thoughts. Many of them probably checked and rechecked the numerous permits and passes that had been issued by various governments to get them into Belgium. And because communication was still unreliable between the London office and the Rotterdam and Brussels offices, each man carried a letter of introduction on CRB stationery, addressed to both offices and signed by Hoover. Each letter gave the student's name and declared that he "has been engaged by this Commission to act upon your instructions in connection with Relief Work in Belgium for this Commission." The letters all ended with the statement that the bearer "has no occupation other than that which you may assign to him." Many of the experienced CRB and CN personnel probably would have agreed with that statement once they saw the young faces of these new delegates.

Even though the Americans were tired from their channel crossing, they were still university men, delighted to find that their first night in Holland happened to be Saint Nicholas's Eve, a major event celebrated by much of Europe. Holland, being neutral and feeling the war's effects only via the Belgian refugees, did not hold back in its annual celebration. In Rotterdam, Nelson wrote: "What a celebration the jolly Dutch had! The crowds thronged every street in town."

He recorded much of the evening's festivities, beginning with two English journalists gathering up the Oxford flock and taking the students to the city's roller rink, "where a great confetti-ball was in progress. At one end was a brass band and a space for skating, and at the other end an orchestra and a space for dancing. About the sides were arranged tables and chairs, and above, a balcony extended about the walls. First the band played and the people with skates began to circle the floor; when they had stopped the orchestra began and the dancers thronged the floor. So they continued alternately all evening, while confetti was showered from the balconies and young fellows in fantastic costumes rushed about winding long strips of colored paper around the couples as they circled, until sometimes they could scarcely be seen for confetti and paper."

Spectators sat at the little tables and watched the skaters and dancers as they drank their Dutch beer and smoked their Dutch cigars. At midnight, the music stilled, and the master of ceremonies announced with a great flourish that it was time for the grand march.

"It bore little resemblance to a grand march as we understand the term," Nelson wrote, "but then the Dutch conception struck me as being fully as enjoyable." The procession was led by Saint Nicholas himself, complete with "red cap and gown and wig, bearing a massive sceptre." He was followed by a boy assistant dressed as an African. Next came the band "playing mostly American ragtime, which begins to strike me as being not only universal but also omnipresent." After that came the dancers and skaters, "not paired off as one would expect, but locked arm in arm with from three to ten in a row."

Suddenly, "the master of ceremonies shouted some command, the band led off with a lively tune and the crowd behind followed in wild disorder. First about the dancing space, then out through a little gate and past the tables to the space for skating. . . . Everyone suddenly flashed forth little Dutch flags and began waving them."

While all the festivities were great fun, they were also a bit frustrating for the Americans.

Being young men, they had spent the entire evening listening "helplessly to the babble of Dutch about us and would have pawned our watches right then and there if we could have received in exchange a knowledge of it sufficient to enable us to go up and talk to some of the pretty Dutch girls we saw on every hand." This interest certainly wasn't one-sided, for Nelson noted, "They smiled at us most delightfully whenever they passed us, for they had us 'spotted' from the start."

As the men fidgeted under the scrutiny of pretty girls, the band surprised them. After it played several ragtime tunes, it suddenly struck up the recently popularized tune "Tipperary," "and to our astonishment the whole crowd sang the English words. They swayed back and forth, they jumped up and down; and when they came to the closing, 'It's a long, long, way to Tipperary, but my heart's right there,' they waved their flags furiously and ended with a great flourish."

Once, however, was not enough—neither for the band nor for the crowd. The tune was repeated three or four times, and by end of the night Nelson guessed that "during the rest of the night, the total would be over twenty-five."

Getting Their Assignments

It's probably best that no one recorded when the men finally got back to the hotel, but the next day, even though it was Sunday, they were up early, dressed appropriately, and ready to find out what all this Belgian work was about. They walked the short distance from the hotel to the CRB office, which was on a "tree-bordered Dutch lane lying beside a busy canal where the schools of herring used to run, and where nowadays market carts and fisherwomen, motor-cars, delivery wagons, and peasant farmers in white-washed wooden shoes clatter leisurely by." To the east, and nearly within throwing distance, was the city's major Maas train station.

The building that the CRB occupied was a 100-year-old mansion first owned by a successful Dutch merchant. The house still bore some luxurious paneled walls and painted ceilings that were adorned with allegorical figures. The dining room had been converted into a waiting room but maintained its "massive fireplace, with long vertical Dutch mirrors and wall paintings in the style of 1750, showing quiet landscapes, Ruskin's 'fat cattle and ditch-water,' or violent storms at sea."

While the house maintained some of its previous accoutrements, it was no longer a quiet, stately mansion; it was the bustling business office of the rapidly growing shipping arm of the CRB. A large staff of Dutch, Belgian, and American clerks were scattered throughout the building, and Dutch and Flemish barge captains and dock laborers were always waiting in line for an audience with someone who could either put them to work or solve a problem they had encountered while employed by the commission. The halls and various offices were filled with a nearly constant cacophony of ringing phones, clattering typewriters, and buzzing conversations.

Overseeing it all was forty-year-old Captain Lucey, who occupied the best office in the building. The large room on the second floor overlooked

The CRB Rotterdam office was located in a 100-year-old mansion that still retained many of its stately qualities, such as ornate fireplaces. (Public domain; *A Journal From Our Legation in Belgium*, Hugh Gibson, Doubleday, Page & Co., 1917.)

the Meuse River and the harbor. From his windows he could see many of the 300 barges that the CRB had already chartered. Some were being loaded by floating elevators, others by hand; others waited for their cargoes while still more were being towed upriver by canal tugs toward Belgium. All were draped with huge canvas flags bearing the protective inscription "Belgian Relief Commission."

Even though it was Sunday, people were working in the office, and Lucey was there to greet the ten Oxford students. As one CRB delegate described Lucey, he was a "nervous, big, beardless American . . . who left his business . . . to organize and direct a great trans-shipping office in an alien land for an alien people." The captain spent little time on the preliminaries, getting straight to work on instructing the ten students as to what he knew of Belgian conditions, what he thought they would be doing, and what he felt needed to be done.

Nelson wrote his parents that Lucey "gave us a fairly good idea of what our work would be like, besides telling us in a general way of the situation in Belgium. You will be surprised when you hear of the magnitude of this undertaking, and of the extraordinary difficulties under which it must be carried on."

Nelson went on to outline in general terms what some of those difficulties were: "Many of the canals are useless for navigation; the military have right of way on all railroads; and lastly the very fact that a war is in progress renders everyone liable to suspicion, arrest, and detention."

In a confident tone that marked so many Americans of the time, Nelson stated, "The Americans have been hampered so far by lack of men and lack of supplies, but when our men get established throughout the country, and the organization is perfected, we will be able to handle the situation, for we already have some thirty or forty ships on the way to Holland."

Nelson was so impressed with the operation and with Lucey that he wrote, "One feels prouder of being an American after meeting and talking with him." The young first-year Rhodes scholar already knew, before he had started doing any relief work, that "our work goes on day and night, seven days a week." He even predicted that for the Oxford students this would not be a six-week jaunt, as they had signed up for: "This job is not a three month's or six month's job; it is a one or two year's job, for even if the war should stop today, the Belgians must be fed until they can gather in the next harvest." And he was already clear on his intentions, even before experiencing one day in occupied Belgium: "I shall very likely stay by this work for six months or longer, if I can arrange matters at Oxford." He had become a convert to the cause and even ended one of his letters to his parents by stating, "I hope North Dakota, which is prospering because of this war, will be generous in her aid to the Belgians."

By the end of Sunday's session with Lucey, it was time for assignments. In a colorful re-creation written later by one of the delegates (Gilchrist Stockton), Lucey assigned some of them their stations.

"'Mr. Hollmann, you have been chosen for Maastricht. I regret to say that you will not go into Belgium.'

"Lucey then turned to twenty-three-year-old Kittredge. 'Mr. Kittredge, it has been decided, partly by chance, that you are to go into Hasselt. Will you choose a companion? There will be two delegates in each province.'

"Simpson, sitting next to Kittredge, plucked his sleeve and whispered, 'Take me with you, Kit, don't leave me in Holland.'

"So Kittredge replied to Captain Lucey, 'I'll take Simpson. He speaks a little French and I speak a little German. Between us I think we can worry along.'"

Kittredge and Simpson would leave the next day, Monday, December 7, for Hasselt, the capital of the Limburg Province. Leaving the same

Unidentified Rhodes scholars in the CRB's Rotterdam office study materials before leaving for Belgium. In the foreground is a prominent Belgian, last name Rolin, delegated by the Comité National to serve in the Rotterdam office. (Public domain; Hoover Institution Archives, Stanford University, California.)

day would be Spaulding and Walter C. Lowdermilk, who were assigned to the Hainaut Province. Many of the other Oxford men would go to Brussels the same day to attend more orientation meetings before receiving assignments from the Brussels office.

As for Nelson, Sunday evening he wrote, "I shall be here at Rotterdam for a few days at least; possibly I shall be attached to the office here for some time. It is all in Capt. Lucey's hands."

But the next day, as the others were leaving, plans had already changed for Nelson. After visiting Lucey again on Monday morning, he was told he would leave that afternoon to go to Liège via Maastricht. Nelson wrote his father, "It is now two-thirty; we will get our pass-ports back from the German consul at four o'clock; and presumably we shall leave on the evening train for Maastricht."

He would travel with twenty-four-year-old Emil Hollmann, who had been assigned to the Dutch town of Maastricht. Hollmann was president of the Oxford Americans Club and had helped Galpin and Bowden organize the first meeting of students interested in joining the CRB. Lucey had tasked Hollmann with establishing a central station and a forwarding and trans-shipping office at Maastricht because all supplies for the provinces of Liège and Limburg, and a lot for Namur, would come by rail or canal barge via Maastricht.

As the two men prepared to leave Rotterdam, Nelson wrote his parents about his change in orders and told them they needed to be careful when writing him. All letters should be sent to Rotterdam in care of Captain Lucey. As for content, Nelson warned "under no condition to write anything which might be called into question by the authorities. The Germans have been very obliging, but when the lives of so many are at stake, we cannot afford to take any chances. Besides, we have to deal not only with the Germans, but also with the British and the French, who from the strictly military point of view are not in favor of the work we are doing, and have even placed considerable difficulties in our way."

Nelson's entry into Belgium would not be the easiest, and it reflected just how confusing the situation still was. When he and Hollmann reached Maastricht on Tuesday, December 8, Hollmann began working on his assignment while Nelson began to arrange for another food train from Holland to Liège in Belgium. To complicate matters, Nelson discovered that the train would not be allowed through the border due to the decision of some Dutch stationmasters south of Maastricht.

Nelson—quickly learning that one of the most important CRB characteristics was improvisation—decided he needed to talk directly with those stationmasters. He found a ride the next day in a motorcar from Maastricht south seven miles to the small Dutch town of Eijsden (not to be confused with the Belgian town of Eisden, which was north of Maastricht), where the train's permits were being held up. Once there, "after scouring the town I got to the burgomaster's chateau and managed to secure a man who could speak English as well as Dutch, French, and German. You need all to deal with a Dutch official. A Dutchman is without question the slowest person on earth." The volunteer he found to help him with the difficult Dutch officials was a "very nice fellow; count or something, I heard them call him. He thanked me very much for what we Americans are doing and wouldn't hear of my thanking him."

Once Nelson and his volunteer had convinced the stationmasters to allow the train through, and secured clearances, permits, and scheduling for the oncoming train, another problem arose. The motorcar that had given him a ride had left, and he had no way to get to his next stop, the Belgian village of Visé, which was across the border and about five miles south of Eijsden. There were no motorcars to be had, and the Dutch stationmaster in Eijsden would not allow him to ride on the train that would come through later: "Verboden, you know," Nelson was told.

The only thing to do was walk. But he had his valise with him, and it was too heavy to carry such a distance. With little confidence he'd ever see it again, the CRB delegate left his suitcase at the station to be for-warded to him whenever possible. "I shall entertain no hope till I actu-ally lay my hands on it again."

Ever the pragmatist, Nelson took a moment "to eat a little lunch be-fore starting on the walk, as rations may be rather scarce in Belgium." At the café, none of his three lan-guages helped much: "The waitress at this little café knows no English, and so little French or German that it is painful to try to get any-thing, but I finally got her to bring forth some bread and cheese and cold meat and, of course, beer. I didn't have to mention that." In the café he had been writing a letter to his family. He signed off, "Well, now for the Germans—with much love to you all. Dave."

On a cold December afternoon, twenty-three-year-old David T. Nelson walked alone into Belgium not knowing what to expect. He had only the clothes on his back and what was in his pockets. (Public domain; Herbert Hoover Presidential Library Archives, West Branch, Iowa.)

On that cold Wednesday afternoon, December 9, as the sun was get-ting low in the sky, Nelson—sans suitcase and carrying only the clothes on his back, his wallet, his ever-present little Lefax notebook, identity pa-pers, and permits to enter Belgium—began his lonely walk into German-held territory.

The Second Wave Hits Belgium

The same day Nelson was walking into Belgium wondering what he had gotten into, the second wave of fifteen Oxford students departed England for Rotterdam. Besides Galpin, Carmichael, and Branscomb, ages twenty-five, twenty-three, and nineteen, respectively, there were six others who would later be officially recognized as having served as CRB delegates: Charles F. Hawkins, age twenty-two, from New York; William W. Flint, also twenty-two, from New Hampshire; Thomas H. Jones, twen-ty-six, from Kentucky; Robert H. Warren, twenty-one, from Michigan;

Charles R. Clason, twenty-four, from Maine; and John L. Glenn, twenty-two, from South Carolina.

Six others, for unknown reasons (which are later discussed), would never be recognized officially as having served with the CRB even though they were part of the second Oxford wave: twenty-two-year-olds George B. Noble, from Florida, and Clarence A. Castle, from Missouri; twenty-three-year-olds Francis L. Patton, from Ohio, William H. Mechling, from Pennsylvania, and Clyde Eagleton, from Texas; and twenty-five-year-old Alexander R. Wheeler, from Pennsylvania.

The group was informally shepherded by Galpin, who had been the primary organizer and decision maker of the Oxford men in the first two waves. Galpin had always wanted to go but had not included himself in the first ten because he was unsure he could give the CRB the minimum amount of six weeks. He felt the six weeks would take away from his Oxford work, which was a thesis in modern English history titled "The Rise of English Political Parties, 1660–1685." He was in his second year, was not a Rhodes scholar, and "felt that it was my duty to continue my plans."

But Hoover and Rickard kept at him to go to Belgium, and his thoughts continued to return to the importance of the work. Ultimately, it was one of Galpin's previous Yale professors, George Burton Adams, then in London, who changed his mind. Galpin went around to see him and asked for advice. "I still remember his telling me that it was perhaps better to go and make a little history than it was to study it."

As part of this second wave, Galpin wrote how the group crossed the channel on Wednesday, December 9, on the SS *Mecklenburg*, a Dutch steamer. Before embarking, they had been screened by Scotland Yard and waited forty-five minutes in line. The experience was a far cry from the strip search endured by Hoover only a couple of weeks before. Galpin noted that "the British officials showed us every courtesy, as in theory Ambassador Page is directly responsible for each one of us." He also found it interesting that "most of the clerks think that I have a commission, or am a Canadian at any rate."

After discussions with Captain Lucey, the men were ready to enter Belgium. As Galpin related to his brother in a final letter home, "Since tomorrow we leave civilization as represented by a good country with cheap cigars that is not at war, I suppose that this will be the last news from me ... for some time. ... Tomorrow we meet militarism in person and then may learn a little of a new phase of existence." Galpin, just like the other new recruits, was taken aback by the sheer magnitude of the endeavor. "The amazing size of the work appalls me more and more for it is worldwide in its organization as you probably know. But I will leave all superlatives to the official press agent."

When the fifteen reached Rotterdam, Lucey assigned Galpin the task of overseeing all the CRB delegates in Belgium. Galpin wrote his brother: "My job will be the general supervision and control of the eleven different distribution centers in Belgium. I will have headquarters in Brussels where the system is working ok, and with a motor and a traffic man to go with me." Galpin would quickly find out that his job, and the jobs of the others, wasn't as well defined and established as he thought.

Galpin and most of the fifteen men were sent on to Brussels rather than assigned to a specific province. When they reached Brussels they met up with many of the first ten from Oxford. The CRB had arranged for all of the Oxford students to stay at the Palace Hotel in the lower, older part of town. *Baedeker's Belgium and Holland* tour book described the hotel as "a new and luxurious establishment opened in 1909" that boasted a bathroom with each room and a "high-class restaurant and frequented taverne." After the city's surrender, the Germans had requisitioned most of the rooms for their officers. For the Oxford students, the luxurious establishment was a far cry from the countryside camping and sleeping on top of train cars that they had initially expected. The Brussels hotel also instantly exposed them to more German officers than they had ever thought they'd see in their six weeks' work.

A humorous personal essay titled "The CRB in Swaddling Clothes," written by delegate Gilchrist Stockton, set a comical scene of those early days of the delegates and their stay at the Palace, where "the balance of the first and second contingents camped all over the place from the Coiffeur [barber] to the Tavern. Robinson Smith had been corralled somewhere and added to the gang. There was [George] Spaulding telling a crowd that if the CRB insisted on their being put up at the best place in town that the Hotel de Ville [city hall] was a lot sweller looking from the outside. [Charles] Clason was asking, 'What the hell is a guy expected to do in this league?' [Carleton] Bowden was complaining that every time he asked for something to do he was asked if he needed any money. Bowden said that he had never refused such an offer before but that he no longer took any interest in shekels. It was too easy. P. C. Galpin looked distracted.

Every now and then he would take out his note-book and check [off] those in sight."

While it was a humorous sketch, it accurately reflected the first couple of weeks, when many of these delegates were ready to get to work, but CRB executives in Brussels had not yet determined how best to utilize them. In these early days, with Heineman's Brussels office often focused more on German relations and Comité National matters than getting the Oxford men moving, the newly created CRB delegates in Brussels didn't have much to do.

As one CRB history related, "In those first days everything was in a very chaotic condition. It was naturally impossible to create a smoothly working organization to handle so tremendous a task in the short space of a few weeks. When the first batch of Rhodes scholars arrived at Brussels . . . no one in the Brussels office seemed to know what they were to do, save that they were to represent the Commission in some matter in the provinces. The only emphatic instructions which they had received were that they were to be punctiliously neutral in every word and deed and were to avoid any sort of friction with the German authorities. This had been intimated to them at London, repeated emphatically and eloquently at Rotterdam by Captain Lucey, and reiterated tearfully but sternly in Brussels by Jarvis Bell. They spent several days, or even weeks, alternating between the Palace Hotel and the Rue de Naples [CRB office] before they were all assigned to their posts and given their instructions."

Heineman's lack of focus in getting the delegates into the field was a serious issue that Captain Lucey and Hoover were concerned about and were trying to deal with in early December. This serious side of having no work for the delegates was also humorously touched on in "The CRB in Swaddling Clothes" through a story about Robinson Smith. Smith was not an Oxford student and was older than most of the early Oxford delegates. Earlier in the year his book, *The Life of Cervantes*, had been published. As one later delegate described Smith, he was "a queer duck. . . . His voice is a 'fog horn drawl' and his favorite hobby is the rescue of fallen women."

According to "The CRB in Swaddling Clothes," while at the Palace Hotel with the other delegates, Smith "wrote a petition to Mr. Whitlock, denouncing Heineman. Everybody signed it with fervor. They were ready to denounce anybody. However, sober second thought came to most of them and they went to Robinson Smith's room, at all hours of the night, and resigned the honor of petitioning the Minister; Heineman was still the boss and none of them wanted to be fired before even getting a job. . . . In the morning nobody was left on the petition except Smith and Carmichael. Smith took it around to the Legation early before Carmichael could change his mind also."

Whitlock was not amused. According to the tale, "The Minister wanted to send Robinson Smith out of the country when he read the petition, but didn't."

The story has never been verified, but it does reflect the frustration the men were feeling about not receiving assignments. The essay relays more of that frustration when it describes how the first days were spent by most of the men. It captures a bit of Galpin as mother hen of the group: "Every morning Galpin conducted the crowd around to the Rue de Naples [Heineman's offices initially used for the CRB]. They would wait around for an hour or so, and then Galpin would come out of [Amos] Johnson's office and say, 'That is all this morning, boys,' and then in despair would add, 'Does anybody need any money?' upon which there was a wild stampede for fresh air."

Kittredge and Simpson Head for Hasselt

There were some lucky Oxford students who already had their assignments and were on the job. Kittredge and Simpson had received their marching orders from Captain Lucey and had left Rotterdam and gone to Hasselt, the capital of the Flemish province of Limburg in the northeast corner of Belgium. The city of approximately 17,000 people had been founded in the seventh century and had maintained many of its ancient buildings, including the late Gothic main church.

When Kittredge and Simpson arrived, they checked into a hotel and began working. Kittredge had been designated as the chief delegate, but that didn't carry much weight, status, or privileges. They both did whatever was needed to move relief efforts forward. Throughout December they ventured into the city and the surrounding region, contacting rural and city officials, provincial committee representatives, and anyone else who they thought they should call on. They also began setting up an office, filing reports with Brussels, and planning how they would fit into the Belgian distribution system that was already basically in place.

Kittredge wrote later in a CRB history that all the young CRB delegates had "come into Belgium keyed up with heroic resolve to devote their

Left: Tracy B. Kittredge. Right: Richard H. Simpson. (Both photos: public domain; Herbert Hoover Presidential Library Archives, West Branch, Iowa.)

whole energy and ability to the work. No one in London, Rotterdam or Brussels could tell them exactly what that work was to be, so out into the provinces they went and there found work a plenty. In those first days they seldom stopped to enquire what their specific duties were. The food was to be distributed to every household in Belgium, and an infinite amount of detailed organization had to be accomplished before this end could be attained. The delegates almost to a man threw themselves into the breach and did what was to be done without enquiring what their authority was, or whether they were expected to attack the problems to which they devoted themselves."

Kittredge went on to describe some of what they did. "There was indeed much to do: ships to be helped through damaged canals; sunken bridges and barges to be lifted out; lightermen to be cajoled or intimidated into obeying orders; warehouses and depots to be installed, filled and protected; communication within the provinces and with Brussels to be established; mills to be controlled; bakers to be constrained into living up to their contracts; systems of distribution, administrative forms, ration cards to be devised and put into effect; local committees to be organized and induced to distribute food according to instructions; complaints to be investigated and difficulties with the Germans to be smoothed out."With great understatement, he concluded, "The task was a formidable one."

While Kittredge and Simpson were at a distinct disadvantage when it came to understanding their region, the food needed, and the details of how the distribution worked, they had two aces in the hole: They were neutral, and they could move about relatively unrestricted. Neutrality afforded them the ability to work with both the Belgians and the Germans. The ability to move about the region was also special because at this early stage in the German occupation very few Belgians were allowed even to leave their own towns or villages. It was true that by December some areas and cities were starting to see tram and train services restarted, but it was also true that communication was still nearly nonexistent and personal movement was highly restricted.

Because Kittredge and Simpson, along with every other CRB man, were able to obtain German passes to travel for the work, they became vital lifelines of information between Belgian relief officials in the larger cities and their counterparts in villages and towns within the surrounding countryside. They could help collect and disseminate information about food stores, canal viability, and soup kitchen statistics regarding those able to pay for their daily rations and those on complete charity. By providing such invaluable services, these December delegates were able to help prove the CRB's worth in the eyes of many Belgians beyond the food that the Americans could provide.

Transportation was by motorcar, whenever available. The CRB and the German authorities were generally the only two groups allowed to use automobiles in Belgium. The Willys-Overland Motor Company, with its well-known Overland motorcars, had donated a fleet of machines for CRB use, but the cars had not yet arrived in early December. Nevertheless, delegates at this time always seemed to find a ride, either with a motorcar and driver donated by a prominent local person or with a sympathetic German officer.

All Belgian and U.S. motorcars used by the CRB were provided with Belgian drivers. This not only gave much-needed employment to Belgians but it also displayed to the public and the Germans the proper level of respect and professionalism that the CRB hoped to achieve in Belgium.

When in use by the CRB, most of the vehicles were initially decked out with American flags on the front fenders and a placard labeled CRB on the engine cowling. A motorcar so decorated never failed to draw crowds of Belgians and even cheers as it traveled throughout the cities and countryside. These displays quickly drew the ire of the German authorities, however, and it wasn't long before they would take action to quash such spontaneous events.

Spaulding and Lowdermilk Land at Chateau de Mariemont

Spaulding and Lowdermilk were two delegates who were not initially provided with a car. They had been assigned the Hainaut Province on Belgium's south-central border with France. The province's capital was Mons, which sat on a hill above the Trouille River and was home to approximately 29,000 French-speaking Walloons. When the two American delegates arrived in Mons on Tuesday night, December 8, they found that arrangements had already been made to put them up with two different families. Spaulding was placed with a "prominent lawyer, well known, not only in Mons but throughout Belgium." The man and his wife, with the last name Heupgen, took Spaulding in "like a son and they could not have been more attentive to my wants and comforts."

As Spaulding recounted, no food imports were due into the province for "several weeks," so he and Lowdermilk were to travel "from city to city to get information on local supplies and to leave instructions for the formation of committees to handle the food when it did come." The two Americans were "handicapped by the lack of a car of our own to get around in," but Spaulding's host loaned them his when he wasn't doing official business allowed by the Germans.

Soon after they arrived in Mons, however, the two CRB delegates had a fortuitous meeting with an important Belgian that changed not only their transportation but their living and working arrangements. It was a story that was indicative of other delegates' experiences throughout Belgium.

In Spaulding and Lowdermilk's meetings with city and provincial officials, they were introduced to Raoul Warocqué, a forty-four-year-old industrialist and philanthropist who had built on two generations of family fortune to become one of the richest men in Europe. Before the war, he had taken the money he had made from coal mines, gas and electric companies, railroads, and other international businesses and had opened schools, an orphanage, a maternity hospital, and a soup kitchen to feed the poor. His business stature and charitable giving made him a natural for supporting Belgian relief through the Comité National, the provincial committee, and the CRB. Even though he was relatively young, Warocqué was not a healthy man. He was overweight and had "serious breathing problems." He would receive "special treatments every morning under the supervision of a physician." Even so, "he was an extremely jovial and friendly fellow . . . [with] quite a zest for life and many interests."

When Warocqué met Spaulding and Lowdermilk, he learned of their need for a motorcar that they could use all the time. Spaulding said that Warocqué "immediately offered us use of one of his with a driver, if we would come and live with him. It seemed a sensible thing to do; so Lowdermilk and I transferred to Chateau de Mariemont."

The estate had been originally created in the sixteenth century by Mary of Hungary as an official royal estate and hunting reserve. The chateau was filled with a large staff that included footmen, butlers, valets, gardeners, maids, and Warocqué's personal secretary and companion. The library had 50,000 books; the basement held a special cellar for growing mushrooms and chicory; and the extensive wine cellar was complete with false walls to hide his best wines and artwork.

The estate's grounds were massive, with manicured lawns and gardens surrounding the chateau and four flower houses, one of which was "a huge glass building, 40–50 feet high and perhaps 150 feet long [that] housed a real tropical jungle." Spaulding was "particularly intrigued by the special hot house for growing delicious purple grapes. The heating and refrigeration were so perfectly timed that there were ripe grapes available every day of the year. As soon as the grapes were ripe in the compartment for the current month, [the compartment] was chilled, causing the leaves to drop. Then the vines were pruned and prepared for a period of dormancy. At just the right time a few months later, the compartment was warmed to start growth and production of a new crop in the month intended."

Farther from the mansion were the ruins of the original castle from 1548 and large tracts of thick forest. Spaulding wrote: "Lowdermilk was taking a forestry course at Oxford; so the trees and shrubs were of special importance to him, but they fascinated me as well. Among the trees were several small lakes populated with many kinds of water fowl."

With such diversions, it's a wonder the two delegates did any work. But Spaulding wrote that they soon had settled into a regular routine. "Immediately after breakfast the car was brought and we were driven to one town after another to get information on the food supplies and to suggest to the burgomasters that they appoint a committee to handle the food when it arrived. Since distances were fairly short, we usually returned for lunch and went out again in the afternoon."

By the end of December, however, the two Americans were traveling deeper into the province, which led to encounters with German soldiers who knew nothing of the relief work and didn't know exactly what to do with these wandering neutrals. Spaulding told of one such trip. "After checking on food supplies in nearby towns, we began to go farther afield. On a snappy morning between Christmas and New Year's Day we took off for Chimay," a small town of 3,000 people in the southernmost tip of Hainaut Province.

"About 11 a.m. we reached the outskirts of Chimay and were stopped by a German sentry who was puzzled about what to do with us. I should say that we carried a small American flag on one of the front fenders of the car and a Belgian flag on the other. One thing for sure, the sentry wasn't going to let us pass without consultation; so he called the officer of the guard who after a few questions decided to escort us personally by motorcycle to the army divisional headquarters located in the chateau of the Prince of Chimay."

At the chateau they were questioned thoroughly about who they were, their business, and what they wanted to do in Chimay. Their papers were looked over carefully. They were questioned again. Finally, as they thought they might end up in some German jail, they were told, "in a tone not to be ignored," that they would have lunch in the officers' mess. "This was so obviously an order that we accepted graciously."

This was no Spartan military lunch. It was held in the main dining room of the chateau. Because it was the Christmas season, the room was "heavily decorated with boughs and festoons of greenery. On the huge elongated oval table were two small Christmas trees prettily trimmed with baubles." The table was set as if to serve royalty, and Spaulding guessed it must be "the Prince's finest china and crystal ware. Gazing down upon us from the surrounding walls were several austere faces of former princes and princesses."

The two delegates must have stumbled upon a special holiday event, for Spaulding estimated there were at least two dozen officers in attendance. "Each one quietly took his allotted place at the table and stood silently and stiffly behind his chair, waiting for the arrival of the commanding officer. He soon entered the room in quick strides, introduced us to the group at large and gave the signal to be seated. We were then immediately engulfed in an outburst of noisy, jovial conversation."

Spaulding concluded the story by writing, "A clearance from Brussels had obviously arrived during lunch for as soon as it was over we were told to go about our business."

Back at Chateau de Mariemont, Spaulding wrote that during most evenings "the dress was informal, but the service was very formal indeed." The two Americans, Warocqué, and any visitors would sit "together at one end of the large oval dining table and were served course after course by a butler in evening dress. The wine steward was particularly formal. As he served the proper wine for the course he would give the vintage of the wine in a low voice and wait for your nod before filling your glass. At first, I couldn't make out what he was saying but after being told it was easy to detect that he was mumbling the vintage date each time around, I distinctly remember two dates—quatre-vingt-dix and quatre-vingt-dix-sept (1890 and 1897)—as two of the fine quality red wines. The truth is that my taste for wine was so spoiled by my first experience in drinking it, that I have never since seemed to be able to find wines that could compare in flavor and smoothness with those offered at Chateau de Mariemont."

All of this opulence was a far cry from what both Americans had known when attending the University of Arizona. They were far more familiar with life in the American West than life in a Belgian chateau. In fact, while the particulars of Spaulding and Lowdermilk's living situation were unique, their general circumstances were not so out of the ordinary compared with many of the other CRB delegates' experiences in Belgium.

Such a life of privilege and wealth was something none of the CRB men would have ever dreamed of when contemplating working in Belgium. And Hoover would have never condoned their living that way if he had had his way. But adequate food, shelter, and transportation were critical for CRB delegates to do their jobs, and most of the wealthy people in Belgium were more than happy to open their homes to these industrious and brash young Americans who only wanted to help Belgium. By supporting the Americans in this way, wealthy Belgians felt they were doing their small part to help their country.

Their reasons for support of the delegates weren't all altruistic, however. Many of them also hoped that by being associated with the Americans they and their properties would be less likely to be abused by the Germans. In the majority of cases that turned out to be true.

For many of the delegates, it was difficult or confusing to be on the receiving end of such largesse. Some felt awkward or embarrassed when experiencing such luxury and comfort in a time when most of the country was on the brink of starvation. A few of the men would struggle mentally with trying to reconcile such extremes, and their health would suffer for it.

Nelson Walks Into Belgium

One person who would have been happy for just a touch of luxury was David Nelson as he walked solo into Belgium for the first time. With no suitcase and little besides the clothes on his back, Nelson was imagining the worst as he approached the Dutch/Belgian border.

What happened next caught him off guard. Nothing. "It was a distinct surprise to me after the picture I had formed of being stopped and obliged to show my papers at every cross-road." Customs officials quickly passed him through to Belgium and the town of Visé. He walked among the ruined parts of town before going to the train station. There he ended up chatting with the German stationmasters before taking a train to nearby Liège. From the station in Liège he caught a ride with a German merchant in his motorcar to the city's Grand Hotel, which sat on one of the major squares, Place Saint Lambert.

Liège was one of Belgium's major cities, and as the capital of Liège Province it boasted a university, a bishop, and more than 175,000 residents. *Baedeker's Belgium and Holland* declared that Liège "lies in a strikingly picturesque situation. The ancient and extensive city rises on the lofty bank of the broad Meuse. . . . Numerous factory-chimneys bear testimony to the industry of the inhabitants, while the richly-cultivated valley contributes greatly to enhance the picturesque effect."

Because Liège was also at the confluence of the Meuse and the Ourthe rivers, an island was part of the city center. It was connected to the right bank by five bridges and to the left bank by six bridges and a small iron footbridge. The main part of town, with its principal buildings and churches, was on the left bank while numerous factories and the homes of workers and artisans were on the right bank.

Before the war Liège had been a prosperous city due to the surrounding coalfields and the numerous manufacturing industries that had grown up over generations. In an unusual turn, one of the city's major businesses had for years utilized laborers' homes. As explained by *Baedeker's*, "One of the chief branches of industry is the manufacture of weapons of all kinds, which have enjoyed both a European and a Transatlantic reputation since the end of the 18th century. The pieces are made and mounted by the workmen in their own houses. These mechanics, 40,000 in number, work at their own risk, for a piece containing the slightest flaw is at once rejected." Additional industries in and around the city included zinc foundries, engine factories, and cycle and motor works. The city was also home to the royal gun factory, the cannon foundry, and the Société de St. Leonard, which made steam locomotives.

The people in such a highly industrialized city were not only hardworking but surprisingly free-spirited and resentful of any authority that tried to restrict them. In a history that included numerous invasions by various countries, the residents of Liège "frequently manifested a fierce and implacable spirit of hostility towards those who have attempted to infringe their privileges."

Couple such spirit with the city's valuable industries and it wasn't surprising that twelve fortresses encircled the city within three to five miles and made Liège one of the most daunting fortifications along the Meuse. It was the first major city the Germans had attacked in their August invasion, primarily because it sat within the Meuse Valley, which they needed to traverse to reach France. Liège's forts and 30,000 troops had slowed down the Germans for a critical twelve days in August, but they were ultimately no match for the German Army and five days of constant bombardment by massive Big Bertha artillery.

As Nelson noted, however, much of the city was still intact. "When I entered Liège I was surprised to find that the city had not suffered at all from the bombardment. It may be that in the outskirts some traces may be found; I have not yet been around the city to any extent. But the main portion of the city is absolutely intact with the exception of a few buildings opposite the University which were destroyed because of a riot, and of course the bridges, several of which were torn down by the Belgians. The Germans, however, are repairing them rapidly."

For Nelson, the first experiences with Germans were what he had hoped for. Unlike most of the CRB delegates, he was self-proclaimed "pro-German" and found it difficult to believe many of the stories he had read about German atrocities. He wrote his parents that during his journey into Belgium he was "stopped by no 'haughty German officers,'" as he had been forewarned about. At Visé, he wrote that two German stationmasters, once they learned he was American, had "brought forth cigars and a bottle of German beer, and we talked, with slight interruptions, for two hours or more. (I speak wretched German and worse French, I might add)."

After nearly a week in Liège, Nelson wrote to his parents more about the Germans: "I have found them uniformly courteous. They mind their own business strictly and give the Belgians great freedom when one considers the tenseness of the situation." The city curfew was at seven in the evening, but Nelson said the Germans were relatively lax about enforcing the exact time, and that "whenever I have observed them in cafés or elsewhere, [they] pay for all they get."

The only thing he didn't like about the Germans were their loud cars. "The military autos go by early and late and their horns make an infernal noise, for they have right of way and must give everyone warning to scatter."

Near the end of his long letter, Nelson wrote: "I suppose you will say that my pro-German sympathies have not vanished yet, but frankly, after seeing what has so far come under my observation, I can honestly say that I now feel justified in not believing the atrocious stories that reached America from London. . . . And I say this not because this letter will come under the eye of the German censor . . . but rather because I think that justice should be rendered where justice is due."

It was Monday, December 14, the first week in Belgium for Nelson, and his feelings for the Germans were practically the same as when he had left America three months before. Shortly, though, he would move in with a Belgian family, become heavily involved in the CRB work, and begin to see the Germans in a different light.

———————

During the month of December, many of the CRB delegates worked tirelessly and surprised everyone—probably even themselves—at what they were accomplishing. As Kittredge summed up later in his CRB history, "One of the best tributes to the efficiency with which these young Americans rose to the issue is the fact that food-supplies were being distributed in every province and in almost every village within six weeks of the time of their arrival on the scene. In all their work at first they had little but moral backing on which to depend, but they were young, fearless, energetic and American, and their initiative inspired confidence in the committees which at first had looked askance at their youth. They commandeered automobiles from the Belgians who were only too willing to offer them. They extracted passports and motor-fuel from the German authorities. They personally patrolled the canals and on occasions even lent a hand to remove debris and clear up channels for the lighters. They personally supervised the early distribution and made sure that the food was sent to the places of ultimate distribution with as much speed as possible. In all this they had but few instructions from the Brussels office."

Without stating it directly, Kittredge was damning the Brussels office for lack of guidance. He got his point across by listing who had done what without help from Brussels. "Jackson in Liège depended almost altogether on Captain Lucey for instructions, and Kittredge, the delegate for Limburg, went directly to his province from Rotterdam and was there at work two weeks before he even visited Brussels. Mr. Edward Eyre Hunt . . . was asked to become the Commission's delegate in Antwerp and he, with the aid of the Antwerp committee, practically worked out his entire distribution system without a word of advice or instruction from Brussels. Mr. Robinson Smith working at Mons, in the Hainaut, in the face of alarming food shortages, was yet able, on his own initiative, to get the Commission's food quickly and effectively distributed in time to prevent any real famine, but he too had little help from Brussels. Glenn and Bowden at Namur, and Wellington and Hawkins in the Luxembourg, spent all their time traveling over their provinces organizing committees, repairing canals, and getting things under way, on their own initiative."

Kittredge was being somewhat generous when he wrote, "At this time the people at the Brussels office were absorbed in completing the general outline of the Commission's distribution system, and had but little understanding of the conditions in the provinces and but little appreciation of the problems by which the delegates were faced."

The delegates—and probably Hoover and Lucey—couldn't help but wonder what was going on in Brussels.

THIRTY-THREE

Antwerp

Hunt Begins Working for the CRB in a "Dead City"

On Friday, December 11, as the second wave of Oxford students were either meeting with Captain Lucey or on their way to Brussels, E. E. Hunt arrived in Antwerp as the new CRB chief delegate for the province of Antwerp. The last time he saw the city, it was reeling from brutal bombardment, was burning and beaten, and was in the process of surrendering to the German invaders.

In Hunt's view, the city had not improved much, for "the hum and the throb of industry were gone; the quays were empty; factories were shut; acres of rusting wagons and rotting ships lined the northern basins; the warehouses were sealed and guarded by German soldiers; labor was dispersed; and the very air was idle and noisome." To him, Antwerp was now "a dead city."

Even though it was the season of Saint Nicholas and a time of gift giving and goodwill toward others, there didn't seem to be much of either.

A notice at the Red Cross set a decidedly sad tone: "This year Saint Nicholas cannot make a proper distribution of presents to the poor children of Belgium. Therefore it will be necessary to have useful things to give to the little ones: a pair of slippers, a warm dress, or something of the sort for distribution through the hospitals, children's refuges, and *crèches* [day nurseries]."

A few shops were still able to sell the usual Christmas cakes and candies. One Belgian treat, *speculoos*, was normally only made around the Saint Nicholas feast of December 6. Fashioned into various holiday shapes, the hard gingerbread biscuit-like *speculoos* came in either thin cookies or thicker pieces that were perfect for dunking in Belgium's traditional chicory-flavored coffee. Normally, bakers would have large window displays of *speculoos* and other confectionery treats, but this December, with the lack of milk, eggs, and flour, displays were modest at best.

In a department store along the city's broad commercial street Place de Meir, Hunt noted that there was a Saint Nicholas dressed in a "bishop's golden mitre and chasuble, white lace cotta and black cassock, mittens, and gold crosier," which gave the place "a touch at least of the Christmas season," but "the good bishop did not resemble our jolly, homely Santa Claus."

What were the residents to do?

"There was nothing to do," Hunt wrote, "but to promenade, so the streets were thronged with women in mourning and idle men who passed aimlessly up and down, or studied the pillar-posts where the German Government posted its regulations in the German, Flemish, and French languages." Beggars still roamed the streets, but no one gave to them anymore, so "they walked aimlessly and indifferently; and their faces were inexpressively sad."

The situation was compounded by refugees returning from Holland. Hunt estimated there were probably 30,000, and many "were without homes, most were without money, all were without work."

With no civilian motorcars allowed and few draft animals left after German requisitioning, the streets were filled with carts and wagons that were dragged over the cobblestone streets by dogs and sometimes men and women. The magnificent Central Station was heavily barricaded with sandbags and protected by "rapid-fire guns" that pointed down the Avenue de Keyzer toward the center of town.

Every day there were long lines of petitioners at the German pass bureau, which was protected by three lines of German sentries. The Belgians in line were all seeking passes to the suburbs, Brussels, or other parts of the country. Each different type of pass had a corresponding fee, which could be substantial. According to Hunt, farmers coming into Antwerp to sell their "scanty stock of vegetables and milk" had to pay their local pass bureau as much as three German marks.

Despite—or more likely because of—Antwerp's condition, Hunt threw himself into the work. The moment he arrived in town he went straight to the *hôtel de ville* to present himself to Burgomaster Jan de Vos and any other officials he could find. To get there, he took the same route the victorious German Army had taken when first marching into

Louis Franck, president of the Comité National's provincial committee in Antwerp. (Public domain; *War Bread,* E. E. Hunt, Henry Holt & Co., 1916.)

the city in October. He walked down Place de Meir, passed by the cathedral with its magnificent tower (now capped by a German flag), and then entered the famous Flemish square, the *grand place*, which was ringed by ornate guild halls and little medieval shops. German sentries guarded the doors to the *hôtel de ville*. As Hunt was allowed into the town hall, "a stench of cabbage soup swam out of the open doors, for most of the guard was at mess, laughing and eating below stairs."

Hunt met with de Vos and was introduced to Louis Franck, the president of the CN's provincial committee, who had organized the city's surrender. Hunt was impressed with the surroundings and with Franck. "He sat in a paneled room of Flemish oak and gold, behind a massive oaken desk, facing a magnificent marble chimney-piece from the old Abbey of Tongerloo; his bold head framed with a cascade of curly, jet-black hair and black Assyrian beard. He was forty-seven years old, in the prime of his strength, with an optimistic faith in the future of Belgium which was contagious."

Hunt's timing was opportune; the first gathering of the CN's Antwerp provincial committee was about to begin. Franck walked Hunt from his office to the building's marriage hall, where the meeting was to be held. "Down upon us from the walls smiled paintings of marriage ceremonies, Gaulish, Roman, Old Flemish, of the time of Rubens, and of the period of the French Revolution." The paintings were the only clear thing Hunt saw, for when he turned to the assembled men, "it was a confused vision of bearded gentlemen, grave as prophets, in long black coats and stiff collars, whom later I was to know as loyal co-workers and patriots. They were aldermen and notable citizens of the city, country burgomasters and provincial deputies; representatives of all three political parties—Catholic, Liberal, Socialist; of all three classes of society— noble, bourgeois, and proletarian; and of a variety of professions and callings."

These were the most notable men of industry, commerce, and politics within the province. Some, such as Franck and Edouard Bunge, vice president of the committee, would become friends, some would not, but all were appreciative of Hunt's presence that day, for he represented in many ways not only America but the entire world. Despite the fact that he was a young, slight, beardless man who was unassuming and spoke little, he was still an American who was attending a Belgian meeting held in German-occupied Belgium. If nothing else, he was a symbol that America and the world cared about what happened to the Belgian people. Hunt might not have contributed a lot during the meeting, but he had already done a great deal just by showing up.

That day the first task for both the provincial committee and Hunt was discussed. It was agreed that information was critical. The committee and the CRB needed to know the status of all the towns and villages within the province of Antwerp. Official reports were needed from every commune on the extent of destitution, employment status, possibilities for putting people to work, prevalence of sickness, and need for food. Hunt wrote that when all that information was collected, a "card-index formula" would be established that would document "the conditions in the province and ultimately the condition of every individual who required relief."

The provincial committee issued its first letter to all 165 communes. It asked each to answer numerous questions and provide the following information:

- The total population of the commune
- Financial resources

- Immediate financial needs
- Inventory of existing foodstuffs of every sort
- Estimated daily necessities in foodstuffs—the basis for flour being not more than 250 grams per day per person
- Estimated daily necessities in fodder for cattle
- Whether there was a building ready to serve as communal food depot
- Whether medicine was needed in the commune

The answers and information were to be attested to by each burgomaster and sealed with the communal seal. Because mail had not yet resumed in Belgium and travel was highly restricted, the questionnaires would reach their destinations via any means possible, including via Belgians allowed to move about, helpful German officers, and even Hunt himself.

After the provincial committee meeting adjourned, Hunt wandered around town. He took a moment to enter the cathedral to see the work that was being done to fix the minor damage sustained during the bombardment. He also noted that the confessional previously marked "English Confessor" was now covered with a card in German script bearing the words, "Field Preacher Confessor Doctor Braun." It was probably hard for many Belgians to comprehend, but even the German soldiers seemed to need spiritual guidance.

Later, Hunt stopped at the American Consulate, where he had watched the victorious Germans march into the city a couple of months before. He talked with "kindly old" U.S. Consul General Henry W. Diederich and Vice Consul Harry Tuck Sherman. Since the city's surrender, they had gone all over Antwerp placing signs that stated "under the protection of the American Consulate," which Hunt believed "may have moderated German thoroughness and which certainly heartened the Belgians."

The two men offered Hunt some space in their offices for his CRB work, but within a few days an insurance company below the consulate offices agreed to donate some rooms. While it was a nice gesture, it was not a major concession for the company because "a caretaker and two or three clerks dismally played at business, keeping the long hours of the ordinary Belgian business-day, dusting, sweeping, casting up accounts, and puzzling over cryptic anagrams which prophesied the Kaiser's death or the capture of Berlin. They were delighted to have me near them, for in their eyes I guaranteed protection from the Germans."

Now that he had an office with a "modest" table, a typewriter, and five chairs, it was time to get to work. But what exactly was he to do?

As was the case with any CRB delegate entering a new region at this time, it was mostly a matter of carving out one's own job. Hunt wrote: "My duties as American delegate were necessarily ill-defined but capable of almost unlimited extension. Holding the power-of-attorney of the American Minister, I was in theory the owner of all supplies imported into the province of Antwerp by the Commission for Relief in Belgium from the time they reached me on the canal boats from Rotterdam up to the time of their consumption by the Belgians."

Because the food was officially consigned to Whitlock, and because Hunt and the others had been "delegated" by the minister through powers-of-attorney to act as consignees for the province, all cargoes of food arriving at Antwerp's port were Hunt's responsibility. He believed he was responsible for the food throughout the process, so "in theory this applied to . . . their transference to the docks or the Commission warehouses in Antwerp, Turnhout, Malines and Tamise; to their transport thence by canals or light railways to the regional warehouses; then to the one hundred and sixty-five communes; and so to the million and more individual consumers" in Antwerp Province.

For the intense journalist-turned-relief-worker, this responsibility was a sacred trust with international ramifications: "The Americans in Belgium were in honor bound to know what became of every item of supplies, for only on terms like these would Great Britain modify her blockade in favor of Belgium."

All this meant that Hunt had to be "familiar in detail not only with the transportation and distribution of imports, but also with the condition and needs of every commune in his province, and to report on these matters regularly to the headquarters of the Commission for Relief in Belgium and to the American Minister."

A Trip to a Village Brings Hope

Hunt decided he needed to venture out of the city and see firsthand what life was like in the small towns and villages. He applied to the German pass bureau for permission to visit the village of Boisschot. He also requested that two members of the provincial committee, Francois Franck and A. Palmans, accompany him. On Wednesday, December 16, the

As chief delegate of the city and province of Antwerp, E. E. Hunt began traveling into the countryside in his CRB motorcar to help determine who needed what and when. (Author's archives.)

three men took off in a borrowed Belgian Minerva limousine and headed southeast for the approximately twenty-five-mile trip to Boisschot. The motorcar was traveling in the area that the Belgians called the Campine, which was flat land covered with scrub pine trees and purple heather etched with slim creeks lined with willows that had been "pollard" pruned to keep them short. The area was considered the "less prosperous part of the province," according to Hunt.

Along the way the three men came to Koningshooikt, a hamlet of 3,000 residents. It had suffered in the invasion when ninety-eight homes had been completely destroyed and twenty-seven more had been partially damaged. Hunt stated the obvious when he wrote, "In so small a village the ruin was enormous."

A little farther on, they reached the town of Heyst op den Berg, and the road rose slightly in altitude. For Hunt, his "heart thrilled at the climb out of the flat Belgian plain, although the Berg is only a little hill. One could imagine oneself for a moment on the roof of the world, after the incessant monotony of the Flemish polders [low-lying land surrounded by dikes] and Campine."

Throughout the trip, Hunt "saw few signs of life. Almost every village through which we passed had been hammered with shells. Chickens and live-stock were rarities. Fear of the Germans was universal."

What he found in Boisschot, he later came to realize, was typical of many small villages in Antwerp Province. According to Hunt, the town hall was a "small, ugly building, not much superior to the old-fashioned Little Red School House of American pioneering days. The Burgomaster's office was a cold, bare rectangle, with sanded floors, a few thin chairs, and a long table piled with papers. A cheap lithograph of King Albert and Queen Elisabeth hung on the whitewashed walls of the room, and a framed proclamation printed in German, Flemish, and French, signed by the commandant of the district."

When the Minerva pulled up in front, it drew a crowd "of wooden-shoed villagers—the first automobile they had seen in four months." Inside, Hunt was "vigorously shaken by the hand and on friendly terms with a big blond Burgomaster named Baron de Gruben and a thin, bearded spectre who was the communal secretary."

Hunt, Franck, and Palmans had come not only to learn more about conditions in the country but to fill out the provincial committee's form. The questionnaire had been written in Flemish, but because of Hunt's lack of comprehension of Flemish, the questions were asked and answered in French.

In the give-and-take that ensued, Hunt was surreptitiously informed by his two companions that Burgomaster de Gruben was a gentleman and was unique because "most of our burgomasters ask for more than they have a right to. He is not so. He is a fine man, that Baron de Gruben."

Franck and Palmans also took this time to warn Hunt that "you must always be on your guard with the Belgian burgomaster. . . . The Belgian is a man who always complains—*qui toujours se plaint*. And he is stubborn, too. Always tell him what he must *not* do, then he will do what you wish. He is a man who goes to the door marked 'Exit' and comes out the door marked 'Entrance!'"

While getting all the details about Boisschot, the Antwerp group also learned other facts that weren't necessarily important to the relief work but provided insight into what the town had been through. Two of the village's teachers had been imprisoned by the Germans while both clergy and twenty other area priests had been taken. Initially, 200 residents had been arrested and transported to Germany. Since then 100 who were under sixteen or older than forty-five had been released; the rest remained prisoners in Germany. While the town and its homes had not been damaged by artillery fire, it had twice been evacuated and twice pillaged by German soldiers.

One of the few bits of good news was that no major sicknesses or diseases had so far appeared in the village. Throughout Belgium there was a growing concern that major health issues could arise due to deteriorating sanitary conditions and weakening individual health. Precautions were being taken at all levels to prevent any epidemics, including giving later CRB delegates the four-shot inoculation for typhoid, which made some of them sick.

As for the need for food relief, Boisschot had a population of 3,300, and 900 of those needed charity. De Gruben told Hunt and the two CN provincial committee members that the commune needed flour, peas, beans, rice, bacon, herring, gasoline, and coal. The residents also needed clothes and blankets. "Send us anything," the burgomaster pleaded. "We have been twice pillaged. We have nothing. We still eat, but we have no clothes."

The town's treasury was down to 2,000 francs but had recently secured a loan of 3,000 francs from a relief group in Antwerp. Franck and Palmans told de Gruben that the CN provincial committee would give the town 1,000 francs a month to provide assistance to its residents. The relief and appreciation by the village officials were nearly palpable.

With repeated assurances that the town had not been forgotten, the three climbed back into their motorcar. They were all painfully aware that they had just brought the town one item that was more valuable than food or clothes: hope.

When Hunt returned to Antwerp, he knew that Boisschot represented only one out of hundreds of villages scattered throughout the Antwerp Province that desperately needed help. How was he, as one man, to attempt supervision of relief efforts for all these villages and more than a million people?

Within ten days of his arrival in Antwerp, he received reinforcements— some by a little confiscation, some by official support.

On Monday, December 21, Hunt was in the office when CRB courier Edward Curtis walked in. He was "covered in mud and smiles and informed me that three new American delegates and three Overland motorcars were on their way from Rotterdam to Brussels."

Hunt was quick to say, "One of those automobiles is mine; *n'est-ce pas?*"

Curtis's reply was not what Hunt wanted to hear: "Brussels say they intend to supply themselves, and afterwards the provinces."

"Tell them two automobiles are coming," Hunt said. "This office has a motto—it's Antwerp first!"

In his efforts to secure one of the motorcars, Hunt had an unlikely assistant—the Germans. As the new delegates were driving down from Rotterdam in the new Overlands, they were arrested in Antwerp on some technicality, probably incorrect permits or passes. They were kept and questioned for three hours at the *kommandantur*, which gave Hunt plenty of time to speak with the Germans, argue his point of ownership, and "confiscate the car I wanted."

That act of confiscation didn't seem to affect support from the Brussels office. They sent three of the Oxford men to help Hunt: William W. Flint along with Oliver C. Carmichael and his nineteen-year-old friend Bennett H. Branscomb. Hunt—the nearly thirty-year-old worldly wise war correspondent—immediately took these young men under his wing and began training them how to be efficient, effective CRB delegates.

The Americans lived together in a "quiet mansion" on Rue Marie-Thérèse. "From the windows we overlooked a little park, and the capped, thoughtful statue of the artist Quinten Metseys. The lintel of our doorway was gashed, where an incendiary shell, striking in the street, had ricocheted and burst." The home had been donated by Bunge, and it had been the same place where Edouard, his three daughters, and their servants had lived during the bombardment of Antwerp.

Life for the Antwerp delegates was anything but ordinary. As Hunt noted, "The conditions of war soon grow to seem normal, but there is an emotional and physical strain about them which eats at one's heart." And home seemed far away, if not completely gone. "We received no letters or newspapers from any one outside of Belgium. We had no new books. We knew little about the progress of the war. Home was almost a myth." This was especially hard to bear for ex–war correspondent Hunt, who had consumed news and newspapers like a perpetually starving man.

But with a new Overland and three enthusiastic recruits, Hunt reported, "We Americans were busy and we were happy." He felt as if the tide was beginning to turn a little in his favor, and that of the Belgians.

THIRTY-FOUR

Elsewhere in Belgium

The story that Hunt had heard while in Boisschot was nearly the same in many other places throughout Belgium: Commune officials were trying to cope with greater and greater need as food stores and financial resources shrank. And many village officials were despairing because they thought they were working alone on the unsolvable problem of providing food for their citizens.

This was true in Luxembourg Province, which covered the southeastern tip of Belgium and was the country's physically largest province with the smallest number of residents. The small population, consisting mainly of Walloons (French-speaking Belgians usually living in the southern and eastern portion of the country), was due in part to the rugged terrain of a large portion of the province known as the Ardennes. This region was covered with dense forests, rolling hills, and steep ridges and was a major source of coal for Belgium and Europe.

Into this mining, industrial province the CRB sent two of its new delegates: Laurence C. Wellington, one of the first ten Oxford students; and Charles F. Hawkins, one of the second wave.

Hawkins had accompanied the first ten students to London for their departure just to see what was going on, but Hoover and his associates were so convincing of the need and urgency for good men that Hawkins had returned to Oxford only to pack and join the second wave. Galpin, in his initial list of potential recruits to Hoover, had described Hawkins as being a first-year Rhodes scholar, able to speak French and German, and "safe and sure." Hawkins, twenty-two, was the eldest son of a farmer in Warwick, New York. He had attended Williams College and graduated from Harvard before sailing on the SS *St. Paul* with Nelson and many other Rhodes scholars in September.

Hawkins's CRB partner, Wellington, was better known to his friends as "Duke," after the famous British Duke of Wellington who had defeated Napoleon at Waterloo, Belgium, in 1815. He was twenty-four and had grown up in Massachusetts as the only child of a professor of chemistry. After graduating from Williams College (just ahead of Hawkins), he had moved to New York City and taken an editorial job with the renowned *Century Magazine*. Deciding he wanted to teach English literature, he left magazine publishing and was accepted at Oxford. He and Galpin were the only two Oxford men in the first two waves who were not "Rhodesters," as Hunt referred to the Rhodes scholars. Good-looking with dark eyes, a small mouth, and blond hair that rarely stayed in place because of a cowlick, Wellington could speak German and a little French.

Hawkins and Wellington motored into the Ardennes as the first two delegates for the Luxembourg Province, wondering what lay before them. Wellington had been designated the chief delegate, possibly because he was two years older, had been in the first wave, had better language skills, or simply had made a better impression on Captain Lucey. At such an early stage, however, such a designation usually meant little—both men would end up doing anything and everything needed to get the job done.

As for the work, a later delegate remembered, "At that time the work was all to be organized, there was no postal system and Belgians were not allowed to circulate so that these two [Hawkins and Wellington] were the intermediaries and couriers between the central committee of intelligent and knowing business men and the small committees which ran the regional stores. All through the bitter months of winter they motored through the snow from region to region, bringing money and instruction, seeing that the shipments had arrived, explaining and organizing."

They also sat in on weekly meetings of the provincial committee, met with local commune officials, and filled out countless reports about what was being stored, what was being shipped, what was being received, what was being consumed, and what was needed to keep up with demand.

One of the biggest challenges for many delegates at this time was simply getting the food to its destinations. While the country's canal system was a slow, steady means of transporting cargo, it had also been purposefully damaged by the Belgians in defense of their country and by the Germans during the invasion. As Ben Allen, Hoover's journalist friend and CRB founding executive, explained, "The network of Belgian canals constitute the only means by which food can be transported into the country, and this system has also suffered from the vicissitudes of war."

According to Allen, in those cold and often wet December days, "it was necessary for the Commission to map and explore the entire canal system, to clear the wreckage from the streams and arrange with the local communes to remove the defensive obstructions. As the Belgian people are restricted by military order from traveling anywhere except within the immediate environs of their own homes, the pioneers of the Commission were compelled to grope their way like explorers in a newly discovered country."

Another delegate remembered: "In the early days of December 1914 the delegates were faced with the most interesting problems. They followed long expected lighters in their cars down the banks of the Meuse, the Sambre and the Scheldt [rivers], they demanded that debris of old bridges be blown up, that pontoon bridges be opened to allow passage of lighters, and did a hundred other interesting things."

Hunt recalled, "As for the canals, some of the dykes had been cut and were not yet repaired; bridges had been blown up for military reasons; barges had been sunk; and at important points the Belgians were not permitted to approach the canal embankments for fear they might attempt to damage the system to the detriment of the German armies."

No one knew for sure which canals were clear and which were blocked. As Hunt noted by middle to late December, "The Rotterdam office had been in operation for eight weeks, yet in that time it had secured practically no information regarding the condition of the Belgian waterways. In sheer desperation Captain Lucey had dispatched canal-boats of flour, rice, peas, and beans, without knowing whether the canals were navigable or blocked."

Lucey also sent Captain Sunderland, the man who had accompanied the first train shipment into Liège, back into Belgium with the urgent request for any information regarding canals. Hunt was determined to help and knew that what was needed was a system to be able to track lighters as they moved through Belgium. This was especially obvious to Hunt because there had been times when he and his Antwerp delegates had "spent days patrolling the canals in search of a lighter which had dropped from sight almost as if swallowed up by Father Scheldt [River] himself."

Hunt came up with a plan. If he could find a spot overlooking the Scheldt where the lighters could be seen as they entered Belgium, that information could be telegraphed to Rotterdam and Brussels for tracking. The lighters would be easy to identify because they all had distinctive names, such as "Marie Germaine," "Louisa," "Ariel," "Deo Gloria," "Dorothea," "Madonna," and "Frederika." He sent one of his new delegates, Flint, to find such a lookout along the shores of the Scheldt. Flint "set out on a river boat and disappeared for five days. Then he returned to Antwerp with a tale of great adventures, arrests, detentions, conferences, and agreements."

Flint had also found Fort Lillo, an ideal place to spot incoming barges. Close to the Dutch border, Fort Lillo was situated high above the river on old earthworks. The only things there were "a few trees, a few small Flemish houses in orderly rows, [and] a single customs house overlooking the river." Hunt and Flint motored out to negotiate for the job they needed. When they got there, "our limousine completely blocked the narrow lane before the customs house and drew all the civil and military population about us. Several Landsturm soldiers [older Germans used for non-combat duties] strolled up, puffing away at their pipes and staring. The Belgian population ranged itself silently about the car. The dead silence, the dropped jaws, the fixed eyes of such crowds were always disconcerting to us, but our Belgian chauffeur seemed as indifferent as a good actor before a crowded house."

Out of the customs house came two officials in their green uniforms and box caps. They "touched their foreheads, and bowed gravely." Hunt and Flint told them what they were after. Once the customs officers knew the two were with the CRB, the Belgians said they would be happy to provide all the names and shipping numbers of passing barges. But how to get the information back to the Antwerp office? The Belgians suggested asking the German officer in charge of the area, who had been helpful in the past.

"We lifted our hats, shook hands all round, and motored to a small bar-room—the office of the commandant." As soon as Hunt saw the German, he was sure of success. "He was a lonely young under-officer who greeted us with obvious pleasure because we broke the monotony of his exile." Once Hunt explained the situation, the German immediately replied: "Certainly, certainly . . . I am pleased to help. I will telephone every day what lighters pass Lillo. It is a pleasure to help."

Tracking One Shipment Through the Canals

Before Hunt's plan was totally in place, Robinson Smith, sometimes known as "Foghorn Smith" because of his distinctive voice, wrote an article that traced the agonizingly slow movements of one shipment of wheat from Rotterdam into Belgium. After the frustrating days of hanging around with the Oxford students at the Palace Hotel in Brussels, Smith had been assigned the position of chief delegate of the Hainaut Province and was placed in charge of the three Rhodes scholars who were already there: Spaulding, Lowdermilk, and Robert H. Warren.

Smith wrote up the tale of the lighter's journey because it was indicative of the frustrations that occurred throughout the process of transporting and supervising cargo within wartime Belgium. As Smith described the start of the trip, the shipment of 520 tons of wheat was loaded into the barge *Hedrina* in Rotterdam. It was bound for Ghent or Bruges, depending upon the need.

When the lighter reached Ghent, it was instructed to continue on to Bruges, which was then in greater need. Before the *Hedrina* could reach that city, however, it was stopped as it tried to enter the war zone known as the "etape," or "etappen." This area had greater restrictions than the rest of occupied Belgium because of its proximity to the ongoing fighting. The lighter was denied entry into the war zone. It turned around and headed back to Ghent.

While the barge was still in transit, the chief delegate at Ghent, Rhodester Scott H. Paradise, received a telegram from the Brussels office stating that he should come at once to Brussels to discuss the barge and where the wheat should go. After getting the proper German permissions

Robinson Smith became chief delegate to the Hainaut Province and was placed in charge of three Rhodes scholars. (Public domain; Hoover Institution Archives, Stanford University, California.)

to travel, he headed for Brussels. At the CRB office, it was decided the *Hedrina's* cargo would be reloaded into two smaller lighters and sent to the two cities in the Hainaut Province that had the greatest need: Tournai and Mons.

Everything was settled, and Paradise headed back to Ghent confident that this was the best course of action. By the time he arrived back in Ghent, however, the barge's 520 tons of wheat had been unloaded at the region's main mill.

As Smith told it, no one could be faulted for the unloading because the bill of lading had stated Bruges or Ghent. And "the Belgian committee at Ghent had had the right, previous to the arrival of the American delegate, to order a discharge." Others—mainly CRB personnel—could have argued that the shipment was not allowed to be touched until the delegate had broken the CRB seals on the barge's holds, but to the hungry Belgians that was a trifling formality easily overlooked under the circumstances.

Regardless of the failure to follow proper procedures, the fact remained that the 520 tons of wheat were not for Ghent and had to be immediately reloaded. Days were ticking away and still the wheat wasn't even close to becoming much-needed bread.

While the millers at Ghent complained, Paradise insisted, and the Ghent provincial committee officials complied. The wheat was reloaded into two smaller barges, the *Trois Freres* (Three Brothers) and the *Poule d'Eau* (Water Hen or Water Chicken).

Another delay occurred, however, because there was "a great scarcity of tugs," and the two smaller barges had to wait for days to get a tug. They finally were pulled from the Ghent wharf fifteen days after they had left Rotterdam.

The story was still not over, however.

As the barges were pulled up the Scheldt, the river was high, and the current was strong. When the barges and their tug came to a place where a downed bridge filled most of the river, the tug had to pull each barge separately through the narrow space. They barely made it.

As the barges were struggling through such obstacles, they made a mighty impression on those who saw them, for they were the first two barges to enter the region since the start of the war. Smith wrote: "When the people knew what they contained, they lined the banks and wept with joy and cried, God bless you. To the American delegate who met them at Tournai [probably Lowdermilk or Spaulding], these two old hulks, against the setting sun, were glorified, for he knew that upon them, and the route which they opened up, the life of a million depended."

The cargo of the *Trois Freres* was unloaded quickly at Tournai, "and in a day the wagons from the [area's] fifty communes were backing up to the mill" to collect their portion of flour.

As to the other lighter?

The *Poule d'Eau* was destined for Mons. Because the canal from Tournai to Mons was too narrow and shallow for tugs, the barge would normally have been pulled the rest of the way by horses. "But not a horse was to be had, so finally four men were engaged for the three days' pull" to Mons. Smith added as an aside that this practice of using men rather than horses "has begun a regular service, cheaper and more charitable than horses."

By now, the word had spread to Mons of the barge's approach. "All Mons was expecting the arrival of the first boat to come to her need, almost literally dying to see her make the bend," according to Smith. But as the barge got within fifteen kilometers (nine miles), the lighterman's wife, who had been "ill," became "more ill and had to go below, and the [lighterman] refused to let anyone else steer the *Poule d'Eau*. So the four pullers had to sit for two days on the bank and await the issue."

The "illness" had a happy result—a baby girl! Mons responded by baptizing the little girl La Poulette ["the Little Hen"], and the city finally had its wheat. Smith summed up the story by writing, "All through December Mons had been living on precisely 77 grams [2.72 ounces] of bread per person per day. Now, for a few days, you could fairly hear that town eat."

Making sure barges got to their destination was just one of the delegates' jobs. Because they were able to move relatively freely, they ended up at times being scroungers of supplies, not only for their own office, but also for Belgians working in the distribution network.

In one instance, Smith drove from Mons up to Brussels for the day to meet with other delegates. While there, he went to the *grand place* because he had things to buy. "A hundred weights must be bought for the warehouses, four reams of cardboard must be loaded into the auto for the bread-tickets; no weights, no cardboard, nothing in the provinces." He also collected a few large American flags from the Brussels office that would be hung on the provincial warehouses and mills to alert the Germans that those establishments were part of the relief work and should be left alone.

It was late afternoon when he and his chauffeur finally were able to get away from Brussels. The motorcar was so loaded with the weights, cardboard, and flags that Smith and the chauffeur could barely fit in. As Smith told it, "The motor speeds in the dark through village after village still as death. It is only eight, but not a light is to be seen; petroleum is dear. It begins to rain."

Suddenly, out of the dark a woman appeared pushing a baby carriage. The driver swerved and just missed her. They drove on, although the image of the woman bothered Smith. He knew he was not allowed to carry unauthorized people in his motorcar. That thought, however, didn't do anything to erase the cold and miserable scene in his head. "It is dark and cold and stormy, yet a moment's hesitation: shall one stop and go back? She is going in the opposite direction: what can one do? But there is the child: 'Chauffeur, *arretez, retournez.*' There she is again, pushing hard along the muddy road."

The chauffeur stopped, turned around, and Smith hopped out. He was ready to assist her and her baby into the car. That's when he got a surprise. "There in the carriage—a sack of potatoes." Smith tipped his hat and got back into the auto, very much aware he should report her to the authorities for possible black market food smuggling. He settled back into his seat knowing no such report would ever be filed.

Later that night, Smith made his last stop at a miller's house. He handed the Belgian one of the large American flags he had brought back from Brussels. The miller knew what it meant to have such a flag hanging from his mill: It was public acknowledgment that he was part of the CRB/CN relief efforts and was relatively safe from German harassment. The miller reverently took the flag from Smith. As the delegate later wrote, "The miller looks at it silently for a moment—then puts it to his lips."

The cold, wet drive had been worth it.

In Antwerp, a few days before Christmas, Hunt, Branscomb, Flint, and Carmichael were startled by an unexpected visitor. Curtis had arrived as part of his usual courier duties, but entering before him was "a man in a raincoat and automobile cap, his serious, boyish face splashed with mud."

"'Mr. Hoover,' explained Curtis, by way of introduction."

As Hunt remembered it, Hoover hardly said a word and "quietly took a chair in a dark corner and required no further attention from me, although I thought he listened carefully to the word Curtis brought me from Rotterdam, and to the messages I sent by him to Brussels."

As Hoover was leaving, he turned to Hunt and said, "You deserve better quarters."

"I have them already," Hunt answered. "Mr. Edouard Bunge, vice-president of our Belgian Committee, has donated an excellent suite of offices in his bank for the Commission's work."

Hoover's only reply: "Um. . . . Good-by."

That was Hunt's first encounter with Herbert Hoover.

Humor Among the Delegates

Despite the serious nature of the relief work, there were moments of levity, which, when told and retold among the delegates, brightened otherwise difficult days. One such moment was at the expense of Richard H. Simpson, the twenty-five-year-old second-year Rhodes scholar who had pleaded with Kittredge in the initial Lucey meeting to take him to the Limburg Province.

Simpson was an only child who was born and raised in Indianapolis. His father was an attorney and was no doubt proud when his son graduated from Harvard and went on to be a Rhodes scholar in 1913. Simpson was of average height and build and had thick dark hair that he parted on the left. His face was open and lively. He was prone to wearing modern Arrow collars that weren't as stiff or high as traditional ones. He was never without a walking stick, which he liked to twirl and jab at others playfully. Through December he was with Kittredge, but at the first of

In the front seats are the Belgian driver and delegate Gilchrist B. Stockton; in the back seat is Richard H. Simpson, the delegate who was accidentally left on the side of the road one cold winter night by his driver. (Author's archives.)

the year he was transferred to the Antwerp Province to help Hunt and his team.

The story that always brought a smile to the delegates' faces happened one late December afternoon while Simpson was still with Kittredge, living in Limburg Province's capital city of Hasselt. Simpson and his chauffeur were on their way to Brussels in their Overland motorcar. When they reached Louvain it was already dark, and the driver suggested that he stop and light the car's headlights. Because it was very cold, and the road from Hasselt to Brussels was paved with bone-rattling Belgian paving blocks, Simpson got out to stretch and move about. He strolled over to look in the window of a closed shop.

As CRB delegate Stockton later wrote of the tale, Simpson was about to get a rude surprise: "When he turned around, he couldn't see his car. He felt he must be dreaming. It couldn't have gotten so dark so suddenly. He walked over to where the car had been, but there was no car."

With nothing to do but walk, he did so, even without his prized walking stick. As he walked, he kept repeating to himself, "It cannot be true, it's too silly."

When he reached a sentry post, the German soldier confirmed that a CRB motorcar had recently passed through on its way to Brussels. Simpson left an address in Louvain where he could be found and told the sentry to give it to his driver when the man returned, adding with a dark tone, "I'll be waiting for him."

A half hour later, still no car or driver. Simpson decided to take the small train that had begun running again between towns. As the train pulled out of the station, Simpson kept a sharp eye out into the darkened countryside, certain that "when his chauffeur missed him he would return slowly, looking for his corpse."

When the train was halfway to Brussels, Simpson spotted his car "barging down the road faster than an Overland ever went before. The chauffeur's head was bent low over the wheel, and he heeded naught else."

The delegate stood up in the train and "began to wave his arms and shout, but the car whizzed on to Louvain and was swallowed up by the darkness. The people on the tram thought that he was crazy."

When the train pulled into Tervueren, southeast of Brussels, Simpson decided to get off and wait for his car, because the main road led right past the station. "He paced up and down for an hour, but the car never came. Then he climbed wearily into another train and started once more for Brussels."

When he finally reached the Palace Hotel late that night, he was shocked to see his luggage waiting for him. The driver had bypassed Tervueren and taken another road into the city.

"Simpson was nearly wild."

He turned to the night desk clerk: "Find my chauffeur and send him to my room."

As Stockton wrote the tale, "The flunkeys and bell-boys thought they saw evidences of a fast approaching tragedy."

When the poor driver was found, he could barely force himself up to Simpson's room and was almost too afraid to knock. But the stouthearted Belgian finally gathered up his courage and knocked.

Before Simpson could vent any of his rage, the man blurted out: "When I reached Brussels and turned around, and you were not there, Monsieur, j'etais tellement saisi! [I was so overcome!]." The man nearly started crying, thinking this was the end of one of the few jobs left in Belgium.

When Simpson finally got him calmed down enough to tell his story, the driver said he had never missed him until he turned around and asked, "Le bureau ou le Palace Hotel, Monsieur?" The poor man had nearly had a heart attack when all he saw was "the overcoat, the hat, the stick on the back seat."

Simpson never reported being abandoned again. That same driver made sure of it.

Just as the delegates were trying to determine their jobs and how they fit into the Belgian distribution system, so the average Belgians were trying to understand what role the Americans were to play in their lives. One short essay by Stockton titled "Relief and Distress" began, "Mr. Hoover decided that 'relief' meant rice, flour, bacon, lard, peas, and beans, but the Belgians interpreted it to mean the opposite of distress or even as a cure to all ills."

In the Antwerp office, Hunt and his team found this meant that when the Germans requisitioned the hay crop, they got a complaint from a farmer. As the Stockton essay related, "We explained that we could not keep them from requisitioning any crops they wished to appropriate." The farmer shook his head and said, no, he didn't want the Germans to stop requisitioning; he was complaining because "he was only receiving seven francs per ton while his neighbors were receiving eight. He knew that Americans were a just people, and 'wouldn't we step in and see fair play!'"

In another instance, "a man came into the Antwerp office and asked us to give him a certificate that he had been born in Liverpool. He said he could get one at the Hotel de Ville for seven francs, but as he was going to get married soon, he was trying to save money. He thought that he might get one from us cheaper!"

The essay also included a story about second-wave Rhodes scholar John L. Glenn. The twenty-two-year-old from South Carolina had gone from Brussels's Palace Hotel to an assignment as delegate in the Namur Province with fellow Rhodester Bowden. Glenn was tall and blond, and as the essay noted, he was "a splendid physical specimen and could stand the test as well as any other man in the Commission of filling the ideal of the terrible Americans who had come to Belgium to feed the people and protect them from the Germans." One day Glenn visited a school and learned that the children had some preconceived ideas of what an American should be like. "When the children were asked what they thought of him, one little boy replied almost disgustedly, 'Ah, where is his pistol?'"

The essay ended, "The Belgians thought that 'Les Délégués Américains' were omniscient and omnipotent—those who did not know us."

THIRTY-FIVE

Brussels

Von Bissing Becomes Governor General

Thursday, December 3, marked a major change for Belgium, but at the time few realized how major. On that day Baron Moritz Ferdinand von Bissing replaced von der Goltz as the governor general of Belgium. A one-sentence *affiche* was plastered all over Brussels and the rest of the country: "His Majesty, the Emperor and King, having deigned to appoint me Governor-General of Belgium, I have to-day assumed the direction of affairs. Baron von Bissing, General of the cavalry."

Von Bissing was a seventy-year-old Prussian military officer who had been born into the German landed gentry. In 1865, at twenty-one, he became a lieutenant in the German cavalry and took part in both the Austro-Prussian and the Franco-Prussian wars. As a young major in 1887 he became the aide-de-camp to the crown prince, who later became Kaiser Wilhelm II. After a distinguished military career, von Bissing retired in 1908 but was recalled to lead the VII Army Corps from August

On the right, next to an unidentified man, is the sword-carrying Baron Moritz Ferdinand von Bissing, who became governor general of Belgium on December 3, 1914. He would rule Belgium ruthlessly. (Public domain; A Journal From Our Legation in Belgium, Hugh Gibson, Doubleday, Page & Co., 1917.)

through November 1914. He was then promoted to *Generaloberst* and appointed by the kaiser to be governor general of Belgium.

A few days after von Bissing's appointment, Brand Whitlock was officially presented to the governor general by Baron Oscar von der Lancken, head of the political department of the occupation government. Whitlock was joined by his Spanish counterpart, the Marquis de Villalobar, and his Dutch counterpart, Mynheer van Vollenhoven. The three men formally met von Bissing in the richly appointed salon of the residence of the Belgian Arts and Sciences minister. For Whitlock it was an inauspicious moment because the man they were meeting, "justly or unjustly, was destined to stand forth to the world as the symbol of one of the darkest, cruelest and most sinister pages of its miserable history."

As Whitlock recorded it, the man that stood before them was "old, and thin, with thick graying, black hair brushed straight back from his forehead and plastered down as with water or with oil on the curiously shaped head that was so straight and sheer behind. His face was hard and its leathern skin, wrinkled and old and weather-beaten, was remorselessly shaved as to chin and throat and high lean cheeks, leaving the thick, heavy moustaches of a Prussian *Reiter* [horseman] to hide somewhat the thin lips of the stern mouth and then flow on, growing across his cheeks to bristle up fiercely by his ears."

The German was "scrupulously clean, one might almost say scrubbed. . . . His brow was high and the lean face tapered to the wedge of a very firm jaw; the visage of an old Prussian dragoon of the school and mentality of Bismarck." Whitlock noted that from such a face "there gleamed a pair of piercing dark eyes that seemed black until one saw that they were blue; they were keen, shrewd eyes, not wholly unkind."

He was not so much dressed as adorned with the accoutrements of a Prussian cavalry officer: "a great heavy sabre that clanked against his thin legs . . . a well-worn uniform . . . blue trousers, caught with straps below the long, pointed boots that were made of soft leather and furnished with great silver spurs. His tunic was light grey and short, and its shabbiness was somehow accentuated by the Iron Cross of the first class that he wore, and by the enameled star of the Order of the Black Eagle, fastened by a cravat about his collar and dangling heavily out at this wrinkled old throat."

While von Bissing was able to speak French, he did not like to, so with the three ministers he "expressed himself with a rough voice in German" and made von der Lancken stand by him translating into French. He shook hands with each man and spoke a few personal words to each before "the brief audience, which had been invested with the formality of a private presentation at Court, ended."

Whitlock and his companions "drove back in the bleak afternoon, with its lowering clouds and gusty winds, under the impression of a strong and possibly a hard personality."

The sense of imperial, harsh royalty that swirled around von Bissing was one that many people had. According to Hunt, von Bissing's new position "carried with it the dignity and authority of royalty. His proclamations were written in the first person: 'I command. . . . I ordain. . . . I decree.' They say that in his youth Governor-General von Bissing was a chum of the Kaiser's and that the Kaiser used to pay the bills at a time when his friend's personal fortune was too small to permit even of the ordinary expenditures of a dashing young army officer. If that is true General von Bissing has advanced a long way since then. He lives in a Belgian palace, he rules a nation, and he stands on a par, under the War Lord, with the petty monarchs of some of the oldest German states."

Von Bissing would immediately make his mark on the Belgians. As Whitlock noted, only seven days after von Bissing's appointment, he decreed that the Belgians must pay 480 million francs as a "contribution of war." To determine how to raise such a sum, the governor general convened a special session of the provincial councils of Belgium for Saturday, December 19, and set guidelines: The session would last only one day; all deliberations were to be held in secret; and the sole objective was to determine a method for raising the money.

Von Bissing's harsh rule had just begun.

It would not be long, however, before certain Belgians—both commoner and exalted—would make him realize his job would not be an easy one.

Whitlock's Take on the Young Delegates

Into the new, brutal world that von Bissing was creating came the young American delegates. As Whitlock in the U.S. Legation in Brussels noted, "Finally the Rhodes scholars began to arrive, clean young fellows whom one could admire unreservedly. They came as volunteers, to work for no other reward than the satisfaction of helping in a great humanitarian cause. The work never could have been done without them, or half so well by men who had been paid for this labour. I suppose the world has never seen anything quite like their devotion; it used to amuse, when it did not exasperate, us, to see the Germans so mystified by it; they could not understand it, and were always trying to find out the real reason for their being there."

The German military authorities were sure they were spies and sometimes treated them as such. They were also convinced the Americans were in the work merely to line their own pockets. Nothing could be further from the truth, according to Whitlock. "It was, in fact, as fine an example of idealism, and I am tempted to add of American idealism, as, in its ultimate organization and direct management, it proved to be of American enterprise and efficiency."

Neutrality was the key to the whole endeavor. The CRB delegates had to maintain their dispassionate approach to both sides for the work to succeed. This was so critical that, as Whitlock reported, "The young men were under the heaviest adjurations from all of us to maintain a strict neutrality, and this they all did. Not one of them was ever guilty of an indiscretion, not one of them ever brought dishonor upon the work, or upon their nation, or its flag, or upon the various universities whose honour they held in their keeping and on which they reflected such credit." In his writing flair, Whitlock was a little loose with the truth, as time, circumstances, and primary source material would later reveal.

But Whitlock hinted at this when he said: "They showed remarkable tact, and they were all neutral, 'strictly neutral,' as their coterie phrase had it. Raymond Swing, a newspaper correspondent, observing them at their work, remarked, however, that some were born neutral, some achieved neutrality, and some had neutrality thrust upon them. The provocation was often very strong, what with the scenes they had to witness and that odour of invasion in which they lived. But they kept their opinions to themselves with a remarkable discretion, and expressed themselves, in public at least, only in the diplomatic phrases befitting neutrals."

Whitlock wrote that many of the men had the hardest time when talking about the German atrocities during the invasion. One particular village seemed to stand out. "I have said that the worst [atrocity] of all was [at] Tamines, but perhaps it only seems the worst because it made such an impression on the minds of the young men of the Commission for the Relief in Belgium. They were always talking of it. 'Yes, but have you seen Tamines,' they would say whenever the conversation, as it did persistently, with a kind of fatal irrelevancy, turned on the atrocities."

"Many of the young men of the Commission," Whitlock continued, "whose experience of human kind had been as fortunate as their own natures were kind, came with the skepticism that did so much credit to their characters; but somehow that little graveyard at Tamines was more potent as proof to them than more direct and positive evidence could have been.

"Tamines is a little mining town on the Sambre [River]," Whitlock explained, "down in what is known as the Borinage, the coal-fields between Namur and Charleroi. The little church stands on the village green overlooking the river, its facade all splotched where the bullets and grape-shot spattered against it. And in the little graveyard beside the church there are hundreds of new-made graves, long rows of them, each with its small wooden cross and its bits of flowers. The crosses stand in serried rows, so closely that they make a very thicket, with scarcely room to walk between them. They were all new, of painted wood, alike except for the names and the ages—thirteen to eighty-four. But they all bore the same sinister date, August 22, 1914."

Regardless of the delegates' efforts to maintain neutrality, what they needed most in those early days of December was guidance, something that was lacking from the Brussels office as run by Heineman. As Hoover had seen in his first visit and learned from reports by Lucey and others, Heineman was too involved with, and tied to, the Comité National and his own business affairs to fully comprehend the necessity of a strong, independent CRB presence in Brussels and across Belgium.

In his CRB history Kittredge wrote, "During the month of December the Commission offices in Belgium were gradually coming into working order; but chaos still reigned in the Rue de Naples." The organization in place was Heineman as director, Hulse as honorary secretary, Macloskie as executive secretary, Baetens as head of shipping, Galpin as supervisor of delegates, and Meert as chief inspector to travel in the provinces.

But as Robinson Smith remarked dryly in a later article, the CRB was then "an organization without one." It was so bad that Kittredge wrote: "The provincial delegates, coming in after strenuous days spent in touring about their provinces in motor-cars, found little tangible assistance at Brussels. . . . [They] usually left Brussels in despair and went ahead on their own initiative to work out plans of distribution in co-operation with the provincial committees. The delegates on going to Brussels would often wait for hours in the corridors of the office, without being able to find anyone who was at all concerned about their difficulties. Every time they would ask for advice, the almost invariable answer would be: 'We will go into the matter; won't you call in to-morrow?' The exasperated delegate would walk out with his problems unsolved and return to his province to win his own battles as best he could."

Something had to be done.

Van Doren Builds His Network

With the coming of December, the advent of winter, and the installation of von Bissing, the occupation took on deeper, darker tones for Belgians everywhere. This was especially true for Eugene van Doren and the Abbé de Moor, who were trying to maintain and even expand their underground activities.

As the book *Underground News* explained it, "Times had changed, and within the past few weeks changed considerably. Every day the German Military Government's grip was tightening and their counter-espionage system was growing in strength, increasing the difficulties and dangers of any clandestine activities. While Burgomaster Max held his office, Brussels had retained a certain degree of liberty. But when he was arrested and deported in Oct. 1914, the iron heel had descended with a vengeance, and since von Bissing's arrival . . . Brussels had become to all intents a vast concentration camp under a harsh and tyrannical rule."

This meant that to "enter or leave the city required a passport obtainable only in exceptional circumstances and at exorbitant cost. Everyone had to carry an identity card bearing a photograph, and men between the age[s] of eighteen and forty were controlled by the Meldeamt [registration office] and had to report themselves regularly at the Kommandantur like ticket-of-leave convicts. The streets were patrolled day and night by armed military police as well as the ordinary city police force, and three special brigades of secret police, employing *agents provocateurs* and Belgian informers, had been organized."

Seemingly arbitrary curfews were imposed with only a few hours notice "and enforced with rifles. The whole life of the city was regulated according to the requirements of 'military necessity,' the only law recognized by the Occupant and one against which there was no appeal."

Information from the outside world, most notably foreign newspapers, was at a premium, although the Belgian black market, like everything else, became more efficient as time went on. Gibson wrote: "A little while ago the *London Times* cost as high as two hundred francs. It has been going down steadily, until it can be had now for four francs and sometimes for as little as two. The penalties are very severe, but the supply keeps up, although the blockade runners are being picked up every day."

Von Bissing and his government of occupation kept posting *affiches* that outlawed or made criminal more and more activities. "It was a crime to take snapshots, to make sketches, 'to put up or expose or distribute any written text, engraving or illustration,' not submitted to the censor." Citizens couldn't even sing or whistle patriotic songs or wear any clothing that was similar to the national colors of the Allies. Each such action was considered a provocation that was punishable by a fine and imprisonment.

Van Doren, de Moor, and Jourdain chafed under such conditions. They also knew that in such a repressive environment they had a greater chance of getting caught. This would be especially true when they began expanding from their simple bulletin to bigger and more aggressive projects. To survive they had to make their organization tighter and more secretive so that it would be less susceptible to detection and breakdown.

But where to start?

The most obvious component to improve and reinforce was distribution. Since their earliest days they had circulated their materials by wandering the city and dropping off individual copies in residential mailboxes. Or they would give the materials to friends who would do the same. Such methods, however, were too open to the possibility of chance observation and capture. The men understood that to stay with the "haphazard letterbox distribution was out of the question; it would be too costly, too dangerous and, with the comparatively small number of copies they could handle, ineffective." They would have to build a distribution network that would be efficient, effective, and protect them from capture as well as possible.

To do so, however, meant they also needed to separate the editorial side of the operation from the printing side, and both of those from the distribution side.

By December, the inner circle of critical people numbered only five: Van Doren; the abbé; the well-known editor and writer Victor Jourdain; his daughter, thirty-five-year-old Julie Jourdain; and Father Paquet, Victor's confessor and "one of the most active charity organizers in the city." Paquet was "a big, benevolent-looking Jesuit past middle age. He spoke little and he had a steady, level gaze that people found disconcerting or soothing according to their individual conscience." Julie Jourdain lived with her elderly father and helped him in all aspects of the work while also attending to her sick mother.

Van Doren was the critical link because he was the only one who knew the four others of the inner circle. The abbé did not know that the two Jourdains and Father Paquet were involved, and they did not know de Moor was working with van Doren and active in underground activities.

After much discussion among the inner circle, the distribution model they settled on was to individually build separate distribution circles, or circles of trust, from one central point, "something like a planetary system of which van Doren was the sun. Van Doren would remain unknown to all except the vital contacts with the next circle, and even to these he would pose as a simple distributor supplied by someone supposedly nearer the source."

As one writer later commented, "The whole system may seem open to criticism. . . . No doubt any thriller writer would be able in five minutes to evolve a method surer, safer and in every way more efficient. But as a piece of pure improvisation, based largely on speculation in the first place and accomplished by tentative groping in the dark, it was a creditable achievement."

Once the team understood the concept of these circles of trust, they began to build them outward, away from themselves. Julie Jourdain gave van Doren a list of people she felt he could rely on to circulate small amounts of whatever was produced. She also carefully began contacting convents and Catholic schools, beginning with the well-known Jesuit

St. Michael College, where her sons attended school, "and going from one to the other with a recommendation from some one in the previous establishment."

Altogether, the team realized quickly that "laying the foundations of the distributing system was a laborious business. It demanded considerable patience and sometimes eloquent persuasion" to enlist people who were frightened or reluctant to tempt the fates and the German authorities.

As the five were building their networks, van Doren continued to work on ways to better conceal material. One day he went to see Victor Jourdain and entered the man's room "jauntily swinging a walking-stick." He was like an excited child with a secret too big to hold in. "He picked up his stick with the air of a conjurer about to produce white rabbits from a hat. . . . He twisted the ferrule [top metal ring] off his stick and withdrew a long cylinder of paper."

He showed Jourdain—and Paquet, who happened to be there—how the cane's secret compartment would be a good hiding place for editorial material being transported to a printer.

As van Doren was showing off his cane, he would have been surprised to know that de Moor had carrier pigeons concealed in his loft and was using them to communicate with British intelligence. The priest had also recently received 10,000 francs from a secret Belgian government courier. The money would be used to pay Belgian railroad men for information about German troop and train movements.

De Moor would have been surprised that Jourdain had finished the book that he had started a month before. The elderly editor had documented eyewitness accounts of the German atrocities during the invasion and titled it *The Pan-Germanic Crime*. During the writing process, van Doren would come by Jourdain's office and collect the most current manuscript pages. He would then carefully seal them up in his new cane and stroll home. Once there, he would laboriously type the handwritten manuscript pages onto very thin paper.

By the end of December the book was completed. It was then time to get it out of Belgium and into the hands of a publisher. Jourdain's eldest son, Paul, volunteered to smuggle it across the Dutch border and take it to England. The book was concealed in the false bottom of an attaché case. On Christmas Eve Paul successfully survived the searches of the German sentries. When he reached London he quickly found a publisher who agreed to publish the book. In early 1915 it was published with the author listed under the pseudonym Paul van Houtte.

This major success did not slow down Jourdain or van Doren in their desire to do more damage to the German occupation. As the manuscript was being completed, Jourdain had struck on a new idea. It would be one that would inspire the nation, drive the Germans—especially von Bissing—crazy, and cause the death of a handful of courageous countrymen. The idea was the aforementioned underground newspaper *La Libre Belgique* (*The Free Belgium*).

The elderly newspaper editor had come up with the concept as a natural extension of his anger at the Germans and his earlier impassioned essay reacting to the German-sponsored newspapers. If the Germans were going to publish such lies, he needed to counteract their propaganda with an underground newspaper that told the truth. Van Doren, the Belgian cardboard manufacturer turned clandestine operator, was all in when he heard the idea. He couldn't wait to tell his friend and underground partner, de Moor. Even though van Doren knew he could not divulge that the famous editor Jourdain was at the helm of the new publication—that would have broken the rules of their newly created circles of trust—that did not dampen his excitement.

When van Doren went to the abbé with the exciting news, he expected his priest friend to immediately and enthusiastically embrace the idea. As *Underground News* later described the scene, de Moor surprised van Doren when he initially said he wasn't sure he would do it. He told van Doren: "I'm sorry, Eugene, but I must think it over. I don't think you realize what you're taking on. Within a week you'll have the Kommandantur, the police and all their spies after you."

"I know that," van Doren retorted. "So much the better. I'm not afraid, if you are."

"I've got responsibilities that don't permit me to take fool risks unless they're worth while," de Moor responded. He was thinking of all the other much more important clandestine activities he was involved in. Taking on this highly dangerous newspaper could jeopardize all his other work.

Van Doren stormed out of the abbé's room. The priest knew "perfectly well that van Doren had not stopped to think of all the difficulties and grim possibilities of the job he was undertaking so blithely. The running of a clandestine newspaper in occupied territory was daring to the point of folly. . . . True, too, that he had helped van Doren with his offensive little pamphlets. But that was only a prank that he could stop at a moment's notice."

On reflection, however, de Moor thought of all that van Doren had done for him, how he had "taken on every venture the Abbé had suggested to him, without a thought to his own safety." A short time later, the priest was at van Doren's door. "Well, hot-head," de Moor started, "after due reflection I've come to offer your vast organization the benefit of my services. Now tell me what it's all about."

Before a first issue could be produced, however, van Doren and his associates would have to find a printer and distributors willing to take on such a dangerous job. The five within the inner circle knew that it was a project that "once begun, must be continued at all costs if the enemy were not to be allowed a victory which would be worse than if the attempt had never been made. It was a tall order." They also knew that what they were planning might cause personal harm, not only to themselves but also to others.

A Young Woman Joins the Cause

None would be more affected by *La Libre Belgique* than a young orphan girl named Gabrielle Alina Eugenia Maria Petit. She had been born on February 20, 1893, to working-class parents in Tournai in the southern province of Hainaut. Her mother had died when she was young, and Petit was raised in a Catholic boarding school in Brugelette, a small village just west of Tournai.

When the war broke out she was twenty-one, living in Brussels, working as a salesgirl, and engaged to a Belgian soldier, Maurice Gobert. Those who knew her said that "with her wild auburn locks and candid brown eyes she looked scarcely seventeen. But beneath that almost puerile gaiety and naïve eagerness for life she concealed a strength of character few men could boast." She was the niece of a man who lived next door to the Abbé de Moor.

When the Germans had invaded, Petit had immediately volunteered at the Red Cross while her fiancé had gone to fight in the battles around Liège. When she heard rumors that Gobert had been wounded and evacuated to a hospital in Charleroi, she simply walked the thirty-five miles to be with him. When she got to Charleroi she found it was occupied by French troops, and she was told that no wounded had been brought

Gabrielle Petit was a twenty-one-year-old Belgian orphan who had successfully escaped to England but chose to return to her country and work in the underground. Because of that decision she would not live to see the end of the war. After the war she became a national hero. (Public domain; multiple sources.)

to Charleroi because the Belgians were falling back to Namur.

Not caring that a war was raging around her, she set off toward the fighting and Namur, twenty-four miles away. During that walk, she stopped to stay the night with friends at the small town of Farciennes. According to one book about her, "That night the Germans entered the town. The horrors of that night and the succeeding days wrought a fundamental change in Gabrielle Petit." From what she saw and experienced, her resolve doubled to somehow find her fiancé and do something to fight the Germans.

Around Namur she could get no new information about Gobert, so she headed back to Brussels, which had become an occupied city since she had left. Returning to the Red Cross she had the good fortune to find her fiancé in a Brussels hospital. He was seriously wounded, and because he was a soldier, he was a prisoner of the German Army.

When Gobert was able to stand and walk, Petit developed a plan to smuggle him out of the hospital and get them both to Holland. In a bold move, she hid a nurse's uniform and cap under her coat for Gobert. The other nurses did not give them up as later they sauntered boldly, "arm in arm, with Gabrielle chatting gaily . . . down the long gloomy corridors under the nose of a German orderly and past the sentry into the street."

For three months Gobert hid in the pension where Petit lived while she sold contraband newspapers to raise money to smuggle him out of the country. "It was a dangerous but profitable business. With a bundle of German papers under her arm she went from café to café. Choosing the customers with discretion, she offered *Kölnishche Zeitung* (*Cologne Gazette*). 'Do you want the latest?' she said with a meaningful glance. And in exchange for two, three or even five francs, she would hand over a week-old German paper in which was concealed a copy of one of the Dutch, French or English dailies."

At this stage, even though Petit's uncle was the neighbor of the Abbé de Moor, the uncle knew nothing of her clandestine work nor of her desire to get her fiancé to Holland. If she had confided in her uncle, he would have no doubt connected her with the abbé. If that had happened, one book speculated, "It would probably have changed the whole course of her life, for . . . her fiancé would have been taken charge of by the Abbé's organization."

Instead, Petit did raise the money, and she and Gobert headed toward the Dutch border. "At the end of December, 1914, after nights of tramping across country, she succeeded in crossing the frontier with her fiancé and reached Flushing." The Dutch port, which sat on the island of Walcheren at the wide mouth of the Scheldt River, was a bustling seaport. Gobert had already decided he needed to make his way to Britain and from there get a boat to France so he could rejoin his regiment. Petit's plan was to accompany him and join the Red Cross at the front.

Together they secured passage across the English Channel to the British seaport of Folkestone. It was there, while the two young people waited to get clearance to board another boat for France, that Petit "met her fate in the person of a man who had known her as a child. The man was an agent in the Allied Intelligence Service."

Because many Belgian women wanted to join their men at the front and the easiest way to do that was to join the Red Cross, Petit's friend warned her how difficult it might be to get permission. Petit reportedly replied, "I don't care . . . I would do anything to fight those brutes—anything!" As one account related, "Suddenly she thought of a woman she had seen led through the street of a village she had hidden in on her way back to Brussels in September. They had tied the woman to a tree and shot her, and the officer in charge of the squad had turned to the villagers watching paralysed with horror and said coldly: 'That is what we do to spies.'"

Thinking of that scene, Petit told her friend, "I would even be a spy."

"Would you be willing to go back to Brussels?" he asked.

"I would go anywhere to serve my country."

The two arranged to meet the next day while Gobert was in barracks with other soldiers waiting to get to France. Petit met her friend, who brought with him an Englishman. Both men questioned her about her travels around Belgium and what she had seen and done.

A couple of weeks later, she broke the news to Gobert that she wanted to return to Belgium and work in the underground against the Germans. He was worried for her but understood that nothing would change her determination. While he was waiting for permission to get to France, the couple had to face saying good-bye. "In the evening of a damp and melancholy day they parted on the front at Folkestone—chill and bleak as their hearts when they broke from this last passionate embrace."

The next morning, Petit, who had then taken the name Miss Legrand, boarded a boat for Flushing and her new life as a spy.

As 1914 came to a close, Petit would begin her clandestine operations in German-occupied Belgium. Not long after, she would finally connect, through her uncle, with the Abbé de Moor and add distributor of *La Libre Belgique* to her secret activities. Meanwhile, her fiancé would rejoin his regiment at the front.

The two young Belgians, Gabrielle and Maurice, would never meet again.

THIRTY-SIX

London

Hoover Fights to Get the Clock Running Again in Belgium

Hoover was strongly affected by his first trip into Belgium in late November. He arrived back in London on December 3 and found that his wife, Lou, had just returned from America. Despite the fact they had not seen each other for months, Hoover immediately took the time to write up an extensive report about his trip, covering everything from canal blockages to how many sacks of wheat were left in Brussels warehouses. Ever mindful of the need to keep Belgium in the public eye, he released the report to the press, and it was picked up by numerous British and overseas newspapers, including the *New York Times*.

In Britain, the *Daily News & Leader* was one of the newspapers that published it. In the article, Hoover reported, "Of a population of about 650,000 remaining in Brussels an average of 218,000 were on the adult canteens and 31,000 babies on the baby canteens last week, or more than one-third of the total population." But these statistics were fleshed out as he recalled the visit to the Brussels canteen: "I can imagine nothing more pitiful than the long lines of mothers we saw, with children in their arms, waiting their turn at these canteens."

Instinctually knowing what sound bites were before they existed, Hoover declared, "The clock has stopped in Belgium," which meant that "practically every Belgian soul will be dependent upon the Commission for bread within thirty days."

The practical, no-nonsense businessman summed up his trip by saying, "It is difficult to describe, without appearing hysterical, the condition of the civil population of Belgium. I do not know that history produces any parallel of a population of seven million people surrounded by a ring of steel."

While there was still much to do, much had been accomplished. According to Kittredge, "By December 1 the German government had agreed not to requisition any imported foods, to temporarily suspend the requisition of native cereals, and to grant the Commission liberty of action within Belgium." The Germans had even indicated they might be agreeable to allowing the Belgians to keep all their projected 1915 harvest if the Allies allowed the CRB to continue the relief work.

In addition, the Allied governments had allowed the work in the first place; the British government had granted an initial subsidy of £100,000; and the Belgian government had advanced large sums to the CRB.

Even with these positive movements, though, victory was far from assured. As CRB delegate Robinson Smith wrote in an article about Hoover, "The supreme test of the man was in those first months of the Belgian Relief. Then he had no certain government support, his responsibility continued to the actual feeding of the people, and the whole thing was new."

Part of the problem was that people simply didn't know exactly what the CRB was. According to Kittredge, "The chief significance of the Commission, and most of the difficulties, arose because of the fact that it was a diplomatic compromise, not only in the beginning but throughout the whole of its activities. As a tremendous business organization it had to carry on its work in a way satisfactory to Powers that were struggling with each other for life and death. It was only Mr. Hoover's ingenuity in persuading or bullying the various Powers into making the concessions demanded by the other groups that made possible the continuance of relief work."

Kittredge went on to explain: "In carrying on these negotiations, the Commission acted from the first as a semi-diplomatic body, sometimes dealing with the governments concerned through its diplomatic patrons, more often acting through personal interviews or correspondence of members of the Commission, and especially of Mr. Hoover, with the competent officials of the various governments. The Commission's work was based on a loose sort of contract between the belligerent governments, with the Commission acting as a negotiator and a depository and the executive agent for enforcing the contract. Such a position has probably never been occupied by a similar body."

British Opposition to the CRB

In December 1914 it was anyone's guess if the CRB would survive from day to day. Since Hoover's return from Belgium, he felt, according to historian Nash, as if "the British posture toward his relief project was hardening." Opposition was gaining momentum as individuals like First Lord of the Admiralty Churchill, Chancellor of the Exchequer David Lloyd George, and Secretary of State for War Lord Kitchener insisted that any relief to Belgium was assisting the enemy. Their contention was that the CRB's work helped the Germans for several reasons:

- The food simply replaced what the Germans were requisitioning.
- Any imports to Belgium indirectly helped support the heavy monetary war levies the Germans were placing on Belgians.
- Without the CRB the Germans would, no doubt, feed the Belgians.
- It relieved the Germans of feeding the Belgians, so it prolonged the war.

Additionally, and well outside the public's earshot, there was another argument circulating among the British military leaders. In a startling statement, Hoover later told Whitlock that "Kitchener had made the cynical and brutal statement that if the Belgians were to be let to starve it would then require more German troops to subdue the revolutions that would break out as a result of hunger, and thereby so much weaken the German forces." In other words, Belgian starvation would create such havoc that the Germans would have to pull troops from the western front to maintain order.

Much of this was laid on the table at a hastily arranged meeting between Hoover and British Prime Minister Asquith on Friday, December 4. Hoover later wrote a memorandum recording what happened at the meeting in which he indicated that Asquith was not very sympathetic to the Belgian cause. He felt the Germans were obligated to take care of the Belgians, and food relief would relieve them of their obligations. He saw no way that the British government could sanction such assistance to the enemy.

By all accounts, Hoover stood up to Asquith. He even hinted—if not downright threatened, depending upon which source is consulted—that the British government could not afford to oppose the relief work because it might jeopardize favorable American public opinion toward the British. Hoover told Whitlock later that before the Asquith meeting he had sent a long cablegram to his journalist friend and CRB executive Will Irwin in New York exposing the Kitchener argument. Hoover had, as he told Whitlock, instructed Irwin to "hold this until I send a cablegram releasing it, then blow the gaff, and let the work of revictualing [supplying] go up in a loud report that shall resound over the world to England's detriment."

Walking into the meeting with Britain's prime minister, Hoover supposedly had the cablegram in his pocket. That letter represented the huge hammer of public opinion. Hoover had known from the very start that it was critical to have public opinion on his side for the CRB and Belgian relief to have any chance of success. None of the governments involved would ever agree to the work without the specter of negative public opinion hovering over them. Believing this, Hoover had been carefully constructing that hammer since October. It was time to see if it had the power he thought it did.

Hoover wasted no time in preliminaries. Once Asquith finished stating that his government would not support Belgian relief, Hoover launched his counteroffensive: "You have America's sympathy only because America feels pity for the suffering Belgians." He then pulled the Irwin letter from his pocket and showed it to the prime minister. "I will send a telegram at once, and tomorrow morning the last vestige of pity for England in America will disappear. Do you want me to do it?"

Asquith was stunned. Hoover said the prime minister told him he was not used to being addressed in such a way, adding, "You told me you were no diplomat, but I think you are an excellent one, only your methods are not diplomatic." Hoover supposedly "expressed regret" to the British head of state, but as historian Nash commented, "It did not sound like the most penitent of confessions."

Three things about this story indicate that the meeting probably didn't take place so cinematically: the prepared cablegram to Irwin has never been found; Hoover was, at times, prone to dramatic retelling for the PR effect; and Whitlock was a born storyteller with a flair for literary drama.

No matter the details, however, the result was that Hoover got Asquith to be more supportive of Belgian relief and the CRB.

British Prime Minister Herbert H. Asquith initially did not believe his government should sanction or financially support Belgian relief. (Public domain; multiple sources.)

On a smaller, everyday scale, Hoover continued to chip away at the arguments opposing relief in every possible way, in every meeting and correspondence with the British government and in every contact with the press. In a later memorandum, Hoover succinctly countered each point. He told the CRB detractors that, as to requisitioning of food, "the Germans had given an undertaking that after the first of January no such requisitions would be made." He also insisted that, to date, the Germans had "impressed none of our actual food."

As for the point that the food indirectly helped the war levies, Hoover was adamant: "We were introducing no new money into Belgium, but were simply giving circulation to the money already existing, and that there was no danger of the Germans taking the money which we collected for foodstuffs because that money was in the possession of the American Minister."

Hoover was also confident that all of his dealings so far with the Germans had shown they would never feed the Belgians. Their reasoning was that they had no legal obligation because they had *conquered*, not *annexed*, the country. As Hoover put it, the Germans believed "there was no clause in the Hague Convention obligating the Germans [as conquerors]

to provision the civil population of Belgium." Furthermore, they felt that
because the Belgians imported most of their goods, it was the British
who were starving them with their blockade. The Germans reasoned that
if the Allies would agree to open the port of Antwerp for international
trade with neutral countries, the Belgians would be fine. Hoover pointed
out that the Germans had not changed their position even after a small
amount of rioting in Belgium, and that the northern French behind
German lines were, in some cases, already starving.

To further strengthen his case, especially when it came to the argument
that relief would prolong the war, Hoover tried to awaken a sense of greatness within the British government and its people. He maintained that
the British had undertaken the war "for the avowed purpose of protecting
the existence of small nations, of vindicating the guaranteed neutrality
by which small nations might exist, for the avowed purpose of guaranteeing to the world the continuance of democracy as against autocracy in
government." It would, therefore, be an "empty victory if one of the most
democratic of the world's races should be extinguished in the process and
ultimate victory should be marked by an empty husk." Hoover told all
those opposed to the work that "the English people were great enough to
disregard the doubtful military value of advantages in favor of assurances
that these people should survive."

Whenever possible, Hoover engaged the press to get these points
across and to keep the plight of Belgium in the forefront of the minds
of the world. At every opportunity he issued press releases; reported activities of the London, Rotterdam, and Brussels offices; and forwarded
messages or information the CRB had received from inside Belgium. He
also gave speeches whenever and wherever possible, despite the fact that
he didn't seem to like public speaking.

As Hoover later recalled to an associate, "I employed myself from the
first of December until Feb. 17th [1915] in constant proselytizing with
Englishmen of importance, and with the Cabinet ministers on this issue. In
the meantime, we have worked up a sentiment in the United States, Canada,
Australia and other countries in favour of the feeding of the Belgian people
to such an extent that it became a worldwide movement of interest, second
only to the war itself. We carried on the most active campaign of publicity
by every device we could invent in England as well as in those countries."

In early December, Hoover publicized letters that were still coming
in from various Belgian communes asking for assistance. On Thursday,

December 3, the British *Daily Telegraph* ran an article titled "A Plea From Belgium 'We have nothing here.'" It opened with, "The following letter, received yesterday by the Commission for Relief in Belgium . . . from the authorities of the Belgian town of Dendermonde, is typical of the pathetic requests which arrive daily from every part of Belgium."

The letter reported that 1,200 homes in the town had been destroyed during the fighting. While many residents had fled during the fighting, people had come back: "With a few exceptions, most of the returned men are workers, and as all the works are closed, now, nobody can work in this country. Consequently, you will quite well understand the situation. We have nothing here. We need most food, beds, clothing, and coals. Even if we could buy a quantity of about 150 tons of wheat at a very low price we should be happy to do so, so that we may be able to feed the hungry poor workpeople."

Only three days later, the London *Sunday Times* ran a major article, "'One Huge Cemetery.' Desolate Belgium. Pitiful Sights." It was a report of what Theodore Waters of the American *Christian Herald* had seen when he had followed a cargo of food that the paper's subscribers had donated to the CRB. Waters said, "In Antwerp I saw over one thousand poorly clad women, one in bedroom slippers . . . standing shivering in the snow and slush, waiting for food to be doled out to them, and this under the shadow of a big hotel where well-fed, well-clad soldiers drank and made merry."

Waters rode in a two-horse carriage from Antwerp to Brussels. On the road "we overtook thousands of refugees tramping dejectedly along, weary and forlorn, returning to villages and towns where there is not now food enough to sustain those who are already there."

Most striking to the American journalist was the fact that "the country was one huge burying ground. Always between the ruined houses we could see graves. Graves, graves, graves! In some would be stuck a bayonet with a Belgian soldier's cap hanging on it. Above other rough [graves were] white crosses rudely inscribed, 'To the memory of a Belgian soldier.' On one grave was a child's shoe, poor little marker of its parents' grief. Graves, graves, orphans, orphans, a country desolate; its trees felled in rows to make way for the gullets, it crops long gone to seed, and sticking leanly up through the snow, dead things in rows like markers in a miniature cemetery."

These accounts of Belgium's misery were, for the most part, true and heartrending. They also served well Hoover's greater purpose of building public sentiment and sympathy so that the relief work could go on.

Four days after the Waters article appeared, Hoover came up with a smart PR move. He sent a telegram to King Albert asking that one man, representing all the American press, be allowed to visit the king at his battlefield command in the little sliver of free Belgium. That journalist happened to be Ben Allen, Hoover's trusted friend who was helping Rickard in the CRB publicity department. Four days later, the king agreed to the interview, and Allen crossed the English Channel. He had to wait days to interview the king, but on December 20 he got his chance. From that trip and that interview, the worldwide media learned more about the suffering Belgians and their tall, dashing, and heroic king.

Hoover himself was becoming prominent, and on Friday, December 18, he gave a major speech at the American Luncheon Club in London, which was picked up by numerous reporters. He was introduced by U.S. Ambassador Page. It was probably one of his first important public speeches.

The *Bristol Times Mirror* covered the event and quoted Hoover, who declared, "The Commission had under charter 32 cargo ships for the transport of foodstuffs, and had delivered into Belgium something like 50,000 tons of food, with a gross value of about £500,000. For future delivery, cargoes aggregating a gross value of about two million sterling were arranged."

But just in case listeners thought the organization was growing too big to need continued individual help, Hoover put those figures into context: "Large as these figures might appear, when contrasted with the required monthly budget of £1,200,000, they were adequate only for a short period."

Hoover also made sure to speak directly to those who thought the Germans were still taking Belgian food. "I wish to make clear with emphasis that the Germans are not interfering with this foodstuff. Not one mouthful, so far as we know, has gone down a German throat yet, nor do I believe we will ever be confronted by such an event."

While Hoover wanted Belgium to be in the press as much as possible, he also wanted the information to come from him or the CRB publicity office. Three days before Christmas multiple newspapers throughout Britain ran an extensive report from William Stratton, one of the CRB delegates inside Belgium. This was probably a Hoover-inspired and CRB-distributed report because of its widespread publication, because of its use of Hooveresque language and statistics, and because the delegate who penned it continued to work for the commission long after the article had been published, which probably would not have happened if it had not been sanctioned or if it had been critical of the CRB in any way.

Stratton, one of the first ten Rhodes scholars into Belgium, was twenty-two, from Utah, and, according to Hunt, "tirelessly energetic and intelligent." In the British newspaper *Morning Advertiser,* Stratton's inside-Belgium report began with a description of the lines of needy in Brussels. "Each morning, between the hours of 11 and 12, some 200,000 persons received their portions of soup and bread, the lines forming and moving through the distribution depots with perfect precision and regularity."

Stratton admitted that "a few—very few—persons of the humbler classes have been driven by hunger to seek food by breaking into the houses left vacant by rich Belgians, who have gone to England for the duration of the war. In some cases they have even been driven by their hunger to the point of rioting with the German troops stationed over them. Fortunately thus far these incidents have been followed by no serious consequences, largely owing in those cases with which I am familiar, to the reasonableness and the good sense displayed by German commanders."

Then, sounding like Hoover when he would imply dire consequences to gain advantage over opponents, Stratton warned about the rioting: "If this sort of thing continues—and it may be more or less expected as long as there is hunger—there is no knowing what may be the result. It might be most terrible."

There was nothing like the vision of food riots to keep the sympathy and charity coming.

With this kind of exciting copy, the newspapers never seemed to tire of running Belgian stories. And Hoover never seemed to run out of stories to send them.

While Hoover was gaining great Belgian publicity around the world and making small inroads with the British government, he was also learning in early December that things were going to hell in Rotterdam and Brussels. Lucey might have had excellent executive abilities, but he also could be a maverick with a loose and informal style. Because he sometimes felt that it was better to break the rules and later apologize rather than to pass up an opportunity to move the relief efforts forward, Lucey undertook many initiatives that had rankled not only the Dutch but also the Germans, the

Belgians, and even some Americans in Brussels. Meanwhile, Hoover's November decision to have Bell handle administrative duties in Brussels while Heineman stayed in place to deal with the Germans was not working well. The two men fought constantly and were driving Whitlock crazy.

Hoover knew it wouldn't be long before he had to cross the English Channel again and set things right.

THIRTY-SEVEN

Brussels

CRB Showdown

After Hoover's first trip to Brussels, he had crafted a typically long but precise document that outlined the CRB, the functions of the delegates, and the relationship with the CN. It had been a diplomatic work of subtlety that had defined functions and responsibilities for people, positions, and organizations that were just beginning to work. Additionally, Hoover had indirectly addressed his desire to replace Heineman by sending Bell to handle the administrative functions of the Brussels office back in November.

The sharing of control between Heineman and Bell had been rocky at best. As early as Sunday, December 6, Whitlock recorded that Bell had come to the legation and told him "a long tale of the disorganization in Heineman's office."

The next morning, Whitlock had a long meeting with Bell, Heineman, Francqui, Villalobar, and others about the relief work. As the diplomatic head of the relief effort, Whitlock saw his role as one of listening to everyone's complaints about everyone else, smoothing out ruffled feathers, and offering ways of compromise or reorganization that might appease the crowd. "I talked with Heineman about making a new organization with the distribution, having it as an annex for the Legation, for I had worried so much about this subject in the night that I could not sleep; and he promised to do so. And then I talked to Bell and tried to have them work in harmony."

At 6 p.m. that same day, the three main forces behind the Brussels office—Heineman, Hulse, and Bell—returned to the legation for another meeting. This time Whitlock did the talking. "As carefully as I could I explained to them my desire to have the details of the distribution of the revictualing, now grown suddenly to such large proportions, organized according to business principles and set forth so simply and clearly that any one could see at a glance what was being done, just how much food had arrived and what was being done with it. I explained to them the necessity of the fullest ventilation, so that there could be no possibility of any abuses or derelictions in any quarter. I explained it very carefully and tried to spare the feelings of Heineman as much as possible, and the balky Bell sat by with a rather dour expression, he preferring, I think, a much more direct and brutal statement, and perhaps the entire elimination of Heineman from the scheme."

The next day, Tuesday, December 8, Whitlock engaged the services of Gibson to further his plan by reinforcing it to the participants. Gibson promised to "undertake it in the morning, first with Heineman, whose feelings we should like to spare, but it must be put on an unquestioned foundation and be done right."

It was all getting to be too much for Whitlock, who admitted in his journal with a touch of melodramatic ego: "I wish I were rid of the dreadful responsibility. Of course I can end it at once, but then the poor Belgians would starve and that must not be." Without his steady hand and wise counsel, he was sure the entire relief program would collapse. Many others, most notably Gibson, Lucey, and Hoover, would probably have disagreed strongly with that feeling.

That didn't mean Whitlock served no purpose. He was best at listening to people and soothing their hurt egos. Later that same Tuesday night, Bell was once again at the legation complaining to Whitlock. The minister wrote in his journal that with Bell's "views of Heineman, growing now into a positive hatred, an exceedingly difficult situation [is] developing. Bell is dreadful; talks all the time, and his sentences never have verbs, no end, no aim, no result . . . and yet Hoover sent him here to take charge. I think he is an ignorant man, and a poseur."

Two days later, Bell was back again. He showed up "early this morning with his jaw still set." Later, though, Bell brought around the new Rhodes scholars. Whitlock wrote in his journal that they were "clean-cut young chaps whom one could admire, very serious and very interested and anxious to serve in the work. I talked to them a long time, impressing upon them the importance of their mission, the necessity of being serious, and of comporting themselves with dignity and tact."

By evening, Whitlock was visited by Heineman, who rang and spent more than two hours talking the situation through with the minister. Whitlock admitted that Heineman "was rather fine about it all. Said he would do anything I asked him to do. . . . I was greatly reassured and felt that it would be unjust to displace him, since it really was he who first thought out this scheme of revictualing. . . . Surely he should not be ousted by Bell."

Within another week or so, Whitlock had had it with Bell and called for his removal. In a letter to Ambassador Page in London, Whitlock complained, "By some sad fate everyone who comes in here feels that he must assume command of the entire situation, oust everybody from all authority, and establish as it were, a government of occupation."

By the end of December, despite Hoover's extensive memorandum on office responsibilities, the problems had grown too big to be ignored, but no one in Brussels was tackling them.

The Ultimate Problem Solver

It was time, once again, for Hoover to step in so that he could deal with the "new administrative difficulties that had arisen." He arrived in Brussels on Sunday, December 20.

Hoover seemed to be able to solve any problem laid before him, whether it be in London, Rotterdam, or Brussels. "Everywhere that he went he found anxious problems to be solved, involved situations to be disentangled, seemingly irresistible obstacles to be overcome, but almost invariably in a very few days he was able to find a ready and satisfactory solution."

Hoover's January 1915 letter to Irwin shows that he felt this was a do-or-die situation that needed drastic action. "We have had great trials over [on] this side through the conduct and attitude of the Belgian Committee and part of our Commission who were in control in Brussels. Things got on to such a footing, that it was brought home to me, that unless an immediate revolution took place we might afford one of the greatest scandals of the War and be in a position that would damn the balance of our lives. After many sleepless nights, I went to Belgium and found everybody dead against me."

This discovery might have daunted lesser men, but for Hoover it was just a complicated engineering problem that he was determined to fix. "I stayed there a little over two weeks, and as a result, I first brought Whitlock to my side within twenty minutes—I had the Belgians my way in 24 hours and in a week the Americans in control were either bashed into line or were eating out of my hand." He accomplished all this by starting with a few intense and straightforward conferences with Francqui, Heineman, Bell, and Whitlock. Whitlock was being kind when he said the Brussels office had been "functioning with so many halts and so much creaking." Francqui admitted in an earlier letter to Hoover, "When the plan you have conceived is carried out, I think the organization of your offices and ours will be complete." The Belgian even praised the provincial delegates in another December letter: "The young Americans already at work are doing splendidly."

Through these conferences Hoover's initial assessments were reconfirmed, and he then knew that six things needed to happen within the Brussels office for that part of the organization to work efficiently and effectively. They must do the following:

- Replace Heineman.
- Reorganize the responsibilities within the Brussels office.
- Find new offices to physically separate the CRB from Heineman and the CN.
- Improve communications and relations between the CRB and the CN in Brussels.
- Improve communications between the Brussels office and Rotterdam and between the Brussels office and the provincial delegates.
- Establish an improved definition of a delegate's duties.

On the first item, Hoover decided that Lucey, who had done a good—albeit loose-cannon—job of organizing the Rotterdam office, would immediately take over as director of the Brussels office until Hoover's chosen replacement for Heineman, Albert N. Connett, could come over from America. Bell would be recalled by the CRB from Belgium to London. (He would leave the CRB in January 1915.)

Lucey almost upset Hoover's plan, though, by initially refusing the position. A highly frustrated Hoover brought Lucey to meet Whitlock for the first time to see if the minister could help. Whitlock's initial impression was of "a fine upstanding bald-faced Irishman." Hoover left the two men alone to talk. With Whitlock's diplomatic, chatty abilities, they found they had numerous mutual friends. When Hoover returned an hour later, Whitlock said, "Why, Lucey is a great friend of mine, and he is going to stay and help me out."

But there was also the delicate matter of getting Heineman out of the top CRB position. He had been an integral part of the relief work since the beginning, and his work and relationships with the Germans had been invaluable. Nevertheless, Hoover sat down with Heineman and thrashed out his stepping aside. As Whitlock said, "Heineman had conceded every point . . . and Hoover felt, as he said, that this was the greatest psychological battle he had ever found and won." (No historical record has ever surfaced of that monumental confrontation.)

On the second item, Hoover implemented an office reorganization that created five departments: the executive, under the director; shipping, under Baetens; the secretariat, under Galpin as secretary; accounts; and statistics.

The third issue was resolved by a somewhat unlikely source. Francqui graciously donated a "rambling suite" of offices on three floors in an office building at 66 Rue des Colonies, across the street from his own Societe Generale bank. It was nearly a stone's throw from the city park and a few blocks from the famous twin-towered cathedral. Maybe Francqui was following the old adage to " keep your friends close and your enemies closer"? Whether or not there were ulterior motives for his offer, Hoover accepted.

To deal with the fourth item, a member of the CN's executive committee, Chevalier Emmanuel de Wouters d'Oplinter was chosen to work with the new CRB director in Brussels to smooth out and coordinate the work between the two groups. He was probably chosen because Hoover had known and gotten along with him during his China mining days.

The CRB office in Brussels was moved to 66 Rue des Colonies, and the space was donated by Émile Francqui, whose bank was across the street. (Public domain; *In Occupied Belgium*, Robert Withington, The Cornhill Co., 1921.)

When the new offices were operational, Lucey and d'Oplinter ended up "sitting at their desks facing one another in the director's room" and worked through every problem that arose.

The answer to the fifth problem was a "regular automobile courier service was established thrice weekly to Rotterdam and once or twice weekly to each of the provinces. . . . Arrangements were made with the German authorities for permission to carry the mails and for the speedy transmission of important messages by telegraph inside Belgium and to Rotterdam." In addition, a biweekly meeting in Brussels for all American delegates in Belgium was decided on. By early 1915, these meetings, which became weekly, would turn into great release valves for the highly stressed CRB delegates stationed in the provinces.

As for the last item, the delegates' duties in the provinces had been a point of contention between the CRB and the CN, and even among the delegates themselves, since the beginning of relief efforts. Despite Hoover's December memorandum that outlined many of the duties and responsibilities, the reality was that the individual "power, influence and duties of the provincial delegates differed according to the efficiency of the provincial committees, the difficulties of the local situation and the personality of the delegate."

Within the ranks of the CRB, this boiled down to two opposing points of view. According to Kittredge's history, "On the one hand was the group led in the beginning by Hunt and Robinson Smith, that believed that the work of relief should be essentially an American affair; that the responsibility for the direction of relief operations rested on the American members of the Commission; that its methods should be those of American business efficiency; and that consequently the head delegate in each province was to be regarded as the manager of relief operations in his province."

On the other side of the discussion "were the majority of provincial delegates and all of the successive directors of the Commission in Brussels. They agreed the work of the Commission was indispensable to the success of the relief operations, and that the American delegates should exercise such supervision and control as to make sure that the food-supplies and benevolent funds were efficiently handled, that they were fairly distributed and that they went solely to the Belgian civil population. But, according to this second point of view, the actual work of distribution was essentially a Belgian domestic problem; the work could be best done by Belgians who, because of their acquaintance with local conditions, habits and ideas, were in a position to conduct the work in a manner agreeable to the Belgians themselves."

Most critical of all, the majority side, which included Hoover, felt that "it was not the duty nor the function of the Americans to reform the Belgians or revolutionise their business methods and their social habits." Therefore, "the delegate should use his power with extreme discretion, should act as a diplomatic intermediary between the Germans and the Belgians and between the various conflicting groups of Belgian committees."

It was easy to know which side Francqui and the CN took—the latter. The few delegates like Hunt and Smith who supported the former were causing quite a concern with Francqui and his group, despite Francqui's occasional compliments about these young men. At a meeting of the CN's executive committee on December 22, as Kittredge in his history noted tactfully, "the activities of the American delegates seemed to have exceeded the anticipations of the Belgian gentlemen of the executive committee, for they seemed to have been somewhat alarmed at the part being played by the American delegates."

This was not the first or last time there would be "rather painful misunderstandings" between the Commission and the Comité National. The basic foundation for disagreement would never change: The Belgians of the CN felt the entire relief work was a domestic issue they were quite capable of handling themselves, and thus there was no need for supervising CRB delegates to be wandering around their country.

In this regard, the Belgians and Germans agreed. The Germans felt relief efforts could be handled by the CN under German supervision, and they "regarded the Americans of the Commission as rather troublesome intruders, who were not to be allowed to have an active voice in the distribution of food and who were to be induced to be content with seeing that the food did not go to the Germans."

While Hoover and most of the delegates understood they were not there to change Belgian ways, this awareness did not mean they agreed that they served no useful function within Belgium. They knew their presence was necessary for the relief to function at all "because of the responsibilities imposed upon [the CRB] by the allied governments." Hoover had personally agreed to, and the CRB had officially accepted, the job through the Allied guarantees of buying, shipping, and supervising the distribution of food and clothes down to the commune level. Hoover and his young and sometimes strident delegates would accept nothing less.

But the Belgian concerns in December about the delegates overstepping their authority were, no doubt, passionately communicated by the CN executives numerous times to the CRB executives. Hoover knew as he sat through meetings in Brussels that it was an issue that begged for definition. He referred to his December 8 memorandum, specifically the point he had made that "as it is, however, impossible for the CRB to create for all of Belgium a sufficiently large organization for handling in all its details the work of storage, milling, short-distance shipments, delivery to communes, etc. all of which is necessary before the merchandise can finally be delivered to the communes, it is proposed that the organization of the Comité Provincial should carry out this work, and that the merchandise be transferred to them (not the ownership or control) for so doing on their order of disposition."

Such finer points, however, were lost among the everyday operations of young American delegates out in a war-ravaged countryside dealing with Belgian businessmen of varying social, religious, and political affiliations. As Kittredge honestly assessed, "In the end, as in the beginning, no definite decision was ever reached as to the exact function of the delegate. . . . His position continued to depend largely upon his personality and upon that of the heads of the province to which he was assigned."

With that said, however, Hoover did take decisive action with the delegates during his second Brussels trip.

On Christmas Eve day, Hoover's final meeting took place at the legation. In attendance were Francqui, Villalobar, Baron Lambert, and Whitlock. As Whitlock recorded, they all had "agreed finally on the last, or what seemed then the last, of the troublesome details" in how the two organizations would work together.

But as Kittredge remarked in his history, the CRB, the CN, and their interdependence "was to be in a continual process of change and of evolution, its tasks, its burdens and obligations were to continually increase, but the clear object of the common effort was never lost from sight."

Whitlock summed up this time with a literary flair. "And so, as the short December days were declining with the year, the great work was set in motion, with infinite toil and pain, with many a psychological problem, with such delicate management and humouring of human feelings, jealousies, susceptibilities, and, what is worst of all in this world to endure, the irritations of '*grands faiseurs de petites choses* [great makers of small things].'"

Though Whitlock wrote about others beset by such petty emotions, perceived slights, and diplomatic stumbles, he himself was afflicted with the same ailments on occasion. His detractors thought he shied away from conflict, felt slighted at the least perceived offense, and cared more for his own reputation and appearance than anything else. Worst of all to some, he was not a man of action. As Galpin later recalled, it was difficult for Gibson, who was definitely a man of action, to "get Mr. Whitlock to take action on a number of things that required the Minister. . . . Mr. Whitlock wasn't quite active enough."

Christmas Under German Occupation

Whitlock did, however, know the proper etiquette for most situations. Since the CRB/CN difficulties had been addressed—not solved, but at least addressed—it was time to acknowledge Christmas. The Whitlocks officially invited Hoover and his wife, Lou, who had accompanied him into Belgium, to share Christmas Eve dinner at the legation. Other guests included Gibson; a U.S. reporter named Frederick Palmer, who had come with the Hoovers; and the three men from the Rockefeller Foundation, Rose, James, and Bicknell, who were wrapping up their fact-finding mission.

The spirit of the event was anything but gay. Gibson wrote that "although there was a bunch of mistletoe over the table, it did not seem a bit Christmasy, but just an ordinary good dinner with much interesting talk."

After dinner, Rose pulled Whitlock aside and told him that after all he and the other two men had seen and done in Belgium over the course of the last few weeks, he was ready to say that the Rockefeller Foundation would support the Belgian relief efforts "to the full extent of its resources."

Even with such positive news, Whitlock felt as if he was on "the eve of the saddest Christmas, in some ways, I had ever known." Over the entire city "there brooded a sadness." Gibson's feelings were similar. "This is the weirdest Christmas that ever was—with no one so much as thinking of saying 'Merry Christmas.' Everything is so completely overshadowed by the war, that had it not been for the children, we should have let it go unnoticed."

A few days before, the war had made itself known in a highly explosive way to the residents of Brussels. Two French aviators had buzzed the city and dropped six bombs on the railway yards at Etterbeck. Gibson reported that "the German forces did their level best to bring the bird men down with shrapnel, but they were flying high enough for safety." Additionally, for three or four days leading up to Christmas, residents had been hearing the big German guns that had been silent for a while. Gibson said: "We don't know what it means. The Germans explain it on the ground that they are testing guns."

Even though the Germans had missed their aerial targets, they were in much better spirits than any of the Belgians in Brussels. Being far from home, they had set up a huge Christmas tree in the royal park "blazing with thousands of electric lights in coloured bulbs, like the one in Madison Square at that season, and German soldiers gathered around it and sang their choruses." Whitlock also recorded that there were "little Christmas trees in all the windows of the Ministry. Hoover says they should sling bayonets on them."

Because of their love of Christmas trees, the Germans had, according to Whitlock, "for weeks been cutting down the fir-trees in the Belgian woods for their Christmas trees; there were celebrations for the soldiers everywhere. . . . I do not know how many were required for the Germans in Brussels . . . but each company had to have one, and at Liège alone seven hundred trees were required."

Christmas Day dawned "stinging cold and sharp, the trees all white with hoar-frost," according to Whitlock. The CRB men in Brussels tried to make the day memorable for the Belgian children.

New CRB delegate Lewis Richards hosted a massive event for the little ones of one neighborhood. Richards was a thirty-three-year-old American professional pianist who lived in a large house on the edge of town with his wife, Berthe Smedt. The couple also owned a café. Richards had recently volunteered his services to the CRB. He and his wife set up a large tree in their house, organized a small orchestra, and opened up their home on Christmas Day for the children of their local commune. Six hundred young Belgians showed up that day, "clattering along in wooden shoes, while the orchestra played the 'Star Spangled Banner,' a tune that all Brussels musicians were practicing in those days," according to Whitlock.

Gibson wrote that the mothers brought their children into the house in groups of 100, and the children "marched around the house, collecting things as they went. In one room each youngster was given a complete outfit of warm clothes. In another, some sort of a toy which he was allowed to choose. In another, a big bag of cakes and candies, and finally, they were herded into the big dining-room, where they were filled with all sorts of Xmas food."

The effect was overwhelming. "The children were speechless with happiness, and many of the mothers were crying as they came by."

For the host of the event, Gibson only had high praise. "Since the question of food for children became acute here, Richards has been supplying rations to the babies in his neighborhood. The number has been steadily increasing, and for some time he has been feeding over two hundred youngsters a day. He has been very quiet about it, and hardly anyone has known what he was doing.

"It is cheering to see a man who does so much to comfort others; not so much because he weighs the responsibility of his position and fortune, but because he had a great-hearted sympathy and instinctively reached out to help those in distress. Otherwise the day was pretty black, but it did warm the cockles of my heart to find this simple American putting some real meaning into Christmas for these hundreds of wretched people. He also gave it a deeper meaning for the rest of us."

Rumors had been floating around Belgium for some time that there was an American Christmas ship on its way. Whitlock recalled, "There had never been a public reference in Belgium to what America was doing [in regard to a Christmas ship] . . . but the news had got abroad and was known everywhere." The ship was filled with donated toys, clothes, and food for Belgian and French children. The gifts would not, however, reach their intended recipients until long after Christmas because of German red tape.

As for New Year's Day, the U.S. minister had "asked that there be no manifestation in America's honour that New Year's Day, for, since assemblages were forbidden, it could only result in embarrassment for the officials of Brussels and difficulties for the people." The Belgians found a way around that little problem. Whitlock later wrote to Hoover, who had already left the city: "I am sorry you were not here on New Year's Day, for something very beautiful occurred. Spontaneously, quietly, all day long a stream of Belgians poured into the Legation signing names in a little book which Baron Lambert provided; over three thousand in all, to express their thanks for what America has done—all sorts and conditions of men, from noblemen whose cards wore high titles down to the poorest woman from the slums who had carefully written her name on a bit of pasteboard, the edge of which still showed the traces of scissors. It was very touching, very moving, and I want you to know of it, for you have done so much more than any of us to help them."

Whitlock expressed it well when he finished by saying, "Nobody need tell me any more that self-interest is the great power that moves man, or that there is no gratitude in the world. Surely in this wonderful work this best of human qualities has brilliantly shown forth."

The Hoovers had left Brussels at 9 a.m. that New Year's morning in a motorcar. They were accompanied by Galpin and CRB courier Curtis. As Galpin later recalled, they drove "through Louvain, where our passes were stamped at the Town Hall, perfect still, then to Namur, along the Meuse, to Liège, no forts visible, but a nice German officer, and on to Maastricht" in Holland.

Before Hoover had left Brussels, however, he had taken one more decisive action. Even though publicly he, Francqui, Whitlock, and Gibson had been complimentary of the young CRB delegates, behind the scenes they were disappointed with some of them. The general consensus was that they were too young, inexperienced, and unqualified for such demanding work. The best of men were being challenged by the complicated combination of business and diplomacy that was required for the job. In the end, as Hoover wrote to Irwin, he had to "remove 10 or 12 idealists from a sphere of labour where they felt they had the chance of their lifetime to do some good."

That was an action that would call for no press releases or demands for media coverage. It was not mentioned in any Hoover-sanctioned CRB materials or histories. It was also not mentioned in what had been planned as the official history, which had been written by Kittredge but never published because Hoover had not liked it. (Hoover had found it unacceptable primarily because it dealt with the difficulties of the CRB-CN relationship.)

Such silence was consistent, however, with the reticence of Hoover and most of the other delegates to ever talk about those who washed out. Even in the CRB's extensive personnel files, there was no overall record made of who was terminated and for what reasons. The only fact that hinted at who might have been removed was the list of names of Oxford students who definitely did go into Belgium but were never placed on official lists of CRB delegates. And even that list was never compiled by CRB personnel. (It was gathered by the author.) For all intents and purposes, those men never existed in the CRB world.

While this lack of transparency was totally counter to Hoover's usual methods of operation, the lessons that were learned from such unacceptable delegates did lead to stronger guidelines in 1915 regarding what made for an acceptable CRB candidate.

Back in Brussels, as the year came to an end, Gibson wrote in his journal: "Here is the end of the vile old year. We could see it out with rejoicing, if there were any prospect of 1915 bringing us anything better. But it doesn't look very bright for Belgium."

Earlier in the month, Gibson had written about one of the few bright lights that had begun to burn in 1914 and that he hoped would burn brighter in 1915. "It is a curious thing to watch the Commission grow. It started as nothing but a group of American mining engineers, with the sympathetic aid of some of our diplomatic representatives and the goodwill of the neutral world. It is rapidly growing into a powerful international entity, negotiating agreements with the Great Powers of Europe, enjoying rights that no Government enjoys, and as the warring governments come to understand its sincerity and honesty, gaining influence and authority day by day."

THIRTY-EIGHT

Cardinal Mercier's Christmas Pastoral Letter

It was nearing Christmas in the ancient town of Malines (Mechelen in Flemish) in the Flemish province of Antwerp. Situated on the tidal River Dyle, the town was home to nearly 60,000 people. Malines was more than 1,000 years old and boasted a *grand place* that was ringed by picturesque gabled houses of the sixteenth and seventeenth century and held the city's fourteenth-century *hôtel de ville*.

Among all the architectural treasures in the city, however, the most famous was the magnificent Saint Rumbold's Cathedral, which had been started at the end of the thirteenth century, completed in 1312, and rebuilt after a massive fire in 1342. A tower that had been planned as the tallest in all of Christendom was incomplete at 318 feet and gave the cathedral its distinctive flat-topped tower. Starting in 1560 the church had been the home of the Catholic archdiocese of Malines, which covered all of Belgium.

During the Christmas season of 1914, within the cathedral's private chambers, the highly outspoken Cardinal Désiré Félicien François Joseph

Mercier sat contemplating the war, the people of Belgium, the Catholic Church, and his personal feelings about the German invaders.

He had been born in Braine-l'Alleud, twenty miles south of Brussels; had been educated at Louvain; and was "proud of being a Walloon," according to U.S. Legation Minister Whitlock.

He was a very tall man, well over six feet, and stood out in any crowd. When Whitlock first met the cardinal, he was impressed because Mercier "entered, advanced, tall and strong and spare, in the long black soutane with the red piping and the sash, not with the stately, measured pace that one associates with the red hat, but with long, quick strides, kicking out with impatience the skirt of his soutane before him as he walked, as though it impeded his movements."

Hunt, when describing Mercier, focused more on his face. It was "thin, scholarly, ascetic, with sparse, grayish-white hair above it . . . and his forehead so white that one feels one looks on the naked bone. His eyes are deep-set, the eyes of a man who sees a great deal. There is a pleasantly humorous look about the corners of the firm mouth, but the expression of his face in conversation is that of a man who knows what he thinks, measures what he says, and feels in advance the exact effect of every remark he makes and of every look he casts upon one."

Mercier had become archbishop of Malines in 1906 and a year later was elevated to cardinal, so that he was both a bishop and a cardinal.

In December 1914, as he sat in his chambers, Mercier could not forget that in late August, as the Germans swept through Belgium, he had had to leave his beloved country and go to Rome to select a new pope, who turned out to be Benedict XV. While in Rome he had heard about the arrest and imprisonment of numerous Belgian priests and civilians, the destruction of many towns and villages, and, most distressing of all, the burning of Louvain and its great university, where he had been an instructor years before.

When Mercier returned to Belgium in September, he found a disheartened and demoralized nation occupied by the German Army and German authorities who seemed uncaring and unresponsive to local needs and requests. The cardinal had immediately traveled to Brussels and paid a visit to Governor General von der Goltz to ask for the return of the Belgian priests and teachers who had been deported at the time of the invasion. He also talked about the refugees who wanted to return home but were afraid their fighting-age men would be arrested or deported.

Cardinal Désiré Félicien François Joseph Mercier wrote a Christmas pastoral letter that stirred the hearts of Belgians, infuriated the Germans, and inspired the world. (Public domain; A Journal From Our Legation in Belgium, Hugh Gibson, Doubleday, Page & Co., 1917.)

Mercier had already negotiated an agreement with the governor of Antwerp, General von Huhne, that the returning Belgians and the civilian guard who had laid down their arms would be left alone. He asked von der Goltz to accept and apply that guarantee nationwide.

The next day von der Goltz traveled to Malines and told Mercier that he would do everything possible to return any innocent Belgian priests and teachers as soon as possible. He also promised to extend von Huhne's guarantees to the whole country. "The Governor expressed his wish to see normal life restored at an early date." The cardinal—never one to hold back what he really wanted to say—stated that a restoration of normal life "was his wish also, but that the people were too deeply impressed by the tragic events which had marked the beginning of hostilities to allow them to feel any confidence." Mercier then brought up specific German atrocities and his feeling that there should be a court of arbitration to deal with them. These remarks "threw the General into an embarrassment which he altogether failed to disguise." The interview ended soon after.

Baron von Bissing, who took over on December 3 for von der Goltz, acknowledged the importance of the Catholic Church in maintaining civilian order when he wrote, "Any German statesman who is appointed to control the German administration in Belgium must realise that Catholicism is, and will remain, a strong and living force in Belgium, and that among the most important requirements for successful German work is an intelligent regard for the Catholic Church and its disciples."

But von Bissing took a roundabout, old-school approach to Cardinal Mercier. Instead of writing to him directly or simply asking for an audience, he wrote to Cardinal Felix von Hartmann of Cologne, Germany. In that letter, dated December 4, he stated, "In a large part of Belgium the Catholic clergy represent a force whose importance cannot be overrated; therefore, I should not wish to ignore negotiating with them and their heads, not only in the interests of my mission, but likewise in the interest of the country and of the Catholic population." He, therefore, asked Cardinal von Hartmann to tell Cardinal Mercier, "I should be very pleased to enter into personal relations with him, whether it be that he give me an interview with him at Malines, for so long as the time at my disposal allows, or that he will have the kindness to pay me a visit at Brussels."

Cardinal von Hartmann quickly forwarded von Bissing's letter to Mercier, along with his own letter endorsing the sincerity of von Bissing's words. "The General, whom I have had the honor of knowing for a long time, is an intelligent, discreet, just and benevolent man, who sincerely feels all he has written in his letter, and whose heart's desire will be to respond to the wishes of the bishops."

Cardinal Mercier did not seem overly impressed with von Bissing's highly formal, indirect approach. He didn't officially reply to von Hartmann or von Bissing about this for nearly three weeks. Then sparks flew.

Meanwhile, Cardinal von Hartmann's words about von Bissing seemed to ring true when the governor general sent Mercier a quick note on Wednesday, December 9, stating that "the ministry of war at Berlin has given orders to set at liberty all priests detained in Germany, provided no charge has been made against them; so that I have every reason to believe that priests who have duties as teachers will return without further delay."

Cardinal Mercier did not dignify the governor general's missive with his own note; he had his secretary reply. In that reply there was no expression of thanks, merely the hope that the people would be released—basically, he'd believe it when he saw it. Mercier didn't stop there, though. His secretary wrote: "But it is not in these alone that the Cardinal is interested. [He] had asked, besides this, for the liberation of lay teachers in primary schools, whom Belgian military law puts on the same footing as members of the clergy. The absence of these teachers from the country is causing great difficulties in the organization of the people's education."

On Wednesday, December 16, Cardinal Mercier went to nearby Brussels and met with von Bissing. The next day, von Bissing went to Malines to meet with Mercier. During those two meetings, von Bissing reiterated that he had seen to the release of the deported priests and would do the same for the lay teachers. And "in order to show his goodwill toward the ecclesiastical authorities, he gave the Cardinal every facility to communicate with the Belgian suffragan bishops [those Belgian bishops subordinate to Mercier]."

Von Bissing appeared to be working hard to gain Mercier's approval. But the cardinal would not be directed away from his message—that no one should forget what had happened during the invasion. "The Cardinal thanked von Bissing for his benevolent attitude, but called his attention to the fact that the Belgians, whatever might be the feelings of the Governor General toward them, would not forget the horrors which had marked the beginning of the invasion."

That was too much for von Bissing. He "cut him short. He said that he could not discuss the conduct of the German Army, which, he maintained, was fully justified by the attitude of the Belgian people." Regaining his composure, von Bissing ended the meeting by offering to personally forward Mercier's response to Cardinal von Hartmann's December 6 letter.

On December 28 Mercier took von Bissing up on his offer with a letter to the governor general and a letter to von Hartmann that was left open so that von Bissing could read it. In his letter to von Bissing, Mercier once again pulled no punches. He gave lip service to the "care which you manifest for the religious interests of the country," but—and there always seemed to be a "but" with Mercier in his relations with the Germans—"I regard it as my strict duty in the interests of truth to add that, no matter what the personal dispositions of Baron von Bissing may be, the Governor General represents amongst us here a usurping and hostile nation, in whose presence we assert our right to independence and respect for our neutrality."

Mercier didn't stop there. "Further, as guardian of the moral and religious interests of Belgium, I protest against the acts of injustice and violence of which my compatriots have been the innocent victims."

The cardinal was no less strident in his letter to von Hartmann and even indirectly called upon the German cardinal to join Mercier's fight. "Your Eminence [Hartmann] will understand that patriotism and justice impose upon me the duty to go on protesting against these crimes until they have been punished; and I will add that if you were in possession of all the evidence that I have gathered, your own sense of righteousness would compel you to unite your protest to ours."

Mercier continued: "It must be stated, furthermore, that the comparative good-will shown us at present in no wise atones for the outrages to which Belgians have been so cruelly subjected. When the Imperial Chancellor in his speech on December 2 dared to say, 'We shall remember after the war the wrongs done to our defenseless compatriots in enemy lands, wrongs which clash with all the laws of civilization,' he went beyond all bounds; and in so far as these words were aimed at Belgium he uttered a monstrous lie."

Mercier was referring to a December 2 speech that was given by German Chancellor Theobald von Bethmann-Hollweg to the German Parliament. In the wide-ranging speech the chancellor talked about the causes of the war ("Britain the Real Aggressor"), the Ottoman Empire joining Germany as an ally on October 28, and the difficulties that German soldiers had to face. The German chancellor had stated: "For we must and will wage this war of defence, in which we are assaulted from all sides, to a successful end for the sake of right and liberty. When that time has come we shall also remember the injustice and ill-treatment dealt out to our defenceless citizens in hostile countries—wrongs which in many cases were an outrage against all the principles of civilization. The world must come to learn that nobody can hurt a hair on a German's head with impunity."

Mercier's two letters created a tremendous amount of frustration and anger in von Bissing. The governor general felt he had tried hard to accommodate Mercier's every request, and all he had received in return were condemnations.

In a letter dated December 31, von Bissing refused to forward Mercier's letter to von Hartmann and took up the gauntlet that Mercier had thrown down. "It is quite impossible for me to grant you the facilities for traveling which you request; for now, I cannot see any common ground on which we can work together with mutual confidence in the interests of the Belgian people." As for the letter to von Hartmann, von Bissing wrote: "It is impossible for me to forward a criticism so unjustifiable and so offensive to the higher authorities, both of the German Empire and of the German Army. I return this letter to your Eminence."

Unbeknownst to von Bissing, while these correspondences and meetings were being held, Cardinal Mercier was also working on a pastoral letter through much of December. In his position as archbishop of Malines, Mercier was following a tradition of writing a yearly pastoral letter to his people. According to Mercier, these once-a-year letters "touched any vital question, social or political, concerning which he felt the church owed a duty of leadership. But primarily, they were messages from the spiritual chief to his flock, intimate and affectionate in their greeting and encouragement, searching in their condemnation, compelling in their exhortation, exalted in their explanation of Catholic doctrine."

The cardinal had many who wanted to hear his thoughts. The majority of Belgians in 1914 were Catholic, and the religion was a driving force in the country, more so in the Walloon south than in the Flemish north. In fact, religion was such a strong influence in Belgium that it mitigated much of the differences that existed over language. And in the critical arena of politics—which seemed to dominate nearly every Belgian's body and soul before the war—the Catholic party had been in power for nearly thirty years.

Hunt wrote: "Throughout Belgium the priest is an important character. A few of the cities and most of the towns are Catholic, and the priest is a political and social as well as a religious director. In the towns and villages he is often more important than the Burgomaster. He is accustomed to relieve distress, and in the volunteer organizations through which the work of the CRB is done the parish priest and the whole Catholic hierarchy, with the Cardinal-Archbishop at their head, are most important elements."

Another CRB delegate reported, "It takes quite a while for an American to realize that in Belgium political beliefs are the standard by which men judge each other and on which they form their friendships and enmities; the first question that a man asks about another is whether he is a liberal or a Catholic."

To this large flock, Mercier sat down to write his pastoral letter, which he titled "Patriotism and Endurance." It became a tour de force that would inspire a nation and excite the world.

When the huge missive was finished, it went to the archbishop's printer. Once copies were made, they were circulated, unbeknownst to the Germans, to all the priests in Belgium via the "seminarists leaving Malines for the Christmas holidays." A note from Mercier was attached telling the priests to read the whole pastoral letter to their congregations "without omitting or erasing any part of it in spite of any orders to the contrary that might be issued by any other power."

On Friday, January 1, 1915, the first section of Mercier's pastoral letter was read aloud by priests in churches all over Belgium. As Hunt noted, the cardinal's "ringing challenge to the nation" was a surprise to everyone, including the German troops attending mass all around the country. "The astonished soldiers could only listen in open-mouthed amazement."

This was no gentle, spiritual guide to love and understanding; this was a document that described within the first pages the destruction of Louvain and "the wholesale shooting of citizens, and tortures inflicted upon women and children, and upon unarmed and undefended men." And later, Mercier said: "The ruins I beheld, and the ashes, were more dreadful than I, prepared by the saddest of forebodings, could have imagined. . . . Churches, schools, asylums, hospitals, convents in great numbers, are in ruins. Entire villages have all but disappeared."

Almost like a newspaper reporter, Mercier listed numerous places and how many homes had been destroyed; then he went on to talk of the thousands of people who had been deported. He also stated, "In my diocese alone I know that thirteen priests or men in orders were put to death."

In painful overview, and surely with tears in his voice, he said: "We can neither number our dead nor compute the measure of our ruins. And what would it be if we turned our sad steps towards Liège, Namur, Andenne, Dinant, Tamines, Charleroi, and elsewhere?"

He reiterated what everyone knew about Belgium at that moment: "All commerce at an end, all careers ruined; industry at a standstill; thousands upon thousands of working-men without employment; working-women, shop-girls, humble servant-girls without the means of earning their bread; and poor souls forlorn on the bed of sickness and fever, crying, 'O Lord, how long, how long, how long?'"

One positive note that the cardinal struck was about the brave Belgian Army. "Our soldiers are our saviours. A first time, at Liège, they saved France; a second time, in Flanders, they arrested the advance of the enemy upon Calais. France and England know it; and Belgium stands before them both, and before the entire world, as a nation of heroes."

And at the head of this brave army was King Albert. "Our King is, in the esteem of all, at the very summit of the moral scale; he is doubtless the only man who does not recognize that fact, as simple as the simplest of his soldiers, he stands in the trenches and puts new courage, by the serenity of his face, into the hearts of those who he requires that they shall not doubt their country."

According to the cardinal, the war had done more than just create a heroic king and army. Before the fighting "there were Belgians, and many

Cardinal Mercier wrote, "As the simplest of his soldiers, [King Albert] stands in the trenches." He became known as the symbol of stouthearted, heroic Belgium. (Public domain; *A Journal From Our Legation in Belgium*, Hugh Gibson, Doubleday, Page & Co., 1917.)

such, who wasted their time and their talents in futile quarrels of class with class, of race with race, of passion with personal passion." But when the Germans invaded, all Belgians had come together: "At once, instantly, we were conscious of our own patriotism."

As to casting blame for the war, the cardinal was not afraid to state what many felt. The treaty of 1839 had established Belgium's neutrality, so "Belgium was thus bound in honor to defend her own independence. She kept her oath. The other Powers were bound to respect and also to protect her neutrality. Germany violated her oath; England kept hers. These are the facts."

With all this damning information, what were Belgians supposed to do?

Buried within the long letter, which could only be partially read in one service, was Mercier's recommendation that Belgians should "abstain from hostile acts against the enemy army, to have that regard for the occupying power which the common weal [well-being] demands and to respect the regulations imposed so long as they did not interfere either with liberty of conscience or offend their patriotic feelings."

After such a recommendation that Belgians should abstain from hostile acts, however, Mercier followed with some of his strongest rhetoric. His voice surely rang to the rafters when he proclaimed: "I do not require of you to renounce any of your national desires. On the contrary, I hold it as part of the obligations of my episcopal office [office of a bishop] to instruct you as to your duty in face of the Power that has invaded our soil and now occupies the greater part of our country. The authority of that Power is no lawful authority. Therefore, in soul and conscience you owe it neither respect, nor attachment, nor obedience."

The cardinal then drove home the point, stating: "The sole lawful authority in Belgium is that of our King, of our Government, of the elected representatives of the nation. This authority alone has a right to our affection, our submission." He then reminded his flock that "occupied provinces are not conquered provinces."

This was no humble speech from a person locked within a brutal German occupation; this was a spiritually free man calling upon Belgians to remember the past, accept the present, and hold within their hearts the knowledge that they were unjustly imprisoned and would someday be set free.

It was not what von Bissing wanted to hear.

That night at midnight Mercier's printer was arrested, and all copies of the pastoral letter were confiscated. At 6:15 a.m. three men sent by von Bissing were at Mercier's door, demanding to see his eminence. The leader of the group was Baron von der Lancken, head of the German political department in Belgium and the governor general's right-hand man.

A spirited discussion ensued, with von der Lancken accusing the cardinal of illegally circulating a communication not approved by German censors. Mercier said he had no knowledge of such a regulation; therefore, he had not broken the law. Von der Lancken insisted the archbishop had incited Belgians to resist the German occupation. He had done no such thing, Mercier shot back, pointing to the passages in the letter telling the Belgians to remain calm and refrain from any hostile acts. Neither side moved from its initial position.

Von Bissing wrote Mercier, "It has caused me a most disagreeable surprise." He then announced: "I have ordered the confiscation of copies of the letter which were found at the printing works, and I have decreed penalties against any one circulating them. It is clear that the reading of the letter has already provoked an agitation among the Belgian people. . . . I am obliged to request your Eminence to at once forbid your clergy to read and to circulate your pastoral."

The cardinal refused to do so.

When the dust had settled, Mercier—who was too prominent and beloved in Belgium to be imprisoned or shot—was, for a short time, restricted from traveling, and the Germans did their best to contain the circulation of the letter.

That would be harder than they probably thought.

Van Doren's Network Takes On the Pastoral Letter

The pastoral letter had become the talk of Belgium. As one writer explained it, "This preliminary skirmish to a long drawn out battle of words and wits between the Cardinal and von Bissing caused great excitement throughout occupied territory. The Cardinal categorically refused to withdraw the letter, and, in fact, reiterated his order that it be read."

But most Belgians had not heard the entire letter, nor read any of it. "The result was that comparably few people actually knew the contents of the Letter about which everyone was talking."

That gave editor Victor Jourdain an idea. He asked van Doren if he could find a printer to do the job and then distribute copies to as many people as possible. Van Doren agreed immediately.

At the same time, the Abbé de Moor, "realizing the value the Cardinal's stirring message would have in stiffening the patriotic spirit of the oppressed people," decided to have 5,000 copies made for distribution in his parish. When he told van Doren about his plans, van Doren told the priest to increase the print run to 25,000, not telling him who the additional copies were for.

The trickiest part was printing such a quantity. Van Doren's little jelly press could not handle such a job. They would need a legitimate printer. But the Germans, "anticipating that attempts might be made to print the Letter secretly, had given instructions to the patrols to keep close watch on all small printing works."

Small printing operations, many of which were also stationery shops, were still allowed to operate throughout Belgium because the Germans wanted business and civilian life to be as normal as possible. While they were banned from printing any public notices or information not approved by the censors, printers were permitted to do small jobs, everything from business and personal stationery to calling cards and birth, marriage, and death announcements. Even with such German approval, however, the print shops were constantly watched and raided by the German police. Those who secretly did take on illegal jobs knew they were playing a dangerous cat-and-mouse game that could land them and their families in jail or before a firing squad.

Armed with an order for 25,000 copies of the pastoral letter, de Moor made some discrete inquiries. A man named Becquaert, with a shop and printing press on Louvain Street in Brussels, agreed to do the job, even though he was "under no illusions as to his fate if he were discovered."

Becquaert took no chances, and because anyone could be a spy, he waited until his staff had gone home before he personally set the type. To make the job as easy as possible, the letter was set in very small type, which meant it could fit on both sides of one piece of paper. Van Doren added another element of safety by sending a note to Becquaert, asking that he print both sides of the paper, a ream at a time, so he could take delivery of 500 copies at a time. This would lessen, van Doren thought, the chances of confiscation.

Unbeknownst to van Doren, the printer didn't like the idea. He wanted to get the complete job done as quickly as possible, so he ignored the request. He ran off 25,000 copies on one side, then sent a note to van Doren that the first 500 would be done the next morning.

When the abbé and van Doren got to the printer's, they waited outside out-of-sight until they saw a woman go in. The priest explained to van Doren that usually when the Germans raided a place, they'd keep even innocent people in the shop to try and apprehend more of the guilty who would walk in unsuspecting. De Moor told his partner: "If she comes out it means we're safe. We'll wait."

A few minutes later, the woman came out. The abbé told van Doren to watch for patrols and headed into the shop. He quickly collected the 500 copies, hid them in the folds of his cassock, gathered up van Doren, and together they strolled leisurely down the street. By 7 p.m. that night they had folded and stuffed each one-page document into an envelope, and with the help of some trustworthy Boy Scouts under de Moor's command, the first bundle had been delivered. Becquaert had told them to come back that night for the second 500. As they happily headed back for the second bundle, they had no idea what was happening at the shop.

In the early dark of December, Madame Becquaert had noticed three men loitering around near the shop. With streetlights not allowed due to possible Allied air raids, she only got a look at one of them as he came toward the shop and into the light of the shop's window. She immediately saw "the unmistakable silhouette of a plain clothed *Poliezi.*

"She rushed to the door of the workshop and screamed: 'Les Boches! sauve-toi! [The Germans! save yourself!]'

"At the same moment the police burst into the shop. As they rushed toward her, she turned the key in the workshop door and threw it over their heads through the shop door into the street."

The printer was just tying up a fresh bundle of printed letters when his wife screamed and locked the door. He bolted out the back and into a side street and then ran a hundred yards to a chemist he knew down the street. Rushing into the shop, he told the old chemist the Germans were after him, he needed a coat, and to take his bundle. "I can't explain," he said. "A priest—a tall, dark fellow, can't mistake him—he'll be going to my place in a minute. Stop him. Give him this and tell him . . . I'm at the Prince d'Orange, Petite Espinette."

As Becquaert slipped into the chemist's coat and went to the door, he watched in horror as down the street in the fading light his wife and child were being led away by the German police. "Don't forget," he called out to the chemist. "Big, dark man—de Moor's his name. He'll be along any minute." In a moment, he had disappeared, leaving behind the frightened old chemist.

Luckily for van Doren and de Moor, when a German car pulled in front of the printer's shop, and men began loading it with bundles of the unfinished pastoral letter, the scene drew a neighborhood crowd. When the two men got there they immediately knew what must have happened and easily merged with the rest of the crowd. It wasn't long before the old chemist, scared and shaking, approached de Moor, confirmed his identity, and then told him of the package he had waiting in his shop. The old man was so nervous, though, that he couldn't remember the specific address Becquaert had given him. All he could remember was Petite Espinette. The priest and van Doren gathered up the bundle and headed home, wondering what would happen to the Becquaert family and whether they were next to be rounded up.

After midnight, there was an "urgent ringing at the abbé's front door." When he got to the door he looked through the peephole and recognized Becquaert's wife. "This, he thought, was a pretty kettle of fish. She must have come straight from the Kommandantur, and had probably been shadowed. If he let her in it would be only a matter of minutes before they were both arrested."

Seeing her on the verge of collapse, however, he let her in. "Her teeth were chattering and her breath came in long sobs. From her incoherent sentences the Abbé gathered that she had been held all the evening at the Kommandantur with her daughter and cross-examined. But she had refused to speak. Finally they had let her go about ten o'clock. She had taken her child to a relative's house and come straight to the Abbé. Did he know what had happened to her husband?"

When de Moor asked her if she knew of a spot on Petite Espinette where her husband might go, she remembered they would occasionally take tea at the Prince d'Orange. De Moor advised the woman to go home and "Go to the old chemist's tomorrow at seven and someone will be there to give you news of him. Meanwhile don't say a word to anyone and don't come here again. You may be watched."

When de Moor related the story to van Doren, they agreed it was best to get Becquaert out of the country. But it would cost money. Van Doren said he knew someone and then went to Jourdain and explained the situation. The editor said he would pay for the man's escape from Belgium. In only a few days Becquaert was equipped with false identity papers, money, and a guide to lead him across the Dutch border. His wife and child stayed in Brussels and continued to run the shop under the ever-present watchful eye of the Germans.

While the experience worked out relatively well in the end, it gave de Moor and van Doren a strong shot of reality. But it also hardened van Doren's resolve to print and distribute the cardinal's letter. He immediately began looking for another printer. This time, however, he was much more cautious. He decided to approach a newsagent named Massardo who owned a bookshop in the St. Hubert arcade, which lay a few blocks northeast of the *grand place*. Van Doren felt he could trust Massardo because he had bought banned foreign newspapers from him before. When he introduced himself, though, van Doren became Mr. Willem. Massardo took Mr. Willem's request and approached the printer who did his legitimate orders. The man agreed on the condition his name would never be revealed.

This time the printing and distribution went without a hitch. Belgians all over Brussels, and later all over the country, began to read the cardinal's inspiring words. It was just the New Year's present they had needed.

As a history of *La Libre Belgique* related, this event was also "a foretaste of what was soon to become an everyday incident in van Doren's life." As a result, he was much more cautious in his underground activities. Just as importantly, though, the incident brought Massardo and his wife into the clandestine community. They would quickly become an integral part of the operations.

While the Germans were trying everything they could think of to stop circulation of Cardinal Mercier's letter in Belgium, they were even more motivated to make sure it never got out of Belgium. If the letter was printed beyond the Belgian borders, it would be a major embarrassment to the German authorities and give the Allies more ammunition to turn worldwide public opinion against them.

The cardinal knew this. He was one step ahead of the Germans and had already made plans to spirit the document out of the country and into the hands of a friend who would make sure it was published in the world press. As Mercier explained years later to a journalist, "I had, of course, foreseen that this letter would displease our occupying friends, and I thought I had better send it out of the country before it should be published in Belgium, and so I did." Six days before the printing and circulation of the letter, with the Germans unaware of what was about to happen, Mercier decided to get his letter to Holland. He had a friend there, "a very good priest, who was my representative among our refugees there."

The cardinal devised three secret pathways for the letter and hoped at least one would be successful. "I sent my letter first by a courageous young man who tried to get into Holland. I never learned whether he did pass." The second method was via a small boat that was going down the Scheldt River. He never found out if that one got through either. The third way, Mercier said, was "most sure of all, and it succeeded." As he explained it, "At the frontier between Holland and Belgium we have a seminary where there are seven or eight hundred students, and for their living they received usually a great quantity of Dutch cheese in boxes. The Germans liked the cheese and let it pass into our country. Well, I thought I could send my letter very surely this way: When the cheeses came to Belgium to the seminary, the papers in which they were wrapped were, of course, crumpled and dirty. I made my letter old and soiled, and it was sent back with all those filthy papers in the boxes to Holland."

After its arrival on Dutch soil, the letter was quickly sent to newspapers in France, England, and America, where it appeared in the *New York Times* on January 22, 1915. Its publication had Mercier's desired effect—world sentiment was strengthened in sympathy for the Belgians, in admiration for the heroic cardinal, and in denunciation of the Germans.

Two Delegates Smuggle Out the Pastoral Letter

Officially, CRB delegates never had any link to the cardinal's letter. They did, of course, hear about it via the Belgian rumor mill, and many of them probably read one of the clandestine copies that circulated for months. Unofficially, however, two of the earliest delegates, Rhodes scholars Carmichael and Branscomb, claimed they smuggled a copy out of Belgium and sent it to England for publication. The tale is supported by statements from both men and recorded in a Carmichael family book, but it has never been verified through third-party sources.

Their story began when the two agreed to give up their planned trip to Scotland to become part of the second wave of Oxford students to enter Belgium. Carmichael penned in his diary at Oxford on December 4 that he had "been in a state of restless tension about the new plan of vacation. I believe I'll get as much done in B as in England but must retire and rise fairly early to get ready to go down to London."

Arriving in Brussels they joined the other CRB delegates at the Palace Hotel waiting for assignments. CRB records showed Carmichael and Branscomb joining Hunt on Monday, December 21, as delegates of the Antwerp Province. Carmichael was immediately assigned by Hunt to personally handle the city of Malines.

According to Carmichael, a few days later he and Branscomb were in Malines "to arrange for a shipment of food" and talked with the acting burgomaster, Francis Dessain. Francis's brother, Charles, was Mercier's printer, but he was then in England, so Francis had been given the responsibility printing the pastoral letter. Francis offered to introduce the two CRB delegates to the cardinal. This was approximately a week before Mercier would deliver his letter to his congregation.

The two Americans jumped at the chance to meet his eminence and were mightily impressed with the man. Carmichael wrote that "he spoke with much feeling of the gratitude of Belgium for America for her great work in relief and sympathy." At the end of the short interview, "the distinguished Divine mentioned the 'letter to his people,' which had just come from the printer and presented us with an autographed copy each."

So far, so good—the Americans had not done anything yet to breech their promise of neutrality.

But then, "a third copy was offered us with the request that we send it across to a friend of the Cardinal in England. Until then, nobody knew, save its author and publisher, what was contained in the document before us, but the thought of what might be there made Mr. Branscomb hesitate while I, to save the situation, accepted the responsibility for the letter

without reserve." Carmichael wrote that Mercier had said: "You gentlemen can do a service to me and the Belgian people by taking a copy out
of Belgium so that the outside world will know its contents. Will you do
it?"

The cardinal had laid in their hands a heavy burden for a nineteen-
and twenty-three-year-old, especially because they had generally given
their word as gentlemen to whomever recruited them to remain absolutely neutral. After returning to Antwerp the excitement of meeting the
archbishop wore off, and they both started wondering what was in the
letter. If they knew what it said, they would have a better understanding
of how much trouble they'd be in if they were caught at the border. They
read the missive.

They realized they could be in serious trouble. "We were not only as-
tounded at the fiery eloquence of the gentle churchman, but we began to
have sinister misgivings as to the wisdom of our promise. . . . Should we
or should we not take the letter along to post to England? At this point,
we hesitated and reviewed briefly the possibilities."

But a promise was a promise, especially one made to a man of God.
"Finally, with a temerity more lucky than wise, we decided to fulfill our
rash promise."

Their time came the next day when "it was necessary for us to make a
trip to Holland on business." With the boldness of youth, they had yet
to make a plan ten miles from the border. But shortly "our plan had been
perfected; it remained only to execute it."

When they reached the frontier guardhouse, it was "reeking with sentries. A couple came out to meet us and to guide us into the cul de sac in
which everything suspicious remains. A few more were on the inside to
receive us while still others took over the Overland (the automobile) to
search for contraband."

From the motorcar they were escorted into the guardhouse. "My friend,
Branscomb, was carrying the document so I preceded him as we entered
the room. While I was receiving the embraces of the diligent guard who
insisted on feeling underneath my waistcoat, up and down my back, Mr.
Branscomb had quietly backed up to a table in the corner and deposited
the Cardinal's letter."

According to Branscomb, he had put the letter inside a folded newspaper. One of the guards saw the paper and went over to look at it. When
he noticed it was in English, he turned away.

As Branscomb was being frisked, Carmichael "eased over to the table where the document laid and in as casual a manner as the circumstances permitted, transferred it to my baggage."

In another moment they were back in the motorcar and driving into Holland. "We breathed a sigh of relief and sent the letter posthaste to its destination in England."

If the story is true, and the men had been caught at the border, it would have had major consequences for the two personally and could have jeopardized the entire relief program—millions of lives might have been affected. Even so, as Carmichael later admitted, "It was not without a certain satisfaction that we felt we had assisted in a small way in letting the truth about Belgium be known to the world."

THIRTY-NINE

Antwerp

E. E. Hunt and Belgian Politics

As Hunt worked with diverse groups of men in the numerous commit-tees and communes, he quickly realized that he was standing in a hurricane's eye, surrounded by the swirling winds of Belgium's social, religious, and po-litical attitudes. He knew he would have to understand and acknowledge the powers of each to effectively fashion a coordinated relief effort.

Belgium had become a nation less than 100 years before, which meant, as Hunt learned, "the commune, not the nation, was the Belgian fa-therland." At odds were "Republicanism against Monarchy, Clericalism against Anti-Clericalism, Flemings against French-speaking Walloons, Socialism against Capitalism. Business, society, every department of life, was divided and subdivided into self-contained cliques. The bitterness of the struggle and the disunion were almost unbelievable."

While the Germans had changed all that and converted the country's fierce generational parochialism into "tenacious patriotism," Hunt acknowledged, "Even in the midst of war men could not be expected to lay aside fundamental principles." The Belgians "still feared and distrusted their fellow Belgians. War exaggerated certain of their suspicions, instead of allaying them."

The CRB was supposed to be above all that. It was, in theory, working for all Belgians, no matter what their religion, political affiliation, or social standing.

That concept was tested when in late December the members of the city district of Turnhout told Hunt privately they did not want to be in the Antwerp provincial committee; they wanted to deal with Brussels directly or just with Hunt. They had not yet received any food from Antwerp and did not trust that a provincial committee could represent them and their needs to the headquarters in Brussels. As Hunt wrote, the town of Turnhout was "rustic, old-fashioned, and Clerical" and did not trust the "merchants of Antwerp." In fact, the representatives of Turnhout were not even clear on what the CRB was supposed to do. As Hunt put it, "It looked on us as an association of benevolent grain-dealers, selling flour to a body of Antwerp business men, who, in turn, would resell it to the Turnhout delegation, of course at a profit to themselves!"

The issue came to a head at a provincial committee meeting. "There was an exciting moment when all the Turnhout delegates were on their feet at once, speaking Flemish instead of French, as they usually did when much excited, protesting . . . and adding that they were appealing to Brussels for complete separation from Antwerp." The room began to feel uncomfortably small, and, as Hunt said, "one of the gentlemen wept in the excess of his feeling, and choruses of recriminations, which I could not understand, were exchanged between the groups." The Turnhout group threw across the room to their colleagues the damning question: "When had Antwerp, rich and pious in the Middle Ages— now subject to tradesmen and freemasons—when had it been generous to Turnhout?"

The representatives of Turnhout were so adamant in their beliefs that they petitioned the CN and the CRB in Brussels to permit a division of the province. Hunt was equally adamant that his province not be divided. He wrote multiple reports about the issue and why it was not a good idea to allow the secession of Turnhout. With major communication difficulties still existing throughout Belgium, Hunt's reports did not reach Brussels in time to affect the decision.

Because the CRB office was still under Heineman, who often seemed to take more of a Belgian perspective than an American one, the CRB Brussels office decision came down allowing Turnhout to break away from the Antwerp provincial committee.

Hunt refused to accept the verdict. He pleaded his case with greater intensity. Within a few days, "more as a favor to me than for any sounder reason, Brussels consented to reverse this judgment." The CRB head office even sent Hunt another assistant, Simpson—the cane-wielding Rhodester who had worked with Kittredge in Hasselt and had been left on the roadside by his driver. He was immediately assigned by Hunt to deal exclusively with Turnhout as a way of alleviating the city's fears of not being properly represented.

Hunt did not stop there, however. He knew that there was truth in what the Turnhout representatives had been saying. The city of Antwerp had too much control over what was happening in the entire province of Antwerp. Hunt decided to take a bold next step in an attempt to address some of their concerns. It was time to take on the powerhouse of Antwerp.

The city had been running relief efforts since the beginning of the war, before the CRB had shown up. City officials had always seen the work as a municipal matter. These officials, however, were "party men. They belonged to the Liberal or Socialist party. No Catholics were among them." And while they had done an admirable job and had "shared with their neighbor communes what food and money the municipality controlled," they saw no reason "why they should surrender their favored position at the center of supplies when food began to come from America instead of the municipal warehouses."

As Hunt stated diplomatically, "As an American delegate I was pledged to a different point of view."

To correct the situation, Hunt realized that "the Antwerp Provincial Relief Committee must be divorced from the Antwerp Town Hall and the group of party men who had so ably ministered to the wants lying close at hand." The separation began, as Hunt noted, rather comically. His youngest assistant, nineteen-year-old Branscomb, was designated as delegate to the city. One of his first jobs had been to reprimand the local committee for the reports they had been handing in. As Hunt wrote, standing before some of the most prominent men of the greatest Flemish cities, Branscomb had held up one of their reports and spoken in a quiet, southern drawl, "We cannot and we will not send another such report as this to Brussels. Reports must have our signature as American delegates. We will not give our signatures to tardy and un-businesslike reports."

The men were taken aback. The controller of Antwerp supposedly told a friend, "I have been accustomed to handle millions of francs every day, and now these young Americans come and ask me what became of such-and-such a bag of flour last week!"

If they were surprised by Branscomb's remarks, they were shocked by what Hunt announced at the next provincial committee meeting. He told the assembly that he had transferred the entire relief work for the city of Antwerp from the town hall to offices in the Bank of the Union and had designated a new delegate, Thomas O. Connett, to serve as the representative for the city of Antwerp. Hunt added that Connett had been instructed to create a census of all bread and flour consumers in the district.

While the transfer was completed in four days, "such precipitate action appalled some of our supporters in the Committee."

After some time, however, their reaction became muted and then turned to praise once they saw what Connett was able to do. As Hunt noted, the "quiet, unobtrusive young Cambridge student, about twenty-two years old," with the help of numerous bank clerks, "had card-indexed the city of Antwerp and reorganized the system of control over food distributions with a saving of about one-fifth of the supplies."

Despite their youth, the American delegates were getting things done. As Hunt noted, "None of us was out of his twenties. We were beardless boys in the assemblies of our elders, but young or old, we were equal participators in a thrilling undertaking and we intended to do our part."

While December had been a little rocky for Hunt and his handful of delegates in the province of Antwerp, they had made a respectable start. And his CRB office had moved into newly donated offices in Edouard Bunge's Bank of the Union of Antwerp at 2 Marché aux Grains.

Little did the Americans know that much harder times were just around the corner in 1915.

The Bunges' Expanding Lives

In his role as vice president of the provincial committee of Antwerp, Bunge met multiple times with Hunt, both in formal gatherings and individually. Although Bunge was considered progressive in his business and societal thinking, he still found it a little disconcerting that Hunt moved to challenge the conventional wisdom of the provincial committee and the local commune leaders. Overall, though, Bunge heartily approved of Hunt and the other CRB delegates he met. It was natural for Bunge to automatically extend an open invitation to any delegate to come out to Hoogboom and Chateau Oude Gracht for moments of much-needed relaxation or to stay the night if journeying around the province.

Hunt, along with many other delegates, took Bunge up on his invitation. It was at Oude Gracht that Hunt met Erica, Eva, and Hilda. All three women volunteered at Antwerp hospitals and worked in either the soup kitchens or in the Little Bees children's canteens. Like most other young Belgian women, they had put away their colorful dresses and only wore dark, subdued colors to mourn their country's occupation. Erica, the eldest of the three, was known as the practical, business-minded one who was forceful and confident—handsome rather than attractive. Eva was the studious, intellectual sister and looked the part with her wire-rimmed glasses and tightly pulled-back hair. Hilda was acknowledged as the prettiest Bunge girl, with a rather adventurous spirit that did not enjoy long, involved political conversations. Before the war the three had been avid readers, and Erica and Eva in particular had been fascinated and engaged in what was happening internationally.

Erica had learned much about business through her discussions with her father. She in particular felt quite forward thinking in her social, religious, and political attitudes. Still, she found she could be quite surprised by the brash and straightforward-speaking young Americans.

At Oude Gracht when delegates were in attendance for dinner, Erica insisted there be no separation after the meal so that the entire group of men and women could adjourn to the parlor for conversing, playing piano, reciting literary passages, or listening to the gramophone. And there was always her nightly game of billiards with her father, who would occasionally invite a delegate to join them.

Many times at Oude Gracht the conversations were about the war, German atrocities during the invasion, or the occupation. It was during those discussions that Erica and Eva especially could get quite frustrated with many of the Americans. Their frustration lay in the fact that Hunt and most of the other Americans refused to talk about their feelings regarding the war, the Germans, or the occupation. They were honor bound as gentlemen to be neutral, and most of them strove hard to maintain that neutrality in all their dealings, whether formal or informal.

Erica had no qualms about telling anyone who would listen how she felt about the Germans, using the disparaging term "dirty Boche," which had no literal translation. Edouard would many times frown when she did so but did not say anything.

The Bunge sisters were, however, at times naïve about some aspects of life simply because of their privileged position as part of the wealthy merchant class. As one delegate, affectionately nicknamed "Pink," later recalled, "[The sisters] thought we were marvelous, a curious lot, and they evidently liked us pretty well because some of them married Americans. They were very wealthy people, and the idea that I, for instance, obviously a college graduate, that I had done menial tasks—of course they didn't believe it to begin with, that I was a farm hand and pitched hay for a dollar a day, and so on. And then I told them about selling the *Saturday Evening Post.* I had my Saturday route to dispose of 150 copies of the *Post*—bought at 3 cents, sold at 5 cents—to make some pocket money.

Edouard Bunge invited all the CRB delegates to think of Chateau Oude Gracht as their home. (Author's archives.)

"And one of these girls would say to another, 'Do you know the latest from Pinkske? He now claims that he was a newsboy.'

"'Oh,' the other one would say, 'don't believe a word he says. You can't believe anything he says.'"

They certainly knew what a newsboy was, but as Pink said, "their picture of a newsboy was some waif standing on the Bowery in New York in a driving snow storm peddling papers."

Despite such innocence, the Bunge sisters were prepared to do much physical work in areas such as nursing and farming for their country and the relief effort. The idea to start a dairy farm, conceived by Edouard and Erica in November, was coming to fruition. The Germans had agreed to allow Edouard to purchase dairy cows from Holland, and he immediately arranged to buy 100 at the exorbitant wartime price of 2,000 francs per head.

E. E. Hunt became good friends with the Bunges and visited them often at Chateau Oude Gracht. Sitting on the chateau's veranda, from left to right, are Hunt, Eva, Edouard, Hilda, and Erica. (Author's archives.)

Building of the dairy facilities was underway at Hoogboom, including two long barns and equipment and storage sheds; all of that would make up what Erica hoped would be a model dairy. She and Hoogboom's farm supervisor, Verheyen, conferred as often as Erica was able to get away from her other responsibilities. To do so, she would rise very early and walk to the farm as she used to do in her prewar morning ritual. This time, though, it seemed harder to rise early. She was so much more tired, and winter's cold and darkness were no longer invigorating as they had been before the war.

As for building the dairy facilities, Verheyen and Erica had no trouble finding labor because so many men were out of work. They also had little difficulty in arranging for the future daily supply of men and wagons to carry the milk into Antwerp. If there were not enough horses, dogs would have to do. If dogs could not handle the loads, men would take their places. The milk would be given to the canteens for children and, when possible, to hospitals. If all went according to plan, the facilities would be completed and the cows brought down from Holland in early 1915.

In Antwerp, Erica and her sisters had finished their hospital course in late December and were then licensed to better assist at the hospitals where they volunteered. Most of their patients were soldiers who had been either disfigured or burned and needed long-term care.

One burn patient of Erica's was known by the nickname Bronze. She wrote in her diary one day that he "read me the cards." While she didn't believe in such nonsense, she went along to please him. He told her six things that she wrote down in her diary on December 28.

"1. You have loved a young man who is at war, but he marches against us.

"2. You have family in a foreign country; a boy will be born there.

"3. You will soon receive a letter with bad news. You will even cry.

"4. There is a young man who loves you. You do not know it. You will never marry.

"5. There is a blond young woman who loves you very much. She owes you some gratitude, which she will show.

"6. You will receive a letter with some money, or you will inherit some. You have a lot of money, and you will have even more (ace of diamonds)."

Erica wrote responses to three of them. For the first one, she simply wrote the last name Pritzelwitz and underlined it. For item two she wrote her older sister's name, Dora, with a question mark. Dora had gone with her husband to Holland at the start of the war. Erica then had written, "My godson Karel is born in Holland." And the last item she responded to by stating, "Received a letter with 200 Fr. from R. Percher for l'Enfant du Soldat." Of course, Erica still did not believe, but she would never forget that reading by the horribly burned soldier.

Even with her various jobs and volunteering, Erica wanted to do more. She was reminded of the war all the time, even on the tranquil Hoogboom estate, where she could often hear the sounds of the large artillery fire from the front. As she wrote in her diary on Sunday, January 3, 1915, "Right up to Christmas we could hear the cannon. Since today it has started rumbling again, having stopped from the 25th to Jan. 2nd." There was also local news that was distressing. One of the servants told the family: "There had been a train accident in Kapellen. Several dead and wounded! Oh God, let there be no one we know! Poor Uncle Ed. is not home yet and Aunt E. is very upset."

Left: Eva and Erica Bunge. The collie was Erica's new dog, Ninia, which Hunt helped pick out. Right: E. E. Hunt. (Both photos: author's archives.)

Only a short time later, she wrote in her diary that she had had a special event with the help of one of the CRB delegates. "I have a dog of my own now! She is a pretty and delightful collie. Mr. Hunt and I went to get her this evening. I will name her Ninia. She is a beauty and a love. She refuses to go to the basement and for the moment she sleeps under the telephone."

A little later, Erica once again wrote in her diary and mentioned the delegates. It was evident that she was very much a young woman not always focused on work. "The Americans (Hunt, Carmichael, Simpson and Connett) are here again. Hunt is the nicest of all, but he was strange tonight. I feel a little guilty and I'm sorry I was sarcastic. He is very sentimental, and so depressed! Why did he talk so much to Eva? Would I be jealous by any chance? May God preserve me from that! He is so nice, I like him very much! Ninia is a love. Mr. Hunt loves her and she licks him, which is a pleasure to see!" She ended on a note of longing that belied her confident public persona. "I wish I were ten years older! My character and my personality would be more stable, more balanced. I get angry and I'm very silly sometimes, and afterwards I regret it! If only I were more sure of myself!"

Such internal conflict and questioning didn't stop Erica from wanting to somehow become more directly involved with the war. In the end, a way to do that came to her. Because of her outspoken views of the Germans, a local underground operator discretely approached her to ask if she might be interested in doing some clandestine work. Of course she would, she replied. What was needed? Besides simply being observant and providing information about any German troop movements she happened to see, she would be called upon on special occasions to ferry men across her property toward the Dutch border.

The task was made doubly dangerous by the fact that there were German troops bivouacked throughout the large property. Hoogboom's proximity to the border—twenty kilometers northwest of Antwerp, on the edge of the sparsely populated, flat Campine region—made it of interest to the Germans, who were clamping down on underground activities between Belgium and Holland.

Erica was used to sharing much with her sisters and her father, but in this case, she would tell no one of her underground activities. No one, that is, except Ninia and her little yellow canary friend, who perched contentedly in its cage near the marble fireplace in her bedroom.

Little did Erica know that Eva had made contact with an agent of British intelligence and had agreed, like her older sister, to work in the underground against the Germans.

It would only be on a cold and wintry night in 1915 that they would discover each other's clandestine activities when they came face-to-face in a dark forest.

FORTY

At the Front

By the end of November, the trenches stretched for hundreds of miles from Switzerland to the North Sea. It had been a brutal four months of death and carnage, and December seemed to be the time when many silently agreed to take a breather from the fighting.

On the civilian front, a group of British suffragettes wrote an open Christmas letter asking for peace and addressed to the "Women of Germany and Austria." On Monday, December 7, Pope Benedict XV called for an official truce and asked that "the guns may fall silent on the night the angels sang." The pope's request was rebuffed by the governments of both sides.

In the trenches, the soldiers who had been fighting and watching their comrades die had a different perspective from their generals and governments. Peace was practically in the air as small sections of the trenches spontaneously arranged truces to collect the dead and to allow troops to move about in some places without fear of being shot at. These truces became more and more prevalent and bolder in their inclusion of activities. In fact, that December became famous for the Christmas Truce of 1914—a series of widespread and unofficial ceasefires up and down the line. Stories tell of enemies exchanging greetings, newspapers, food, and drink. Men from both sides sang songs together and even played soccer matches in the no-man's-land between the trenches.

It seemed as if the men were so tired they didn't care anymore, while the generals and the governments wanted nothing to do with such peaceful activities.

The world would never again see such fraternization during World War I. And the bloodshed—which up to that time had shocked the world— would be equaled, and then some, during 1915.

FORTY-ONE

The Story Continues in 1915, Book Two

From October through December 1914 the Germans were generally help-ful to the work of the CRB and the CN. But as one CRB history records, "As the work of the Commission grew in volume and importance the atti-tude in general and von Bissing in particular became less accommodating. The change was due in part to the fear that this neutral body was becom-ing too powerful in territory where, theoretically at least, German rule was absolute, and in part to disapproval of the enthusiasm with which the Belgian people greeted the Americans wherever they went on their tours of inspection. Whatever the cause, the German tendency to deny the Americans reasonable freedom of movement raised a serious issue, for without that freedom, the Commission could not discharge its responsi-bility of guaranteeing the proper distribution of relief."

The issues would soon lead to a clash of wills that would threaten the entire relief effort.

When Hoover returned to London from his late December trip to Belgium, he found that the CRB was still on precarious financial footing. "By January 1 [1915] it had become evident that the program of the Commission, requiring as it did a monthly expenditure which now approached a million and a half pounds, could not be carried out unless a large governmental subsidy could be secured. The appeal to charity had brought great results, but these seemed very small in comparison with the amount of money needed to continue the provisionment of Belgium. Hoover therefore resolved to make sure of every resource at his command to overcome the opposition of the British Government to his proposal that the allied governments should subsidise the work of the Commission by means of loans to the Belgian Government."

It all came to a head on Thursday, January 21, when Hoover had a meeting with some of Britain's highest officials, including Attorney General Sir John Simon, Lord Alfred Emmott of the Committee on Trading with the Enemy, and Lord Eustace Percy of the Foreign Office. Leading the group was David Lloyd George, the British chancellor of the Exchequer who would later become prime minister.

As Hoover wrote later, the meeting was to discuss "the question of the exchange of money with Belgium." This was the concept that moneys outside of Belgium and inside of Belgium could be interconnected without having to physically exchange paper money or gold. Without such an arrangement, the relief program would not be able to function on the scale necessary.

Hoover knew that Lloyd George was an opponent of the CRB, but he also felt that the work and the CRB agreements had advanced far enough that this meeting was about pounding out details regarding his financial exchange plan.

He was in for a rude surprise. As historian Nash stated, "A routine appointment now turned into a battle of survival."

Lloyd George—the man who controlled Britain's purse strings—told Hoover outright that he was totally opposed to any relief to Belgium because it assisted the enemy. The chancellor of the Exchequer was sure that the war would be won by economic pressures. The first one to cave under such financial weight would lose the war. By helping the Belgians with food, the CRB would be relieving the Germans of an economic obligation that it would no doubt take up if the CRB was not in place.

British Chancellor of the Exchequer David Lloyd George was totally opposed to the CRB when he met Hoover on January 21, 1915. It would be a defining moment for Hoover, the CRB, and the Belgian people. (Both photos: public domain; multiple sources.)

One of Britain's toughest politicians, known for his strong stands on issues, had basically told Hoover he was going to shut down the CRB. It would be a defining moment for Herbert Hoover, the CRB, and the Belgian people.

Hoover took a breath and turned to his powerful opponent.

The end of 1914 saw the trio of van Doren, de Moor, and Jourdain making some good strides in the fight against German occupation, with no security breakdowns in their growing network of underground activities. That would all change in 1915, as the three upped the ante with the creation and distribution of *La Libre Belgique.*

They distributed only 1,000 copies of the first issue, dated February 1, 1915. The initial small press run—which would later grow into tens of thousands—did not lessen its effect.

As the book *Underground News* stated, "February 1, 1915, was a date Governor-General von Bissing and the members of his government were never allowed to forget. It marked the beginning of a battle of wits in which the best brains of the German Secret Service, all the forces of the German Military Police and all the powers of intimidation and coercion of which a tyrannical Governor disposed, pitted themselves in vain against that elusive, venomous *Libre Belgique*."

Adding insult to injury, van Doren and de Moor would fuel von Bissing's hatred with a routine that began right from the first issue—the delivery of a copy of each issue onto the governor general's desk or directly into his hands.

The first issue was delivered in a bold way. De Moor had a "young and pretty sister on whose discretion and quick wit he knew he could rely." She lived with her parents in a house that was not too far from van Doren's home.

On the day of delivery of the first issue, as de Moor walked over to see her and ask if she would participate in his plan, he stopped and bought a "large pale pink envelope lined with pastel-tinted paper; the kind of envelope never addressed by any but a feminine hand."

The moment she heard the idea she was in. With a laugh she picked out one of her finest dresses that accented her womanly charms; then she addressed the pink envelope de Moor had brought in her most attractive handwriting.

A short time later, she stood in front of the Ministry of Agriculture, where von Bissing had his offices. Wearing a heavy veil, she "looked coyly at the stalwart sentry posted at the door" and then boldly walked past him into the imposing building. She approached a young orderly who sat at a table in the vestibule.

"'Is the Freiherr von Bissing in?' she inquired in hesitating German with an attractively soft accent. 'It's a very personal matter . . .' she added with a hint of shyness, taking from her handbag a delicately perfumed, pink envelope.

"A grin spread slowly over the orderly's face, and his eyelids flickered.

"'Yes, Fräulein,' he said. 'His Excellency is in. What can I do for you?'

"'You would be very kind to hand him this,' she said sweetly. 'It is very important. It is for him personally.'

"'I will hand it to His Excellency myself, Fräulein. Is there any answer?'

"'I shall be calling back tomorrow,' she said, and thanking him, walked demurely away.

"A few minutes later the orderly, true to his word, handed von Bissing the pink envelope containing issue no. 1 of the *Libre Belgique*."

LA LIBRE BELGIQUE

FONDÉE
LE 1ᵉʳ FÉVRIER 1915

BULLETIN DE PROPAGANDE PATRIOTIQUE — RÉGULIÈREMENT IRRÉGULIER

NE SE SOUMETTANT A AUCUNE CENSURE

ADRESSE TÉLÉGRAPHIQUE :

KOMMANDANTUR - BRUXELLES

BUREAUX ET ADMINISTRATION
ne pouvant être en emplacement
de tout repos, ils sont installés
dans une cave automobile

ANNONCES : Les affaires étant nulles
sous la domination allemande, nous
avons supprimé la page d'annonces et
conseillons à nos clients de réserver
leur argent pour des temps meilleurs.

AVIS.

SON EXCELLENCE LE GOUVERNEUR Bᵒⁿ VON BISSING
ET SON AMIE INTIME

NOTRE CHER GOUVERNEUR, ÉCŒURÉ PAR LA LECTURE
DES MENSONGES DES JOURNAUX CENSURÉS, CHERCHE LA VÉRITÉ
DANS LA « LIBRE BELGIQUE »

L'ORDRE SOCIAL TOUT ENTIER DÉFENDU
PAR LA BELGIQUE.

PRIÈRE DE FAIRE CIRCULER CE BULLETIN

In 1915, long before Photoshop existed, the underground newspaper La Libre Belgique
*faked an image that made a mockery of Governor General von Bissing by showing him
reading the paper. It enraged the seventy-one-year-old Prussian military officer.* (Public
domain; Herbert Hoover Presidential Library Archives, West Branch, Iowa.)

The game had just become very personal, and von Bissing would ultimately vow to many, including the kaiser, that he would crush the paper and silence its creators.

By the end of December, the CRB and the CN had begun to bring food and clothes into Belgium to help its nearly 7 million citizens. But these weren't the only people desperate and trapped within the German occupation. Two million French were also behind German lines. In many cases they were living in even worse conditions than the Belgians.

While most Belgians were within what the Germans called the Occupation Zone, most of the 2 million French were in a fifty-mile-wide strip of land between Verdun and the North Sea that was called the Army Zone. This area was not under the control of von Bissing; it was controlled by several German armies. Additionally the Army Zone was separated into the Operation Zone, which extended about twelve miles back from the front lines, and the Etape Zone, which ran between the Operation Zone and the Occupation Zone. Military law ruled in these two zones, and life was brutal. Nothing in these two zones remained of "civil institutions or personal freedom. The armies assumed proprietorship of property, of food, of currency; they arrested all French male citizens of military age; they forbade the inhabitants to leave their own communes, and in general restricted the conduct of private affairs to such an extent that the people had scarcely any greater liberty than actual prisoners of war."

As one CRB history stated, "The situation in occupied regions of France was no less desperate than in Belgium. Industrialized, densely populated, and effectively cut off from the world, the two million of French people behind the German lines quickly came to the end of their food resources and stood like their Belgian neighbors to the north in the face of starvation."

If Hoover was to win his January 1915 fight with Lloyd George and keep the CRB alive, he knew that his next impossible task would be to somehow immediately expand the operations to include the 2 million desperate people of northern France.

Hoover was painfully aware that the CRB had not yet been completely successful in feeding 7 million Belgians. He wondered how he and his young band of Yanks would ever include 2 million French.

As the Belgians turned to a new year, there was the hope that came with the CN and the CRB's young, brash Americans. But conditions were still bad. As delegate Robinson Smith wrote in his article "How Does It Feel?," if an American wanted to feel a little of what the Belgians were feeling, "all he has to do is skip his dinner. That will make him feel exactly as millions of Belgians are feeling at the present hour. They have each day something to eat, but it is not enough. They have their litre of soup and their half-pound of bread and some potatoes and rice, but when five o'clock comes, they are hungry; some of them very hungry."

But according to Smith, skipping dinner didn't tell the whole story. "It is only when you have come to know this people, that you can realize the terror of their plight. When you picture Belgium, think not only of the black lines before the soup-kitchens, of the black groups of men without work in the squares by day, of the villages pitch-black by night; think too of the tens of thousands of the once well-to-do, who now have lost or are losing all that they have hitherto enjoyed. Surely and with almost mathematical progress poverty is penetrating into every home of the land, and all that [middle] class[,] who in America form the suburbs[,] can now count the months that their little capital will hold out."

His conclusion was simple but powerful, "Belgium is like a person slowly bleeding to death, and only the care of the whole world can save her."

In 1915, Erica Bunge would continue volunteering at Antwerp hospitals, soup kitchens, and children's canteens while at the same time work with Verheyen at Hoogboom preparing for the arrival of the dairy cows. Any spare moment during the day was spent talking with, or thinking about, the men of the CRB.

And then there were her clandestine activities. On special evenings throughout 1915, Erica would slip out of bed when all the family and servants were asleep and pull on her darkest clothes from the bedroom's large armoire. Taking a moment to whisper a farewell to her little canary and scratch behind Ninia's ears as recompense for locking her in the room on these nights, she would push down the large brass handle of her door and quietly enter the long hallway. Walking down the hall, her steps muffled by a plush pale blue and beige carpet, she would pass the lift and briskly take the one flight of stairs to the first floor. She would collect her coat, gloves, and hat from the *vestiaire* (cloakroom) in the right front tower and slip out into the dark of night. She would meet her contact at various locations around the property and then ferry people through a portion of her family's property.

She always had to be alert to skirt the German Landsturm guards who patrolled through and around the Hoogboom estate. Often, however, she wasn't too concerned. The Landsturm were older men not fit for trench warfare, so they were assigned relatively unimportant duties behind the lines. Their age and non-combat duties meant that they were more interested in staying warm, smoking their pipes, catching a little sleep, or finding food than they were in capturing Belgians of the underground.

All was going relatively well for Erica when she walked into an Antwerp bakery one late afternoon in 1915. It was not her usual bakery, and it was across town in a section of the city she didn't know well. Located on a side street that looked a bit abandoned, the shop was small and dimly lit. She had been on an errand and had tried taking a shortcut that hadn't worked out. When she stumbled across the place she thought she'd stop in, ask directions, and see if it had anything that might surprise her father for breakfast. She knew she'd have to pay dearly for whatever she bought, and it would probably be made from black market flour, not authorized CRB flour, but she wanted to see her father smile and she knew she would never tell any of her CRB gentlemen friends, so where was the harm?

Inside she found a handful of Flemish men and women. Their faces were set and firm with an anger forged by nearly a year of privation and German occupation. They barely glanced up when she entered; their full attention was on a young German foot soldier. He must have been only twenty or so, but he was obviously very drunk and very upset. He was swearing and in rambling loud words was telling them that he wanted some bread, and he would have it, and he would not pay for it because he and his friends had fought and died for it, and they could all go to hell, and he would have his bread now or start shooting. He began to fumble with the rifle that was slung over one shoulder.

The handful of people were all yelling at once, telling him to go to hell and take the kaiser with him and to get out of their bakery. Erica backed into a corner and with horror watched as an old lady grabbed the rifle the solider was trying to level at the baker. The German shoved her away as the rest of the men and women moved in and started punching him. The small bakery filled with the fury of the Belgians and the screams for help from the German.

It would be a long time before Erica emerged from the bakery. She hurried down the dark lane, hoping she would someday forget what she had just seen and done.

(Author note: The above bakery story comes from Erica Bunge Brown approximately a week before she died at Whitehall Farm in Maryland in 1986. She told the tale in a rambling deathbed confession to her grandson, Vernon C. Miller Jr. No documentary evidence has ever been found to corroborate the event. In the above re-created scene, the author has added many details to what was a very sketchy story with few details.)

Belgian children were the most affected by the war and the relief program. Not far behind were the destitute, who had little before the war and had practically nothing during the German occupation. Without the CRB and the CN, millions of Belgian and French civilians would have probably died. Because of them, more than 9 million were saved from starvation. (Both photos: public domain; children, Herbert Hoover Presidential Library Archives, West Branch, Iowa; adults, *The Millers' Belgian Relief Movement*, William C. Edgar, Northwestern Miller, 1915.)

Sources

The following list comprises primarily the titles cited in the notes. Because the author researched World War I, Belgium, and the CRB sporadically since the 1980s (fulltime 1986–1988 and 2012–2014) and because he researched the entire time period (1914–1918), a comprehensive list of sources would be excessively long. He has chosen what he considers to be the most appropriate research materials to list for this book and its coverage of August 1914 through December 1914.

Books and Major Articles

Baedeker, Karl. *Baedeker's Belgium and Holland.* Lipzig: Karl Baedeker, 1910.

Beatty, Jack. *The Lost History of 1914: Reconsidering the Year the Great War Began.* New York: Walker and Co., 2012.

Bissing, Mortiz Ferdinand von. *General von Bissing's Testament: A Study in German Ideals.* London: T. Fisher Unwin, Ltd., no date.

Bland, J. O. P., translator. *Germany's Violations of the Laws of War, 1914–1915: Compiled under the Auspices of the French Ministry of Foreign Affairs.* London: William Heinemann, 1915.

Cammaerts, Emile. *Through the Iron Bars (Two Years of German Occupation in Belgium)*. London: The Bodley Head, 1917.

Carmichael, Erskine, M.D. *One Generation: Portrait of a Family—Scrapbook, 1879–1990*. Birmingham, AL: Blue Rooster Press, 2013.

Collier, Price. *Germany and the Germans From an American Point of View*. London: Duckworth and Co., 1914.

Danielson, Elena S. "Herbert Hoover." In *The United States in the First World War: An Encyclopedia*, ed. Anne Cipriano Benzon. Garland Press, 1995.

Davis, Arthur N. *The Kaiser as I Know Him*. New York: Harper and Brothers, 1918.

Fuehr, Alexander. *The Neutrality of Belgium: A Study of the Belgian Case Under Its Aspects in Political History and International Law*. New York: Funk and Wagnalls Co., 1915.

Galpin, Perrin C., ed. *Hugh Gibson, 1883–1954, Extracts From His Letters and Anecdotes From His Friends*. New York: Belgian American Educational Foundation, 1956.

Gay, George I., and H. H. Fisher. *Public Relations of the Commission for Relief in Belgium: Documents*, 2 vols. Stanford University: Stanford University Press, 1929.

Gibson, Hugh. *A Journal From Our Legation in Belgium*. New York: Doubleday, Page and Co., 1917.

Graves, Dr. Armgaard Karl, with collaboration of Edward Lyell Fox. *The Secrets of the German War Office*. New York: McBride, Nast and Co., 1914.

Gray, Prentiss, Sherman Gray (son), and Prentiss Gray (grandson), eds. *Fifteen Months in Belgium: A CRB Diary*. Princeton, NJ: self-published, 2014.

Green, Horace. *The Log of a Noncombatant*. New York: Houghton Mifflin, 1915.

Hamill, John. *The Strange Career of Mr. Hoover Under Two Flags*. Google Book. No location: no publisher, n.d.

Harpur, Patrick, ed. *The Timetable of Technology*. New York: Hearst Books, 1982.

Hendrick, Burton J., ed. *The Life and Letters of Walter H. Page*, 4 vols. New York: Doubleday, Page and Co., 1924.

Hoover, Herbert. *The Memoirs of Herbert Hoover: Years of Adventure, 1874–1920*. New York: MacMillan and Co., 1951.

Horne, John, and Alan Kramer. *German Atrocities, 1914: A History of Denial*. New Haven, CT: Yale University Press, 2001.

Houtte, Paul Van (pen name for famous Belgian journalist, Victor Jourdain). *The Pan-Germanic Crime: Impressions and Investigations in Belgium During the German Occupation*. London: Hodder and Stoughton, 1915.

Humphreys, Arthur L. "The Heart of Belgium." A collection of four articles that appeared earlier in the *London Times*. London: Arthur L. Humphreys, 1915.

Hunt, Edward Eyre. *War Bread: A Personal Narrative of the War and Relief in Belgium*. New York: Holt and Co., 1916.

Kellogg, Charlotte. *Bobbins of Belgium: A Book of Belgian Lace, Lace-workers, Lace-schools and Lace-villages*. New York: Funk and Wagnalls Co., 1920.

Kellogg, Charlotte. *Mercier: The Fighting Cardinal of Belgium*, New York: D. Appleton and Co., 1920.

Kellogg, Charlotte. *Women of Belgium: Turning Tragedy to Triumph*. New York: Funk and Wagnalls Co., 1917.

Kellogg, Vernon. *Fighting Starvation in Belgium*. New York: Doubleday, Page and Co., 1918.

Kellogg, Vernon. *Headquarters Nights: A Record of Conversations and Experiences at the Headquarters of the German Army in France and Belgium*. Boston: Atlantic Monthly Press, 1917.

Kellogg, Vernon. *Herbert Hoover: The Man and His Work*. New York: D. Appleton and Co., 1920.

Kellogg, Vernon; Arthur W. Page, ed. *Washington in War Time: The World's Work: Americans to the Rescue: The First Chapter of the Authentic Story of the Commission for Relief in Belgium. Written from Mr. Hoover's Records by Vernon Kellogg, of the Commission*. New York: Doubleday, Page and Co., 1917.

Kittredge, Tracy B. *The History of the Commission for Relief in Belgium, 1914–1917*. Unpublished, n.d.

Liddell, R. Scotland. *The Track of the War*. London: Simpkin, Marshall, Hamilton, Kent and Co., 1915.

Lipkes, Jeff. *Rehearsals: The German Army in Belgium, August 1914*. Leuven: Leuven University Press, 2007.

Marshall, Brigadier General S. L. A. *The American Heritage History of World War I*. New York: American Heritage Publishing Co./Bonanza Books, 1982.

Massart, Jean. *Belgians Under the Eagle*. New York: E.P. Dutton and Co., 1916.

Maurice, Arthur Bartlett. *Bottled Up in Belgium: The Last Delegate's Informal Story*. New York: Moffat, Yard and Co., 1917.

Mears, E. Grimwood. *The Destruction of Belgium: Germany's Confession and Avoidance*. Google book: no original location, publisher, or date shown.

Mercier, Cardinal D. J. *Cardinal Mercier's Own Story*. New York: George H. Doran Co., 1920.

Millard, Oscar E. *Underground News: The Complete Story of the Secret Newspaper That Made War History*. New York: Robert M. McBride and Co., 1938.

Nash, George H. *The Life of Herbert Hoover: The Humanitarian, 1914–1917*. New York: W. W. Norton and Co., 1988.

Nelson, John P., ed. *Letters and Diaries of David T. Nelson, 1914–1919*. Iowa: The Amtndsen Publishing Co., 1996.

Nevins, Allan, ed. *The Letters and Journal of Brand Whitlock*, 2 vols. New York: D. Appleton-Century Co., 1936.

O'Regan, John Rowan Hamilton. *The German War of 1914: Illustrated by Documents of European History, 1815–1915*. London: Oxford University Press, 1915.

Patterson, David S. *The Search for Negotiated Peace: Women's Activism and Citizen Diplomacy in World War I*. New York: Routledge, 2008.

Powell, E. Alexander. *Fighting in Flanders*. New York: Charles Scribner's Sons, 1914.

Proctor, Tammy M. *Civilians in a World at War, 1914–1918*. New York: New York University Press, 2010.

Proctor, Tammy M. *Female Intelligence: Women and Espionage in the First World War*. New York: New York University Press, 2003.

Reynolds, Francis J., and C. W. Taylor, eds. *Collier's Photographic History of the European War, Including Sketches and Drawings Made on the Battle Fields*. New York: P. F. Collier and Son, 1917.

Russell, Thomas H., John J. Pershing, William Dunseath Eaton, and James Martin Miller. *America's War for Humanity: Pictorial History of the World War for Liberty*. No location: no publisher, 1919.

Smith, Richard Norton. *An Uncommon Man: The Triumph of Herbert Hoover*. New York: Simon and Schuster, 1984.

Stallings, Laurence, ed. *The First World War: A Photographic History*. New York: Simon and Schuster, 1933.

Surface, Frank M., and Raymond L. Bland. *American Food in the World War and Reconstruction Period: Operations of the Organizations Under the Direction of Herbert Hoover, 1914–1924*. Stanford University: Stanford University Press, 1931.

Taggart, George, and Wallace Winchell. *A Yankee Major Invades Belgium: The Chronicle of a Merciful and Peaceful Mission to Europe During the World War*. New York: Fleming H. Revell Co., 1916.

Taillandier, Madame Saint-Rene. *The Soul of the "C.R.B.": A French View of the Hoover Relief Work*. New York: Charles Scribner's Sons, 1919.

Toynbee, Arnold Joseph. *The Belgian Deportations*. London: T. Fisher Unwin, Ltd., no date.

Toynbee, Arnold Joseph. *The German Terror in Belgium: An Historical Record*. London: George H. Doran, 1917.

Tuchman, Barbara M. *The Guns of August: The drama of August 1914, a month of battle in which war was waged on a scale unsurpassed and whose results determined the shape of the world in which we live today*. New York: Random House, 1962.

Ville, Father Jean de. *Back from Belgium: A Secret History of Three Years Within the German Lines.* New York: H. K. Fly Co., 1918.

Vincent, C. Paul. *The Politics of Hunger: The Allied Blockade of Germany, 1915–1919.* Ohio: Ohio University Press, 1985.

Whitlock, Brand. *Belgium: A Personal Narrative,* 2 vols. New York: D. Appleton and Co., 1919.

Whitlock, Brand. "Belgium, Before the Storm," "The Storm Breaks," and "Belgium, Under the German Heel." *Everyone's Magazine,* multiple issues, February 1918.

Wickes, Mariette, ed. *Love in the Time of War.* No location: self-published, no date.

Williams, Albert Rys. *In the Claws of the German Eagle.* New York: E. P. Dutton and Co., 1917.

Wilson, Woodrow. *The President's War Message—Delivered at a Joint Session of the Two Houses of Congress, April 2, 1917.* New York: Grosset and Dunlap, 1917.

Withington, Robert. *In Occupied Belgium.* Boston: The Cornhill Co., 1921.

Zuckerman, Larry. *The Rape of Belgium: The Untold Story of World War I.* New York: New York University Press, 2004.

CRB Reports

Gay, George I. *Statistical Review of Relief Operations: Five Years, November 1, 1914, to August 31, 1919 and to Final Liquidation.* Stanford University: Stanford University Press, n.d.

No author or editor. "Balance Sheet and Accounts, French Government Accounts, Belgian Government Accounts, Supporting Schedules, Covering six years from commencement of operations, October, 1914, to 30th September, 1920." No location: CRB, 1921.

No author or editor. "First Annual Report, November 1st 1914 to October 31st 1915, Part I: Provisioning Department." No location: CRB, 1916.

Individual Papers

The author reviewed more than fifty individual collections or papers in numerous research libraries before he began writing this book and planning the two others in the series. Following are the two main research institutions he used and the names of those whose collections were the most important in the writing of *Behind the Lines.*

Herbert Hoover Presidential Library Archives, West Branch, Iowa: Ben S. Allen, Hugh Gibson, Prentiss Gray, Joseph Green, Herbert C. Hoover, Edward Eyre Hunt, George Spaulding (found in the Alan Hoover papers), and Brand

Whitlock. Also extremely useful were the comprehensive clip books that contained hundreds of CRB-related newspaper clippings from the United Kingdom.

Hoover Institution Archives, Stanford University, California: Ben S. Allen, Robert Arrowsmith, Perrin C. Galpin, Hugh Gibson, Emil Hollmann (HIA catalogued under "Emile Holman"), Edward Eyre Hunt, Robert A. Jackson, Tracy B. Kittredge, David T. Nelson, Gilchrist B. Stockton, Robinson Smith, and Robert Withington. Also extremely useful were the Herbert Hoover Oral History Program interviews and the more than 500 boxes of files under the name Commission for Relief in Belgium.

Author's Archives Are Available

The author's archives are open to any legitimate researcher. They include hundreds of letters and a diary written by his grandfather, Milton M. Brown, while he was a CRB delegate (January 1916 to April 1917), as well as a small diary written by, and numerous photos taken by, his grandmother, Erica Bunge Brown. In addition, the author has Edouard Bunge's extensive personal account, "What I Saw of the Bombardment and Surrender of Antwerp, October 1914," which details Bunge's participation in the surrender of the city to the Germans. The translation of the document was done by Milton Brown, son-in-law to Edouard. For more information about what the author has in his archives, or to obtain access, contact Jeff Miller at jbmwriter@aol.com or 303-503-1739.

Notes

Abbreviations

HIA   Hoover Institution Archives, Stanford University, Stanford, California.
HHPLA   Herbert Hoover Presidential Library Archives, West Branch, Iowa.

1. A Story Few Have Heard 1–3
"THERE ONCE WAS A NICE TOWN IN THAT PLACE" 1–3
   The scene in the Hotel Astoria and all quotes used are from Edward Eyre Hunt, *War Bread*, (Holt and Co., 1916), 167–168.

──────────────── AUGUST 1914: INVASION ────────────────

2. Setting the Stage 5–24
PRACTICALLY INEVITABLE 5–8
   "To understand Germany": An unnamed German officer in Arthur Bartlett Maurice, *Bottled Up in Belgium* (Moffat, Yard & Co., 1917), 96.
   Five German armies: John Horne and Alan Kramer, *German Atrocities, 1914: A History of Denial* (Yale University Press, 2001), 9.
   Largest invasion force: Horne and Kramer, *German Atrocities*, 9.
   150,000 men: Brigadier General S.L.A. Marshall, *The American Heritage History of World War I* (American Heritage Publishing Co./Bonanza Books, 1982), 43.
   "I have faith in our destiny": Brand Whitlock, "Belgium, Before the Storm," *Everyone's Magazine*, issue 2, first installment (Feb. 1918).

"a scrap of paper": "The Scrap of Paper, Aug. 4, 1914," Charles F. Horne, ed., *Source Records of the Great War, vol. I* (National Alumni, 1923).

BELGIUM PREPARES FOR INVASION 8–10

80,000 maps: Credited to D. L. Blount in "Saw Burning of Louvain," *New York Times*, Sept. 7, 1914.
garde civique: Hugh Gibson, *A Journal From Our Legation in Belgium* (Doubleday, Page & Co., 1917), 64–65.

BELGIAN WOMAN ERICA BUNGE—"WE ARE DESPERATE" 10–15

"all the little German cafes": R. Scotland Liddell, *The Track of the War* (Simpkin, Marshall, Hamilton, Kent & Co., 1915), 28.
Erica Bunge's information and diary entries come from the author's personal knowledge, family oral history, and the unpublished papers of both Erica Bunge and her future husband, Milton M. Brown. Erica Bunge's diary was edited and translated by her eldest daughter, Erica Miller.

FRANC-TIREURS—"WHOLLY AGAINST THE LAWS OF WAR" 15–18

"True strategy consists": Father Jean de Ville, *Back from Belgium* (H. K. Fly Co., 1918), 264.
"We learned it": An unnamed German officer to an unnamed CRB delegate, Madame Saint-Rene Taillandier, *The Soul of the CRB* (Charles Scribner's Sons, 1919), 214.
"That means hard fighting": No author, "The Kaiser Summons All Germans to Arms to Defend Fatherland Against 'Reckless Assault,'" *New York Times*, Aug. 7, 1914.
"Belgium was represented": Paul van Houtte (pen name for famous Belgian journalist, Victor Jourdain), *The Pan-Germanic Crime: Impressions and Investigations in Belgium During the German Occupation* (Hodder and Stoughton, 1915), 34.
"The soldiers, as they set out": Houtte, *The Pan-Germanic Crime*, 66.
Franc-tireur was a word; and "civilian resistance": Horne and Kramer, *German Atrocities*, 17–18.
"the population of Belgium": Horne and Kramer, *German Atrocities*, 18; referenced by them as: "Politisches Archiv des Auswartiges Amts (PAAA) Bonn, R 20880, fols. 8-9: commentary by the kaiser on a message from the Belgian government informing the German government of the uniforms worn by the garde civique (Aug. 9, 1914—i.e., date of receipt)."
"Men of all professions": The German *White Book*, as quoted in Brand Whitlock, "The Reign of Terror," no. 5, *Everyone's Magazine*, (vol.38, May 1918).
"The reports of unprovoked": Horace Green, *The Log of a Noncombatant*, (Houghton Mifflin, 1915).
"The controversy over" and "For many, Belgium": Larry Zuckerman, *The Rape of Belgium: The Untold Story of World War I* (New York University Press, 2004), 23.

VISÉ—"VANISHED FROM THE MAP" 18–19

"the suicide of civilized Europe": *His Holiness Pope Benedict XV on the Great War: A Collection of the Holy Father's Utterances in the Cause of Peace* (Bums & Oats, 1916).
By evening six columns: George I. Gay and H. H. Fisher, *Public Relations of the Commission for Relief in Belgium: Documents*, 2 vols. (Stanford University Press, 1929), chapter 1: 1.
"Around noon, the Germans": Arnold Joseph Toynbee, *The German Terror in Belgium: An Historical Record* (George H. Doran, 1917), 25; and Zuckerman, *The Rape*, 22.
Belgian soldiers withdrew: Horne and Kramer, *German Atrocities*, 13; Toynbee, *The German Terror*, 22.

"Monsieur Istas": Jeff Lipkes, *Rehearsals: The German Army in Belgium, August 1914* (Leuven University Press, 2007), 92.

"that his body": Lipkes, *Rehearsals: The German Army*, 92.

sixteen-year-old Belgian girl: Zuckerman, *The Rape*, 22.

By August 18, the town: Horne and Kramer, *German Atrocities*, 24.

"first systematic destruction": Horne and Kramer, *German Atrocities*, 24.

"heaps of bricks": Emil Hollmann, "Relief Work in Belgium," referring to another CRB delegate; Emile Holman papers, Hoover Institution Archives (HIA), Stanford University.

"vanished off the map": Toynbee, *The German Terror*, 25, which cites "An der Spitze Meiner Kimpagnie, Three Months of Campaigning," by Paul Oskar Hocker, Ullstein and Co., Berlin and Vienna, 1914"; Zuckerman, *The Rape*, says Hocker was a captain who commanded a reserve company and rode through Visé three hours after the fires started on Aug. 15, 1914.

DINANT—"THE TOWN IS *GONE*" 20–21

"curiously Oriental spire": Whitlock, "Reign of Terror."

"soldiers of the 108th": "The Martyrdom of Dinant," text of the 11th Report of the Committee of Inquiry, Hugh Gibson collection, box 80, HIA.

The murder of Wasseige: Gibson, *A Journal*, 329; the official list of those killed, "Neccrologe Dinantais Aout 1914," Perrin Galpin collection, box 3, #57015-913, file, "German Occupation of Belgium. Atrocities Perpetrated," HIA.

"We saw the wall": Prentiss Gray, *Fifteen Months in Belgium: A CRB Diary*, (self-published, 2014), 96.

"Those killed": Gibson, *A Journal*, 329.

"killed 674 people": Zuckerman, *The Rape*, 30.

"Dinant is far worse": Gray, *Fifteen Months*, 96.

"The town is *gone*": Gibson, *A Journal*, 327.

LOUVAIN—"WE SHALL MAKE THIS PLACE A DESERT" 21–24

Statistics on Louvain: Horne and Kramer, *German Atrocities*, reports the library contained 300,000 volumes, 39; Toynbee, *The German Terror*, says the library contained 250,000 volumes, 116.

"brewers, lacemakers": Richard Harding Davis, "The Burning of Louvain," *New York Tribune*, Aug. 31, 1914; and Karl Baedeker, *Baedeker's Belgium and Holland* (Baedeker, 1910), 239.

"a dull place": Baedeker, *Belgium*, 239.

Belgian troops purposefully: Toynbee, *The German Terror*, 89.

"All necessary measures": Zuckerman, *The Rape*, 38, which footnoted "Wieland, *Belgien 1914*, p. 34. See also PAAA, Bonn, R 20882, fol. 75-87; report by Dillen, Prior of the Dominican Order at Louvain, Sept. 4, 1914."

"Die Wacht am Rhein": Horne and Kramer, *German Atrocities*, 39.

"were indeed terrified": Toynbee, *The German Terror*, 89.

15,000: Horne and Kramer, *German Atrocities*, 39.

"Stampeded": Toynbee, *The German Terror*, 100–101.

"Hubert David-Fishbach": Horne and Kramer, *German Atrocities*, 39; Toynbee, *The German Terror*, 119–120.

By some accounts: Horne and Kramer, *German Atrocities*, 39.

Sixth of the city's buildings: Horne and Kramer, *German Atrocities*, 38 and 40.

Three others with Gibson: Bulle and Posette, the Mexican and Swedish charges d'affairés, and D. L. Blount, an American businessman living in Brussels, from Gibson, *A Journal*, 155; and "Saw Burning of Louvain," *New York Times*, Sept. 7, 1914.

"The road was black": Gibson, *A Journal*, 156.
"A lot of the houses": Gibson, *A Journal*, 158.
"We shall make this place": Gibson, *A Journal*, 162.
"May I take a picture?": Gibson, *A Journal*, 161.
"Belgium's ordeal": Arthur L. Humphreys, "the Whispered 'When!'" as part of "The
    Heart of Belgium" (a collection of four articles, the *London Times,* no month, 1915), in
    the Nina Eloesser papers, box 1, HIA, 44.

3. Marching Into Brussels 25–33
"Big Bertha": Patrick Harpur, ed., *The Timetable of Technology* (Hearst Books, 1982), 42.

A CHANCE MEETING OF A BUSINESSMAN AND AN ABBÉ 26–27
"monstrous grey reptile": Oscar E. Millard, *Underground News, The Complete Story of The
    Secret Newspaper That Made War History,* (Robert M. McBride and Co.,1938), 23.
"for a Belgian": Millard, *Underground News*, 22.
Vicar of Saint Albert: Charlotte Kellogg, *Mercier, the Fighting Cardinal of Belgium*
    (D. Appleton and Co., 1920), 68.
"no ordinary priest" and "with black hair": Millard, *Underground News*, 23.
"In that chance meeting": Millard, *Underground News*, 23.
Gabrielle Petit: Millard, *Underground News*, entire book.

BRAND WHITLOCK, U.S. LEGATION MINISTER 27–31
"tense look": Hunt, *War Bread*, 187.
to write literary novels: Allan Nevins, ed., *The Letters and Journal of Brand Whitlock*
    (D. Appleton-Century Co., 1936), Letter to Rutger B. Jewett, April 9, 1914, 179.
"the dim, familiar": Whitlock, "Before the Storm."
"all our patience": Whitlock, "Before the Storm."
Story of young couple: Whitlock, "Before the Storm."
Americans joining Whitlock: J. H. Fleming letter, Fleming papers, box 341, HIA.
"Funds were raised": Whitlock, "Before the Storm."
"riding in column": Brand Whitlock, "Belgium, The Storm Breaks," *Everybody's Magazine,*
    no. 3, March 1918.
"And this was Germany!": Whitlock, "The Storm Breaks."

HUGH GIBSON, U.S. LEGATION SECRETARY 31–33
"his wit" and the busiest person: Hunt, *War Bread*, 186.
Gibson's observations on Germans marching in: Gibson, *A Journal,* 100, 102, 103, 104.
"the humiliation": Gibson, *A Journal*, 105.

4. London 34–41
AMERICAN TOURISTS IN HARM'S WAY 34–35
Story of Mrs. Kahn: "Mrs. Kahn Reaches London," *New York Times,* Aug. 5, 1914.
Story of W. E. Walters: "American Refugees Report Adventures," *New York Times*, Aug.
    6, 1914.

ORGANIZED ASSISTANCE STUMBLES INTO EXISTENCE 35–38
Page telegram: George H. Nash, *The Life of Herbert Hoover: The Humanitarian, 1914–1917*
    (W. W. Norton & Co., 1988), 5.
"It is estimated": "Tourists Leaders Finding the Way," *New York Times,* Aug. 5, 1914.
$200,000: "Tourists Leaders Finding the Way," *New York Times,* Aug. 5, 1914.

"Quaker settlement" and "breakfasts": Richard Norton Smith, *An Uncommon Man: The Triumph of Herbert Hoover* (Simon and Schuster, 1984), first section of photo pages between 56 and 57.

"eighteen financial": Elena S. Danielson, "Herbert Hoover," in *The United States in the First World War: An Encyclopedia*, ed. Anne Cipriano Benzon (Garland Press, 1995) 283–289.

"his dress never varies": Robinson Smith, "Hoover—The Man of Action" (unpublished), Robinson Smith papers, HIA.

Hoovers work in London: Smith, *An Uncommon Man*, 80.

"He didn't want": John L. Simpson, "Activities in a Troubled World: War Relief, Banking, and Business," an interview conducted by Suzanne B. Riess, 1978, Regional Oral History Office, The Bancroft Library, University of California, Berkeley, California.

How Hoover got involved: Nash, *The Life of Herbert Hoover*, 5.

"gathering all the cash": Nash, *The Life of Herbert Hoover*, 5-6.

"The all-male": Nash, *The Life of Herbert Hoover*, 6.

HOOVER MAKES HIS MOVE FOR DOMINANCE 38–41

Hoover personally gave: Nash, *The Life of Herbert Hoover*, 7.

"Another who did": "American Refugees Report Adventures," *New York Times*, Aug. 6, 1914.

"moved rapidly": Nash, *The Life of Herbert Hoover*, 7.

Edward Curtis: Gibson, *A Journal*, 340.

"with the object": "Prepare for Rush from Continent . . . New Relief Organization," *New York Times*, Aug. 8, 1914.

Page had not agreed: Nash, *The Life of Herbert Hoover*, 7.

"worked mainly with banks": Nash, *The Life of Herbert Hoover*, 8.

Action by congress: "Gold Cruiser to Sail Today," *New York Times*, Aug. 6, 1914.

American Relief Expedition: "Tennessee off with $5,867,000," *New York Times*, Aug. 7, 1914.

"take over the entire": Nash, *The Life of Herbert Hoover*, 10.

Transfer to Hoover's group: "Refugees' Bureau Finishes Its Work," *New York Times*, Aug. 20, 1914.

During the week of: "Refugees' Bureau Finishes Its Work," *New York Times*, Aug. 20, 1914.

"Many were absolutely": "Another Big Crowd of Refugees Sails," *New York Times*, Aug. 30, 1914.

5. Back in America 42–45

Census figures: *Statistical Abstract of the United States, 1913* (no. 36, Department of Commerce, Washington Printing Office, 1914), 46–47.

Quotes from Wilson: Extracts from Wilson's speech given to congress on Aug. 19, 1914; multiple sources.

Urban dwellers: *Statistical Abstract of the United States, 1913*, 41; total number of farms, online at agclassroom.org; total population, online, *The Bulletin of the American Geographic Society*.

People per square mile: Tracy B. Kittredge, *The History of the Commission for Relief in Belgium, 1914-1917* (unpublished), 8.

City sizes: *Statistical Abstract of the United States, 1913*, 43.

Wages: *Statistical Abstract of the United States, 1913*, 505.

Reading statistic: *Statistical Abstract of the United States, 1913*, 107.

"The lamps": Marshall, *American Heritage History*, 39.

——— SEPTEMBER 1914 : BEGINNINGS OF HUNGER AND RETALIATION ———

6. The First Major Battles 49–53

E. E. HUNT LOOKS FOR A GOOD STORY 49–50

Letter to Steff: March 3, 1914, letter to Steff, E. E. Hunt papers, box 1, HHPLA.

INVASION MOVES TOWARD TRENCH WARFARE 50–53

twenty-five miles from Paris: Horne and Kramer, *German Atrocities*, 70.
spotted by British pilot: Marshall, *American Heritage History*, 51.
"there is no more": Marshall, *American Heritage History*, 56.
suffered a nervous breakdown: Multiple sources, including "The Battle of the Marne," Wikipedia.
"knew at last" and "began slowly": Marshall, *American Heritage History*, 57.
"You will be home": Marshall, *American Heritage History*, 41.
"Even the most pessimistic": Kittredge, *History of CRB*, 14.

7. Antwerp 54–62

THE CITY BRACES FOR ATTACK 54–57

"one of the most": Baedeker, *Belgium*, 169.
the most prosperous: Baedeker, *Belgium*, 169.
"Antwerp was almost": E. Alexander Powell, *Fighting in Flanders* (Charles Scribner's Sons, 1914), 28.
The busiest ports: *Statistical Abstract of the United States, 1913*, 704.
"situated on the broad": Baedeker, *Belgium*, 169.
"Antwerp is the principal": Baedeker, *Belgium*, 171.
the kaiser ordered: Marshall, *American Heritage History*, 74.

ERICA BUNGE—"THE DAYS PASS AND ARE NEVER THE SAME" 57–59

all Erica Bunge diary entries: Author's archives.

"THE PEOPLE DID NOT SMILE" 59–62

"No other city": Powell, *Fighting in Flanders*, 30.
"it is estimated": Powell, *Fighting in Flanders*, 29.
"groups of Belgians": Green, *The Log*, 6.
"the devastation was": Green, *The Log*, 6.
"acres and acres": Powell, *Fighting in Flanders*, 31.
"the darkness of London": Powell, *Fighting in Flanders*, 58.
"became about as": Powell, *Fighting in Flanders*, 57.
"The people did not": Powell, *Fighting in Flanders*, 59.
"spy-mad": Powell, *Fighting in Flanders*, 44.
"slept rolled up": Powell, *Fighting in Flanders*, 38.
"I don't quite": Powell, *Fighting in Flanders*, 38.
The Belgian army: Horne and Kramer, *German Atrocities*, 24.
"I watched the": Green, *The Log*, 12.

8. Brussels 63–87

GERMAN OCCUPATION STARTS THE WAR OF THE WILLS 63–69

"trudging by in": Brand Whitlock, "Belgium, Under the German Heel," *Everyone's Magazine*, no. 6, June 1918.
"one of the finest": Baedeker, *Belgium*, 128.
Begun in 1402: Baedeker, *Belgium*, 128.

"is a great": Baedeker, *Belgium*, 131.
"we go to bed": "A City in Sadness," *Scotsman* newspaper, Nov. 23, 1914, clip books, HHPLA.
"Oh, I see": Gibson, *A Journal*, 244.
"played as large": Whitlock, "Under the German Heel."
all quotes from von der Goltz's *affiche*: Gibson, *A Journal*, 188.
"had a somewhat": Whitlock, "Under the German Heel."
"regarded as a": Gibson, *A Journal*, 241.
"made everybody furious": Gibson, *A Journal*, 241.
"I ask the": Gibson, *A Journal*, 242.
"he could not": Gibson, *A Journal*, 242.
"rushed off to": Gibson, *A Journal*, 242.
Max becoming hero: Whitlock, "Under the German Heel."

Van Doren and de Moor Team Up 69–72
"assist him": Millard, *Underground News*, 23.
"Nurse Cavell organization": Millard, *Underground News*, 10.
"Allied Intelligence": Millard, *Underground News*, 24.
"there was apparently": Millard, *Underground News*, 24.
"satisfy an urge": Millard, *Underground News*, 24.
"ironical little sheets": Millard, *Underground News*, 25.
"to avoid the": Millard, *Underground News*, 20.
The owners and editors: Millard, *Underground News*, 20.
"prohibiting of": Gibson, *A Journal*, 200.
"no newspapers were": Whitlock, "Under the German Heel."
"threatening the": Millard, *Underground News*, 25.

Whitlock and Gibson Tackle Neutrality 72–75
responsible for picking up: Whitlock, *The Letters*, 178.
"solid blocks of": Whitlock, "Before the Storm."
"a house with": Whitlock, *The Letters*, 178.
"we also need": Whitlock, *The Letters*, 178.
Whitlock staff: Whitlock, *The Letters*, on the Dramatis Personae page.
Omer called up: Whitlock, "Before the Storm."
U.S. Legation representing others: Gibson, *A Journal*, 246; Gibson does not mention who they were, but they included Belgium, Britain, and Japan.
a "little jaunt": Gibson, *A Journal*, 200.
"bearing a napkin": Whitlock, "Under the German Heel."
Gibson story about pillow: Gibson, *A Journal*, 268; also "Lunch at 66 Rue des Colonies," Gilchrist Stockton papers, box 9, HIA.
"We began to note": Whitlock, "Under the German Heel."

Belgians Begin Organizing to Stave off Starvation 75–80
population densities: Kittredge, *History of CRB*, 8.
"To the Belgian": Arthur L. Humphreys, four articles that ran in the London *Times* and later compiled into a 46-page pamphlet *The Heart of Belgium*.
"Famine sweeps over": Smith, "Hoover—The Man in Action," Robinson Smith papers, HIA.
"The whole machinery": Kittredge, *History of CRB*, 10.
"Waves of refugees": Hunt, *War Bread*, 189.
"It was practically": Kittredge, *History of CRB*, 11, 17.
"began to establish": Kittredge, *History of CRB*, 11.

"purchasing agents": Hunt, *War Bread*, 180.
"sometimes in place": Kittredge, *History of CRB*, 10, 11.
"No communication": Kittredge, *History of CRB*, 10.
preliminary meeting: Whitlock, "The Storm Breaks."
"main rival": History of the Francqui Foundation on its website.
"the iron man": John Hamill, *The Strange Career of Mr. Hoover Under Two Flags* (Faro, Inc., 1931), 316.
"a type familiar": Hunt, *War Bread*, 272.
Americans in the room: Kittredge, *History of CRB*, 13.

AMERICANS IN BELGIUM GET INVOLVED 81–86

Heineman details: From the biography of Heineman on the American Physical Society's website.
"suggested to Francqui": Kittredge, *History of CRB*, 13.
Max asks: Whitlock, "Under the German Heel."
"strong private body": Kittredge, *History of CRB*, 13.
"private body [that]": Kittredge, *History of CRB*, 11.
3 or 4 cents: The "money-table," Baedeker, *Belgium*, frontispiece.
completely destitute: Kittredge, *History of CRB*, 14.
"This appeal was": Kittredge, *History of CRB*, 14, 15.
"The food supply": Gibson, *A Journal*, 243, 246.
"Belgium was gutted": Hunt, *War Bread*, 180.
chosen to take next step: Kittredge, *History of CRB*, 12.
Shaler biography: Obituary in the *Daily Journal-World*, Lawrence, Kansas, Dec. 16, 1942.
a three-piece suit: His CRB portrait photo; interpretation by the author and a "cow-puncher" reference in "A Day in the London Office," by Milton M. Brown, in author's archives.
Shaler biography: Obituary in the *Daily Journal-World*, Lawrence, Kansas, Dec. 16, 1942.
"An American engineer": Smith, *An Uncommon Man*, 81.
"It is not": Gibson, *A Journal*, 243.
Mr. Couchman: Gibson, *A Journal*. Gibson mentions him only by last name a few times, placing Couchman with Shaler in London on the first trip to secure food. This author was never able to find Couchman's first name, history, or what he did for the CRB; Kittredge, *History of the CRB*, says Couchman was Shaler's "assistant," 35.

SEARCHING FOR FOOD IN BELGIUM 86–87

"one fine September": *History of CRB*, 16.
"the Brussels [food]": Kittredge, *History of CRB*, 15.
two days of flour left: Kittredge, *History of CRB*, 16; Heineman to Max, Sept. 22, 1914, Heineman's Report.
By the end of the month: Kittredge, *History of CRB*, 16; Reports of Comité Executif to Comité Central, Oct. 15, 1914, Dec. 1, 1914.

9. London 88–92

A FORMIDABLE AMERICAN FORCE EMERGES 88–90

more than 100,000: Nash, *The Life of Herbert Hoover*, 12.
"Here was a team": Nash, *The Life of Herbert Hoover*, 13, footnote 70: "New York Times, August 7, Breckinridge, Report, p. 38."
He officially changed: Nash, *The Life of Herbert Hoover*, 13, footnote 78 "The American Committee: Report Embracing the Work of Committee from Its Inception on August 4th [*sic*] 1914, to September 25th, 1915 (booklet, 1915), especially p. 18, in CRB Miscellaneous Files."

Shaler's Mission Hits Roadblocks 90–92

"in view of": Kittredge, *History of CRB*, 35.

"These are parlous": Gibson, *A Journal*, 243, 246, 248.

Shaler and Belgian minister: Kittredge, *History of CRB*, 35.

"The British authorities": "Preliminaries of Organization," Gay and Fisher, *Public Relations*.

"Belgium has deserved": Purnell, "The Great War: Part 128," Joe Green papers, Seeley G. Mudd Manuscript Library, Princeton University, New Jersey.

10. Coming From America 93–96

sailing on SS *St. Paul*: Passenger manifest for the *St. Paul*; also Oxford University entrance records of the individuals mentioned.

David T. Nelson details: John P. Nelson, ed., *Letters and Diaries of David T. Nelson, 1914–1919* (The Amtndsen Publishing Co., 1996), 8; a copy of the book was given to the author by John P. Nelson. The motorcycle was made by the Indian Motorcycle Manufacturing Co.

"a lifetime habit": Nelson, *Letters and Diaries*, 10, 11.

"gave the usual": Nelson, *Letters and Diaries*, 17.

"Everybody cheered": Nelson, *Letters and Diaries*, 18.

11. Resistance Is Futile 97–99

Burgomaster Max Gets Arrested 97–98

Max's story and Luttwitz's *affiche*: Gibson, *A Journal*, 251–253.

"We Shall Never Forgive!" 99

"they may not": Humphreys, *The Heart of Belgium*.

"Of course I hate": Humphreys, *The Heart of Belgium*.

_____ October 1914: Stumbling Toward Organization _____

12. The Fall of Antwerp 103–125

"October blessed": Will Irvin, "Babes in Belgium," an article copyrighted by the CRB for mass publication.

"54 fortresses": Edouard Bunge, "What I saw of the bombardment and surrender of Antwerp," October 1914; an original document never published but held by this author. The translation of the document was done by the author's grandfather, Milton M. Brown, husband to Erica Bunge and son-in-law to Edouard.

150,000 troops: Marshall, *American Heritage History*, 74.

"the hospitals": Powell, *Fighting in Flanders*, 179.

Churchill to Antwerp: Powell, *Fighting in Flanders*, 181.

"A most spectacular": Powell, *Fighting in Flanders*, 181.

"At sundown": Green, *The Log*, 71–72.

"Reservee": Green, *The Log*, 73–74.

General de Guise placard: Bunge, "What I saw."

"having taken": Gibson, *A Journal*, 265.

"Hundreds, thousands": Bunge, "What I saw."

"Winston Churchill": Gibson, *A Journal*, 267. Date confirmed by Marshall, *American Heritage History*, 75.

"The King": Marshall, *American Heritage History*, 75.

THE BUNGES AND E. E. HUNT   109–125
   Bunge sisters: Bunge, "What I saw."
   turned down barony: Bunge obituary, Milton M. Brown's papers, author's archives.
   Edouard activities: Bunge's obituary, author's archives.
   "The three": Bunge, "What I saw."
   "Horace Green": Hunt, *War Bread*, 84.
   "thin-faced Westerner": Hunt, *War Bread*, 84–85.
   "a little man": Powell, *Fighting in Flanders*, 15.
   "By using": Powell, *Fighting in Flanders*, 14.
   "a hotel always": Hunt, *War Bread*, 85.
   "Thompson's Fort": Green, *The Log*, 91.
   "We had kept": Bunge, "What I saw."
   "I gave to": Bunge, "What I saw."
   "every pane" and following scenes are paraphrased or quoted: Hunt, *War Bread*, 87–90.
   "I stood": Hunt, *War Bread*, 90.
   Hunt experiences: Hunt, *War Bread*, 92-93.
   "When one of": Powell, *Fighting in Flanders*, 172.
   "thousands of": Hunt, *War Bread*, 97.
   "continued to": Bunge, "What I saw."
   "There was panic": Hunt, *War Bread*, 98.
   "the regular nurses": Bunge, "What I saw."
   "wish to abandon": Bunge, "What I saw."
   "They told us": Bunge, "What I saw."
   "The only authority": Bunge, "What I saw."
   "there remains": Bunge, "What I saw."
   "It was an": Bunge, "What I saw."
   "It was a common": Hunt, *War Bread*, 104–105.
   "magnificent and": Hunt, *War Bread*, 100.
   "The infantry came": Bunge, "What I saw."
   royal palace: Powell, *Fighting in Flanders*, 226.
   Deutschland song: Hunt, *War Bread*, 112.
   "I think that": Powell, *Fighting in Flanders*, 227–228.
   Erica bird scene: recreated from material in Bunge's "What I saw" and from author's oral
      family history.
   "In fact": Powell, *Fighting in Flanders*, 32, 33.
   "All this": Bunge, "What I saw."
   "The citizens of": Powell, *Fighting in Flanders*, 47, 48.

13. The Refugees   127–133
   Bunge escort: Bunge, "What I saw." Bunge noted the others as "the Burgomaster,
      Monsieur Franck, Senator Rychmans, Carlier, Robert Osterrieth and myself. Some
      of these men, not wishing to start out alone, willing comrades joined them, so that
      there were, if I am not mistaken, eight instead of six men—a plan which General von
      Schutz upon being consulted, ratified without any difficulty."
   "Chance or perhaps": Bunge, "What I saw."
   "Pillage had": Bunge, "What I saw."
   "It is the": Bunge, "What I saw."

AMERICAN JOURNALISTS JOIN THE REFUGEES   129–133
   "I managed to": Green, *The Log*, 104.
   "The war?": Hunt, *War Bread*, 116.

"pedaling for": Hunt, *War Bread*, 115.

"I never before": Hunt, *War Bread*, 119–120.

"little peasant": Hunt, *War Bread*, 120.

"absolute terror": Hunt, *War Bread*, 120.

"The car": Hunt, *War Bread*, 120–121.

Hunt and Bunge passing: Bunge, "What I saw." As he wrote, "Chance, or perhaps the Germans' information, willed that the sector which they assigned to me should be ground on which I was at home: Merxem, Schooten, Brasschaet and Capellen." Hunt's account of the incident says that the car was coming from Fort Starbroeck, which was less than three miles from Capellen on the only main road in the area. Hunt's account specifically states two officers and a civilian were in the car. Circumstantially, these two accounts indicate it was Bunge in the German motorcar. The assumption that Bunge was feeling strongly about the refugees being pushed aside comes from all his various writings that show his great sympathy for them.

"Most of": Hunt, *War Bread*, 122.

"in every": Hunt, *War Bread*, 129.

Hunt cables story: Hunt, *War Bread*, 71.

14. Battle of the Yser and the First Battle of Ypres 134–136

"uniforms, rifles": Hunt, *War Bread*, 113.

"quiet little": Baedeker, *Belgium*, 47–48.

"Belgium units": Marshall, *American Heritage History*, 75–76.

swampy: Marshall, *American Heritage History*, 75.

"It was not": Marshall, *American Heritage History*, 75–76.

impassable barrier: Marshall, *American Heritage History*, 75–76.

"every supreme": Marshall, *American Heritage History*, 77.

15. London, October 1–17 137–145

Shaler purchase: Gay and Fisher, *Public Relations*, 2 and doc. 20.

Rickard details: London *Financial Times*, November 14, 1914; Smith, *An Uncommon Man*, 76, 81, 150.

closest friend: Smith, *An Uncommon Man*, 150.

living in London: Smith, *An Uncommon Man*, 76, 81, 150.

"immediately impressed": Gay and Fisher, *Public Relations*, 2.

"promised to help": Kittredge, *History of CRB*, 37.

waiting for him: Gibson, *A Journal*, 260–261.

"some talk": Gibson, *A Journal*, 261.

"a most energetic": Kittredge, *History of CRB*, 36.

diplomat inaction: Gibson, *A Journal*, 261.

"At this point": Nash, *The Life of Herbert Hoover*, 19.

"It was an": Nash, *The Life of Herbert Hoover*, 19.

Hoover's help: Gay and Fisher, *Public Relations*, 2.

"the idea of": Kittredge, *History of CRB*, 37–38.

Heineman vice-chair: Kittredge, *History of CRB*, 38.

Hoover Stimulates Public Opinion 142–145

"Already America": Kittredge, *History of CRB*, 39.

"Starving Belgium": Smith, *An Uncommon Man*, 81.

"In two weeks": Gay and Fisher, *Public Relations*, doc. 9.

"the diplomatic": Kittredge, *History of CRB*, 36.

"a comprehensive": *New York Times*, October 18, 1914; Kittredge, *History of CRB*, 40–41.

16. Brussels 146–149

"extend its services": Kittredge, *History of CRB*, 43.
"Francqui therefore": Kittredge, *History of CRB*, 43.
national scale: Nash, *The Life of Herbert Hoover*, 23.
"now that Antwerp": Kittredge, *History of CRB*, 42.
Comité details: Gay and Fisher, *Public Relations*, doc. 7.
"lay the situation": Gibson, *A Journal*, 276.
"carry the weight": Gibson, *A Journal*, 277.
"in three motors": Gibson, *A Journal*, 278.

17. London, October 18–22 150–161

HOOVER AND FRANCQUI MEET AGAIN 151–154

two neutral patrons: Gibson, *A Journal*, 279–280.
Francqui poor symbol: Nevins, *The Journal*, 55.
"impressed men": Kittredge, *History of CRB*, 48.
"Hoover, with": Kittredge, *History of CRB*, 47.
Hoover wrapping himself up: Laurence Wellington, oral history, Duke University,
    Durham, North Carolina.
"He can be": Hunt, *War Bread*, 193.
"What!": Joe Green, "Some Portraits: Emile Francqui," Feb. 15, 1917, Joseph C. Green
    papers, Seeley G. Mudd Manuscript Library, Princeton University, New Jersey. Green
    was not there when Francqui learned of Hoover's participation in Belgian relief, but
    this sounds very much like something Francqui would have said.
"the gossips said": Brand Whitlock, *Belgium: A Personal Narrative*, vol. 1 (D. Appleton and
    Co., 1919), 398–399.
Poem: Rudyard Kipling, "The Ballad of East and West"; Whitlock, *Belgium*, vol. 1: 399.

OUTLINING THE AMERICAN ORGANIZATION 154–161

"'Of course'": Gibson, *A Journal*, 284.
"Yes, I'll": Gibson, *A Journal*, 280.
"absolute command" and "knitting bee": Herbert Hoover, *The Memoirs of Herbert Hoover:
    Years of Adventure, 1874-1920* (MacMillan and Co., 1951), 155; Nash, *The Life of Herbert
    Hoover*, 26.
Smith, *An Uncommon Man*, 81.
"constitution" of CRB: Gay and Fisher, *Public Relations*, 3.
eight numbered items: Gay and Fisher, *Public Relations*, doc. 13.
"But the war": Gay and Fisher, *Public Relations*, doc. 13.
"The Brussels Committee": Gay and Fisher, *Public Relations*, doc. 13.
"To assist in": Gay and Fisher, *Public Relations*, doc. 13.
"in order to": Gay and Fisher, *Public Relations*, doc. 13.
"Furthermore, it is": Gay and Fisher, *Public Relations*, doc. 13.
"an endeavor": Gay and Fisher, *Public Relations*, doc. 13.
"wholly inadequate": Gay and Fisher, *Public Relations*, doc. 13.
"if this was": Gay and Fisher, *Public Relations*, doc. 13.
"It appears that": Gay and Fisher, *Public Relations*, doc. 13.
Allen at meeting: Victoria F. Allen (Ben Allen's wife), "The Outside Man," Ben Allen
    papers, box 12, HHPLA.
"set up an": Gay and Fisher, *Public Relations*, doc. 15.
"worked earnestly": Gay and Fisher, *Public Relations*, doc. 17.
expanded membership: Vernon Kellogg, *Fighting Starvation in Belgium* (Doubleday, Page
    & Co., 1918), 25.

18. Rotterdam 162–166

Lucey Begins Building a Trans-shipping Business 162

two shipments: Gay and Fisher, *Public Relations,* chapter II, First Measures, November 1914.

Rotterdam: Kellogg, *Fighting Starvation,* 27; Gay and Fisher, *Public Relations,* chapter II, 2.

Lucey details: Biographical sketch, *Mining and Oil Bulletin,* 7, July 1921.

"possessed the": Kittredge, *History of CRB,* 67.

temporary office: Kittredge, *History of CRB,* 68.

two-day trip: "Distress in Belgium," British *The Morning Post,* Oct. 28, 1914.

150 safe-conduct: Kittredge, *History of CRB,* 70, 72.

"handle, for the": Kittredge, *History of CRB,* 68.

lighters in Holland: Kittredge, *History of CRB,* 69.

"Appeals, rumors": Gay and Fisher, *Public Relations,* chapter II: 1. First Measures, November 1914.

accompanied by: British *Daily Telegraph,* Nov. 7, 1914, clip books, HHPLA.

"he brought no": Kittredge, *History of CRB,* 70.

"detailed information": Kittredge, *History of CRB,* 70.

"The people are": Gay and Fisher, *Public Relations,* chapter II: doc. 24.

19. London, October 23–31 167–174

"Well, there was": Milton M. Brown, oral history, HHPLA.

"There's no use": Milton M. Brown, oral history, HHPLA.

Hoover and minister story: Lewis R. Freeman, *Outlook* magazine article, Sept. 8, 1915; Hunt, *War Bread,* 194–196; Gibson, *A Journal,* 301.

"Mr. Hoover is": Smith, "The Man in Action," Robinson Smith papers, HIA.

"He will squarely": Smith, "The Man in Action," Robinson Smith papers, HIA.

The Work Starts Having an Impact 169–172

"All day": "Race with Food," British *Standard,* Oct. 28, 1914, clip books, HHPLA.

steamer details: "For Starving Belgium: First Shipment of Food Leaves To-morrow," British *Standard,* Oct. 27, 1914, clip books, HHPLA.

arrival time: Jarvis Bell statement in British *Daily Citizen,* Nov. 14, 1914, clip books, HHPLA.

"It is a": "Belgium and America. Message from King Albert," British *Northern Whig,* Nov. 2, 1914, clips books, HHPLA.

"Accompanying this": "Belgium and America. Message from King Albert," *Northern Whig,* Nov. 2, 1914; clips books, HHPLA.

"We have worked": Letter from Hoover to Oscar T. Crosby, June 30, 1915 when Crosby took over as director in Brussels, Gilchrist Stockton papers, HIA.

totals on food: Gay and Fisher, *Public Relations,* doc. 20.

"considerably less": Gay and Fisher, *Public Relations,* doc. 20.

Britain Gets Behind Belgian Relief 172–174

1,500 refugees: "Refugees in Earl's Court," British *The Standard,* Oct. 24, 1914, clip books, HHPLA.

card index: "Tracing Lost Relations," British *The Daily News,* Oct. 27, 1914, clip books, HHPLA.

"There were crowds": "Belgians in Exile and at Home," British *The Daily Chronicle,* Oct. 28, 1914, clip books, HHPLA.

specific donations: "Articles Received for Sale on Behalf of the Belgian Christmas Fund,"
   British *Daily Telegraph,* Oct. 24, 1914, clip books, HHPLA.
"A whole people": no headline, British *Westminster Gazette,* Oct. 24, 1914, clip books,
   HHPLA.
opposition to relief: Elena S. Danielson, overview article on the CRB, *The United States
   in the First World War: An Encyclopedia.*
"In an effort": Danielson, overview article on the CRB, *The United States in the First World
   War: An Encyclopedia.*
"favorite expressions": Letter from Hoover to Oscar T. Crosby, June 30, 1915, Gilchrist
   Stockton papers, HIA.

20. Brussels 175–179
"since the time": Kittredge, *History of CRB,* 75.
"As you perceive": Kittredge, *History of CRB,* 76.
"The members of": Gibson, *A Journal,* 283.
"The Belgian population": Kittredge, *History of CRB,* 76.
"emphasized the": Kittredge, *History of CRB,* 76.

Van Doren Gains Another Partner 177–179
recruited Boy Scouts: Millard, *Underground News,* 27.
"It probably would": Millard, *Underground News,* 21.
"the most": Millard, *Underground News,* 19–20.
"more than a": Millard, *Underground News,* 20.
"personal responsibility": Millard, *Underground News,* 20.
"torn and twisted": Millard, *Underground News,* 21.
"For the first": Millard, *Underground News,* 21.
"it was a": Millard, *Underground News,* 21.

21. At Oxford 180–182
"stared at us": Nelson, *Letters and Diaries,* 19.
"We are not": Nelson, *Letters and Diaries,* 19.
"builds your fires": Nelson, *Letters and Diaries,* 19.
"two Fords": Nelson, *Letters and Diaries,* 20.
"All you need": Nelson, *Letters and Diaries,* 24.
"After lunch I": Nelson, *Letters and Diaries,* 25.
"very interesting": Nelson, *Letters and Diaries,* 25.
Red Cross train: Nelson, *Letters and Diaries,* 26.
"many of them": Nelson, *Letters and Diaries,* 26.
100,000: no headline, *The Times,* London, Oct. 13, 1914; Nash, *The Life of Herbert Hoover,*
   19.
Louvain professors: Nelson, *Letters and Diaries,* 26.
"One feels the": Nelson, *Letters and Diaries,* 26.
"War is a": Nelson, *Letters and Diaries,* 20.

22. Speeding Toward the Belgian Border 183–186
as guest: Hunt, *War Bread,* 138.
"mostly women": "Distress in Belgium," British *The Morning Post,* Oct. 28, 1914, clip books,
   HHPLA.
"all available": Hunt, *War Bread,* 138.
"For a week": Hunt, *War Bread,* 142.

"They filled": Hunt, *War Bread*, 142.

"paradise compared": Hunt, *War Bread*, 144.

"civilian refugees": Hunt, *War Bread*, 146.

"most of the": Hunt, *War Bread*, 147.

"sluiced and spotched": Hunt, *War Bread*, 150.

"My fiancée's": Letter from Hunt to Mr. Forman, Nov. 14, 1914, E. E. Hunt papers, box 1, HHPLA. Given the time it took letters to get back and forth at this time—usually three weeks at minimum—this meant the death occurred probably sometime in October.

———————————— NOVEMBER 1914: COMING TOGETHER ————————————

23. Rotterdam 189–192

Bell's quotes: Britain's *Daily Citizen* newspaper, Nov. 14, 1914, clip books, HHPLA; *The Scotsman*, Nov. 11, 1914, clip books, HHPLA.

"with great kindness": Britain's *Daily Citizen* newspaper, Nov. 14, 1914, clip books, HHPLA.

"This first trip": Kittredge, *History of CRB*, 70.

Curtis details: Passport application; two birth certificates show 1891 and 1892 as dates of birth. He used 1892 on all passport applications. The online Harvard Directory does not list a graduation date for Curtis, but does show he entered in 1910; Author interpretations from Curtis photos and writings and stories by others; Gibson, *A Journal*, 340; Edgar Rickard letter to Curtis' father, Feb. 16, 1917, Edgar Rickard papers, HIA.

"Consigned to": British *Daily Citizen*, Nov. 14, 1914, clip books, HHPLA.

Members of canal trip: British *Daily Citizen*, Nov. 14, 1914, clip books, HHPLA; Kittredge, *History of CRB*, 70.

24. Into Occupied Belgium 193–203

"STARING AT OUR FLOTILLA AS IF IT WAS SOME MIRAGE" 193–196

Bell's quotes on trip: British *Daily Citizen*, Nov. 14, 1914, clip books, HHPLA.

Canal network details and quotes: Kittredge, *History of CRB*, 69–70.

LIÈGE—"WE ARE NOW THREATENED BY FAMINE" 196–200

"a small portion": British *Daily Mail*, Oct. 10, 1914, clip books, HHPLA.

Morning Post quotes: British *Morning Post*, Nov. 7, 1914, clip books, HHPLA.

"Their description": British *Daily Citizen*, Oct. 30, 1914, clip books, HHPLA.

train departure: Telegram from Henry van Dyke to Hoover, Nov. 11, 1914, says the train left at 4 a.m., World War I document archive, online; Kittredge, *History of CRB*, says 5 a.m., 72.

Gibson quotes: Gibson, *A Journal*, 304–305.

"quite late": Telegram from Henry van Dyke to Hoover, Nov. 11, 1914, WWI Document Archive, online.

train story: Ben Allen, "Feeding Seven Million Belgians: The Work of the American Commission for Relief," *The World's Work*, April 1915, Ben Allen papers, HIA.

Gibson story of ceremony: Gibson, *A Journal*, 308; the Belgian franc to U.S. dollar conversion from the "Money-table," Baedeker, *Belgium*, frontispiece.

Sunderland report: Kittredge, *History of CRB*, 72.

REFUGEES BEGIN RETURNING HOME 200–202

King Albert message: Central News dispatch, Oct. 29, 1914, clip books, HHPLA.

"a stream of": British *Daily Telegraph*, Nov. 7, 1914, clip books, HHPLA.

LUCEY FINDS SOME FOOD 202–203
> Lucey telegram to Hoover: British *Morning Post*, Nov. 28, 1914, clips books, HHPLA.
> "Days and even": Kittredge, *History of CRB*, 70.
> After negotiations with: Kittredge, *History of CRB*, 70–71.
> "could give Lucey": Gay and Fisher, *Public Relations*, chapter II: 1.

25. Brussels 204–215
> "endeavored to get": Kittredge, *History of CRB*, 70.
> "The absence of": Kittredge, *History of CRB*, 72.

FRANCQUI BEGINS BUILDING THE CN 205–207
> "should be impartially": Kittredge, *History of CRB*, 77.
> "enjoy entire": Kittredge, *History of CRB*, 77.
> "The Commission": Kittredge, *History of CRB*, 77.
> "this attitude of": *History of CRB*, 86.
> Francqui financial arrangements: Kittredge, *History of CRB*, 75–76.

A WEAK CRB OFFICE IN BRUSSELS CAUSES PROBLEMS 207–210
> "had been engaged": Kittredge, *History of CRB*, 86.
> "offered to provide": *History of CRB*, 70.
> "During these first": Kittredge, *History of CRB*, 73.
> "hardly realized": Kittredge, *History of CRB*, 73.
> "Heineman himself": Kittredge, *History of CRB*, 86.

WHERE DID THE GERMANS STAND ON RELIEF? 210–211
> All quotes in "Where Did the Germans Stand on Relief?: Kittredge, *History of CRB*, 78–79.

VAN DOREN TAKES PRECAUTIONS 211–214
> All quotes in "Van Doren Takes Precautions": Millard, *Underground News*, 31, 35, 38, 39, 42, 43.

THE GERMAN OCCUPATION GETS TOUGHER 214–215
> All quotes in "The German Occupation gets Tougher": Gibson, *A Journal*, 309, 310–311, 312, 314, 318.

26. London 216–224
> All quotes and stats on use of non-neutral ships: Kittredge, *History of CRB*, 56.

THE BRITISH AND THE CRB 218–221
> "given its consent": Gay and Fisher, *Public Relations*, doc. 21.
> "consigned to": Gay and Fisher, *Public Relations*, doc. 22.
> "the following letter": British *The Daily Citizen*, Nov. 9, 1914, clip books, HHPLA.
> "official approval": Gay and Fisher, *Public Relations*, doc. 22.
> "the German Government": Kittredge, *History of CRB*, 56.
> Hoover story on request for one representative from British: Kittredge, *History of CRB*, 56.

HOOVER COMES OUT SWINGING AT FRANCQUI 221–224
> All quotes and information in "Hoover Comes Out Swinging at Francqui": Gay and Fisher, *Public Relations*, doc. 26.

27. Hoover Fights for U.S. Dominance 225–237

"All these efforts": Kittredge, *History of CRB*, 61.
"During the first few": Kittredge, *History of CRB*, 61.

Two Major Competitors 226–230

"A few modest": Edward T. Devine, "Belgian Relief Efforts," *The American Review
of Reviews*, vol. L, no. 6 (Dec. 1914): 689–693. Devine said the Belgian Relief
Committee was founded "Early in the summer" when the war didn't even start until
August 1914.

de Forest starts committee: Devine, "Belgian Relief Efforts," 689–693.

$50,000 sent to Page: *New York Times*, Oct. 23, 1914, online.

first grant of $100,000: The Rockefeller Foundation's history, on its website.

"give millions of dollars": "Plan Co-Operation in Belgian Relief," *New York Times*, Nov. 3,
1914, online.

All *Times* quotes on this story: "Plan Co-Operation in Belgian Relief," *New York Times*,
Nov. 3, 1914, online.

"arranged to provide": "Rockefeller Pier for Relief Ships," *New York Times*, Nov. 9, 1914,
online.

"in these arrangements": Kittredge, *History of CRB*, 62.

"War Relief Commission": "Rockefeller Pier for Relief Ships," *New York Times*, Nov. 9,
1914, online.

"The arrangements": "Rockefeller Pier for Relief Ships," *New York Times*, Nov. 9, 1914,
online.

"Belgian Relief Efforts," 689–693.

"We Must Centralise Efforts" 230–234

"To the embarrassment": Kittredge, *History of CRB*, 62.

$150,00 from CRB: "$300,000 Quick Help to Hungry Belgians," *New York Times*, Oct. 31,
1914, online.

"It's a fine idea": Kittredge, *History of CRB*, 62.

"Stronger action": Kittredge, *History of CRB*, 62.

"arranged to have": Kittredge, *History of CRB*, 62.

"The Commission for": Kittredge, *History of CRB*, 63.

"Mr. Hoover never": Robinson Smith, "The Man of Action," Robinson Smith papers,
HIA.

"The Commission for": Kittredge, *History of CRB*, 63.

"central committee": *Washington Post*, Nov. 12, 1914, online.

"Nobody it seemed": Nash, *The Life of Herbert Hoover*, 58.

died a quick death: Multiple sources, but Nash, *The Life of Herbert Hoover*, 58–59, does
the best job of summarizing what happened.

Shipping Becomes the Key to Preeminence 234–236

"If the various": Kittredge, *History of CRB*, 57.

"Hoover informed": Nash, *The Life of Herbert Hoover*, 50.

"The New York": Kittredge, *History of CRB*, 64.

"The Commission would": Kittredge, *History of CRB*, 64.

"With the securing": Nash, *The Life of Herbert Hoover*, 62.

"I do not wonder": Hoover to Bates, Feb. 19, 1915, CRB Correspondence, box 2, HIA.

"You can always": Hoover to Bates, Feb. 19, 1915, CRB Correspondence, box 2, HIA.

Hoover Turns to Finding Delegates 236–237

Delegate names and universities: Multiple sources, including official CRB lists; Kellogg *Fighting Starvation*, list; Oxford's archives of past students; Gay and Fisher, *Public Relations*, footnote 209.

"It occurred to": George Spaulding, "The Commission for Relief in Belgium and the Chateau de Mariemont," Alan Hoover Collection, box 8, HHPLA.

28. At Oxford 238–251

All quotes from Nelson in this chapter: At Oxford: Nelson, *Letters and Diaries*, 28–30.

All Carmichael details and quotes in this chapter: Erskine Carmichael, M.D., *One Generation, Portrait of a Family—Scrapbook, 1879–1990* (Blue Rooster Press, 2013), 74–76.

Perrin Galpin Hears From Hoover 241–243

"Dear Sir": Hoover to Galpin telegram, Nov. 24, 1914, Galpin papers, box 1, HIA.

There is some question: Letter from Perrin to his brother Harry, Nov. 27, 1914, and another on Dec. 1, 1914, Galpin papers, Harry file, HIA. There is no evidence that Galpin told his brother that he had seen something in the newspaper and approached the CRB. It was only forty-three years later that Galpin mentions a newspaper piece. The CRB did post newspaper requests for men, but they were later in its history and were published in America. Lastly, it's reasonable to assume that Hoover, in his first telegram to Galpin, might have mentioned Galpin's initial inquiry, if that had happened. Hoover didn't, which doesn't mean it didn't happen, but it is another piece of circumstantial evidence that Hoover approached Galpin, not the other way around.

"Would be glad": Hoover to Galpin, Nov. 26, 1914, Galpin papers, box 1, HIA.

"I am going": Letter from Perrin to his brother Harry, Nov. 27, 1914, Galpin papers, Harry file, HIA.

The spelling of Hollmann: Oxford had a required form that all entering students had to fill out "in his own handwriting." On that form, Emil (without an e) spelled his last name Hollmann. Soon after that, documents begin to show a spelling of Hollman and, finally, Holman. The author chose to use the original spelling throughout this book.

"Hoover telegraphs": Millard Hunsiker to Galpin, Nov. 28, 1914, Galpin papers, box 1, HIA.

What Would the Students Do in Belgium? 243–245

Meeting: Galpin to CRB, Nov. 29, 1914, Galpin papers, box 1, HIA.

"will see that": British *Daily Telegraph*, Nov. 7, 1914, clip books, HHPLA.

"collection information": Spaulding, "The CRB," Allan Hoover papers, box 8, HIA.

twenty-five offered to go: Galpin to CRB, Nov. 29, 1914, Galpin papers, box 1, HIA.

"more in a spirit": Galpin, "Early Days of Rhodes Scholars with CRB," Galpin Papers, HIA.

"passed by ourselves": Galpin to CRB telegram, Nov. 29, 1914, Galpin papers, box 1, HIA.

"whether the men": Galpin to Hoover, Nov. 29, 1914, Galpin papers, box 1, HIA.

The Possibility of Bad Seeds in the CRB 245–247

"Tyler Dernett": Hoover to Galpin, Dec. 1, 1914, Galpin papers, box 1, HIA. From the various communications, there are three different spellings: Dernett, Denett, Dennett. The author was never able to find any information on the man.

"We telegraphed": Hoover to Galpin, Dec. 1, 1914, Galpin papers, box 1, HIA.

"Know nothing of": Galpin to Hoover, Dec. 2, 1914, Galpin papers, box 1, HIA.

"Have decided": Hoover to Galpin, Dec. 2, 1914, Galpin papers, box 1, HIA.

"we are rather": Rickard to Galpin, Dec. 2, 1914, Galpin papers, box 1, HIA.

"I could not": Telegram and letter from Galpin to CRB, both Dec. 3, 1914, Galpin papers, box 1, HIA.

Hoover chose all delegates: Joe Green papers, Seeley G. Mudd Manuscript Library, Princeton University, New Jersey.

"We propose to": Hoover to Galpin, Nov. 30, 1914, Galpin papers, box 1, HIA.

official records: The six recorded by Galpin as having gone into Belgium on the second wave of Oxford students, but who are not listed on any official CRB lists, are George B. Noble, Francis L. Patton, William H. Mechling, Clyde Eagleton, Alexander R. Wheeler, and Clarence A. Castle. Galpin to CRB London office, Dec. 4, 1914, Galpin Papers, box 1, HIA.

The First Ten Chosen 247–251

first ten: Galpin to CRB, Dec. 2, 1914, Galpin Papers, box 1, HIA.

"While thus": Spaulding, "The CRB," Alan Hoover papers, box 8, HHPLA.

"I have given": Galpin to CRB, Dec. 2, 1914, Galpin papers, box 1, HIA.

"I trust that": Galpin to CRB, Dec. 2, 1914, Galpin papers, box 1, HIA.

"undertake the": British *Evening Standard*, Dec. 5, 1914, clip books, HHPLA.

"These young men": British *Daily Telegraph*, Dec. 5, 1914, clip books, HHPLA.

"When this war" and "You must forget": Ben Allen, "Feeding Seven Million Belgians: The Work of the American Commission for Relief," *The World's Work*, April 1915, Ben Allen papers, HIA.

"not only": Allen article, "Feeding Seven Million"; these statements are also repeated in Allen, *The Outside Man*, 143, but she attributes the last paragraph to Hoover when in Ben's article it is attributed to Ben. The first two paragraphs definitely sound like Hoover, while the last paragraph has more of the ring of a journalist making good PR.

"the chief": Francis C. Wickes, oral history taken by Raymond Henle for HHPLA and HIA, Oct. 26, 1970.

each carried: Spaulding, "The CRB," Alan Hoover papers, HHPLA.

"What we were": Emile Holman papers, folder 1, HIA.

"Hoover just returned": CRB to Galpin telegraph, Dec. 4, 1914, Galpin papers, box 1, HIA.

29. E. E. Hunt Joins the CRB 252–255

"I hate like": letter to Mr. Forman, Oct. 31, 1914, E. E. Hunt papers, box 1, HHPLA.

"could write you": letter to Miss Holly, Nov. 23, 1914, E. E. Hunt papers, box 1, HHPLA.

"I've so much": letter to Mr. Forman, Nov. 23, 1914, E. E. Hunt papers, box 1, HHPLA.

"As an American": Hunt, *War Bread*, 201.

"the suggestion was": Hunt, *War Bread*, 201.

"Incidentally": letter to Miss Holly, Nov. 23, 1914, E. E. Hunt papers, box 1, HHPLA.

"He added": letter to Mr. Forman, Nov. 23, 1914, E. E. Hunt papers, box 1, HHPLA.

"There once was": Hunt, *War Bread*, 167.

"It was": Hunt, *War Bread*, 156.

"the landscape": Hunt, *War Bread*, 158.

"I was fated": Hunt, *War Bread*, 158.

"It was a living": Hunt, *War Bread*, 160.

"They looked": Hunt, *War Bread*, 161.

"Women holding": Hunt, *War Bread*, 164–165.

"besieged the": Hunt, *War Bread*, 165–166.

30. Brussels 256–270

"This order": Kittredge, *History of CRB*, 80.
"The German": Kittredge, *History of CRB*, 80.
"in the interest": Kittredge, *History of CRB*, 81.
"for the moment": Kittredge, *History of CRB*, 81.
Times article interviewing two Germans: Kittredge, *History of CRB*, 82; *The New York Times Current History: The European War*, vol. 2 (New York Times, 1917), 785, although this source says the article ran Nov. 6, 1914, but the dates of the responses to this article fit better with a Nov. 22 published date than a Nov. 6 published date.
"If America": Kittredge, *History of CRB*, 82; *The New York Times Current History: The European War*, vol. 2: 785.
"If it is": Kittredge, *History of CRB*, 82.
"It seems that": Kittredge, *History of CRB*, 82.
"The Germans": Kittredge, *History of CRB*, 82.

Hoover Decides It's Time to Visit Brussels 259–265

"see for yourself": Kittredge, *History of CRB*, 90.
"had already": Whitlock, *Belgium*, vol. 1: 402.
strip searched: Smith, *An Uncommon Man*, 82.
"possibly the rather": Hoover, *Years of Adventure*, 159.
"German soldiers": Hoover, *Years of Adventure*, 159.
Hoover accompanied by: Gibson, *A Journal*, 318.
"more impressed": Kittredge, *History of CRB*, 91–92.
"very direct": Nevins, *The Journal*, 70.
"in response": Whitlock, *Belgium*, vol. 1: 400.
"too busily": Kittredge, *History of CRB*, 92.
overwhelmed by: Kittredge, *History of CRB*, 92.
"the only Belgian": Kittredge, *History of CRB*, 92.
"agreed that": Nevins, *The Journal*, 70.
"The work, however": Kittredge, *History of CRB*, 92.
"From the bottom": Kittredge, *History of CRB*, 91.
"a man of": Kittredge, *History of CRB*, 91.
great difficulties lay ahead: Kittredge, *History of CRB*, 91.
"At the Central": British *Morning Post*, Nov. 9, 1914, clip books, HHPLA.
"dismal rain": Whitlock, *Belgium*, vol. 1: 402.
those who accompanied Hoover and Whitlock: Gibson, *The Journal*, 70.
The soup itself: British *Daily Graphic*, Nov. 9, 1914, clip books, HHPLA.
"They stood with": Whitlock, *Belgium*, vol. 1: 403.
expand Little Bees: Kittredge, *History of CRB*, 16.

The Bunges in Antwerp—If the Germans Would Only Agree 265–270

bombs in Bunge office: Bunge, "What I saw."
turned down barony: Bunge obituary, author's archives.
Edouard consulted Erica: Oral history of the Bunge, Brown, and Miller families.
Bunge vice president: Hunt, *War Bread*, 262.
Bunge purchase of coffee: Hunt, *War Bread*, 347.
wounded soldiers transferred: Erica Bunge's diary, Jan. 3, 1915, author's archives.
wounded soldiers information: Oral history of the Bunge, Brown, and Miller families.
Erica helping to run farm: Oral history of the Bunge, Brown, and Miller families.
Chateau Oude Gracht and Isidore: Oral history of the Bunge, Brown, and Miller families.

Isidore details: Oral history of the Bunge, Brown, and Miller families.

Details of rooms in Chateau Oude Gracht: After World War II, the chateau's library and study were removed piece by piece, brought to America, and attached to Milton and Erica Bunge Brown's house, Whitehall, on the Eastern Shore of Maryland. The two rooms were kept exactly as they were in World War I—from the rugs and furniture to the books and artwork—and photos from the early 1900s of the rooms prove it. The author grew up knowing these two rooms intimately and knowing how much they meant to Milton, Erica, and the Bunge family.

A plan for a dairy farm: Oral history and a large, three-panel presentation piece that was awarded to Erica Bunge after the war for providing milk to the children of Antwerp; Robert Withington, *In Occupied Belgium* (Cornhill Co. 1921), 34, "one built a model dairy on his estate, and a barn to accommodate the herd; and under the personal supervision of his daughter, the milk was distributed daily to the hospitals of Antwerp, which otherwise would have gone without."

31. Rotterdam 271

Rotterdam office: Kittredge, *History of CRB*, 73; Maurice, *Bottled Up*, 23.

────────────── DECEMBER 1914: UNCERTAINTY PREVAILS ──────────────

32. The Students Head Into Belgium 275–298

ROTTERDAM GREETING 275–279

All personal quotes in "Rotterdam Greeting" from Nelson, *Letters and Diaries*, 37–40.

Hotel overlooks Maas: Baedeker, *Belgium*, 300.

CRB letter with students: Nelson, *Letters and Diaries of David T. Nelson*; Nelson's letter signed by Hoover is so formal and impersonal that the author assumes all ten Oxford students carried one.

GETTING THEIR ASSIGNMENTS 279–284

"tree-bordered": Hunt, *War Bread*, 199.

"massive fireplace": Hunt, *War Bread*, 199.

CRB banners: Hunt, *War Bread*, 200.

"nervous, big": Hunt, *War Bread*, 200.

"gave us a": Nelson, *Letters and Diaries*, 34.

"Many of the": Nelson, *Letters and Diaries*, 34.

"The Americans": *Letters and Diaries of David T. Nelson*, 35–36.

"One feels prouder": Nelson, *Letters and Diaries*, 36, 39.

re-created assignment scene: Gilchrist Stockton, "The CRB in Swaddling Clothes," Gilchrist Stockton papers, box 9, HIA.

Nelson quotes on his assignment and entering Belgium: Nelson, *Letters and Diaries*, 36–37, 42.

THE SECOND WAVE HITS BELGIUM 284–288

"felt that it": Perrin C. Galpin, "Reminiscences," oral history, Perrin Galpin papers, Research Office, Columbia University, 1957, 2.

"I still remember": Galpin, "Reminiscences," 2.

"the British": Letter from Galpin to Harry, Dec. 9, 1914, Galpin papers, HIA.

"Since tomorrow": Galpin letter to Harry, Dec. 10, 1914, Galpin papers, HIA.

"My job will": Galpin letter to Harry, Dec. 8, 1914, Galpin papers, HIA.

"a new and": Baedeker, *Belgium*, 89.

"In those first": Kittredge, *History of CRB*, 92–93.

Kittredge and Simpson Head for Hasselt 288–291
Hasselt details: Baedeker, *Belgium*, 209.
quotes in "Kittredge and Simpson Head for Hasselt": Kittredge, *History of CRB*, 93.

Spaulding and Lowdermilk Land at Chateau de Mariemont 291–295
Arrival in Mons: Delegate work list, Robert Arrowsmith papers, HIA.
All quotes not otherwise marked in "Spaulding and Lowdermilk Land at Chateau de Mariemont": George F. Spaulding, "The CRB and the Chateau de Mariemont," unpublished, in the Alan Hoover papers, box 8, topical files, HHPLA.
Chateau de Mariemont's history: Baedeker, *Belgium*; Spaulding, "Chateau de Mariemont," 5.

Nelson Walks Into Belgium 295–298
Liège statistics: Baedeker, *Belgium*, 247.
"One of the": Baedeker, *Belgium*, 248.
"frequently manifested": Baedeker, *Belgium*, 248.
All quotes from Nelson in "Nelson Walks Into Belgium": Nelson, *Letters and Diaries*, 43–44.
"One of the Best": Kittredge, *History of CRB*, 93.
"Jackson in Liège": Kittredge, *History of CRB*, 94.
"At this time": *History of CRB*, 94.

33. Antwerp 299–308

Hunt Begins Working for the CRB in a "Dead City" 299–304
"a dead city": Hunt, *War Bread*, 202, 203.

A Trip to a Village Brings Hope 304–308
"which was flat": Hunt, *War Bread*, 211.
"In so small": Hunt, *War Bread*, 215.
"heart thrilled": Hunt, *War Bread*, 215.
"saw few signs": Hunt, *War Bread*, 211.
"small, ugly": Hunt, *War Bread*, 211–212.
typhoid shots: Fred Eckstein letters, Feb. 5–23, 1916, Fred Eckstein papers, HHPLA.
"We have been": Hunt, *War Bread*, 214.
"Tell them": Hunt, *War Bread*, 218.
"confiscate the": Hunt, *War Bread*, 219.
three Oxford students join Hunt: Delegate work list, Robert Arrowsmith papers, HIA; Hunt, *War Bread*, 219.
"From the windows": Hunt, *War Bread*, 262.
"We received": Hunt, *War Bread*, 262.
"We Americans": Hunt, *War Bread*, 262.

34. Elsewhere in Belgium 309–320
"Safe and": Galpin to Hoover, Nov. 29, 1914, Galpin papers, HIA.
"At that time": Earl Osborn journal, Nov. 11, 1915, Osborn and Dodge Family papers, Seeley G. Mudd Manuscript Library, Princeton University, New Jersey.
"The network of": Allen, "Feeding Seven Million Belgians."
"it was necessary": Allen, "Feeding Seven Million Belgians."
"In the early": William Hallam Tuck, 13 of 15-page document on delegate's duties, Gilchrist Stockton papers, HIA.
"As for canals": Hunt, *War Bread*, 220.
"The Rotterdam office": Hunt, *War Bread*, 221.

"spent days": Hunt, *War Bread,* 222.
"set out on": Hunt, *War Bread,* 221–222.
"our limousine": Hunt, *War Bread,* 222.
"He was a": Hunt, *War Bread,* 223.
"Certainly": *War Bread,* 223.

TRACKING ONE SHIPMENT THROUGH THE CANALS 313–317

All quotes other than those noted: Robinson Smith, article 6 of a series of articles titled "The Feeding of Belgium," no publisher, in Maurice Pate papers, box 13, folder 11, Seeley G. Mudd Manuscript Library, Princeton University, New Jersey.
[probably Lowdermilk or Spaulding]: Delegate chart, Robert Arrowsmith papers, HIA.
"'Mr. Hoover'": Hunt, *War Bread,* 223.
Hoover's only: Hunt, *War Bread,* 224.

HUMOR AMONG THE DELEGATES 317–320

Simpson walking stick: Photos of Simpson and numerous references; the Arrow collar, Hunt, *War Bread,* 258.
"when he turned": Gilchrist Stockton, "Abandoned," Gilchrist Stockton papers, box 9, HIA.
"the overcoat": Gilchrist Stockton, "Abandoned," Gilchrist Stockton papers, box 9, HIA.
"Mr. Hoover": Gilchrist Stockton, "Relief and Distress," Gilchrist Stockton papers, box 9, HIA.
"he was only": Gilchrist Stockton, "Relief and Distress," Gilchrist Stockton papers, box 9, HIA.
"a man came": Gilchrist Stockton, "Relief and Distress," Gilchrist Stockton papers, box 9, HIA.
"when the children": Gilchrist Stockton, "Relief and Distress," Gilchrist Stockton papers, box 9, HIA.
"The Belgians thought": Gilchrist Stockton, "Relief and Distress," Gilchrist papers, box 9, HIA.

35. Brussels 321–334

VON BISSING BECOMES GOVERNOR GENERAL 321–324

"His Majesty": Gibson, *A Journal,* 321; Whitlock, *Belgium,* vol. 1: 392.
von Bissing history: Zuckerman, *The Rape,* 93; Jean Massart, *Belgians Under the Eagle* (E.P. Dutton & Co., 1916), 23.
"justly or unjustly": Whitlock, *Belgium,* vol. 1: 393.
"old, and thin,": Whitlock, *Belgium,* vol. 1: 393.
"there gleamed": Whitlock, *Belgium,* vol. 1: 393.
"a great heavy": Whitlock, *Belgium,* vol. 1: 393–394.
"carried with it": Hunt, *War Bread,* 171.
"contribution of war": Whitlock, *Belgium,* vol. 1: 395–396.

WHITLOCK'S TAKE ON THE YOUNG DELEGATES 324–326

"Finally the Rhodes": Whitlock, *Belgium,* vol. 1: 409.
"It was": Whitlock, *Belgium,* vol. 1: 409.
"the young men": Whitlock, *Belgium,* vol. 1: 409–410.
"They showed": Whitlock, *Belgium,* vol. 1: 410.
"Tamines is": Whitlock, "Reign of Terror."
"During the month": Kittredge, *History of CRB,* 95.
"The provincial delegates": Kittredge, *History of CRB,* 97.

VAN DOREN BUILDS HIS NETWORK 326–331
"Times had": Millard, *Underground News*, 37.
"enter or leave": Millard, *Underground News*, 37–38.
"A little": Gibson, *A Journal*, 335.
"It was": Millard, *Underground News*, 38.
"a big, benevolent-looking": Millard, *Underground News*, 32.
"something like a": Millard, *Underground News*, 40.
"The whole system": Millard, *Underground News*, 40–41.
"and going from": Millard, *Underground News*, 41.
"laying the": Millard, *Underground News*, 41.
"He picked up": Millard, *Underground News*, 33.
10,000 francs: Millard, *Underground News*, 30.
Once there: Millard, *Underground News*, 25.
pseudonym Paul van Houtte: Millard, *Underground News*, 25; a copy of the book in author's archives.
"I'm sorry": Millard, *Underground News*, 36.
"I've got": Millard, *Underground News*, 36.
"perfectly well": Millard, *Underground News*, 39.
"taken on": Millard, *Underground News*, 39.
"Well, hot-head": Millard, *Underground News*, 39.
"once begun": Millard, *Underground News*, 38.

A YOUNG WOMAN JOINS THE CAUSE 331–334
All quotes in "A Young Woman Joins the Cause" from Millard, *Underground News*, 67–70.

36. London 335–344

HOOVER FIGHTS TO GET THE CLOCK RUNNING AGAIN IN BELGIUM 335–337
"I can imagine": British *Daily News & Leader*, Dec. 7, 1914, clip books, HHPLA.
"The clock has": British *Daily News & Leader*, Dec. 7, 1914, clip books, HHPLA.
"It is difficult": Herbert Hoover, quoted in the British *Daily News & Leader*, Dec. 7, 1914, clip books, HHPLA.
"The Germans": Kittredge, *History of CRB*, 100.
"The supreme": Smith, "The Man of Action."
"The chief": Kittredge, *History of CRB*, 105.
"In carrying": Kittredge, *History of CRB*, 106.

BRITISH OPPOSITION TO THE CRB 337–344
"The British": Nash, *The Life of Herbert Hoover*, 71.
"Kitchener had": Nevins, *The Journal*, 77.
Hoover and Asquith meeting: Nash, *The Life of Herbert Hoover*, 69.
"Hold this until": Nevins, *The Journal*, 77–78.
"I will send": Nevins, *The Journal*, 78.
"You told me": Nevins, *The Journal*, 78.
"It did not": Nash, *The Life of Herbert Hoover*, 70.
"impressed none": Gay and Fisher, *Public Relations*, chapter IV" doc. 129.
"we were": Gay and Fisher, *Public Relations*, chapter IV" doc. 129.
Hoover pointed out: Gay and Fisher, *Public Relations*, chapter IV: doc. 129.
"empty victory": Gay and Fisher, *Public Relations*, chapter IV: doc. 129.
"The English people": Gay and Fisher, *Public Relations*, chapter IV: doc. 129.
"I employed myself": Letter from Hoover to Oscar T. Crosby, June 30, 1915, Gilchrist Stockton papers, HIA.

"It opened with": British *Daily Telegraph,* Dec. 3, 1914, clip books, HHPLA.
"One Huge": London *Sunday Times,* Dec. 6, 1914, clip books, HHPLA.
"The country": London *Sunday Times,* Dec. 6, 1914, clip books, HHPLA.
Allen trip to interview Belgian king: Victoria Allen, *The Outside Man,* unpublished, 167-200, Ben Allen papers, HHPLA.
"The Commission": British *Bristol Times Mirror,* Dec. 21, 1914, clip books, HHPLA.
"Large as": British *Bristol Times Mirror,* Dec. 21, 1914, clip books, HHPLA.
"I wish to": British *Bristol Times Mirror,* Dec. 21, 1914, clip book, HHPLA.
"tirelessly energetic": Hunt, *War Bread,* 255.
"Each morning": British *Morning Advertiser,* Dec. 22, 1914, clip books, HHPLA.
"a few": British *Morning Advertiser,* Dec. 22, 1914, clip books, HHPLA.
"If this sort": British *Morning Advertiser,* Dec. 22, 1914, clip books, HHPLA.

37. Brussels 345–357

CRB SHOWDOWN 345–347

a long tale: Nevins, *The Journal,* 74.
"I talked with": Nevins, *The Journal,* 74–75.
"As carefully as": Nevins, *The Journal,* 75–76.
"undertake it in": Nevins, *The Journal,* 76.
"I wish I": Nevins, *The Journal,* 76.
"view of": Nevins, *The Journal,* 76.
"clean-cut": Nevins, *The Journal,* 77.
"was rather": Nevins, *The Journal,* 77.
"By some": Whitlock to Walter Page, Dec. 19, 1914, Nash, *The Life of Herbert Hoover,* 77.

THE ULTIMATE PROBLEM SOLVER 347–353

"new administrative": Gay and Fisher, *Public Relations,* 15.
Hoover arrives Dec. 20: Gibson, *A Journal,* 341.
"Everywhere that": Kittredge, *History of CRB,* 97.
"We have had": Letter from Hoover to Will Irwin, Jan. 18, 1915, CRB Correspondence, box 1, HIA.
"functioning with": Whitlock, *Belgium,* vol. 1: 411.
"when the plan": Kittredge, *History of CRB,* 94.
Connett coming from America: Nevins, *The Journal,* 81; Kittredge, *History of CRB,* 97.
"Why, Lucey": Nevins, *The Journal,* 82–83.
"Heineman had": Nevins, *The Journal,* 82.
CRB five departments: Kittredge, *History of CRB,* 98.
Francqui donated offices to CRB: Kittredge, *History of CRB,* 97; Hunt, *War Bread,* 199.
"sitting at their": Kittredge, *History of CRB,* 97.
"regular automobile": Kittredge, *History of CRB,* 98.
"On the other": Kittredge, *History of CRB,* 96.
"were the majority": Kittredge, *History of CRB,* 96.
"It was not": Kittredge, *History of CRB,* 96.
"regarded the": Kittredge, *History of CRB,* 104.
"as it is": Gay and Fisher, *Public Relations,,* doc. 27.
"In the end": Kittredge, *History of CRB,* 96.
"agreed finally": Whitlock, *Belgium,* vol. 1: 414.
"was to be": Kittredge, *History of CRB,* 99.
"And so": Whitlock, *Belgium,* vol. 1: 412.
"get Mr. Whitlock": Galpin, "Reminiscences," 16.

CHRISTMAS UNDER GERMAN OCCUPATION 353–357
   Christmas guests: Gibson, *A Journal*, 341.
   "although there": Gibson, *A Journal*, 342.
   "to the full": Whitlock, *Belgium*, vol. 1: 414.
   "the eve of": Whitlock, *Belgium*, vol. 1: 413.
   "this is the": Gibson, *A Journal*, 342.
   "the German forces": Gibson, *A Journal*, 341.
   "We don't": Gibson, *A Journal*, 341.
   "blazing with": Whitlock, *Belgium*, vol. 1: 413.
   "little Christmas": Nevins, *The Journal*, 79.
   "for weeks been": Whitlock, *Belgium*, vol. 1: 413–414.
   "clattering along": Whitlock, *Belgium*, vol. 1: 415.
   "marched around": Gibson, *A Journal*, 343.
   "The children": Gibson, *A Journal*, 343.
   "It is cheering": Gibson, *A Journal*, 343–344.
   Christmas ship: Whitlock, *Belgium*, vol. 1: 415.
   "asked that there": Whitlock, *Belgium*, vol. 1: 417.
   "nobody need": Kittredge, *History of CRB*, 99.
   "through Louvain": Galpin letter to brother Harry, Jan. 2, 1915, HIA.
   "remove 10 or 12": Letter from Hoover to Will Irwin, Jan. 18, 1915, Nash, *The Life of Herbert Hoover*, 80.
   "Here is the": Gibson, *A Journal*, 344.

38. Cardinal Mercier's Christmas Pastoral Letter 358–375
   Malines details: Baedeker, *Belgium*, 159–160.
   "entered, advanced": Whitlock, *Belgium*, vol. 1: 420.
   "thin, scholarly,": Hunt, *War Bread*, 237.
   asked von der Goltz: Cardinal D. J. Mercier, *Cardinal Mercier's Own Story*, 3–24 (George H. Doran Co., 1920): 23–24.
   "threw the German": Mercier, *Own Story*, 24.
   "Any German": Moritz Ferdinand von Bissing, *General von Bissing's Testament: A Study in German Ideals* (T. Fisher Unwin Ltd., no date).
   "He, therefore": Mercier, *Own Story*, 25.
   "The General": Mercier, *Own Story*, 26.
   "the ministry": Mercier, *Own Story*, 27.
   "But it is": Mercier, *Own Story*, 28.
   "in order to": Mercier, *Own Story*, 29.
   "The Cardinal": Mercier, *Own Story*, 29.
   "cut him short": Mercier, *Own Story*, 29.
   "I regard": Mercier, *Own Story*, 30–31.
   "Further, as": Mercier, *Own Story*, 31.
   "Your Eminence": Mercier, *Own Story*, 33.
   "We shall remember": Mercier, *Own Story*, 32.
   "For we must": German chancellor's speech to the German Reichstag, Dec. 2, 1914, multiple sources.
   "It is impossible": Mercier, *Own Story*, 50.
   "touched any vital": Kellogg, *Mercier*, 51.
   "throughout Belgium": Hunt, *War Bread*, 341.
   "It takes quite": Earl Osborn journal, Jan. 27, 1916, Osborn and Dodge Family papers, Seeley G. Mudd Manuscript Library, Princeton University, New Jersey.
   "seminarists": Mercier, *Own Story*, 45.

"without omitting": Mercier, *Own Story*, 45.

"ringing challenge": Hunt, *War Bread*, 238.

"the ruins I": Cardinal Mercier's "Patriotism and Endurance" pastoral letter as replicated in Kellogg, *Mercier*, 206–248. All following quotes from his pastoral letter, not otherwise sourced, came from this source.

"abstain from": Mercier, *Own Story*, 45.

"It has caused": Mercier, *Own Story*, 50.

Van Doren's Network Takes On the Pastoral Letter 368–372

"This preliminary": Millard, *Underground News*, 26.

"The result was": Millard, *Underground News*, 26.

"realizing the value": Millard, *Underground News*, 26.

"anticipating that": Millard, *Underground News*, 26.

print shops and illegal jobs: Well-known facts, multiple sources.

Louvain Street: Kellogg, *Mercier*, 64

"under no": Millard, *Underground News*, 26.

Becquaert took no chances: Millard, *Underground News*, 26–27. The author made certain assumptions about the printing through the descriptions read. The small type was never stated, but it was stated that the job was done on one sheet, front and back. Because the pastoral letter was long, it had to have been set in small type, even if it was only excerpts of the document.

"If she comes": Millard, *Underground News*, 27.

"At the same": Millard, *Underground News*, 27.

Luckily for van Doren: Millard, *Underground News*, 28–29.

"Her teeth": Millard, *Underground News*, 30.

"go to the": Millard, *Underground News*, 31.

"a foretaste of": Millard, *Underground News*, 31.

"I had, of course": Kellogg, *Mercier*, 80.

Two Delegates Smuggle Out the Pastoral Letter 372–375

Carmichael and Branscomb story and all quotes in "Two Delegates Smuggle out the Pastoral Letter": Erksine Carmichael, M.D. (nephew of Oliver), *One Generation, Portrait of a Family Scrapbook: 1879-1990*, self-published, 2013, a copy of which was given to this author by Dr. Carmichael, 112–115.

39. Antwerp 376–385

E. E. Hunt and Belgian Politics 376–379

"the commune": Hunt, *War Bread*, 243.

"Republicanism": Hunt, *War Bread*, 246.

"even in the": Hunt, *War Bread*, 243, 246.

"still feared": Hunt, *War Bread*, 246.

"rustic": Hunt, *War Bread*, 249.

"When had": Hunt, *War Bread*, 248–249.

"more as a": Hunt, *War Bread*, 249.

"party men": Hunt, *War Bread*, 250.

"shared with": Hunt, *War Bread*, 250–251.

"the Antwerp Provincial": Hunt, *War Bread*, 251.

"We cannot": Hunt, *War Bread*, 251–252.

"I have been": Hunt, *War Bread*, 252.

"Such precipitate": Hunt, *War Bread*, 252.

"had card-indexed": Hunt, *War Bread*, 253.

"None of us": Hunt, *War Bread*, 252.

CRB office in Bunge bank: Hunt, *War Bread*, 224, 261.

THE BUNGES' EXPANDING LIVES 379–385

"their picture of": John L. "Pink" Simpson, oral history, for HHPLA and HIA, Sept. 20, 1967, John L. Simpson papers, box 21, HIA.

Bunge buying dairy cows: Withington, *In Occupied Belgium*, 34.

milk given to Antwerp children: Withington, *In Occupied Belgium*, 34; three-paneled presentation given to Erica Bunge after the war for the milk the Bunges and their dairy farm had provided, author's archives; oral history of the Bunge, Brown, and Miller families.

"read me the cards": Erica Bunge diary, Dec.28, 1914, author's archives.

"I have a dog": Erica Bunge diary, Jan. 17, 1915, author's archives.

"I wish I were": Erica Bunge diary, Feb. 21, 1915, author's archives.

Erica Bunge's work in the underground: Oral history of the Bunge, Brown, and Miller families.

Eva work in the underground and the two sisters meeting one night in the woods: Oral history of the Bunge and Brown families, from both the American and South American sides of the family; after the war Eva received a medal from the British for her work in British intelligence.

40. At the Front 386–387

"Women of": David S. Patterson, *The Search for Negotiated Peace: Women's Activism and Citizen Diplomacy in World War I* (Routledge, 2008), 52.

"the guns may": Thomas Löwer, "Demystifying the Christmas Truce," The Heritage of the Great War website.

41. The Story Continues in 1915, Book Two 388–396

"As the work": Gay and Fisher, *Public Relations*, 18.

"By January 1": Kittredge, *History of CRB*, 111.

"the question of": Gay and Fisher, *Public Relations*, doc. 129.

"A routine appointment": Nash, *The Life of Herbert Hoover*, 84.

"Feb. 1, 1915": Millard, *Underground News*, 43.

"young and pretty": Millard, *Underground News*, 43.

"large pale pink": Millard, *Underground News*, 43.

"A few minutes": Millard, *Underground News*, 44.

"civil institutions": Gay and Fisher, *Public Relations*, chapter IV.

"The situation in": Gay and Fisher, *Public Relations*, chapter IV.

"Belgium is like": Robinson Smith, article 5, "How Does It Feel?" of "The Feeding of Belgium," no publisher, in Maurice Pate papers, box 13, folder 11, Seeley G. Mudd Manuscript Library, Princeton University, New Jersey.

Index

433

CPSIA information can be obtained at www.ICGtesting.com
Printed in the USA
LVOW10s1704080115

422027LV00020B/1516/P